P9-DTG-960

Changing Values and Beliefs in 85 Countries

European Values Studies

The *European Values Studies* is a series based on a large-scale, cross-national and longitudal research program. The program was initiated by the European Value Systems Study Group (EVSSG) in the late 1970s, at that time an informal grouping of academics. Now, it is carried on in the setting of a foundation, using the (abbreviated) name of the group (EVS). The Study group surveyed basic social, cultural, political, moral, and religious values held by the populations of ten Western European countries, getting their work into the field by 1981. Researchers from other countries joined the project, which resulted in a 26-nations data set. In 1990 and 1999/2000, the study was replicated and extended to other countries. By now, all European countries are involved in one or more waves of the study, including those in Central and Eastern Europe. This series is based on the survey data collected in this project. For more information see: www.europeanvalues.nl.

VOLUME 11

Changing Values and Beliefs in 85 Countries

Trends from the Values Surveys from 1981 to 2004

Loek Halman, Ronald Inglehart, Jaime Díez-Medrano,
Ruud Luijkx, Alejandro Moreno and Miguel Basáñez

BRILL

LEIDEN • BOSTON
2008

This book is printed on acid-free paper.

Library of Congress Cataloging-in-Publication Data

Changing values and beliefs in 85 countries : trends from the values surveys from 1981 to 2004 / Loek Halman ... [et al.].
p. cm. — (European values studies, ISSN 1568-5926 ; 11)
Includes bibliographical references.
ISBN 978-90-04-15778-1 (hardback : alk. paper) 1. Values. I. Halman, Loek. II. Title. III. Series.

BD435.C495 2007
303.3'7209048—dc22

2007036360

ISSN 1568-5926
ISBN 978 90 04 15778 1

Copyright 2008 by Koninklijke Brill NV, Leiden, The Netherlands. Koninklijke Brill NV incorporates the imprints Brill, Hotei Publishing, IDC Publishers, Martinus Nijhoff Publishers and VSP.

All rights reserved. No part of this publication may be reproduced, translated, stored in a retrieval system, or transmitted in any form or by any means, electronic, mechanical, photocopying, recording or otherwise, without prior written permission from the publisher.

Authorization to photocopy items for internal or personal use is granted by Koninklijke Brill NV provided that the appropriate fees are paid directly to The Copyright Clearance Center, 222 Rosewood Drive, Suite 910, Danvers, MA 01923, USA.
Fees are subject to change.

PRINTED IN THE NETHERLANDS

CONTENTS

LIST OF TABLES

Pection C: Work

Section D: Family

Section E: Politics and Society

Section F: Religion and Morale

Section G: National Identity

SERIES EDITORS' PREFACE

This trend book is the eleventh volume in the series on European Values published by Brill Academic Publishers. The books in this series focus on human values, attitudes, beliefs and ideas in contemporary society and are based on the survey data collected within the framework of the European Values Study, a large-scale cross-national and longitudinal research project on fundamental values in Western societies. The project started at the end of the 1970s, aiming at empirically investigating the main fundamental value patterns of Europeans and exploring the changes in these value orientations. Since then, the project has expanded worldwide and has developed into a project in which the European Values Study (EVS) and the World Values Surveys (WVS) try to conduct surveys in as many countries all over the world. EVS focuses on Europe, while WVS aims at conducting surveys also in countries outside Europe. For more information about the start of the European Values Study and recent developments, see the EVS website: www.europeanvalues.nl. For information on the world values surveys, we refer to their website: www.worldvaluessurvey.org.

This book is, as mentioned before, the eleventh volume in this series. Volumes one to five in this series are based on data from the 1990 and/or 1981 survey waves, and are published by Tilburg University Press. The first volume is *The Individualizing Society; Value Change in Europe and North America* (1993; revised edition 1994), edited by Peter Ester, Loek Halman and Ruud de Moor. The second book *Values in Western Societies* (1995) is edited by Ruud de Moor, and the third book *Political Value Change in Western Democracies* (1996) is edited by Loek Halman and Neil Nevitte. The fourth volume *From Cold War to Cold Peace* (1997) is a comparison of Russian and European values. The authors are Peter Ester, Loek Halman and Vladimir Rukavishnikov. This book was also published in Russian in 1998. In 1999, a fifth volume was released on *Religion in Secularizing Society*, edited by Loek Halman and Ole Riis. A second printing of this book appeared in 2003 in the re-established series on the European Values Study now at Brill Academic Publishers. In the sixth volume, edited by Wil Arts, Jacques Hagenaars and Loek Halman, *The Cultural Diversity of European Unity. Findings, Explanations and Reflections from the European Values Study* (2003), Europe's values are examined from economic, political, social, and religious-moral points of view. The seventh volume, *European Values at the Turn of the Millennium* (2004) is edited by Wil Arts and Loek Halman. It contains chapters in which authors from all quarters of Europe try to identify, explain and interpret patterns in the basic values and attitudes of Europeans in and around the year 2000. The emphasis in this volume is on phenomena connected with civil society and citizenship, family and work, and religion and morality. In 2005, an *Atlas of European Values* was produced as the eighth volume in this series. This publication differs from the existing books in the series in the sense that it presents the ideas, values, and beliefs of Europeans in more accessible forms for a general readership, using graphs, charts, and maps in place of advanced statistical analyses. The Atlas provides answers to questions such as: Who are the Europeans? How do they think? What values do they hold dear? What binds them and what divides them? The Atlas presents data primarily from the 1999/2000 European Values Study but also from the World Values Surveys along with data from selected Eurobarometer surveys. It covers all European countries; from Iceland to Turkey, and from Portugal to Azerbaijan. The authors are Loek Halman, Ruud Luijkx and Marga van Zundert (see also: www.atlasofeuropeanvalues.com). Tony Fahey, Bernadette C. Hayes and Richard Sinnott have written the ninth volume in the series. Their study on *Conflict and Consensus. A study of values and attitudes in the Republic of Ireland and Northern Ireland*, presents a detailed comparison of cultural values and attitudes in the Republic of Ireland and Northern Ireland. It is based on survey data covering the period from the 1970s to 2003, but focuses especially on the European Values Study (EVS) as fielded in the two parts of Ireland in 1999–2000. Their study confirms the deep divisions in identity and political allegiance that separate the Catholic and Protestant communities in Northern Ireland, but it also shows that, on many issues, Protestants and Catholics on the island of Ireland are culturally more similar to each other than to any other national population in Europe, including Britain. The tenth volume in this series, edited by Peter Ester, Michael Braun and Peter Mohler, titled *Globalization, Value Change, and*

Generations, addresses a number of very interesting comparative themes: whether value convergence or divergence has occurred; whether traditional values are indeed on the decline as predicted in so many theories of modernization; and whether younger generations play the proverbial vanguard role in culture shifts.

This eleventh book in the series is, like the *Atlas of European Values*, quite different from the other books in this series. It contains mainly tables providing insights into the shifts in the basic values and attitudes of the peoples of more than 80 countries around the world. In collaboration, EVS and WVS have produced an integrated data file containing all available data of all the countries in which the values surveys have been conducted through the years. This post hoc harmonization of all Values Surveys data since 1981 was realized by ASEP/JDS in Madrid and EVS-Tilburg, and the result is a huge dataset of almost 269,000 cases in 85 countries from all over the world. The data can be downloaded free of charge, from both the EVS and WVS websites (www.europeanvalues.nl; www.worldvalussurvey.org) or from ASEP/JDS (www.jdsurvey.net). The original data from the European Values Study surveys in 1981, 1990 and 1999, as well as the integrated dataset of the three waves, are available from Zentralarchiv in Cologne (http://zacat.gesis.org/webview/index.jsp).

We would like to use this opportunity to announce a shift in editorship of this series. Since the series moved from Tilburg University Press to Brill Academic Publishers, we have been series editors. The first editor retired last year and we thought it timely to invite others who are still active in the project to take over his role. We are happy to announce that Paul de Graaf, recently appointed at Tilburg University and Chair of the Theory Group in the European Values Study project, and Koen van Eijck, recently appointed at the Catholic University of Leuven in Belgium and EVS Program Director in Belgium, have both agreed to act as series editors next to Loek Halman who remains editor in this series. The collaboration of these three series editors emphasizes the strong ties between Tilburg University and Catholic University of Leuven which have continued since the start of the European Values Study project.

Wil Arts & Loek Halman
Gouda & Tilburg, March 2007

ACKNOWLEDGEMENTS

This trend book reflects the combined efforts of a large network of social scientists in more than 80 societies, collaborating in a unique project on basic human values that originated at the end of the seventies and continued with a number of repeated studies in the last two and a half decades, in a growing number of countries around the world. The first surveys, fielded in 1981, were confined to countries that belonged to the European Community. In subsequent years, researchers from several countries have joined the project, making it the largest comparative survey research project on values ever carried out, producing survey data from 26 European and non-European countries. Repeat surveys were organized in 1989–1993, 1995–1997 and 1999–2004 in an expanding number of countries. The 1999–2004 wave took place in more than 80 countries in all continents of the world. The data from it enables the examination of stability and change in the beliefs and values of publics around the world.

This trend book is based on these unique survey data collected by researchers from both the European Values Study (EVS) and World Values Survey (WVS). It goes without saying that the authors wish to express their thanks to all EVS and WVS participants that were and are involved in the project, for creating and sharing this rich data set. Mentioning only those who were involved in the most recent data collection would not do justice to those who were involved in the previous waves, let alone to the Founding Fathers of the project, who had the visionary gift to begin such a study on (European) values. They could not have imagined that the project would develop and expand into a truly global study on basic human values, producing such a rich data set that would be drawn on extensively by a wide range of users, including scholars, policymakers, decision takers and politicians, and the general publics. Of course we are indebted to all who in subsequent years became involved in the project. A full list of the current participants in the values study can be found on the websites of EVS (www.europeanvalues.nl) and WVS (www.worldvaluesurveys.org).

We are also grateful to those who have been involved in producing the integrated data file on which this trend book is based. Again it would not be fair to only express our gratitude to the persons and institutes that were involved in the most recent wave of data collection. The first data collection in 1981–1984 was coordinated by Gallup in London; the repeat study between 1989 and 1993 in Europe was coordinated by the Institut für Demoskopie in Allensbach, Germany, and the surveys outside Europe were then coordinated by Ron Inglehart. The 1995–1997 data collection was organized and coordinated by the World Values Surveys and the most recent data collection in 1999–2004 was organized and coordinated by the European Values Study in Europe while the surveys in other countries were the responsibility of the World Values Surveys. Two institutes in particular played an important role in producing the integrated data set: the Central Archive (ZA) in Cologne, Germany and ASEP/JD Systems in Madrid, Spain. The integrated data set containing all available survey data collected within the framework of the EVS and WVS has been prepared by Ruud Luijkx (Tilburg University, the Netherlands) and Jaime Díez-Medrano (JD Systems and ASEP in Madrid). It is accessible via the websites of both EVS (www.europeanvalues.nl) and WVS (www.worldvaluesurveys.org).

This trend book would not have been possible without the imagination, encouragement and generosity of many concerned and enlightened sponsors: charitable trusts and foundations, companies, church organizations and private individuals, as well as some national governments. It would be impossible to mention all organizations, enterprises, and individuals who have contributed to the project, not only because they are too numerous, but also because some of them prefer to remain anonymous. Therefore we can only express our deepest appreciation in a very general way for their support in enabling us to conduct these surveys.

Loek Halman, Ronald Inglehart,
Jaime Díez-Medrano, Ruud Luijkx,
Alejandro Moreno and Miguel Basáñez

INTRODUCTION

The Values Surveys

This trend book examines continuity and changes in people's beliefs and values in countries on all six inhabited continents from 1981 to 2004. It uses the combined data from the European Values Study (EVS) and the World Values Survey (WVS) from more than 80 societies containing more than 85 per cent of the world's population. These surveys cover all of the world's major cultures, and explore the full range of economic and political variation, from societies with per capita incomes as low as $300 per year, to societies with per capita incomes one hundred times that high; and from long-established democracies with market economies, to authoritarian states and ex-socialist states. This project has carried out four waves of representative national surveys, in 1981–84 (the 1981 wave), 1989–1993 (the 1990 wave), 1995–1997 (the 1995 wave), and 1999–2004 (the 2000 wave), and is about to carry out a fifth wave of surveys. An overview of countries involved in the completed survey waves is displayed in the overview on the next page.

For information about the origins of the European Values Study and how the values surveys were and are organized, see the websites of both projects and also: Harding, Phillips and Fogarty (1986), Barker, Halman and Vloet (1992), Ester, Halman and de Moor (1994), and Halman (2001). For more information about the World Values Survey, see: Inglehart, Basáñez and Moreno (1998), and Inglehart, Basáñez, Díez-Medrano, Halman and Luijkx (2004). The integrated data file, on which this trend book is based, can be downloaded free of charge from the websites of EVS and WVS as well as from www.jdsurvey.net.

The Values Surveys are carried out by a global network of social scientists. They constitute the largest cross-national investigation of human beliefs and values that has ever taken place. Despite various indications that changes in mass beliefs were occurring, no global research had been carried out on this topic until the founding of the Values Surveys. These surveys provide substantial evidence that the basic norms and motivations of people throughout the world are changing, in ways that have important social and political implications. These changes involve values concerning religion, political life, work motivations, gender roles, and tolerance of other groups. Since 1981, the Values Surveys have monitored these changes and analyzed their implications for social policy.

How to read the tables

In order to present the findings concisely in the tables that follow, the responses to each question are dichotomized, with only the percentage ranking "high" being shown. For example, the first table presented shows the responses to the question, "How important is your family in your life?" Only the percentage saying that the family is "very important" is shown here; the other three response categories ("fairly important," "not very important," and "not at all important") are not shown. This sacrifice of detail brings a huge gain in conciseness: if we were to report each response category for each variable, it would require a very large and unwieldy book, since some questions have ten response categories.

The countries surveyed are listed in alphabetical order, and the responses in each year for which data are available are shown under the appropriate columns, from 1981 to 2000. As the reader will note, in every one of the 85 countries for which data are available, the public places great importance on the family, with the proportions of respondents saying that the family is "very important" ranging from as low as 61 percent in China to as high as 99 percent in the Philippines. The almost universally positive attitudes shown here are quite unusual: few other topics evoke such a broad positive response. Moreover, the data show no sign that the importance attached to the family is declining.

For all countries from which data are available at more than one time point, the "Change" column shows the net change from the first available time point to the most recent one. This does not take into account the information contained in the intermediate time points, but that information is there in the tables if one wishes to examine the trend in detail. The "Change" column sums up the amount of change found in each country. It is of course tempting to calculate a mean shift figure that summarizes how the trend is moving (or if there is no overall trend) for all the countries as a whole. However, since the countries for which data are available vary from one table to another,

Overview of number of cases in the countries in the four waves

	1981	1990	1995	2000
Albania (al)			999	1000
Algeria (dz)				1282
Argentina (ar)	1005	1002	1079	1280
Armenia (am)			2000	
Australia (au)	1228		2048	
Austria (at)		1460		1522
Azerbaijan (az)			2002	
Bangladesh (bd)			1525	1500
Belarus (by)		1015	2092	1000
Belgium (be)	1145	2792		1912
Bosnia & Herz. (ba)			1200	1200
Brazil (br)		1782	1149	
Bulgaria (bg)		1034	1072	1000
Canada (ca)	1254	1730		1931
Chile (cl)		1500	1000	1200
China (cn)		1000	1500	1000
Colombia (co)			6025	
Croatia (hr)			1196	1003
Czech Rep. (cz)		3033	1147	1908
Denmark (dk)	1182	1030		1023
Dominican Rep. (do)			417	
Egypt (eg)				3000
El Salvador (sv)			1254	
Estonia (ee)		1008	1021	1005
Finland (fi)		588	987	1038
France (fr)	1200	1002		1615
Georgia (ge)			2008	
Germany (East; dee)		1336	1009	999
Germany (West; dew)	1305	2101	1017	1037
Great Britain (gb)	1167	1484	1093	1000
Greece (gr)				1142
Hungary (hu)	1464	999	650	1000
Iceland (is)	927	702		968
India (in)		2500	2040	2002
Indonesia (id)				1004
Iran (ir)				2532
Iraq (iq)				2325
Ireland (ie)	1217	1000		1012
Israel (il)				1199
Italy (it)	1348	2018		2000
Japan (jp)	1204	1011	1054	1362
Jordan (jo)				1223
Korea Rep. (kr)	970	1251	1249	1200

	1981	1990	1995	2000
Kyrgyzstan (kg)				1043
Latvia (lv)		903	1200	1013
Lithuania (lt)		1000	1009	1018
Luxembourg (lu)				1211
Macedonia (mk)			995	1055
Malta (mt)	467	393		1002
Mexico (mx)		1531	2364	1535
Moldova (md)			984	1008
Montenegro (mon)			240	1060
Morocco (ma)				2264
Netherlands (nl)	1221	1017		1003
New Zealand (nz)			1201	
Nigeria (ng)		1001	1996	2022
Northern Ireland (nir)	312	304		1000
Norway (no)	1051	1239	1127	
Pakistan (pk)			733	2000
Peru (pe)			1211	1501
Philippines (ph)			1200	1200
Poland (pl)		1920	1153	1095
Portugal (pt)		1185		1000
Puerto Rico (pr)			1164	720
Romania (ro)		1103	1239	1146
Russian Fed. (ru)		1961	2040	2500
Saudi Arabia (sa)				1502
Serbia (ser)			1280	1200
Singapore (sg)				1512
Slovakia (sk)		1602	1095	1331
Slovenia (si)		1035	1007	1006
South Africa (za)		2736	2935	3000
Spain (es)	2303	4147	1211	2409
Sweden (se)	954	1047	1009	1015
Switzerland (ch)		1400	1212	
Taiwan (tw)			780	
Tanzania (tz)				1171
Turkey (tr)		1030	1907	4607
Uganda (ug)				1002
Ukraine (ua)			2811	1195
Uruguay (uy)			1000	
USA (us)	2325	1839	1542	1200
Venezuela (ve)			1200	1200
Vietnam (vn)				1000
Zimbabwe (zw)				1002
Total	25249	62771	78678	101172

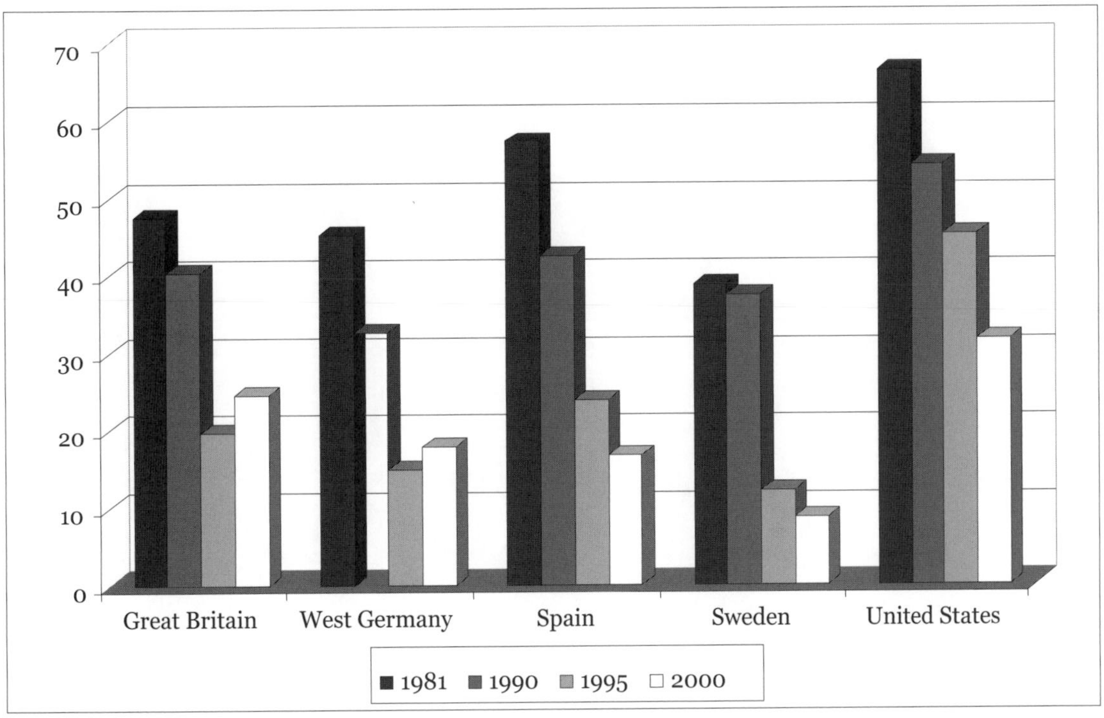

Figure 1 Percentages saying that homosexuality is never justifiable, in Britain, West Germany, Spain, Sweden and the United States

such a "Mean shift" would not be comparable from one table to another.

Changing beliefs and values

Many basic human values are changing. Evidence from the four waves of the Values Surveys demonstrate that people's orientations concerning politics, religion, gender roles, work motivations, and sexual norms are changing—along with their opinions on child-rearing, their attitudes towards marginalized groups and their views on science and technology. However, the idea that similar transformations have occurred in all value domains and all value orientations cannot be substantiated by empirical evidence. For instance, with respect to moral standards and views on parent-child ties, the changes are not dramatic and typical values appear to remain rather strict. The traditional views seem to survive in this domain, whereas de-traditionalization trends can be observed in particular with regard to religious norms, political opinions and most of all with regard to people's moral convictions. Increasingly, sexual and ethical behaviors are considered a private concern that does not allow the interference of other people or institutions.

Figure 1 provides one example, showing the percentage of respondents saying that homosexuality is "Never" justifiable. The respondents in each country were shown a ten-point scale on which 1 means that homosexuality is never justifiable, and 10 means that it is always justifiable, with the eight intermediate points indicating intermediate positions. As this figure demonstrates, in 1981 about half of those surveyed in five Western countries took the extreme negative position, placing themselves at point 1 on the scale (the publics of developing countries were on average even less tolerant of homosexuality). But attitudes changed substantially in subsequent years. By the time of the 2000 survey, only about 25 percent of the West Europeans and 32 percent of Americans took this position. Although attitudes toward sexual orientation are relatively deeply-rooted, they are changing—largely through a process of intergenerational population replacement. Recently, changing attitudes in this field have led to societal-level changes, such as the emergence of same-sex marriages in some countries, and in certain cities in the U.S. This, in turn, mobilized a strong reaction by people with traditional values—giving rise to a widespread belief that the public in general is becoming increasingly hostile to gays and lesbians. The opposite is true. The publics of western societies are increasingly accepting of non-traditional patterns of behavior.

The public and political discourses on changing values are often fuelled by a preoccupation with the

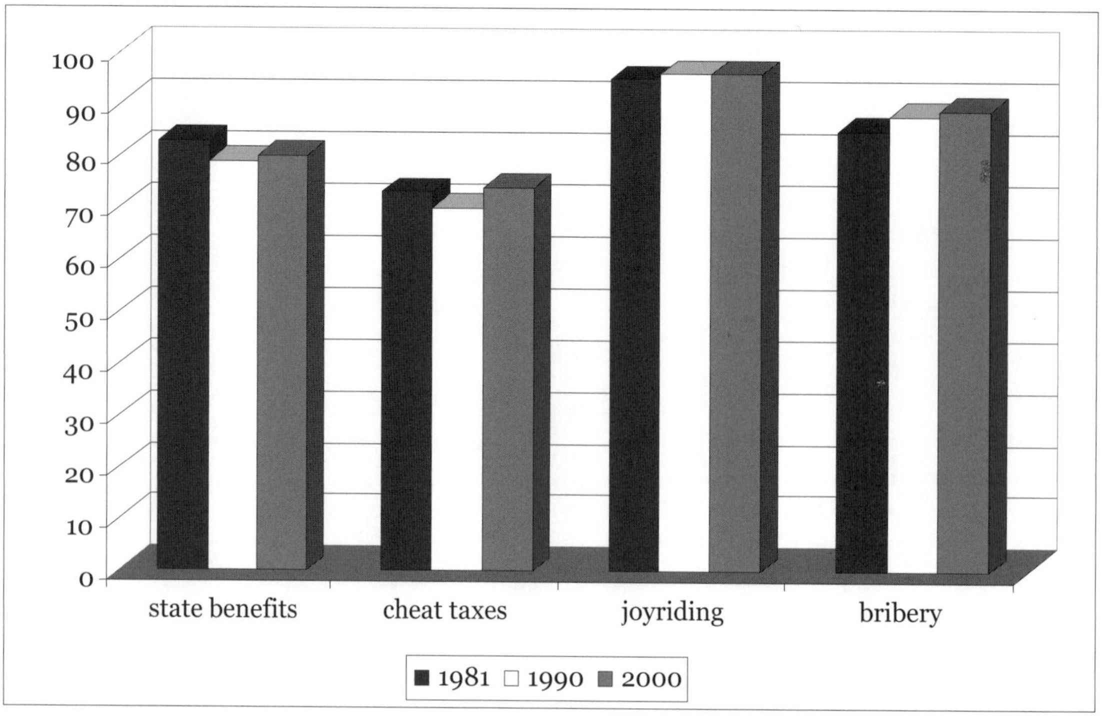

Figure 2 Percentages saying that claiming state benefits illegally, cheating on taxes, joyriding, or bribery are "never" or "almost never" justifiable, in 13 Western European countries

decline of values, in particular those values that are assumed to make us good citizens, and thus make society, and even more broadly human life, good (Ester, Mohler & Vinken 2006: 17; Bellah, Madsen, Sullivan, Swidler & Tipton 1992; Etzioni 1996; 2001; Fukuyama 2000; Putnam 2000; 2002). Many social observers, and politicians claim that contemporary citizens are increasingly indifferent or skeptical towards societal life, and too narrowly focused on pure self-interest. This is considered a severe threat for the respect for human rights and human dignity, liberty, equality, solidarity, and for active community life.

The observed trend of more leniency towards different kinds of sexual and ethical behaviors does not mean a loosening of moral standards. The growing acceptance of homosexuality and other sexual behaviors seems to reveal that increasingly people can accept and understand others to be engaged in such perhaps contrasting behaviors. However, public opinion is notably discriminating on which types of behaviors it will now condone, and which it still condemns. That a personal morality of 'anything goes' has not developed in contemporary society is suggested, among other findings, from the low level of acceptance of behaviors such as claiming state benefits illegally, cheating on taxes, joyriding and accepting bribery. Such behaviors are rarely accepted in the western world and some of these behaviors have even become typically less acceptable during the last two decades. From Figure 2 it appears that an overwhelming majority of Western Europeans would never consider acceptable behaviors such as claiming state benefits illegally, cheating on taxes, joyriding or bribery.

What the data do reveal is that human values are changing gradually but that these changes do not occur in a uniform fashion in all domains and in all countries. Comparing the trends in Western developed societies with the trends in non-Western less developed countries yields evidence that values are changing relatively rapidly in developed countries, and slowly in developing countries.

What is driving these changes? One body of theory developed by Inglehart and others (Inglehart, 1977, 1990, 1997; Inglehart & Baker, 2000; Inglehart & Norris, 2003; Norris & Inglehart, 2004; Inglehart & Welzel, 2005) argues that basic material survival is such a central goal that when it is insecure, one's entire life strategy is shaped by the need to maximize economic and physical security. In advanced industrial societies in recent decades, a large segment of the population has grown up taking survival for granted, leading them to give increasingly high priority to self-expression, individual autonomy and quality of life issues.

Such developments seem to be triggered and strongly driven partly by rising levels of education of the population. More education increases people's abilities and cognitive, political and social skills. This makes them less dependent on the traditional suppliers of values, norms, and beliefs, and more amenable to new ideas and arguments, and to alternative providers of meanings, values and norms. Increasingly, people's actions and behaviors are rooted in and legitimized by people's own personal preferences, convictions and goals. The endeavor to pursue private needs and aspirations is said to result in assigning highest priority to personal need fulfillment and self-expression. Self-development and personal happiness have become the ultimate criteria for individual actions and attitudes. Thus, opinions, beliefs, attitudes, and values have gradually become personal concerns emphasizing personal autonomy, self-reliance, and individual freedom and the Self (Giddens, 1991). Rules and prescriptions imposed by traditional institutions are no longer taken for granted. The traditional options are less likely to be selected by an increasing number of people. The 'disciplined, self-denying, and achievement-oriented norms... are giving way to an increasingly broad latitude for individual choice of lifestyles and individual self-expression' (Inglehart, 1997: 28).

The individual in advanced, post-industrial and post-modern society also faces a multitude of alternatives as a consequence of internationalization, transnationalization, globalization and the rapid evolution of modern communication technology. Technological developments and rapid innovations in telecommunications, the spread and popularity of computers, and also the increased mobility of major companies and people, as well as growing exposure to television, radio, video and films, etc., have intensified worldwide social relations and flows of information. The modern world has become a 'global village,' where people encounter a great variety of alternative cultural habits and a broad range of lifestyles and modes of conduct. As such, globalization 'exhausted the old ideas, the traditional ideas, which had therefore lost their truth on the power to persuade' (Rush, 1992: 187). Globalization makes people aware of an expanding range of beliefs and moral convictions and thus furnishes them with a plurality of choices. Individualization and secularization have liberated people from the constraints imposed by traditional institutions (e.g., religion), and globalization implies that people can pick and choose what they want from a global cultural marketplace.

The emancipation of the individual, the growing emphasis on personal autonomy and individual freedom, the de-unification of collective standards and the fragmentation of private pursuits seem advantageous to 'a declining acceptance of the authority of hierarchical institutions, both political and non-political' (Inglehart, 1997: 15). Citizens are increasingly questioning traditional sources of authority and no longer bound by common moral principles. From this, a society has emerged where people are mainly concerned with their private lives and no longer feel committed to the public case. As Fukuyama (2000: 14) says, 'a culture of intense individualism... ends up being bereft of community'. The calculating citizen chooses to 'bowl alone' and is increasingly disconnected from his once strong social ties. Because social responsibilities have declined and individual citizens are less embedded in associative relations, a process of deinstitutionalization has occurred, manifesting itself in weaker social bonds, detachment from society, non-affiliation and lack of loyalty to the wider community. Such a society is easily threatened with disintegration and the individual with anomie. Durkheim recognized this problem a long time ago, and, more recently, among others Fukuyama warned that a 'society dedicated to the constant upending of norms and rules in the name of increasing individual freedom of choice will find itself increasingly disorganized, atomized, isolated, and incapable of carrying out common goals and tasks' (Fukuyama, 2000: 15).

Such theories have helped to shape the design of the Values Surveys. But the content of these surveys has also been shaped by scores of people on all six inhabited continents, and the surveys capture a wide variety of other concerns including religious decline and religious change (e.g., Dobbelaere, 2002; Davie, 2002; Martin, 2005; Norris & Inglehart 2004; Halman & Pettersson, 2006), the evolution of social capital and confidence in institutions (Fukuyama, 2000; Putnam, 2000, 2002; Putnam & Gross, 2003), factors underlying cultural and technological creativity (Florida, 2002, 2005), changing public attitudes toward science and technology (Miller, Pardo & Niwa, 1997; Miller & Pardo, 2000), links between values and the erosion of political support (Dalton, 2004), the growth of critical citizens (Norris, 1999), and the evolution of work orientations from intrinsic to extrinsic (Ester, Halman & De Moor, 1994; Harding & Hikspoors, 1995; Zanders 1994; De Witte, Halman & Gelissen, 2004). One interpretation of changing values argues that new information technology and the emergence of a network society have given rise to feminism and environmentalism and other movements that are transforming human relationships, and which are reshaping religion, ethnicity and people's sense of identity (Castells, 1996, 1997, 1998). Another perspective emphasizes the fact that the functional requirements of industrial society and people's daily life experiences in it are profoundly different from those of 'post-industrial society,' and the emerging knowledge society: this is reshaping basic values and worldviews (Bell, 1973, 1976). Still another view holds that new perceptions of risk are leading to the development and spread of new values (Beck, 1992).

The Values Surveys make it possible for social scientists to test the implications of these and other theories of individual-level and societal-level value change (e.g., Arts, Hagenaars & Halman, 2003; Arts & Halman, 2004; Ester, Braun & Mohler, 2006). Data from the Values Surveys make it clear that many of the most basic values and motivations of publics throughout the world *are* changing, and that they are changing in coherent and, to some extent, predictable patterns. Few intellectual tasks are more challenging than the effort to understand *why* these changes are taking place, and in doing so, to gain a clearer understanding of their implications. By measuring these values over time, in societies with a wide range of economic, cultural and political conditions, this project makes it possible to analyze these changes from a variety of theoretical perspectives.

Cross-national variation and trajectories of changing beliefs and values

One of the most basic findings from the Values Surveys is the fact that there are pervasive differences between the beliefs and values of the publics of rich countries, and those of low income countries. But even within the European context, a rich variety of cultures exists. This variety reflects the distinctive religious, cultural, economic and social heritage of each society. Countries and their populations have remained quite distinctive in many ways and nation states remain important sources of differences in people's attitudes, values, beliefs and behaviors.

People's beliefs and values differ in thousands of ways, but two dimensions of cross-cultural variation appear particularly important. Each dimension can be linked with one of the two waves of economic development that have transformed the world economically, socially and politically in modern times: (1) the transition from agrarian society to industrial society that began to emerge two hundred years ago and is now transforming China, India, Malaysia, Mexico, Brazil, and many other countries; and (2) the transition from industrial society to the post-industrial or knowledge based society that emerged some fifty years ago and is now reshaping the socioeconomic systems of the U.S., Canada, Western Europe, Japan, Australia and other economically advanced societies.

These processes of economic and technological change give rise to two major dimensions of cross-cultural variation. The *Traditional/Secular-Rational* dimension reflects the contrast between the relatively religious and traditional values that generally prevail in agrarian societies, and the relatively secular, bureaucratic and rational values that prevail in urban, industrialized societies. Traditional societies emphasize the importance of religion, deference to authority, parent-child ties and two-parent traditional families, and absolute moral standards; they reject divorce, abortion, euthanasia, and suicide, and tend to be patriotic and nationalistic. In contrast, societies with secular-rational values display the opposite preferences on all of these topics. The other dimension, *Survival/Self-expression*, also captures a wide range of beliefs and values, reflecting an inter-generational shift from an emphasis on economic and physical security above all, towards increasing emphasis on concerns of self-expression, subjective well-being, and quality of life. Societies that rank highly on Survival values tend to emphasize materialist orientations and traditional gender roles; they are relatively intolerant of foreigners, gays and lesbians and other marginalized groups, show relatively low levels of subjective well-being, rank relatively low on interpersonal trust, and emphasize hard work, rather than imagination or tolerance, as important values to teach a child. Societies that emphasize Self-Expression values display the opposite preferences on all of these topics.

These dimensions are robust aspects of cross-cultural variation, and they enable us to locate any society on a two-dimensional map that reflects their relative positions at any given time. But gradual shifts are occurring along these dimensions, transforming many aspects of society. One of the most important of these changes is the fact that the shift toward increasing emphasis on Self-expression values makes democratic political institutions increasingly likely to emerge and flourish.

These changes are closely linked with the economic changes experienced by a given society. Economic development is associated with predictable changes away from absolute norms and values, toward a syndrome of increasingly rational, tolerant, trusting, and post-industrial values. Throughout most of history, survival has been uncertain for most people. But the remarkable economic growth in the era following World War II, together with the rise of the welfare state, brought fundamentally new conditions in advanced industrial societies. The post-war birth cohorts in these countries grew up with unprecedented levels of prosperity, and the welfare state reinforced the feeling that survival was secure, producing an intergenerational value change that is gradually transforming the politics and cultural norms of advanced industrial societies. An important aspect of this change is the shift from Materialist to Post-materialist priorities. A massive body of evidence gathered from 1970 to the present demonstrates that an intergenerational shift from Materialist to Post-materialist priorities is transforming the behaviors and goals of the people of advanced industrial societies (Inglehart, 1997; Inglehart & Welzel, 2005). Recent research demonstrates that this trend is only one aspect of an even broader cultural shift from Survival values to Self-expression values.

The last graph of Figure 3b shows a two-dimensional cultural map on which the value systems of the societies are depicted in the survey years, using the most recent data available for each country (mostly from the 2000 wave but in some cases from the 1995 wave). The vertical dimension represents the Traditional/Secular-rational dimension, and the horizontal dimension reflects the Survival/Self-expression values dimension. It is obvious that both dimensions are strongly linked to economic development, with the value systems of rich countries differing systematically from those of poor countries. Thus, Germany, France, Britain, Italy, Japan, Sweden, the U.S., and all other societies with a 1995 annual per capita GNP over $15,000 rank relatively highly on both dimensions: without exception, they fall in a broad zone near the upper right-hand corner.

Conversely, every one of the societies with per capita GNPs below $2,000 falls into a cluster at the lower left of the map; India, Bangladesh, Pakistan, Nigeria, Zimbabwe, Morocco, Brazil and Peru all fall into this economic zone, which cuts across the African, South Asian, ex-Communist, and Orthodox cultural zones. The remaining societies fall into intermediate cultural-economic zones. Economic development seems to pull societies in a common direction regardless of their cultural heritage.

These two dimensions and the relative position of countries along them are remarkably robust. There is a strong correlation between the positions of given countries on the Traditional/Secular-rational values dimension from one wave of the surveys to the next. With the Survival/Self-expression dimension, the positions of given countries are even more stable: their positions in the earlier wave are correlated with their positions five years later. Although major changes are occurring along these dimensions, the relative positions of given countries are very stable. If one compares the map based on the 1990 surveys with the map based on the 1995 surveys or the 2000 surveys, at first glance they seem to be the same map, showing given clusters of countries (such as Protestant Europe, the English-speaking countries, the Latin American societies, the Confucian societies) in the same relative position—although each successive wave of surveys was not only carried out roughly five years later than the previous one, but included many countries not covered in previous surveys.

Figures 3a and b shows how each society for which we have at least two time points has changed during the last two decades. For most societies, the trend points upward and to the right, thus indicating that they are moving away from an emphasis on tradition and survival, in the direction of rational secular and well-being values. Some societies show opposite trends. For example, the public of Russia has come to emphasize survival and traditional values more heavily since 1990. The same is true for Germany (both East and West), Latvia, Slovakia, Bulgaria, Romania, Hungary, Turkey, Malta, Argentina and Nigeria. Most of these countries have experienced economic collapse or political upheaval, or in some cases, both of these. Since modernization and post-modernization are strongly driven by economic development, economic collapse tends to pull values in the opposite direction. The broad picture, however, substantiates the theoretical expectations. A vast majority of the societies seem to move upwards and to the right in the graph. However, this Figure also demonstrates that although most societies develop in the expected direction, they do so following their own trajectory of change.

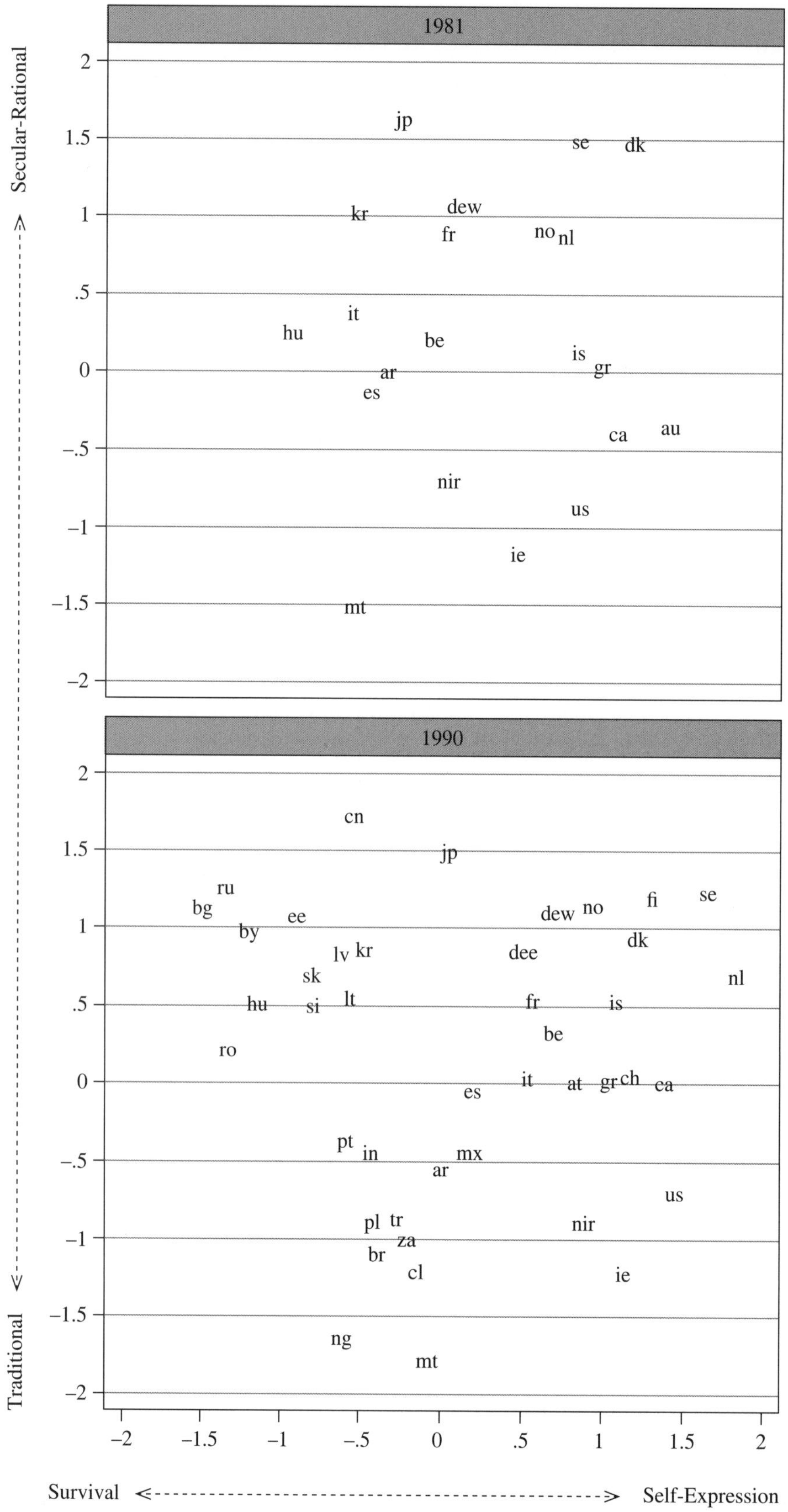

Figure 3a Cultural maps of the world in 1981 and 1990

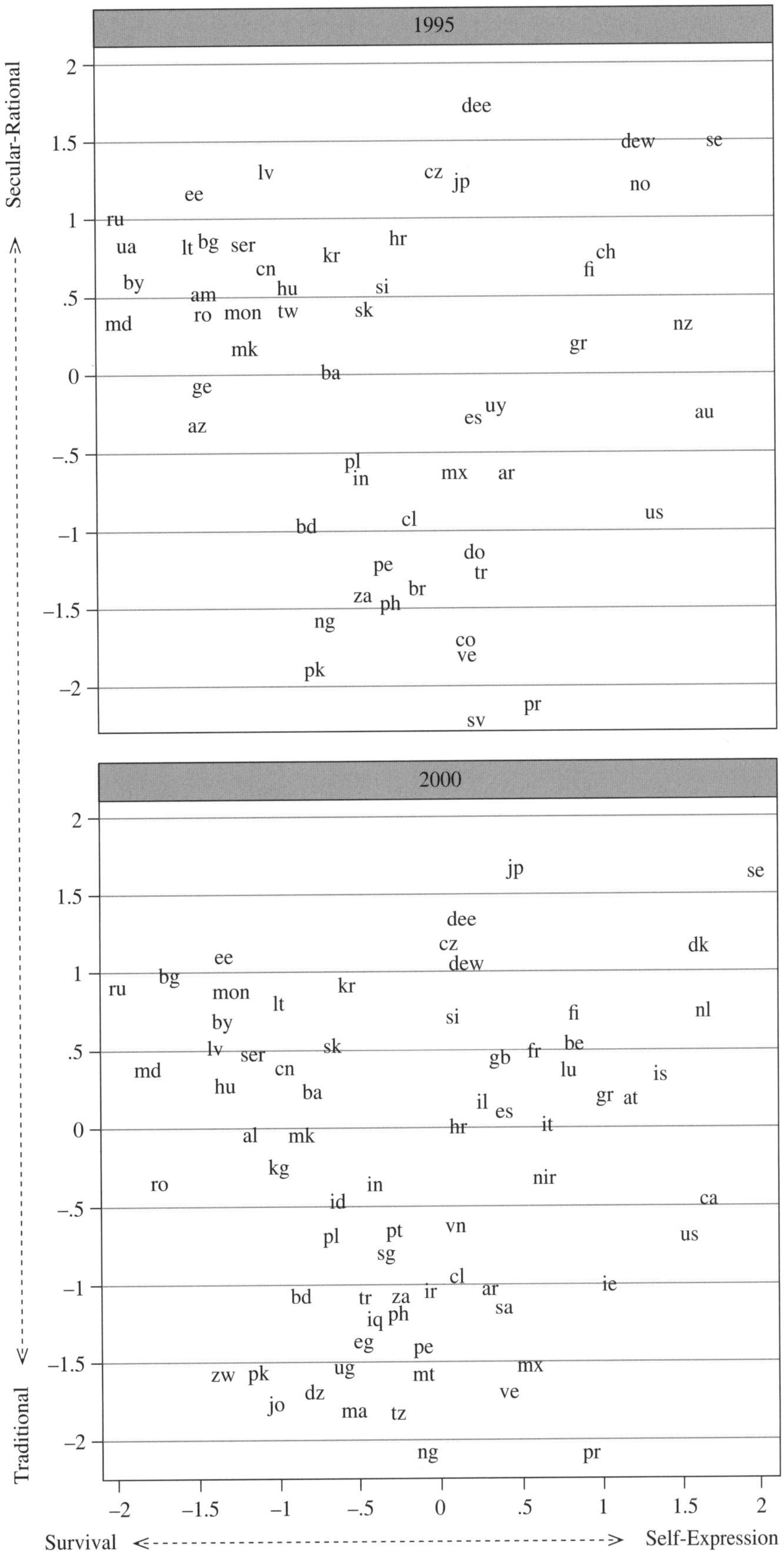

Figure 3b Cultural maps of the world in 1995 and 2000

Economic development interacts with a society's cultural heritage

Nevertheless, two centuries after the industrial revolution began, distinctive cultural zones persist. Different societies follow different trajectories, even when they are subjected to the same forces of economic development, because situation-specific factors, such as a society's cultural heritage, *also* shape how a particular society develops. Huntington (1996) has emphasized the role of religion in the contemporary world and argues that major dividing lines are nowadays defined by culture and no longer defined by ideological, economic and political features. 'In the post-Cold War world, the most important distinctions among peoples are not ideological, political, or economic. They are cultural.... The most important groupings of states are no longer the three blocs of the Cold War but rather the world's seven or eight major civilizations' (Huntington, 1996: 21): Western Christian, Orthodox, Islamic, Confucian or Sinic, Japanese, Hindu, African, and Latin American. Despite the forces of modernization, these zones were shaped by religious traditions that are still, and in Huntington's view increasingly, powerful today.

Although the two dimensions of cultural change are closely linked with economic development, a society's cultural heritage also plays a role. Thus, all eleven Latin American societies fall into a coherent cluster, showing relatively similar values: they rank highly on traditional religious values, but are characterized by a stronger emphasis on Self-expression values than their economic levels would suggest. Economic factors are only part of the story; these countries' common Iberian colonial heritage seems to have left an impact that persists centuries later.

Similarly, despite their wide geographic dispersion, the English-speaking countries constitute a compact cultural zone. In the same way, the historically Roman Catholic societies of Western Europe (e.g., Italy, Portugal, Spain, France, Belgium and Austria) display relatively traditional values when compared with Confucian or ex-Communist societies. And virtually all of the historically Protestant societies (e.g. Denmark, Norway, Sweden, Finland and Iceland) rank more highly on both the traditional-secular rational dimension and the survival/self-expression dimension than do the historically Roman Catholic societies. All four of the Confucian-influenced societies (China, Taiwan, South Korea, and Japan) have relatively secular values, constituting a Confucian cultural zone, despite substantial differences between them in wealth. As Huntington claimed, the Orthodox societies constitute another distinct cultural zone.

A society's religious and colonial heritage seems to have had an enduring impact on its contemporary value system. But a society's culture also reflects, more broadly, its entire historical heritage. A central historical event of the twentieth century was the rise and fall of a Communist empire that once ruled a third of the world's population. Communism left a clear imprint on the value systems of those who lived under it. East Germany remains culturally close to West Germany despite four decades of Communist rule, but its value system has been drawn toward the Communist zone. And, although China is a member of the Confucian zone, it also falls within a broad Communist-influenced zone. Similarly, Azerbaijan, though part of an Islamic cluster, also falls within the Communist superzone that dominated it for decades. Changes in GNP and occupational structure have important influences on prevailing world views, but traditional cultural influences persist.

The ex-communist societies of Central and Eastern Europe all fall into the upper left-hand quadrant of our cultural map, ranking high on the Traditional/Secular-rational dimension (toward the secular pole), but low on the Survival/Self-expression dimension (falling near the survival-oriented pole). Despite different cultural traditions, all of the societies that have experienced Communist rule, form a reasonably coherent group. Although by no means the poorest countries in the world, many Central and Eastern European societies have recently experienced the collapse of Communism, shattering their economic, political and social systems and bringing a pervasive sense of insecurity. Thus, Russia, Ukraine, Bulgaria, Romania and Moldova rank lowest of any countries on the Survival/Self-expression dimension, exhibiting lower levels of subjective well-being than much poorer countries such as India, Bangladesh, Zimbabwe, Uganda and Pakistan. People who have experienced stable poverty throughout their lives tend to emphasize survival values, but those who have experienced the collapse of their economic and social systems experience a sense of unpredictability and insecurity that leads them to emphasize Survival values even more heavily than those who are accustomed to a lower standard of living, in absolute terms.

Not surprisingly, Communist rule seems conducive to the emergence of a relatively secular-rational culture: the ex-Communist countries in general, and those that were members of the Soviet Union in particular, rank higher on secular-rational values than non-communist countries. And, to an equally striking extent, ex-communist countries in general, and former Soviet countries in particular, tend to emphasize survival values far more heavily than societies that have not experienced communist rule. Thus it has been argued (Inglehart & Baker, 2000) that a history of Communist rule continues to account for a significant share of the cross-cultural variance in basic values.

A society's position on the Survival/Self-expression values dimension has important political implications; for example, it is strongly linked with the level of democracy found in each society. The pursuit of self-expression values generates a democratic reform potential, because people tend to emphasize individual freedom and self expression and become more critical towards actual democratic performance. Self-expression values motivate the crucial social force involved in the rise of effective democracy. As such the spread of emancipative self-expression values constitutes the key link in the process of human development, linking socioeconomic development with democratic institutions. Inglehart and Welzel demonstrate that if democratic institutions are in place but emphasis on self-expression values is weak, democracy tends to be ineffective. Self-expression values motivate people to press for freedom, effective civil and political rights, and genuinely responsive government (Inglehart & Welzel, 2005).

The finding that European countries are close to each other on the two dimensions does not mean that they have similar or the same values. On the contrary, despite resemblances, European countries are diverse in this respect (Arts, Hagenaars & Halman, 2003; Arts & Halman, 2004; Halman, Luijkx & Van Zundert, 2005; Ester, Braun & Mohler, 2006). For example, permissiveness with regard to homosexuality is high in the Netherlands and Sweden, but very low in Romania, Lithuania, Latvia and Turkey (Halman, Luijkx & Van Zundert, 2005: 108).

The dimensions of modernization and post-modernization provide an outline of the broad patterns of changes that seem to be occurring among the publics of countries around the world. But the tables that follow in this sourcebook provide a vastly more detailed picture of the ways in which human beliefs and values are changing—and of the fact that many beliefs and values have remained remarkably stable in recent years.

References

Arts, Wil, Jacques Hagenaars & Loek Halman (Eds.) 2003. *The Cultural Diversity of European Unity: Findings, Explanations and Reflections from the European Values Study*. Leiden and Boston: Brill.

Arts, Wil & Loek Halman (Eds.) 2004. *European Values at the End of the Millennium*. Leiden and Boston: Brill.

Beck, Ulrich 1992. *Risk Society: Toward a New Modernity*. London: Sage.

Bell, Daniel 1973. *The Coming of Post-Industrial Society*. New York: Basic Books.

—— 1976. *The Cultural Contradictions of Capitalism*. New York: Basic Books.

Bellah, Robert N., Richard Madsen, William M. Sullivan, Ann Swidler & Steven M. Tipton 1992. *The Good Society. Individualism and Commitment in American Life*. New York: Vintage Books.

Castells, Manuel 1996. *The Information Age: Economy, Society and Culture. The Rise of the Network Society*. Oxford: Blackwell.

—— 1997. *The Information Age: Economy, Society and Culture. The Power of Identity*. Oxford: Blackwell.

—— 1998. *The Information Age: Economy, Society and Culture. End of Millennium*. Oxford: Blackwell.

Dalton, Russell J. 2004. *Democratic Challenges. Democratic Choices*. Oxford: Oxford University Press.

Davie, Grace 2002. *Europe: The Exceptional Case*. London: Darton, Longmann and Todd Ltd.

De Witte, Hans, Loek Halman & John Gelissen 2004. European Work Orientations at the End of the Twentieth Century. Pp. 255–279 in Wil Arts & Loek Halman (Eds.) *European Values at the End of the Millennium*. Leiden and Boston: Brill.

Dobbelaere, Karel 2002. *Secularization: An Analysis at Three Levels*. Brussels: P.I.E. Peter Lang.

Ester, Peter, Michael Braun & Peter Mohler (Eds.) 2006. *Globalization, Value Change and Generations*. Leiden and Boston: Brill.

Ester, Peter, Peter Mohler & Henk Vinken 2006. Values and the Social Sciences: A Global World of Global Values? Pp. 3–29 in Peter Ester, Michael Braun & Peter Mohler (Eds.) *Globalization, Value Change, and Generations*. Leiden, Boston: Brill.

Ester, Peter, Loek Halman & Ruud de Moor (Eds.) 1994. *The Individualizing Society. Value Change in Europe and North America*. Tilburg: Tilburg University Press.

Etzioni, Amatai 1996. *The New Golden Rule. Community and Morality in a Democratic Society*. New York: Basic Books.

—— 2001. *The Monochrome Society*. Princeton: Princeton University Press.

Florida, Richard 2002. *The Rise of the Creative Class*. New York: Basic Books.

—— 2005. *The Flight of the Creative Class*. New York: Harper Collins.

Fukuyama, Francis 2000. *The Great Disruption: Human Nature and the Reconstitution of Social Order*. New York: Simon and Schuster.

Giddens, Anthony 1991. *Modernity and Self Identity*. Stanford: Stanford University Press.

Halman, Loek 2001. *The European Values Study: A Third Wave. Source book of the 1999/2000 European Values Study Surveys*. Tilburg: EVS, WORC, Tilburg University.

Halman, Loek, Ruud Luijkx & Marga van Zundert 2005. *Atlas of European Values*. Leiden: Brill.

Halman, Loek & Thorleif Pettersson 2006. A Decline of Religious Values? Pp. 31–60 in Peter Ester, Michael Braun & Peter Mohler (Eds.) 2006. *Globalization, Value Change and Generations*. Leiden and Boston: Brill.

Harding, Stephen, David Phillips with Michael Fogerty 1986. *Contrasting Values in Western Europe: Unity, Diversity and Change*. London: MacMillan.

Harding, Steven & Frans Hikspoors 1995. New Work Values: Theory and Practice. *International Social Science Journal* 145: 441–455.
Huntington, Samuel 1996. *The Clash of Civilizations and the Remaking of the World Order*. New York: Simon & Schuster.
Inglehart, Ronald 1977. *The Silent Revolution: Changing Values and Political Styles among Western Publics*. Princeton: Princeton University Press.
—— 1990. *Culture Shift in Advanced Industrial Society*. Princeton: Princeton University Press.
—— 1997. *Modernization and Postmodernization. Cultural, Economic and Political Change in 43 Societies*. Princeton: Princeton University Press.
Inglehart, Ronald & Wayne Baker 2000. 'Modernization, Cultural Change and the Persistence of Traditional Values'. *American Sociological Review* 65:19–51.
Inglehart, Ronald, Miguel Basáñez, Jaime Díez-Medrano, Loek Halman & Ruud Luijkx (Eds.) 2004. *Human Values and Beliefs: A Cross-Cultural Sourcebook based on the 1999–2001 Values Surveys*. Mexico City: Siglo XXI.
Inglehart, Ronald, Miguel Basáñez & Alejandro Moreno 1998. *Human Values and Beliefs*. Ann Arbor: The University of Michigan Press.
Inglehart, Ronald & Pippa Norris 2003. *Rising Tide: Gender Equality and Cultural Change Around the World*. New York and Cambridge: Cambridge University Press, 2003.
Inglehart, Ronald & Christian Welzel 2005. *Modernization, Cultural Change and Democracy*. New York and Cambridge: Cambridge University Press.
Martin, David 2005. *On Secularization. Towards a Revised General Theory*. Aldershot: Ashgate.
Miller, Jon D. & Rafael Pardo 2000. Civic Scientific Literacy and Attitude to Science and Technology: A Comparative Analysis of the European Union, the United States, Japan, and Canada. Pp. 81–129 in Meinolf Dierkes & Claudia von Grote (Eds.) *Between Understanding and Trust: The Public, Science, and Technology*. Amsterdam: Harwood Academic Publishers.
Miller, Jon D., Rafael Pardo & Fujio Niwa 1997. *Public Perceptions of Science and Technology: A Comparative Study of the European Union, the United States, Japan, and Canada*. Madrid: BBV Foundation.
Norris, Pippa (Eds.) 1999. *Critical Citizens. Global Support for Democratic Governance*. Oxford: Oxford University Press.
Norris, Pippa & Ronald Inglehart 2004. *Sacred and Secular: Reexamining the Secularization Thesis*. New York and Cambridge: Cambridge University Press.
Putnam, Robert. 2000. *Bowling Alone. The Collapse and Renewal of American Community*. New York: Simon and Schuster.
—— (Eds) 2002. *Democracies in Flux: The Evolution of Social Capital in Contemporary Society*. Oxford: Oxford University Press.
Putnam, Robert & Kristin A. Goss 2002. Introduction. Pp. 3–19 in Robert Putnam (Eds.) *Democracies in Flux: The Evolution of Social Capital in Contemporary Society*. Oxford: Oxford University Press.
Rush, Michael 1992. *Politics and Society. An Introduction to Political Sociology*. New York, London, Toronto, Sydney, Tokyo, Singapore: Prentice Hall.
Zanders, Harry 1994. Changing Work Values. Pp. 129–153 in Peter Ester, Loek Halman & Ruud de Moor (Eds.), *The Individualizing Society*. Tilburg: Tilburg University Press.

TABLES

Family Important

(A001) *For each of the following aspects, indicate how important it is in your life: Family*

Very important (%)

	1981	1990	1995	2000	Change
Albania			96	96	0
Algeria				95	
Argentina			87	90	3
Armenia			86		
Australia			90		
Austria		85		89	4
Azerbaijan			85		
Bangladesh			94	97	3
Belarus		77	84	78	1
Belgium		84		87	3
Bosnia and Herz.			97	99	2
Brazil		91	93		2
Bulgaria		76	89	83	7
Canada		91		94	3
Chile		85	90	96	11
China		62	77	61	–1
Colombia			86		
Croatia			85	79	–6
Czech Republic		86	91	85	–1
Denmark		88		87	–1
Dominican Rep.			86		
Egypt				96	
El Salvador			97		
Estonia		69	78	68	–1
Finland		84	81	80	–4
France		82		88	6
Georgia			95		
Germany (East)		84	83	78	–6
Germany (West)		71	75	82	11
Great Britain		88		89	1
Greece				83	
Hungary		89	90	89	0
Iceland		91		94	3
India		77	91	93	16
Indonesia				99	
Iran				95	
Iraq				98	
Ireland		91		91	0
Israel					
Italy		88		90	2
Japan		78	91	93	15
Jordan				97	
Korea Republic		93	90	90	–3
Kyrgyzstan				87	
Latvia		73	68	72	–1
Lithuania		65	74	66	1
Luxembourg				88	
Macedonia			98	98	0
Malta		96		95	–1
Mexico		85	72	97	12
Moldova			79	86	7
Montenegro			88	92	4
Morocco				93	
Netherlands		80		80	0
New Zealand			93		
Nigeria		94	98	99	5
Northern Ireland		94		90	–4
Norway		88	88		0
Pakistan			81	93	12
Peru			88	83	–5
Philippines			96	99	3
Poland		91	90	92	1
Portugal		65		84	19
Puerto Rico			93	96	3
Romania		83	89	85	2
Russian Fed.		79	84	76	–3
Saudi Arabia				95	
Serbia			89	92	3
Singapore				92	
Slovakia		88	91	87	–1
Slovenia		81	83	82	1
South Africa		90	93	95	5
Spain		83	82	86	3
Sweden		87	90	90	3
Switzerland		88	81		–7
Taiwan			78		
Tanzania				93	
Turkey		87	97	97	10
Uganda				91	
Ukraine			87	82	–5
Uruguay			91		
USA		92	95	95	3
Venezuela			98	98	0
Vietnam				82	
Zimbabwe				97	

Friends Important

(A002) *For each of the following aspects, indicate how important it is in your life: Friends*

Very important (%)

	1981	1990	1995	2000	Change
Albania			19	32	13
Algeria				36	
Argentina			49	50	1
Armenia			45		
Australia			63		
Austria		35		44	9
Azerbaijan			35		
Bangladesh			16	32	16
Belarus		37	32	27	–10
Belgium		46		48	2
Bosnia and Herz.			72	71	–1
Brazil		57	58		1
Bulgaria		38	41	37	–1
Canada		51		60	9
Chile		19	28	29	10
China		22	30	20	–2
Colombia			34		
Croatia			48	36	–12
Czech Republic		23	39	27	4
Denmark		53		55	2
Dominican Rep.			36		
Egypt				37	
El Salvador			65		
Estonia		23	27	26	3
Finland		43	56	51	8
France		41		50	9
Georgia			74		
Germany (East)		32	40	45	13
Germany (West)		37	47	49	12
Great Britain		48		58	10
Greece				42	
Hungary		27	38	34	7
Iceland		49		48	–1
India		30	38	40	10
Indonesia				56	
Iran				30	
Iraq				60	
Ireland		54		61	7
Israel					
Italy		38		36	–2
Japan		34	51	48	14
Jordan				47	
Korea Republic		52	46	45	–7
Kyrgyzstan				48	
Latvia		16	24	25	9
Lithuania		19	22	17	–2
Luxembourg				47	
Macedonia			50	50	0
Malta		29		32	3
Mexico		25	26	38	13
Moldova			21	35	14
Montenegro			48	43	–5
Morocco				42	
Netherlands		59		60	1
New Zealand			57		
Nigeria		53	53	64	11
Northern Ireland		53		65	12
Norway		68	59		–9
Pakistan			27	19	–8
Peru			22	25	3
Philippines			39	37	–2
Poland		21	26	27	6
Portugal		20		30	10
Puerto Rico			29	33	4
Romania		25	21	26	1
Russian Fed.		29	29	27	–2
Saudi Arabia				53	
Serbia			48	57	9
Singapore				40	
Slovakia		28	32	34	6
Slovenia		38	41	42	4
South Africa		23	27	34	11
Spain		45	41	43	–2
Sweden		69	70	71	2
Switzerland		52	59		7
Taiwan			29		
Tanzania				32	
Turkey		55	71	74	19
Uganda				75	
Ukraine			35	39	4
Uruguay			58		
USA		54	70	64	10
Venezuela			42	53	11
Vietnam				22	
Zimbabwe				35	

Leisure Time Important

(A003) *For each of the following aspects, indicate how important it is in your life: Leisure Time*

Very important (%)

	1981	1990	1995	2000	Change
Albania			12	14	2
Algeria				24	
Argentina			27	36	9
Armenia			24		
Australia			45		
Austria		37		39	2
Azerbaijan			30		
Bangladesh			11	23	12
Belarus		37	30	25	–12
Belgium		41		40	–1
Bosnia and Herz.			46	43	–3
Brazil		51	54		3
Bulgaria		36	22	23	–13
Canada		42		38	–4
Chile		33	43	54	21
China		14	11	7	–7
Colombia			40		
Croatia			34	25	–9
Czech Republic		24	26	21	–3
Denmark		48		45	–3
Dominican Rep.			31		
Egypt				9	
El Salvador			62		
Estonia		25	22	19	–6
Finland		47	35	39	–8
France		31		37	6
Georgia			36		
Germany (East)		36	33	23	–13
Germany (West)		40	32	34	–6
Great Britain		45		51	6
Greece				43	
Hungary		32	34	31	–1
Iceland		36		34	–2
India		16	11	29	13
Indonesia				17	
Iran				30	
Iraq				32	
Ireland		32		40	8
Israel					
Italy		33		29	–4
Japan		24	44	44	20
Jordan				17	
Korea Republic		25	23	24	–1
Kyrgyzstan				25	
Latvia		21	20	17	–4
Lithuania		17	19	15	–2
Luxembourg				38	
Macedonia			49	42	–7
Malta		47		50	3
Mexico		28	32	51	23
Moldova			23	25	2
Montenegro			26	25	–1
Morocco				40	
Netherlands		50		53	3
New Zealand			47		
Nigeria		68	51	52	–16
Northern Ireland		31		46	15
Norway		42	39		–3
Pakistan			13	5	–8
Peru			29	23	–6
Philippines			14	15	1
Poland		31	24	25	–6
Portugal		16		20	4
Puerto Rico			47	53	6
Romania		25	27	24	–1
Russian Fed.		29	26	20	–9
Saudi Arabia				31	
Serbia			26	31	5
Singapore				26	
Slovakia		29	26	32	3
Slovenia		28	33	33	5
South Africa		29	32	36	7
Spain		38	30	35	–3
Sweden		55	52	54	–1
Switzerland		47	46		–1
Taiwan			26		
Tanzania				12	
Turkey		24	41	43	19
Uganda				45	
Ukraine			26	25	–1
Uruguay			47		
USA		43	43	43	0
Venezuela			61	66	5
Vietnam				7	
Zimbabwe				28	

Politics Important

(A004) *For each of the following aspects, indicate how important it is in your life: Politics*

Very important (%)

	1981	1990	1995	2000	Change
Albania			23	31	8
Algeria				52	
Argentina			31	24	–7
Armenia			50		
Australia			50		
Austria		35		41	6
Azerbaijan			37		
Bangladesh			50	51	1
Belarus		37	41	30	–7
Belgium		26		32	6
Bosnia and Herz.			49	36	–13
Brazil		42	51		9
Bulgaria		46	26	31	–15
Canada		48		41	–7
Chile		31	20	31	0
China		59	63	68	9
Colombia			32		
Croatia			26	29	3
Czech Republic		37	26	31	–6
Denmark		43		42	–1
Dominican Rep.			39		
Egypt				50	
El Salvador			38		
Estonia		42	28	21	–21
Finland		26	20	20	–6
France		33		35	2
Georgia			46		
Germany (East)		55	47	40	–15
Germany (West)		42	55	39	–3
Great Britain		43		34	–9
Greece				37	
Hungary		26	27	18	–8
Iceland		26		36	10
India		40	34	40	0
Indonesia				39	
Iran				44	
Iraq				55	
Ireland		28		32	4
Israel					
Italy		31		34	3
Japan		54	66	68	14
Jordan				47	
Korea Republic		71	66	51	–20

	1981	1990	1995	2000	Change
Kyrgyzstan				47	
Latvia		44	27	24	–20
Lithuania		51	28	41	–10
Luxembourg				41	
Macedonia			32	36	4
Malta		31		38	7
Mexico		41	48	46	5
Moldova			28	36	8
Montenegro			29	28	–1
Morocco				25	
Netherlands		53		57	4
New Zealand			44		
Nigeria		39	44	52	13
Northern Ireland		28		35	7
Norway		50	45		–5
Pakistan			21	14	–7
Peru			38	44	6
Philippines			49	55	6
Poland		39	31	30	–9
Portugal		22		27	5
Puerto Rico			36	40	4
Romania		21	25	25	4
Russian Fed.		37	28	38	1
Saudi Arabia				56	
Serbia			25	25	0
Singapore				47	
Slovakia		33	29	29	–4
Slovenia		25	15	15	–10
South Africa		58	46	50	–8
Spain		21	24	22	1
Sweden		45	47	55	10
Switzerland		41	38		–3
Taiwan			44		
Tanzania				71	
Turkey		27	52	40	13
Uganda				55	
Ukraine			30	38	8
Uruguay			36		
USA		52	59	57	5
Venezuela			27	34	7
Vietnam				78	
Zimbabwe				42	

Work Important

(A005) *For each of the following aspects, indicate how important it is in your life: Work*

Very important (%)

	1981	1990	1995	2000	Change
Albania			80	82	2
Algeria				93	
Argentina			70	74	4
Armenia			67		
Australia			51		
Austria		62		66	4
Azerbaijan			54		
Bangladesh			83	92	9
Belarus		55	48	49	–6
Belgium		58		63	5
Bosnia and Herz.			81	75	–6
Brazil		82	84		2
Bulgaria		57	54	62	5
Canada		59		52	–7
Chile		75	66	76	1
China		64	65	50	–14
Colombia			72		
Croatia			55	48	–7
Czech Republic		58	49	53	–5
Denmark		51		40	–11
Dominican Rep.			66		
Egypt				72	
El Salvador			95		
Estonia		32	61	51	19
Finland		54	49	52	–2
France		61		69	8
Georgia			58		
Germany (East)		61	61	63	2
Germany (West)		35	41	41	6
Great Britain		51		42	–9
Greece				59	
Hungary		59	51	57	–2
Iceland		56		54	–2
India		86	83	78	–8
Indonesia				89	
Iran				79	
Iraq				86	
Ireland		65		51	–14
Israel					
Italy		62		62	0
Japan		40	53	49	9
Jordan				65	
Korea Republic		69	58	62	–7
Kyrgyzstan				55	
Latvia		33	56	70	37
Lithuania		42	46	54	12
Luxembourg				53	
Macedonia			87	76	–11
Malta		83		76	–7
Mexico		67	62	87	20
Moldova			53	43	–10
Montenegro			55	59	4
Morocco				89	
Netherlands		51		48	–3
New Zealand			48		
Nigeria		94	87	89	–5
Northern Ireland		57		42	–15
Norway		73	59		–14
Pakistan			68	61	–7
Peru			75	69	–6
Philippines			83	93	10
Poland		68	64	78	10
Portugal		35		58	23
Puerto Rico			75	75	0
Romania		69	59	71	2
Russian Fed.		46	49	59	13
Saudi Arabia				63	
Serbia			63	55	–8
Singapore				53	
Slovakia		64	48	61	–3
Slovenia		73	55	62	–11
South Africa		79	81	80	1
Spain		65	59	59	–6
Sweden		67	65	54	–13
Switzerland		52	47		–5
Taiwan			45		
Tanzania				96	
Turkey		59	77	75	16
Uganda				79	
Ukraine			49	62	13
Uruguay			71		
USA		62	56	54	–8
Venezuela			94	93	–1
Vietnam				57	
Zimbabwe				90	

Religion Important

(A006) *For each of the following aspects, indicate how important it is in your life: Religion*

Very important (%)

	1981	1990	1995	2000	Change
Albania			25	28	3
Algeria				91	
Argentina			35	47	12
Armenia			27		
Australia			23		
Austria		24		20	–4
Azerbaijan			30		
Bangladesh			82	88	6
Belarus		12	22	12	0
Belgium		15		18	3
Bosnia and Herz.			35	34	–1
Brazil		57	65		8
Bulgaria		12	16	16	4
Canada		31		30	–1
Chile		51	43	47	–4
China		1	4	3	2
Colombia			49		
Croatia			26	26	0
Czech Republic		9	9	7	–2
Denmark		9		8	–1
Dominican Rep.			51		
Egypt				97	
El Salvador			87		
Estonia		4	8	5	1
Finland		14	13	14	0
France		14		11	–3
Georgia			49		
Germany (East)		12	6	4	–8
Germany (West)		13	15	10	–3
Great Britain		16		13	–3
Greece				33	
Hungary		23	22	20	–3
Iceland		24		19	–5
India		49	49	57	8
Indonesia				98	
Iran				80	
Iraq				94	
Ireland		48		33	–15
Israel					
Italy		34		33	–1
Japan		6	7	7	1
Jordan				96	
Korea Republic		26	20	23	–3
Kyrgyzstan				32	
Latvia		7	13	11	4
Lithuania		16	13	14	–2
Luxembourg				16	
Macedonia			35	48	13
Malta		71		66	–5
Mexico		34	44	68	34
Moldova			31	35	4
Montenegro			24	19	–5
Morocco				94	
Netherlands		22		17	–5
New Zealand			20		
Nigeria		85	92	93	8
Northern Ireland		34		28	–6
Norway		15	12		–3
Pakistan			80	82	2
Peru			55	53	–2
Philippines			78	87	9
Poland		52	47	45	–7
Portugal		17		27	10
Puerto Rico			71	76	5
Romania		42	38	51	9
Russian Fed.		12	14	12	0
Saudi Arabia				89	
Serbia			26	29	3
Singapore				36	
Slovakia		25	24	27	2
Slovenia		17	16	12	–5
South Africa		66	68	70	4
Spain		23	25	19	–4
Sweden		10	10	11	1
Switzerland		24	15		–9
Taiwan			13		
Tanzania				85	
Turkey		61	83	81	20
Uganda				74	
Ukraine			21	22	1
Uruguay			23		
USA		53	56	57	4
Venezuela			61	64	3
Vietnam				10	
Zimbabwe				78	

Feeling of Happiness

(A008) *Taking all things together, would you say you are*

Very happy (%)

	1981	1990	1995	2000	Change
Albania			3	10	7
Algeria				17	
Argentina	17	33	29	33	16
Armenia			6		
Australia	35		43		8
Austria		30		36	6
Azerbaijan			11		
Bangladesh			18	15	–3
Belarus		6	4	5	–1
Belgium	33	40		43	10
Bosnia and Herz.			14	22	8
Brazil		21	22		1
Bulgaria		7	9	8	1
Canada	35	30		44	9
Chile		33	27	36	3
China		28	23	12	–16
Colombia			47		
Croatia			9	13	4
Czech Republic		7	9	11	4
Denmark	31	43		45	14
Dominican Rep.			32		
Egypt				18	
El Salvador			56		
Estonia		3	5	7	4
Finland		20	24	24	4
France	20	25		31	11
Georgia			12		
Germany (East)		13	16	21	8
Germany (West)	11	16	21	19	8
Great Britain	38	38	32		–6
Greece				19	
Hungary	11	11	14	17	6
Iceland	44	41		47	3
India		24	30	26	2
Indonesia				21	
Iran				25	
Iraq				13	
Ireland	40	44		42	2
Israel				28	
Italy	11	16		18	7
Japan	16	18	34	29	13
Jordan				13	
Korea Republic		10	12	10	0

	1981	1990	1995	2000	Change
Kyrgyzstan				20	
Latvia		2	5	7	5
Lithuania		4	4	5	1
Luxembourg				36	
Macedonia			14	19	5
Malta	13	40		31	18
Mexico		26	28	57	31
Moldova			4	6	2
Montenegro			14	9	–5
Morocco				26	
Netherlands	34	46		46	12
New Zealand			33		
Nigeria		40	46	67	27
Northern Ireland	40	37		47	7
Norway	28	29	30		2
Pakistan			28	20	–8
Peru			28	31	3
Philippines			40	38	–2
Poland		10	18	18	8
Portugal		13		18	5
Puerto Rico			43	53	10
Romania		6	5	4	–2
Russian Fed.		6	6	6	0
Saudi Arabia				44	
Serbia			14	12	–2
Singapore				29	
Slovakia		6	7	8	2
Slovenia		9	14	16	7
South Africa		24	35	39	15
Spain	20	21	19	20	0
Sweden	29	41	40	37	8
Switzerland		36	40		4
Taiwan			30		
Tanzania				57	
Turkey		29	51	31	2
Uganda				26	
Ukraine			5	6	1
Uruguay			21		
USA	32	40	47	39	7
Venezuela			55	57	2
Vietnam				49	
Zimbabwe				20	

State of Health

(A009) *All in all, how would you describe your state of health these days? Would you say it is…*

Very good/good (%)

	1981	1990	1995	2000	Change
Albania			72	75	3
Algeria				44	
Argentina	51	60	62	65	14
Armenia			51		
Australia	75		80		5
Austria		64			
Azerbaijan			58		
Bangladesh			47	58	11
Belarus		27	27		0
Belgium	70	72			2
Bosnia and Herz.			58	65	7
Brazil		69	70		1
Bulgaria		51	58		7
Canada	81	80		82	1
Chile		54	61	69	15
China		56	68	61	5
Colombia			76		
Croatia			51		
Czech Republic		49	53		4
Denmark	73	78			5
Dominican Rep.			68		
Egypt				68	
El Salvador			67		
Estonia		36	39		3
Finland		76	72		–4
France	59	66			7
Georgia			49		
Germany (East)		54	56		2
Germany (West)	54	56	61		7
Great Britain	72	75			3
Greece					
Hungary	35	31	47		12
Iceland	69	74			5
India		63	57	63	0
Indonesia				74	
Iran				76	
Iraq				77	
Ireland	78	81			3
Israel					
Italy	50	55			5
Japan	44	44	56	55	11
Jordan				83	
Korea Republic	33		79	78	45
Kyrgyzstan				61	
Latvia		32	36		4
Lithuania		43	45		2
Luxembourg					
Macedonia			73	71	–2
Malta	57				
Mexico		69	56	62	–7
Moldova			32	30	–2
Montenegro			54	59	5
Morocco				73	
Netherlands	71	71			0
New Zealand			79		
Nigeria		78	75	89	11
Northern Ireland	76	77			1
Norway	75	74	79		4
Pakistan			63	66	3
Peru			51	49	–2
Philippines			52	57	5
Poland		37	41		4
Portugal		44			
Puerto Rico			68	73	5
Romania		47	53		6
Russian Fed.		26	26		0
Saudi Arabia				89	
Serbia			52	53	1
Singapore					
Slovakia		47	52		5
Slovenia		43	46		3
South Africa		67	68	78	11
Spain	49	56	70	76	27
Sweden	71	80	77		6
Switzerland		80	85		5
Taiwan			48		
Tanzania				64	
Turkey		60	61	65	5
Uganda				72	
Ukraine			27		
Uruguay			77		
USA	76	79	79	84	8
Venezuela			74		
Vietnam				58	
Zimbabwe				63	

Respect Parents

(A025) *With which of these two statements do you tend to agree? A. Regardless of what the qualities and faults of one's parents are, one must always love and respect them. B. One does not have the duty to respect and love parents who have not earned it by their behavior and attitudes*

Ten to agree with statement A (%)

	1981	1990	1995	2000	Change
Albania			92	87	–5
Algeria				93	
Argentina	67	75	82	88	21
Armenia			93		
Australia			74		
Austria		74		65	–9
Azerbaijan			92		
Bangladesh			90	90	0
Belarus		83	84	71	–12
Belgium	81	76		65	–16
Bosnia and Herz.			89	91	2
Brazil		90	93		3
Bulgaria		83	89	82	–1
Canada	70	69		78	8
Chile		88	84	87	–1
China		75	80	94	19
Colombia			91		
Croatia			74	71	–3
Czech Republic		76	78	74	–2
Denmark	41	47		36	–5
Dominican Rep.			86		
Egypt				95	
El Salvador			94		
Estonia		62	83	72	10
Finland		40	73	63	23
France	80	77		75	–5
Georgia			91		
Germany (East)		77	69	70	–7
Germany (West)	60	62	47	49	–11
Great Britain	59	68		65	6
Greece				69	
Hungary	70	81	81	83	13
Iceland	61	61		61	0
India		84	85	89	5
Indonesia				90	
Iran				89	
Iraq					
Ireland	80	78		72	–8
Israel					
Italy	82	84		79	–3
Japan	70	78	74	72	2
Jordan				94	
Korea Republic	90	94	94	92	2

	1981	1990	1995	2000	Change
Kyrgyzstan				94	
Latvia		72	79	77	5
Lithuania		80	80	83	3
Luxembourg				59	
Macedonia			83	91	8
Malta	92	90		91	–1
Mexico		78	76	90	12
Moldova			89	90	1
Montenegro			89	87	–2
Morocco				97	
Netherlands	44	42		32	–12
New Zealand			64		
Nigeria		87	88	94	7
Northern Ireland	76	80		78	2
Norway	50	45	52		2
Pakistan			94	94	0
Peru			93	91	–2
Philippines			96	94	–2
Poland		89	94	87	–2
Portugal		77		83	6
Puerto Rico			92	97	5
Romania		83	88	84	1
Russian Fed.		76	90	84	8
Saudi Arabia				92	
Serbia			83	87	4
Singapore				93	
Slovakia		82	81	74	–8
Slovenia		82	86	78	–4
South Africa		88	90	91	3
Spain	73	81	86	83	10
Sweden	51	51	57	44	–7
Switzerland		70	66		–4
Taiwan			93		
Tanzania				91	
Turkey		82	86	86	4
Uganda				90	
Ukraine			90	86	–4
Uruguay			78		
USA	74	75	77	77	3
Venezuela			91	94	3
Vietnam				99	
Zimbabwe				96	

Parents' Responsibilities

(A026) *Which of the following statements best describes your views about parents' responsibilities to their children?*

Parents duty is to do their best for their children even at the expense of their own well-being (%)

	1981	1990	1995	2000	Change
Albania			80	75	–5
Algeria				78	
Argentina	69	79	77	81	12
Armenia			64		
Australia			75		
Austria		60		71	11
Azerbaijan			59		
Bangladesh			61	68	7
Belarus		65	53	49	–16
Belgium	68	64		78	10
Bosnia and Herz.			81	88	7
Brazil		81	82		1
Bulgaria		58	58	75	17
Canada	66	67		82	16
Chile		80	76	85	5
China		61	56	67	6
Colombia			87		
Croatia			86	90	4
Czech Republic		56	47	60	4
Denmark	51	52		60	9
Dominican Rep.			83		
Egypt				94	
El Salvador			89		
Estonia		55	65	58	3
Finland		49	56	70	21
France	75	81		75	0
Georgia			76		
Germany (East)		71	68	55	–16
Germany (West)	59	54	46	59	0
Great Britain	73	74		76	3
Greece				57	
Hungary	53	62	79	65	12
Iceland	69	50		64	–5
India		78	77	79	1
Indonesia				84	
Iran				61	
Iraq					
Ireland	78	73		76	–2
Israel					
Italy	67	79		72	5
Japan	54	40	43	40	–14
Jordan				84	
Korea Republic	67	38	49	51	–16

	1981	1990	1995	2000	Change
Kyrgyzstan				67	
Latvia		51	50	76	25
Lithuania		37	45	39	2
Luxembourg				68	
Macedonia			80	82	2
Malta	90	91		91	1
Mexico		74	63	81	7
Moldova			71	75	4
Montenegro			86	86	0
Morocco				85	
Netherlands	60	68		61	1
New Zealand			71		
Nigeria		89	83	98	9
Northern Ireland	75	81		81	6
Norway	76	73	77		1
Pakistan			84	93	9
Peru			85	84	–1
Philippines			91	90	–1
Poland		67	75	72	5
Portugal		84		80	–4
Puerto Rico			89	92	3
Romania		85	66	89	4
Russian Fed.		51	62	56	5
Saudi Arabia				83	
Serbia			76	82	6
Singapore				80	
Slovakia		58	63	60	2
Slovenia		72	85	74	2
South Africa		88	77	82	–6
Spain	77	77	81	80	3
Sweden	68	63	72	67	–1
Switzerland		69	59		–10
Taiwan			75		
Tanzania				78	
Turkey		71	79	79	8
Uganda				84	
Ukraine			63	63	0
Uruguay			80		
USA	72	75	75	85	13
Venezuela			92	90	–2
Vietnam				87	
Zimbabwe				91	

Child Qualities: Good Manners

(A027) *Here is a list of qualities which children can be encouraged to learn at home. Which, if any, do you consider to be especially important?*

Good manners (%)

	1981	1990	1995	2000	Change
Albania			94		
Algeria				83	
Argentina	48	78	74	83	35
Armenia			76		
Australia	53		80		27
Austria		79		78	–1
Azerbaijan			53		
Bangladesh			95		
Belarus		71	15	60	–11
Belgium	47	72		78	31
Bosnia and Herz.			72		
Brazil		77	52		–25
Bulgaria		72	86	69	–3
Canada	54	75			21
Chile		90	82		–8
China		53	67		14
Colombia			84		
Croatia			64		
Czech Republic		87	79	87	0
Denmark	50	66		72	22
Dominican Rep.			85		
Egypt				78	
El Salvador			82		
Estonia		74	67	78	4
Finland		83	82	90	7
France	21	53		69	48
Georgia			61		
Germany (East)		69	74	67	–2
Germany (West)	42	67	66	63	21
Great Britain	67	89		92	25
Greece				76	
Hungary	48	77	83	71	23
Iceland	60	90		74	14
India		94	82		–12
Indonesia				85	
Iran				89	
Iraq				90	
Ireland	66	75		87	21
Israel				77	
Italy	55	79		75	20
Japan	69	83	81		12
Jordan				95	
Korea Republic	69	93	91		22

	1981	1990	1995	2000	Change
Kyrgyzstan					
Latvia		53	51	72	19
Lithuania		35	33	34	–1
Luxembourg				83	
Macedonia			91		
Malta	70	80		82	12
Mexico		73	75		2
Moldova			63		
Montenegro			80		
Morocco				91	
Netherlands	59	80		81	22
New Zealand			77		
Nigeria		97	94	95	–2
Northern Ireland	80	95		89	9
Norway	60	77	75		15
Pakistan			57	67	10
Peru			88		
Philippines			80		
Poland		45	63	58	13
Portugal		83		77	–6
Puerto Rico			87		
Romania		92	91	80	–12
Russian Fed.		57	52	58	1
Saudi Arabia				71	
Serbia			80		
Singapore					
Slovakia		88	77	73	–15
Slovenia		89	81	77	–12
South Africa		81	86		5
Spain	53	82	85	86	33
Sweden	55	78	67	70	15
Switzerland		59	66		7
Taiwan			70		
Tanzania					
Turkey		92	90	92	0
Uganda					
Ukraine			49	56	7
Uruguay			81		
USA	63	76	73		10
Venezuela			90		
Vietnam					
Zimbabwe					

Child Qualities: Independence

(A029) *Here is a list of qualities that children can be encouraged to learn at home. Which, if any, do you consider to be especially important?*

Independence (%)

	1981	1990	1995	2000	Change
Albania			32	57	25
Algeria				26	
Argentina	42	43	42	36	–6
Armenia			32		
Australia	25		53		28
Austria		65		70	5
Azerbaijan			60		
Bangladesh			57	78	21
Belarus		31	30	32	1
Belgium	20	36		41	21
Bosnia and Herz.			37	56	19
Brazil		27	20		–7
Bulgaria		62	38	42	–20
Canada	24	44		62	38
Chile		31	34	53	22
China		84	50	74	–10
Colombia			27		
Croatia			64		
Czech Republic		52	22	69	17
Denmark	55	81		81	26
Dominican Rep.			40		
Egypt				73	
El Salvador			36		
Estonia		43	54	22	–21
Finland		58	56	58	0
France	16	27		29	13
Georgia			51		
Germany (East)		67	45	70	3
Germany (West)	46	73	58	70	24
Great Britain	23	43	49	53	30
Greece				58	
Hungary	50	70	44	71	21
Iceland	38	89		76	38
India		30	37	56	26
Indonesia				76	
Iran				53	
Iraq				29	
Ireland	29	43		50	21
Israel				69	
Italy	22	31		41	19
Japan	47	64	64	82	35
Jordan				22	
Korea Republic	45	54	60	77	32
Kyrgyzstan				55	
Latvia		73	38	51	–22
Lithuania		81	72	77	–4
Luxembourg				49	
Macedonia			62	59	–3
Malta	8	32		31	23
Mexico		47	43	42	–5
Moldova			36	56	20
Montenegro			52	59	7
Morocco				34	
Netherlands	27	49		53	26
New Zealand			54		
Nigeria		16	20	26	10
Northern Ireland	16	37		51	35
Norway	53	86	89		36
Pakistan			20	13	–7
Peru			21	39	18
Philippines			51	66	15
Poland		12	32	22	10
Portugal		24		22	–2
Puerto Rico			28	51	23
Romania		24	51	30	6
Russian Fed.		29	28	31	2
Saudi Arabia				70	
Serbia			51	61	10
Singapore				75	
Slovakia		48	22	61	13
Slovenia		33	71	70	37
South Africa		16	31	62	46
Spain	24	36	25	39	15
Sweden	18	36	61	69	51
Switzerland		42	42		0
Taiwan			66		
Tanzania				42	
Turkey		19	16	15	–4
Uganda				31	
Ukraine			34	32	–2
Uruguay			49		
USA	31	52	45	61	30
Venezuela			23	45	22
Vietnam				56	
Zimbabwe				26	

Child Qualities: Hard Work

(A030) *Here is a list of qualities that children can be encouraged to learn at home. Which, if any, do you consider to be especially important?*

Hard work (%)

	1981	1990	1995	2000	Change
Albania			57	64	7
Algeria				67	
Argentina	49	53	56	57	8
Armenia			84		
Australia	12		36		24
Austria		14		10	–4
Azerbaijan			77		
Bangladesh			8	59	51
Belarus		80	84	92	12
Belgium	33	36		38	5
Bosnia and Herz.			54	54	0
Brazil		51	47		–4
Bulgaria		91	92	86	–5
Canada	20	35		53	33
Chile		12	17	26	14
China		65	73	86	21
Colombia			18		
Croatia			64		
Czech Republic		84	79	73	–11
Denmark	2	2		2	0
Dominican Rep.			50		
Egypt				38	
El Salvador			38		
Estonia		92	87	82	–10
Finland		6	15	12	6
France	36	53		50	14
Georgia			82		
Germany (East)		18	14	20	2
Germany (West)	22	15	6	23	1
Great Britain	16	29	38	39	23
Greece				31	
Hungary	29	70	34	71	42
Iceland	24	78		44	20
India		67	72	85	18
Indonesia				66	
Iran				62	
Iraq					
Ireland	25	28		37	12
Israel				24	
Italy	13	27		36	23
Japan	16	31	24	27	11
Jordan				45	
Korea Republic	40	64	62	72	32

	1981	1990	1995	2000	Change
Kyrgyzstan				87	
Latvia		91	86	85	–6
Lithuania		92	89	86	–6
Luxembourg				58	
Macedonia			24	37	13
Malta	32	59		42	10
Mexico		23	36	30	7
Moldova			87	87	0
Montenegro			68	82	14
Morocco				70	
Netherlands	13	14		14	1
New Zealand			37		
Nigeria		82	83	80	–2
Northern Ireland	20	29		41	21
Norway	4	7	11		7
Pakistan			53	56	3
Peru			63	59	–4
Philippines			58	74	16
Poland		87	16	86	–1
Portugal		68		69	1
Puerto Rico			30	52	22
Romania		71	64	82	11
Russian Fed.		93	91	91	–2
Saudi Arabia				42	
Serbia			68	75	7
Singapore				64	
Slovakia		83	70	75	–8
Slovenia		32	33	29	–3
South Africa		30	59	75	45
Spain	41	37	64	45	4
Sweden	4	5	7	4	0
Switzerland		36	40		4
Taiwan			42		
Tanzania				83	
Turkey		73	69	74	1
Uganda				86	
Ukraine			83	89	6
Uruguay			29		
USA	27	49	52	61	34
Venezuela			55	27	–28
Vietnam				76	
Zimbabwe				85	

Child Qualities: Feeling of Responsibilities

(A032) *Here is a list of qualities that children can be encouraged to learn at home. Which, if any, do you consider to be especially important?*

Feeling of responsibility (%)

	1981	1990	1995	2000	Change
Albania			31	68	37
Algeria				58	
Argentina	57	80	80	77	20
Armenia			69		
Australia	29		66		37
Austria		85		86	1
Azerbaijan			66		
Bangladesh			39	53	14
Belarus		81	62	77	–4
Belgium	37	73		80	43
Bosnia and Herz.			61	74	13
Brazil		72	65		–7
Bulgaria		68	64	76	8
Canada	41	75		77	36
Chile		88	74	84	–4
China		67	34	64	–3
Colombia			77		
Croatia			67		
Czech Republic		61	69	66	5
Denmark	63	86		81	18
Dominican Rep.			84		
Egypt				51	
El Salvador			67		
Estonia		76	77	79	3
Finland		84	87	86	2
France	39	72		74	35
Georgia			68		
Germany (East)		84	91	80	–4
Germany (West)	63	85	93	85	22
Great Britain	24	48	67	56	32
Greece				83	
Hungary	45	66	85	73	28
Iceland	49	94		81	32
India		60	48	68	8
Indonesia				82	
Iran				72	
Iraq				76	
Ireland	22	61		54	32
Israel				65	
Italy	46	82		82	36
Japan	68	84	86	91	23
Jordan				65	
Korea Republic	54	91	88	92	38

	1981	1990	1995	2000	Change
Kyrgyzstan				78	
Latvia		75	80	74	–1
Lithuania		72	74	76	4
Luxembourg				78	
Macedonia			74	74	0
Malta	38	56		77	39
Mexico		77	65	77	0
Moldova			66	83	17
Montenegro			67	68	1
Morocco				63	
Netherlands	55	86		87	32
New Zealand			59		
Nigeria		36	27	33	–3
Northern Ireland	10	38		54	44
Norway	64	90	92		28
Pakistan			71	50	–21
Peru			77	79	2
Philippines			58	65	7
Poland		68	78	73	5
Portugal		78		60	–18
Puerto Rico			84	74	–10
Romania		56	83	62	6
Russian Fed.		70	70	76	6
Saudi Arabia				57	
Serbia			65	71	6
Singapore				84	
Slovakia		64	69	67	3
Slovenia		71	70	76	5
South Africa		45	49	59	14
Spain	63	78	70	83	20
Sweden	63	89	88	87	24
Switzerland		77	80		3
Taiwan			81		
Tanzania				41	
Turkey		66	59	63	–3
Uganda				52	
Ukraine			66	75	9
Uruguay			81		
USA	44	72	69	72	28
Venezuela			74	88	14
Vietnam				70	
Zimbabwe				48	

Child Qualities: Imagination

(A034) *Here is a list of qualities that children can be encouraged to learn at home. Which, if any, do you consider to be especially important?*

Imagination (%)

	1981	1990	1995	2000	Change
Albania			11	29	18
Algeria				12	
Argentina	23	31	26	24	1
Armenia			16		
Australia	13		26		13
Austria		25		24	–1
Azerbaijan			14		
Bangladesh			14	36	22
Belarus		7	9	10	3
Belgium	8	18		23	15
Bosnia and Herz.			24	27	3
Brazil		12	8		–4
Bulgaria		16	7	19	3
Canada	10	23		33	23
Chile		32	24	36	4
China		27	22	35	8
Colombia			19		
Croatia			17		
Czech Republic		5	5	7	2
Denmark	10	37		37	27
Dominican Rep.			12		
Egypt				15	
El Salvador			10		
Estonia		13	9	11	–2
Finland		27	24	28	1
France	12	23		18	6
Georgia			10		
Germany (East)		27	27	27	0
Germany (West)	14	32	40	30	16
Great Britain	11	18		38	27
Greece				22	
Hungary	7	9	13	11	4
Iceland	6	49		18	12
India		22	11	28	6
Indonesia				29	
Iran				11	
Iraq					
Ireland	7	14		25	18
Israel				23	
Italy	8	15		12	4
Japan	11	24	28	35	24
Jordan				5	
Korea Republic	6	6	8	33	27

	1981	1990	1995	2000	Change
Kyrgyzstan				38	
Latvia		11	10	7	–4
Lithuania		6	7	5	–1
Luxembourg				25	
Macedonia			12	13	1
Malta	2	12		7	5
Mexico		31	29	24	–7
Moldova			13	26	13
Montenegro			17	12	–5
Morocco				9	
Netherlands	11	22		32	21
New Zealand			28		
Nigeria		6	6	11	5
Northern Ireland	9	13		31	22
Norway	12	31	37		25
Pakistan			7	7	0
Peru			19	23	4
Philippines			10	14	4
Poland		10	11	13	3
Portugal		20		15	–5
Puerto Rico			13	19	6
Romania		17	39	14	–3
Russian Fed.		11	6	7	–4
Saudi Arabia				31	
Serbia			13	10	–3
Singapore				14	
Slovakia		8	5	3	–5
Slovenia		10	8	12	2
South Africa		8	11	20	12
Spain	24	38	22	29	5
Sweden	16	40	39	40	24
Switzerland		30	23		–7
Taiwan			15		
Tanzania				61	
Turkey		23	22	22	–1
Uganda				11	
Ukraine			11	11	0
Uruguay			31		
USA	9	27	27	30	21
Venezuela			13	24	11
Vietnam				20	
Zimbabwe				11	

Child Qualities: Tolerance and Respect for Other People

(A035) *Here is a list of qualities that children can be encouraged to learn at home. Which, if any, do you consider to be especially important?*

Tolerance and respect for other people (%)

	1981	1990	1995	2000	Change
Albania			81	80	–1
Algeria				54	
Argentina	44	78	74	70	26
Armenia			48		
Australia	67		81		14
Austria		67		71	4
Azerbaijan			59		
Bangladesh			69	71	2
Belarus		80	60	72	–8
Belgium	45	70		83	38
Bosnia and Herz.			61	72	11
Brazil		65	59		–6
Bulgaria		52	46	59	7
Canada	53	80		81	28
Chile		79	61	76	–3
China		62	43	73	11
Colombia			68		
Croatia			64		
Czech Republic		66	60	63	–3
Denmark	58	81		87	29
Dominican Rep.			68		
Egypt				65	
El Salvador			59		
Estonia		70	60	71	1
Finland		80	82	83	3
France	59	78		85	26
Georgia			54		
Germany (East)		72	86	70	–2
Germany (West)	42	77	91	74	32
Great Britain	62	79	86	84	22
Greece				53	
Hungary	31	62	64	66	35
Iceland	58	93		84	26
India		59	52	63	4
Indonesia				63	
Iran				59	
Iraq				78	
Ireland	56	76		75	19
Israel				82	
Italy	43	66		75	32
Japan	41	60	59	71	30
Jordan				67	
Korea Republic	25	55	47	65	40
Kyrgyzstan				65	
Latvia		70	73	69	–1
Lithuania		57	54	58	1
Luxembourg				78	
Macedonia			71	75	4
Malta	24	41		61	37
Mexico		64	57	71	7
Moldova			63	78	15
Montenegro			64	57	–7
Morocco				65	
Netherlands	57	88		91	34
New Zealand			78		
Nigeria		75	63	59	–16
Northern Ireland	60	80		75	15
Norway	32	64	66		34
Pakistan			55	53	–2
Peru			63	73	10
Philippines			48	60	12
Poland		76	82	80	4
Portugal		70		65	–5
Puerto Rico			74	61	–13
Romania		56	72	58	2
Russian Fed.		70	69	67	–3
Saudi Arabia				56	
Serbia			51	64	13
Singapore				70	
Slovakia		55	57	57	2
Slovenia		74	72	70	–4
South Africa		61	70	74	13
Spain	44	73	76	80	36
Sweden	71	91	90	93	22
Switzerland		77	79		2
Taiwan			59		
Tanzania				84	
Turkey		69	59	63	–6
Uganda				57	
Ukraine			61	65	4
Uruguay			70		
USA	52	71	75	79	27
Venezuela			57	80	23
Vietnam				68	
Zimbabwe				78	

Child Qualities: Thrift, Saving Money and Things

(A038) *Here is a list of qualities that children can be encouraged to learn at home. Which, if any, do you consider to be especially important?*

Thrift, saving money and things (%)

	1981	1990	1995	2000	Change
Albania			67	55	–12
Algeria				18	
Argentina	16	15	16	15	–1
Armenia			38		
Australia	15		19		4
Austria		54		48	–6
Azerbaijan			59		
Bangladesh			51	57	6
Belarus		53	53	46	–7
Belgium	36	36		43	7
Bosnia and Herz.			41	37	–4
Brazil		29	39		10
Bulgaria		39	43	39	0
Canada	14	21		27	13
Chile		29	31	34	5
China		56	62	57	1
Colombia			25		
Croatia			29		
Czech Republic		39	44	32	–7
Denmark	15	19		10	–5
Dominican Rep.			11		
Egypt				8	
El Salvador			30		
Estonia		35	30	45	10
Finland		38	29	23	–15
France	32	36		38	6
Georgia			32		
Germany (East)		61	65	45	–16
Germany (West)	31	46	41	35	4
Great Britain	9	26	28	33	24
Greece				30	
Hungary	33	49	42	41	8
Iceland	13	69		21	8
India		24	42	62	38
Indonesia				52	
Iran				30	
Iraq				28	
Ireland	15	22		23	8
Israel				20	
Italy	19	29		35	16
Japan	32	40	38	48	16
Jordan				19	
Korea Republic	34	53	66	68	34
Kyrgyzstan				43	
Latvia		46	41	45	–1
Lithuania		37	39	42	5
Luxembourg				48	
Macedonia			44	40	–4
Malta	32	41		53	21
Mexico		33	49	39	6
Moldova			42	42	0
Montenegro			25	38	13
Morocco				37	
Netherlands	17	29		22	5
New Zealand			25		
Nigeria		8	10	10	2
Northern Ireland	8	25		26	18
Norway	12	22	13		1
Pakistan			60	55	–5
Peru			19	23	4
Philippines			30	45	15
Poland		44	57	38	–6
Portugal		32		36	4
Puerto Rico			23	24	1
Romania		37	61	31	–6
Russian Fed.		61	55	51	–10
Saudi Arabia				31	
Serbia			29	31	2
Singapore				44	
Slovakia		38	44	39	1
Slovenia		58	40	35	–23
South Africa		17	29	37	20
Spain	11	23	19	32	21
Sweden	32	48	42	31	–1
Switzerland		42	35		–7
Taiwan			49		
Tanzania				54	
Turkey		36	32	29	–7
Uganda				11	
Ukraine			49	50	1
Uruguay			27		
USA	10	29	27	23	13
Venezuela			45	39	–6
Vietnam				48	
Zimbabwe				21	

Child Qualities: Determination, Perseverance

(A039) *Here is a list of qualities that children can be encouraged to learn at home. Which, if any, do you consider to be especially important?*

Determination, perseverance (%)

	1981	1990	1995	2000	Change
Albania			41	53	12
Algeria				17	
Argentina	17	29	28	22	5
Armenia			57		
Australia	18		36		18
Austria		39		36	–3
Azerbaijan			47		
Bangladesh			53	36	–17
Belarus		40	41	49	9
Belgium	21	39		44	23
Bosnia and Herz.			43	46	3
Brazil		26	35		9
Bulgaria		41	44	56	15
Canada	21	38		48	27
Chile		31	34	44	13
China		45	36	16	–29
Colombia			19		
Croatia			44		
Czech Republic		31	35	29	–2
Denmark	11	31		32	21
Dominican Rep.			27		
Egypt				9	
El Salvador			14		
Estonia		51	49	50	–1
Finland		39	44	50	11
France	18	39		38	20
Georgia			37		
Germany (East)		55	45	51	–4
Germany (West)	27	49	37	46	19
Great Britain	17	31	36	40	23
Greece				54	
Hungary	17	12	62	29	12
Iceland	13	75		29	16
India		28	29	46	18
Indonesia				44	
Iran				28	
Iraq					
Ireland	10	26		28	18
Israel				31	
Italy	17	27		34	17
Japan	24	59	61	69	45
Jordan				17	
Korea Republic	27	31	36	42	15

	1981	1990	1995	2000	Change
Kyrgyzstan				51	
Latvia		40	48	36	–4
Lithuania		34	36	35	1
Luxembourg				39	
Macedonia			47	43	–4
Malta	4	21		17	13
Mexico		37	42	33	–4
Moldova			29	33	4
Montenegro			42	44	2
Morocco				16	
Netherlands	16	32		34	18
New Zealand			39		
Nigeria		21	39	23	2
Northern Ireland	10	18		34	24
Norway	12	33	35		23
Pakistan			33	29	–4
Peru			24	34	10
Philippines			29	37	8
Poland		27		35	8
Portugal		23		24	1
Puerto Rico			22	24	2
Romania		40	63	19	–21
Russian Fed.		40	41	40	0
Saudi Arabia				40	
Serbia			44	41	–3
Singapore				40	
Slovakia		29	31	25	–4
Slovenia		42	48	54	12
South Africa		28	30	42	14
Spain	13	22	21	29	16
Sweden	17	33	32	29	12
Switzerland			48		
Taiwan			34		
Tanzania				57	
Turkey		20	19	21	1
Uganda				35	
Ukraine			42	46	4
Uruguay			42		
USA	15	36	41	45	30
Venezuela			19	45	26
Vietnam				50	
Zimbabwe				35	

Child Qualities: Religious Faith

(A040) *Here is a list of qualities that children can be encouraged to learn at home. Which, if any, do you consider to be especially important?*

Religious faith (%)

	1981	1990	1995	2000	Change
Albania			30	36	6
Algeria				77	
Argentina	19	28	35	43	24
Armenia			12		
Australia	22		21		–1
Austria		23		20	–3
Azerbaijan			19		
Bangladesh			78	70	–8
Belarus		6	15	12	6
Belgium	17	16		14	–3
Bosnia and Herz.			20	25	5
Brazil		46	57		11
Bulgaria		11	16	15	4
Canada	24	31		31	7
Chile		54	46	40	–14
China		1	3		2
Colombia			42		
Croatia			19		
Czech Republic		9	9	7	–2
Denmark	8	9		8	0
Dominican Rep.			59		
Egypt				87	
El Salvador			67		
Estonia		3	5	6	3
Finland		13	11	16	3
France	11	13		8	–3
Georgia			31		
Germany (East)		13	6	6	–7
Germany (West)	17	20	17	15	–2
Great Britain	13	19	17	18	5
Greece				39	
Hungary	8	24	18	19	11
Iceland	9	50		10	1
India		29	36	47	18
Indonesia				93	
Iran				71	
Iraq				92	
Ireland	42	57		39	–3
Israel				29	
Italy	22	37		31	9
Japan	6	7	6	7	1
Jordan				84	
Korea Republic	14	19	17	21	7
Kyrgyzstan				23	
Latvia		9	14	12	3
Lithuania		21	22	22	1
Luxembourg				17	
Macedonia			22	27	5
Malta	43	54		56	13
Mexico		40	42	53	13
Moldova			28	43	15
Montenegro			13	22	9
Morocco				78	
Netherlands	14	15		9	–5
New Zealand			16		
Nigeria		74	72	68	–6
Northern Ireland	33	44		40	7
Norway	11	14	12		1
Pakistan			81	86	5
Peru			52	56	4
Philippines			63	59	–4
Poland		63		43	–20
Portugal		26		24	–2
Puerto Rico			72	69	–3
Romania		43	58	59	16
Russian Fed.		8	9	9	1
Saudi Arabia				71	
Serbia			13	21	8
Singapore				30	
Slovakia		31	28	33	2
Slovenia		21	19	18	–3
South Africa		49	61	61	12
Spain	22	26	22	20	–2
Sweden	5	6	5	5	0
Switzerland		24	21		–3
Taiwan			9		
Tanzania				75	
Turkey		44	51	47	3
Uganda				68	
Ukraine			20	18	–2
Uruguay			17		
USA	39	55	54	52	13
Venezuela			43	45	2
Vietnam				8	
Zimbabwe				74	

CHILD QUALITIES: UNSELFISHNESS

(A041) *Here is a list of qualities that children can be encouraged to learn at home. Which, if any, do you consider to be especially important?*

Unselfishness (%)

	1981	1990	1995	2000	Change
Albania			12	12	0
Algeria				17	
Argentina	7	5	16	13	6
Armenia			31		
Australia	38		40		2
Austria		8		5	–3
Azerbaijan			17		
Bangladesh			16	16	0
Belarus		27	17	17	–10
Belgium	14	28		29	15
Bosnia and Herz.			29	38	9
Brazil		28	32		4
Bulgaria		22	45	14	–8
Canada	20	42		45	25
Chile		8	25	34	26
China		31	28	37	6
Colombia			37		
Croatia			29		
Czech Republic		37	32	37	0
Denmark	23	51		56	33
Dominican Rep.			12		
Egypt				22	
El Salvador			28		
Estonia		25	17	17	–8
Finland		21	18	21	0
France	22	40		40	18
Georgia			20		
Germany (East)		8	6	11	3
Germany (West)	4	8	5	6	2
Great Britain	40	57		60	20
Greece				26	
Hungary	14	26	29	21	7
Iceland	21	75		35	14
India		32	23	37	5
Indonesia				47	
Iran				29	
Iraq					
Ireland	23	53		49	26
Israel				49	
Italy	2	39		41	39
Japan	27	44	42	53	26
Jordan				32	
Korea Republic	12	11	11	15	3

	1981	1990	1995	2000	Change
Kyrgyzstan				24	
Latvia		16	20	12	–4
Lithuania		33	28	29	–4
Luxembourg				26	
Macedonia			61	47	–14
Malta	18	40		46	28
Mexico		11	36	50	39
Moldova			9	11	2
Montenegro			33	40	7
Morocco				10	
Netherlands	9	23		28	19
New Zealand			33		
Nigeria		17	15	23	6
Northern Ireland	29	49		50	21
Norway	6	10	11		5
Pakistan			31	38	7
Peru			16	50	34
Philippines			31	39	8
Poland		9	14	12	3
Portugal		29		40	11
Puerto Rico			40	28	–12
Romania		20	23	7	–13
Russian Fed.		24	21	21	–3
Saudi Arabia				52	
Serbia			29	35	6
Singapore				30	
Slovakia		22	19	19	–3
Slovenia		33	29	38	5
South Africa		20	22	29	9
Spain	4	8	14	12	8
Sweden	10	29	24	33	23
Switzerland		37	30		–7
Taiwan			21		
Tanzania				46	
Turkey		28	20	22	–6
Uganda				31	
Ukraine			19	15	–4
Uruguay			55		
USA	18	37	36	39	21
Venezuela			38	53	15
Vietnam				39	
Zimbabwe				33	

Child Qualities: Obedience

(A042) *Here is a list of qualities that children can be encouraged to learn at home. Which, if any, do you consider to be especially important?*

Obedience (%)

	1981	1990	1995	2000	Change
Albania			58	54	–4
Algeria				56	
Argentina	19	32	32	37	18
Armenia			18		
Australia	41		29		–12
Austria		26		17	–9
Azerbaijan			25		
Bangladesh			19	19	0
Belarus		22	35	34	12
Belgium	28	37		43	15
Bosnia and Herz.			41	44	3
Brazil		41	59		18
Bulgaria		19	20	16	–3
Canada	21	28		30	9
Chile		52	46	55	3
China		9	29	15	6
Colombia			43		
Croatia			21		
Czech Republic		21	14	17	–4
Denmark	14	20		14	0
Dominican Rep.			51		
Egypt				53	
El Salvador			62		
Estonia		19	27	29	10
Finland		26	28	30	4
France	18	53		36	18
Georgia			23		
Germany (East)		26	14	17	–9
Germany (West)	15	22	11	11	–4
Great Britain	37	39	50	49	12
Greece				11	
Hungary	31	45	31	33	2
Iceland	14	68		17	3
India		56	70	56	0
Indonesia				53	
Iran				41	
Iraq				74	
Ireland	33	35		48	15
Israel				16	
Italy	27	34		28	1
Japan	6	10	6	4	–2
Jordan				46	
Korea Republic	13	18	14	13	0
Kyrgyzstan				37	
Latvia		15	19	20	5
Lithuania		25	23	20	–5
Luxembourg				26	
Macedonia			18	11	–7
Malta	24	56		41	17
Mexico		45	50	60	15
Moldova			39	41	2
Montenegro			41	47	6
Morocco				53	
Netherlands	23	34		26	3
New Zealand			22		
Nigeria		71	71	73	2
Northern Ireland	51	56		58	7
Norway	26	31	26		0
Pakistan			32	44	12
Peru			50	61	11
Philippines			44	44	0
Poland		42	49	32	–10
Portugal		46		39	–7
Puerto Rico			52	56	4
Romania		19	14	19	0
Russian Fed.		26	34	34	8
Saudi Arabia				67	
Serbia			39	33	–6
Singapore				47	
Slovakia		36	27	26	–10
Slovenia		40	28	25	–15
South Africa		42	50	52	10
Spain	30	43	44	49	19
Sweden	13	25	16	13	0
Switzerland		20	24		4
Taiwan			33		
Tanzania				76	
Turkey		31	36	42	11
Uganda				72	
Ukraine			38	35	–3
Uruguay			29		
USA	28	39	38	32	4
Venezuela			50	51	1
Vietnam				56	
Zimbabwe				68	

Abortion When Woman not Married

(A048) *Do you approve or disapprove of abortion under the following circumstances? Where the woman is not married*

Approve (%)

	1981	1990	1995	2000	Change
Albania					
Algeria					
Argentina		18			
Armenia					
Australia					
Austria		16		45	29
Azerbaijan					
Bangladesh					
Belarus				58	
Belgium	24	27		50	26
Bosnia and Herz.					
Brazil		13			
Bulgaria		63		68	5
Canada	23	32			9
Chile		7			
China		76			
Colombia					
Croatia				62	
Czech Republic		51		66	15
Denmark	60	57		81	21
Dominican Rep.					
Egypt					
El Salvador					
Estonia		25		49	24
Finland		67		59	–8
France	35	30		69	34
Georgia					
Germany (East)		18		76	58
Germany (West)	24	22		50	26
Great Britain	32	35		51	19
Greece				68	
Hungary		43		65	22
Iceland	16	22		60	44
India		71			
Indonesia					
Iran					
Iraq					
Ireland	6	8		17	11
Israel					
Italy	27	23		39	12
Japan		57			
Jordan					
Korea Republic					

	1981	1990	1995	2000	Change
Kyrgyzstan					
Latvia		46		53	7
Lithuania		28		57	29
Luxembourg				39	
Macedonia					
Malta	4	4		10	6
Mexico		17			
Moldova					
Montenegro					
Morocco					
Netherlands	28	30		64	36
New Zealand					
Nigeria		16			
Northern Ireland	12	16		24	12
Norway	35	45			10
Pakistan					
Peru					
Philippines					
Poland		14		30	16
Portugal		21		44	23
Puerto Rico					
Romania		51		59	8
Russian Fed.		42		61	19
Saudi Arabia					
Serbia					
Singapore					
Slovakia		45		45	0
Slovenia		44		69	25
South Africa		11			
Spain	16	28		44	28
Sweden	40	41		90	50
Switzerland					
Taiwan					
Tanzania					
Turkey				44	
Uganda					
Ukraine				51	
Uruguay					
USA	26	30			4
Venezuela					
Vietnam					
Zimbabwe					

ABORTION IF NOT WANTING MORE CHILDREN

(A049) *Do you approve or disapprove of abortion under the following circumstances? Where a married couple do not want to have any more children*

Approve (%)

	1981	1990	1995	2000	Change
Albania					
Algeria					
Argentina		25			
Armenia					
Australia					
Austria		28		44	16
Azerbaijan					
Bangladesh					
Belarus				68	
Belgium	23	23		40	17
Bosnia and Herz.					
Brazil		15			
Bulgaria		77		81	4
Canada	24	30			6
Chile		14			
China		93			
Colombia					
Croatia				56	
Czech Republic		56		77	21
Denmark	69	63		72	3
Dominican Rep.					
Egypt					
El Salvador					
Estonia		73		71	–2
Finland		61		52	–9
France	50	48		63	13
Georgia					
Germany (East)		50		78	28
Germany (West)	37	31		50	13
Great Britain	35	41		48	13
Greece				55	
Hungary		69		75	6
Iceland	28	27		50	22
India		61			
Indonesia					
Iran					
Iraq					
Ireland	5	8		15	10
Israel					
Italy	30	26		31	1
Japan		50			
Jordan					
Korea Republic					

	1981	1990	1995	2000	Change
Kyrgyzstan					
Latvia		67		64	–3
Lithuania		45		63	18
Luxembourg				36	
Macedonia					
Malta	4	3		15	11
Mexico		19			
Moldova					
Montenegro					
Morocco					
Netherlands	22	27		50	28
New Zealand					
Nigeria		28			
Northern Ireland	14	17		18	4
Norway	43	46			3
Pakistan					
Peru					
Philippines					
Poland		28		36	8
Portugal		36		39	3
Puerto Rico					
Romania		67		57	–10
Russian Fed.		67		75	8
Saudi Arabia					
Serbia					
Singapore					
Slovakia		45		52	7
Slovenia		70		75	5
South Africa		12			
Spain	16	30		42	26
Sweden	59	52		85	26
Switzerland					
Taiwan					
Tanzania					
Turkey				41	
Uganda					
Ukraine				62	
Uruguay					
USA	25	26			1
Venezuela					
Vietnam					
Zimbabwe					

How often Discusses Political Matters

(A062) *When you get together with your friends, would you say you discuss political matters frequently, occasionally or never?*

Frequently/Occasionally (%)

	1981	1990	1995	2000	Change
Albania			82	78	–4
Algeria				74	
Argentina	79		64	51	–28
Armenia			78		
Australia	65		69		4
Austria		69		74	5
Azerbaijan			53		
Bangladesh			76	74	–2
Belarus		91	80	80	–11
Belgium	44	53		63	19
Bosnia and Herz.			83	73	–10
Brazil		55	58		3
Bulgaria		88	71	74	–14
Canada	69	75		64	–5
Chile		60	46	57	–3
China		89	71	70	–19
Colombia			54		
Croatia			84	80	–4
Czech Republic		89	81	87	–2
Denmark	79	79		80	1
Dominican Rep.			80		
Egypt				57	
El Salvador			38		
Estonia		95	80	82	–13
Finland		82	71	74	–8
France	62	65		65	3
Georgia			72		
Germany (East)		93	88	88	–5
Germany (West)	79	84	90	83	4
Great Britain	64	66	68	49	–15
Greece				79	
Hungary	68	76	73	54	–14
Iceland	74	78		78	4
India		73	66	58	–15
Indonesia				68	
Iran				69	
Iraq				65	
Ireland	52	58		59	7
Israel				86	
Italy	51	58		68	17
Japan	47	66	57	64	17
Jordan				50	
Korea Republic	55	88	83	75	20
Kyrgyzstan				75	
Latvia		96	85	77	–19
Lithuania		94	79	85	–9
Luxembourg				69	
Macedonia			76	80	4
Malta	59	54		62	3
Mexico		74	66	55	–19
Moldova			76	81	5
Montenegro			71	79	8
Morocco				32	
Netherlands	73	75		80	7
New Zealand			84		
Nigeria		63	68	74	11
Northern Ireland	63	56		66	3
Norway	76	88	86		10
Pakistan			57	57	0
Peru			63	77	14
Philippines			77	76	–1
Poland		83	68	76	–7
Portugal		53		51	–2
Puerto Rico			47	60	13
Romania		66	76	62	–4
Russian Fed.		83	76	75	–8
Saudi Arabia				72	
Serbia			71	77	6
Singapore				59	
Slovakia		84	80	86	2
Slovenia		82	75	72	–10
South Africa		70	64	62	–8
Spain	70	52	54	55	–15
Sweden	76	79	81	80	4
Switzerland		86	78		–8
Taiwan			70		
Tanzania				79	
Turkey		56	67	54	–2
Uganda				78	
Ukraine			70	78	8
Uruguay			53		
USA	65	72	73	75	10
Venezuela			53	56	3
Vietnam				75	
Zimbabwe				48	

Belong Social Welfare Service

(A064) *Please look carefully at the following list of voluntary organizations and activities and say... which, if any, do you belong to? Social welfare services for elderly, handicapped or deprived people*

Belong to (%)

	1981	1990	1995	2000	Change
Albania				14	
Algeria				11	
Argentina		2		5	3
Armenia					
Australia					
Austria		5		7	2
Azerbaijan					
Bangladesh				17	
Belarus				1	
Belgium	5	12		12	7
Bosnia and Herz.				2	
Brazil		10			
Bulgaria		4		1	–3
Canada	13	8		13	0
Chile		5		7	2
China		4		3	–1
Colombia					
Croatia				2	
Czech Republic		5		7	2
Denmark	5	6		7	2
Dominican Rep.					
Egypt					
El Salvador					
Estonia		2		3	1
Finland		11		10	–1
France	4	7		6	2
Georgia					
Germany (East)		9		3	–6
Germany (West)	13	7		4	–9
Great Britain	9	7		7	–2
Greece				6	
Hungary		2		2	0
Iceland	20	16		17	–3
India				7	
Indonesia					
Iran					
Iraq					
Ireland	10	7		6	–4
Israel					
Italy	4	4		6	2
Japan		2		9	7
Jordan					
Korea Republic		6		9	3
Kyrgyzstan				8	
Latvia		2		1	–1
Lithuania		1		1	0
Luxembourg				14	
Macedonia				7	
Malta	2	2		2	0
Mexico		5		7	2
Moldova				4	
Montenegro				4	
Morocco				1	
Netherlands	12	16		21	9
New Zealand					
Nigeria					
Northern Ireland	10	9		4	–6
Norway	13	11			–2
Pakistan					
Peru				4	
Philippines				8	
Poland		3		3	0
Portugal		5		2	–3
Puerto Rico				12	
Romania		2		2	0
Russian Fed.		2		1	–1
Saudi Arabia					
Serbia				3	
Singapore				7	
Slovakia		4		7	3
Slovenia		1		5	4
South Africa				9	
Spain	6	3		3	–3
Sweden	7	8		21	14
Switzerland		9			
Taiwan					
Tanzania				27	
Turkey				0	
Uganda				12	
Ukraine				2	
Uruguay					
USA	12	9		17	5
Venezuela				7	
Vietnam				27	
Zimbabwe				9	

Belong Church Organizations

(A065) *Please look carefully at the following list of voluntary organizations and activities and say... which, if any, do you belong to? Religious or church organizations*

Belong to (%)

	1981	1990	1995	2000	Change
Albania				20	
Algeria				7	
Argentina		7		16	9
Armenia					
Australia					
Austria		16		25	9
Azerbaijan					
Bangladesh				43	
Belarus				2	
Belgium	9	12		12	3
Bosnia and Herz.				8	
Brazil		22			
Bulgaria		2		2	0
Canada	33	25		29	–4
Chile		18		21	3
China		1		4	3
Colombia					
Croatia				13	
Czech Republic		5		7	2
Denmark	4	7		12	8
Dominican Rep.					
Egypt					
El Salvador					
Estonia		4		7	3
Finland		18		47	29
France	4	6		4	0
Georgia					
Germany (East)		19		12	–7
Germany (West)	13	16		14	1
Great Britain	22	16		5	–17
Greece				7	
Hungary		11		12	1
Iceland	35	50		71	36
India				18	
Indonesia					
Iran					
Iraq					
Ireland	31	14		16	–15
Israel					
Italy	7	8		10	3
Japan		7		11	4
Jordan					
Korea Republic		39		42	3

	1981	1990	1995	2000	Change
Kyrgyzstan				5	
Latvia		3		5	2
Lithuania		3		5	2
Luxembourg				10	
Macedonia				11	
Malta	15	13		14	–1
Mexico		14		23	9
Moldova				14	
Montenegro				3	
Morocco				1	
Netherlands	35	35		35	0
New Zealand					
Nigeria					
Northern Ireland	51	25		24	–27
Norway	9	11			2
Pakistan					
Peru				25	
Philippines				31	
Poland		7		6	–1
Portugal		11		6	–5
Puerto Rico				42	
Romania		5		4	–1
Russian Fed.		1		2	1
Saudi Arabia					
Serbia				3	
Singapore				20	
Slovakia		14		17	3
Slovenia		3		7	4
South Africa				54	
Spain	15	5		7	–8
Sweden	9	10		71	62
Switzerland		11			
Taiwan					
Tanzania				57	
Turkey				1	
Uganda				42	
Ukraine				4	
Uruguay					
USA	55	49		57	2
Venezuela				23	
Vietnam				10	
Zimbabwe				76	

Belong Cultural Activities

(A066) *Please look carefully at the following list of voluntary organizations and activities and say... which, if any, do you belong to? Education, arts, music or cultural activities*

Belong to (%)

	1981	1990	1995	2000	Change
Albania				14	
Algeria				12	
Argentina		6		9	3
Armenia					
Australia					
Austria		8		13	5
Azerbaijan					
Bangladesh				29	
Belarus				2	
Belgium	10	17		20	10
Bosnia and Herz.				4	
Brazil		5			
Bulgaria		4		4	0
Canada	10	18		21	11
Chile		9		9	0
China		7		2	–5
Colombia					
Croatia				6	
Czech Republic		6		10	4
Denmark	6	13		17	11
Dominican Rep.					
Egypt					
El Salvador					
Estonia		11		8	–3
Finland		20		14	–6
France	6	9		8	2
Georgia					
Germany (East)		8		6	–2
Germany (West)	7	12		8	1
Great Britain	7	10		10	3
Greece				21	
Hungary		3		3	0
Iceland	8	14		15	7
India				15	
Indonesia					
Iran					
Iraq					
Ireland	6	10		10	4
Israel					
Italy	4	4		10	6
Japan		6		11	5
Jordan					
Korea Republic		11		19	8

	1981	1990	1995	2000	Change
Kyrgyzstan				11	
Latvia		7		4	–3
Lithuania		7		2	–5
Luxembourg				17	
Macedonia				12	
Malta	5	7		5	0
Mexico		11		8	–3
Moldova				12	
Montenegro				9	
Morocco				3	
Netherlands	12	34		45	33
New Zealand					
Nigeria					
Northern Ireland	6	11		8	2
Norway	7	13			6
Pakistan					
Peru				13	
Philippines				5	
Poland		2		2	0
Portugal		8		3	–5
Puerto Rico				13	
Romania		2		3	1
Russian Fed.		5		1	–4
Saudi Arabia					
Serbia				3	
Singapore				14	
Slovakia		6		7	1
Slovenia		3		9	6
South Africa				17	
Spain	5	5		7	2
Sweden	13	13		26	13
Switzerland		7			
Taiwan					
Tanzania				28	
Turkey				1	
Uganda				21	
Ukraine				3	
Uruguay					
USA	14	20		37	23
Venezuela				18	
Vietnam				17	
Zimbabwe				7	

Belong Labor Unions/Trade Unions

(A067) *Please look carefully at the following list of voluntary organizations and activities and say…which, if any, do you belong to? Labor unions/trade unions*

Belong to (%)

	1981	1990	1995	2000	Change
Albania				9	
Algeria					
Argentina		1		3	2
Armenia					
Australia					
Austria		20		20	0
Azerbaijan					
Bangladesh				15	
Belarus				39	
Belgium	15	16		18	3
Bosnia and Herz.				7	
Brazil		6			
Bulgaria		19		6	–13
Canada	11	12		14	3
Chile		6		3	–3
China		2		7	5
Colombia					
Croatia				11	
Czech Republic		24		10	–14
Denmark	41	49		54	13
Dominican Rep.					
Egypt					
El Salvador					
Estonia		59		5	–54
Finland		36		32	–4
France	10	5		4	–6
Georgia					
Germany (East)		55		8	–47
Germany (West)	16	15		7	–9
Great Britain	21	14		8	–13
Greece				8	
Hungary		32		7	–25
Iceland	52	60		60	8
India				8	
Indonesia					
Iran					
Iraq					
Ireland	14	9		10	–4
Israel					
Italy	8	6		6	–2
Japan		7		6	–1
Jordan					
Korea Republic		7		6	–1
Kyrgyzstan				12	
Latvia		52		11	–41
Lithuania		43		2	–41
Luxembourg				12	
Macedonia				6	
Malta	9	9		9	0
Mexico		4		6	2
Moldova				14	
Montenegro				16	
Morocco				1	
Netherlands	16	19		22	6
New Zealand					
Nigeria					
Northern Ireland	16	12		6	–10
Norway	35	42			7
Pakistan					
Peru				4	
Philippines				4	
Poland		22		10	–12
Portugal		5		2	–3
Puerto Rico				4	
Romania		20		9	–11
Russian Fed.		62		24	–38
Saudi Arabia					
Serbia				14	
Singapore				4	
Slovakia		22		16	–6
Slovenia		19		17	–2
South Africa				10	
Spain	6	3		4	–2
Sweden	44	59		64	20
Switzerland		6			
Taiwan					
Tanzania				29	
Turkey				2	
Uganda				7	
Ukraine				21	
Uruguay					
USA	13	9		14	1
Venezuela				3	
Vietnam				11	
Zimbabwe				3	

Belong Political Parties or Groups

(A068) *Please look carefully at the following list of voluntary organizations and activities and say... which, if any, do you belong to? Political parties or groups*

Belong to (%)

	1981	1990	1995	2000	Change
Albania				15	
Algeria				6	
Argentina				5	
Armenia					
Australia					
Austria		12		11	–1
Azerbaijan					
Bangladesh				24	
Belarus				1	
Belgium	3	6		7	4
Bosnia and Herz.				7	
Brazil		5			
Bulgaria		11		4	–7
Canada	6	7		6	0
Chile		5		2	–3
China		35		8	–27
Colombia					
Croatia				4	
Czech Republic		5		4	–1
Denmark	7	7		7	0
Dominican Rep.					
Egypt					
El Salvador					
Estonia		8		2	–6
Finland		14		7	–7
France	2	3		2	0
Georgia					
Germany (East)		11		3	–8
Germany (West)	8	7		3	–5
Great Britain	5	6		2	–3
Greece				8	
Hungary		2		2	0
Iceland	13	15		19	6
India				11	
Indonesia					
Iran					
Iraq					
Ireland	4	4		4	0
Israel					
Italy	6	5		4	–2
Japan		2		3	1
Jordan					
Korea Republic		5		3	–2

	1981	1990	1995	2000	Change
Kyrgyzstan				2	
Latvia		18		2	–16
Lithuania		7		1	–6
Luxembourg				6	
Macedonia				11	
Malta	9	8		6	–3
Mexico		5		4	–1
Moldova				5	
Montenegro				20	
Morocco				1	
Netherlands	9	10		9	0
New Zealand					
Nigeria					
Northern Ireland	3	2		2	–1
Norway	14	14			0
Pakistan					
Peru				5	
Philippines				4	
Poland		2		1	–1
Portugal		5		1	–4
Puerto Rico				6	
Romania		3		2	–1
Russian Fed.		11		1	–10
Saudi Arabia					
Serbia				7	
Singapore				0	
Slovakia		3		7	4
Slovenia		3		3	0
South Africa				12	
Spain	3	2		2	–1
Sweden	14	10		11	–3
Switzerland		9			
Taiwan					
Tanzania				26	
Turkey				3	
Uganda				9	
Ukraine				2	
Uruguay					
USA	12	14		19	7
Venezuela				4	
Vietnam				29	
Zimbabwe				7	

Belong Local Community Action

(A069) *Please look carefully at the following list of voluntary organizations and activities and say...which, if any, do you belong to? Local community action on issues like poverty, employment, housing, racial equality*

Belong to (%)

	1981	1990	1995	2000	Change
Albania				12	
Algeria				6	
Argentina		1		3	2
Armenia					
Australia					
Austria		2		3	1
Azerbaijan					
Bangladesh				26	
Belarus				0	
Belgium		5		5	0
Bosnia and Herz.				1	
Brazil		8			
Bulgaria		2		1	–1
Canada		5		8	3
Chile		4		5	1
China		1		2	1
Colombia					
Croatia				2	
Czech Republic		2		3	1
Denmark		5		6	1
Dominican Rep.					
Egypt					
El Salvador					
Estonia		4		2	–2
Finland		3		3	0
France		3		2	–1
Georgia					
Germany (East)		3		1	–2
Germany (West)		2		1	–1
Great Britain		4		4	0
Greece				4	
Hungary		1		1	0
Iceland		2		2	0
India				6	
Indonesia					
Iran					
Iraq					
Ireland		3		5	2
Israel					
Italy		2		2	0
Japan		0		1	1
Jordan					
Korea Republic		13		7	–6

	1981	1990	1995	2000	Change
Kyrgyzstan				7	
Latvia		5		1	–4
Lithuania		2		1	–1
Luxembourg				5	
Macedonia				6	
Malta		3		3	0
Mexico		4		5	1
Moldova				3	
Montenegro				1	
Morocco				1	
Netherlands		5		7	2
New Zealand					
Nigeria					
Northern Ireland		2		3	1
Norway		3			
Pakistan					
Peru				7	
Philippines				7	
Poland		2		2	0
Portugal		2		1	–1
Puerto Rico				9	
Romania		1		1	0
Russian Fed.		2		1	–1
Saudi Arabia					
Serbia				1	
Singapore				2	
Slovakia		3		8	5
Slovenia		6		9	3
South Africa				9	
Spain		1		2	1
Sweden		2		9	7
Switzerland		3			
Taiwan					
Tanzania				24	
Turkey				0	
Uganda				9	
Ukraine				2	
Uruguay					
USA		5		13	8
Venezuela				10	
Vietnam				26	
Zimbabwe				5	

Belong Third World Development/Human Rights

(A070) *Please look carefully at the following list of voluntary organizations and activities and say... which, if any, do you belong to? Third world development or human rights*

Belong to (%)

	1981	1990	1995	2000	Change
Albania				6	
Algeria				3	
Argentina		0		1	1
Armenia					
Australia					
Austria		1		3	2
Azerbaijan					
Bangladesh				11	
Belarus				1	
Belgium	1	6		9	8
Bosnia and Herz.				0	
Brazil		1			
Bulgaria		2		0	–2
Canada	3	5		5	2
Chile		1		2	1
China		1		0	–1
Colombia					
Croatia				1	
Czech Republic		1		1	0
Denmark	3	3		4	1
Dominican Rep.					
Egypt					
El Salvador					
Estonia		1		0	–1
Finland		6		6	0
France	1	3		1	0
Georgia					
Germany (East)		1		0	0
Germany (West)	1	2		1	0
Great Britain	1	2		3	2
Greece				5	
Hungary		0		0	0
Iceland	3	3		8	5
India				3	
Indonesia					
Iran					
Iraq					
Ireland	1	2		2	1
Israel					
Italy	1	1		3	2
Japan		0		2	2
Jordan					
Korea Republic		2		2	0

	1981	1990	1995	2000	Change
Kyrgyzstan				3	
Latvia		1		1	0
Lithuania		1		0	–1
Luxembourg				11	
Macedonia				3	
Malta	0	0		0	0
Mexico		1		2	1
Moldova				2	
Montenegro				1	
Morocco				0	
Netherlands	3	14		23	20
New Zealand					
Nigeria					
Northern Ireland	0	3		2	2
Norway	4	5			1
Pakistan					
Peru				2	
Philippines				5	
Poland		0		0	0
Portugal		1		1	0
Puerto Rico				5	
Romania		0		1	1
Russian Fed.		0		0	0
Saudi Arabia					
Serbia				1	
Singapore				1	
Slovakia		0		0	0
Slovenia		0		1	1
South Africa				4	
Spain	1	1		3	2
Sweden	3	9		15	12
Switzerland					
Taiwan					
Tanzania				19	
Turkey				0	
Uganda				5	
Ukraine				1	
Uruguay					
USA	5	2		5	0
Venezuela				9	
Vietnam				2	
Zimbabwe				2	

Belong Conservation, the Environment, Ecology, Animal Rights

(A071) *Please look carefully at the following list of voluntary organizations and activities and say… which, if any, do you belong to? Conservation, the environment, ecology, animal rights*

Belong to (%)

	1981	1990	1995	2000	Change
Albania				10	
Algeria				4	
Argentina				2	
Armenia					
Australia					
Austria				9	
Azerbaijan					
Bangladesh				20	
Belarus				1	
Belgium	3			11	8
Bosnia and Herz.				2	
Brazil					
Bulgaria				1	
Canada	5			9	4
Chile				3	
China				1	
Colombia					
Croatia				2	
Czech Republic				7	
Denmark	6			13	7
Dominican Rep.					
Egypt					
El Salvador					
Estonia				2	
Finland				4	
France	1			2	1
Georgia					
Germany (East)				2	
Germany (West)	3			3	0
Great Britain	5			1	–4
Greece				11	
Hungary				2	
Iceland	5			5	0
India				7	
Indonesia					
Iran					
Iraq					
Ireland	3			3	0
Israel					
Italy	2			4	2
Japan				3	
Jordan					
Korea Republic				6	
Kyrgyzstan				3	
Latvia				1	
Lithuania				1	
Luxembourg				11	
Macedonia				5	
Malta	2			2	0
Mexico				4	
Moldova				5	
Montenegro				4	
Morocco				1	
Netherlands	11			43	32
New Zealand					
Nigeria					
Northern Ireland	3			1	–2
Norway	4				
Pakistan					
Peru				3	
Philippines				8	
Poland				1	
Portugal				0	
Puerto Rico				4	
Romania				1	
Russian Fed.				1	
Saudi Arabia					
Serbia				1	
Singapore				1	
Slovakia				3	
Slovenia				3	
South Africa				4	
Spain	1			2	1
Sweden	3			11	8
Switzerland					
Taiwan					
Tanzania				20	
Turkey				0	
Uganda				10	
Ukraine				1	
Uruguay					
USA	5			16	11
Venezuela				12	
Vietnam				8	
Zimbabwe				2	

Belong Professional Association

(A072) *Please look carefully at the following list of voluntary organizations and activities and say... which, if any, do you belong to? Professional associations*

Belong to (%)

	1981	1990	1995	2000	Change
Albania				11	
Algeria				9	
Argentina		3		2	–1
Armenia					
Australia					
Austria		6		7	1
Azerbaijan					
Bangladesh				21	
Belarus				1	
Belgium	4	7		9	5
Bosnia and Herz.				2	
Brazil		5			
Bulgaria		5		2	–3
Canada	12	16		18	6
Chile		3		3	0
China		26		1	–25
Colombia					
Croatia				3	
Czech Republic		6		6	0
Denmark	14	12		11	–3
Dominican Rep.					
Egypt					
El Salvador					
Estonia		4		4	0
Finland		15		6	–9
France	4	5		3	–1
Georgia					
Germany (East)		6		3	–3
Germany (West)	8	9		5	–3
Great Britain	9	11		2	–7
Greece				14	
Hungary		6		4	–2
Iceland	11	15		19	8
India				9	
Indonesia					
Iran					
Iraq					
Ireland	4	5		8	4
Israel					
Italy	3	4		7	4
Japan		4		5	1
Jordan					
Korea Republic		13		9	–4

	1981	1990	1995	2000	Change
Kyrgyzstan				6	
Latvia		6		1	–5
Lithuania		3		1	–2
Luxembourg				6	
Macedonia				7	
Malta	4	3		3	–1
Mexico		3		3	0
Moldova				7	
Montenegro				6	
Morocco				3	
Netherlands	8	13		16	8
New Zealand					
Nigeria					
Northern Ireland	7	7		4	–3
Norway	14	16			2
Pakistan					
Peru				6	
Philippines				4	
Poland		4		4	0
Portugal		4		1	–3
Puerto Rico				11	
Romania		2		2	0
Russian Fed.		2		1	–1
Saudi Arabia					
Serbia				3	
Singapore				4	
Slovakia		7		5	–2
Slovenia		6		7	1
South Africa				6	
Spain	5	3		2	–3
Sweden	7	12		14	7
Switzerland		13			
Taiwan					
Tanzania				23	
Turkey				1	
Uganda				9	
Ukraine				2	
Uruguay					
USA	15	15		28	13
Venezuela				9	
Vietnam				13	
Zimbabwe				4	

BELONG YOUTH WORK

(A073) *Please look carefully at the following list of voluntary organizations and activities and say…which, if any, do you belong to? Youth work (e.g. scouts, guides, youth clubs, etc.)*

Belong to (%)

	1981	1990	1995	2000	Change
Albania				12	
Algeria				10	
Argentina		2		3	1
Armenia					
Australia					
Austria		3		3	0
Azerbaijan					
Bangladesh				12	
Belarus				1	
Belgium	5	8		8	3
Bosnia and Herz.				2	
Brazil		4			
Bulgaria		2		1	–1
Canada	10	10		11	1
Chile		6		5	–1
China		9		1	–8
Colombia					
Croatia				2	
Czech Republic		5		7	2
Denmark	8	5		7	–1
Dominican Rep.					
Egypt					
El Salvador					
Estonia		2		2	0
Finland		5		7	2
France	6	3		2	–4
Georgia					
Germany (East)		3		1	–2
Germany (West)	3	4		2	–1
Great Britain	7	4		6	–1
Greece				5	
Hungary		2		1	–1
Iceland	20	8		7	–13
India				6	
Indonesia					
Iran					
Iraq					
Ireland	9	6		7	–2
Israel					
Italy	2	3		4	2
Japan		1		2	1
Jordan					
Korea Republic		7		4	–3
Kyrgyzstan				5	
Latvia		2		1	–1
Lithuania		5		2	–3
Luxembourg				9	
Macedonia				5	
Malta	5	2		2	–3
Mexico		4		4	0
Moldova				6	
Montenegro				3	
Morocco				1	
Netherlands	6	7		7	1
New Zealand					
Nigeria					
Northern Ireland	8	11		6	–2
Norway	8	6			–2
Pakistan					
Peru				6	
Philippines				7	
Poland		2		2	0
Portugal		3		1	–2
Puerto Rico				9	
Romania		1		1	0
Russian Fed.		3		1	–2
Saudi Arabia					
Serbia				1	
Singapore				8	
Slovakia		3		7	4
Slovenia		2		4	2
South Africa				10	
Spain	3	2		2	–1
Sweden	6	9		7	1
Switzerland		4			
Taiwan					
Tanzania				18	
Turkey				0	
Uganda				21	
Ukraine				1	
Uruguay					
USA	12	13		26	14
Venezuela				8	
Vietnam				15	
Zimbabwe				5	

BELONG SPORTS OR RECREATION

(A074) *Please look carefully at the following list of voluntary organizations and activities and say... which, if any, do you belong to? Sports or recreation*

Belong to (%)

	1981	1990	1995	2000	Change
Albania				11	
Algeria				14	
Argentina		5		8	3
Armenia					
Australia					
Austria		19		23	4
Azerbaijan					
Bangladesh				25	
Belarus				2	
Belgium		20		25	5
Bosnia and Herz.				11	
Brazil		8			
Bulgaria		4		4	0
Canada		23		27	4
Chile		12		15	3
China		4		3	–1
Colombia					
Croatia				12	
Czech Republic		18		23	5
Denmark		33		33	0
Dominican Rep.					
Egypt					
El Salvador					
Estonia		14		9	–5
Finland		23		24	1
France		16		16	0
Georgia					
Germany (East)		22		17	–5
Germany (West)		32		30	–2
Great Britain		18		3	–15
Greece				15	
Hungary		4		4	0
Iceland		30		34	4
India				11	
Indonesia					
Iran					
Iraq					
Ireland		24		28	4
Israel					
Italy		10		12	2
Japan		9		14	5
Jordan					
Korea Republic		17		25	8
Kyrgyzstan				7	
Latvia		9		7	–2
Lithuania		8		3	–5
Luxembourg				25	
Macedonia				13	
Malta		6		9	3
Mexico		8		9	1
Moldova				5	
Montenegro				11	
Morocco				5	
Netherlands		40		51	11
New Zealand					
Nigeria					
Northern Ireland		17		14	–3
Norway		33			
Pakistan					
Peru				11	
Philippines				12	
Poland		4		3	–1
Portugal		14		9	–5
Puerto Rico				8	
Romania		3		2	–1
Russian Fed.		5		4	–1
Saudi Arabia					
Serbia				8	
Singapore				15	
Slovakia		11		18	7
Slovenia		8		17	9
South Africa				24	
Spain		5		8	3
Sweden		32		37	5
Switzerland					
Taiwan					
Tanzania				29	
Turkey				1	
Uganda				24	
Ukraine				2	
Uruguay					
USA		20		36	16
Venezuela				21	
Vietnam				19	
Zimbabwe				8	

Belong Women's Groups

(A075) *Please look carefully at the following list of voluntary organizations and activities and say…which, if any, do you belong to? Women's groups*

Belong to (%)

	1981	1990	1995	2000	Change
Albania				14	
Algeria				4	
Argentina		1		1	0
Armenia					
Australia					
Austria		4		4	0
Azerbaijan					
Bangladesh				14	
Belarus				0	
Belgium		9		9	0
Bosnia and Herz.				3	
Brazil		2			
Bulgaria		2		1	–1
Canada		7		8	1
Chile		3		5	2
China		3		3	0
Colombia					
Croatia				2	
Czech Republic		4		2	–2
Denmark		2		2	0
Dominican Rep.					
Egypt					
El Salvador					
Estonia		2		2	0
Finland		3		4	1
France		1		0	–1
Georgia					
Germany (East)		7		4	–3
Germany (West)		6		4	–2
Great Britain		5		2	–3
Greece				4	
Hungary		1		0	–1
Iceland		7		6	–1
India				6	
Indonesia					
Iran					
Iraq					
Ireland		5		4	–1
Israel					
Italy		0		0	0
Japan		3		4	1
Jordan					
Korea Republic		3		4	1

	1981	1990	1995	2000	Change
Kyrgyzstan				3	
Latvia		1		0	–1
Lithuania		3		0	–3
Luxembourg				6	
Macedonia				6	
Malta		1		1	0
Mexico		2		3	1
Moldova				3	
Montenegro				3	
Morocco				2	
Netherlands		7		5	–2
New Zealand					
Nigeria					
Northern Ireland		5		4	–1
Norway		3			
Pakistan					
Peru				6	
Philippines				10	
Poland		5		1	–4
Portugal		0			
Puerto Rico				3	
Romania		0		0	0
Russian Fed.		2		0	–2
Saudi Arabia					
Serbia				1	
Singapore				1	
Slovakia		4		7	3
Slovenia		0		2	2
South Africa				9	
Spain		1		2	1
Sweden		3		3	0
Switzerland					
Taiwan					
Tanzania				24	
Turkey				0	
Uganda				16	
Ukraine				1	
Uruguay					
USA		8		14	6
Venezuela				5	
Vietnam				28	
Zimbabwe				10	

BELONG PEACE MOVEMENT

(A076) *Please look carefully at the following list of voluntary organizations and activities and say...which, if any, do you belong to? Peace movement*

Belong to (%)

	1981	1990	1995	2000	Change
Albania				7	
Algeria					
Argentina		0			
Armenia					
Australia					
Austria		1		1	0
Azerbaijan					
Bangladesh				23	
Belarus				0	
Belgium		2		2	0
Bosnia and Herz.				0	
Brazil		2			
Bulgaria		1		1	0
Canada		2		2	0
Chile		1		2	1
China		1		1	0
Colombia					
Croatia				1	
Czech Republic		1		1	0
Denmark		2		1	–1
Dominican Rep.					
Egypt					
El Salvador					
Estonia		1		0	–1
Finland		2		1	–1
France		0		0	0
Georgia					
Germany (East)		2		0	–2
Germany (West)		2		0	0
Great Britain		1		1	0
Greece				4	
Hungary		1		0	–1
Iceland		1		1	0
India				5	
Indonesia					
Iran					
Iraq					
Ireland		1		2	1
Israel					
Italy		1		1	0
Japan		1		2	1
Jordan					
Korea Republic		2		2	0
Kyrgyzstan				2	
Latvia		1		0	–1
Lithuania		1		0	–1
Luxembourg				2	
Macedonia				5	
Malta		0		0	0
Mexico		1		3	2
Moldova				2	
Montenegro				1	
Morocco				0	
Netherlands		3		3	0
New Zealand					
Nigeria					
Northern Ireland		1		2	1
Norway		1			
Pakistan					
Peru				1	
Philippines				11	
Poland		0		1	1
Portugal		1		1	0
Puerto Rico				1	
Romania		0		0	0
Russian Fed.		1		0	–1
Saudi Arabia					
Serbia				0	
Singapore				1	
Slovakia		2		0	–2
Slovenia		0		1	1
South Africa				6	
Spain		1		1	0
Sweden		3		1	–2
Switzerland					
Taiwan					
Tanzania				5	
Turkey				0	
Uganda				10	
Ukraine				0	
Uruguay					
USA		2		4	2
Venezuela				6	
Vietnam				9	
Zimbabwe				3	

Belong Organizations Concerned with Health

(A077) *Please look carefully at the following list of voluntary organizations and activities and say... which, if any, do you belong to? Voluntary organizations concerned with health*

Belong to (%)

	1981	1990	1995	2000	Change
Albania				13	
Algeria					
Argentina		2		2	0
Armenia					
Australia					
Austria		4		8	4
Azerbaijan					
Bangladesh				22	
Belarus				1	
Belgium		4		5	1
Bosnia and Herz.				3	
Brazil		3			
Bulgaria		2		1	–1
Canada		9		11	2
Chile		3		3	0
China		2		3	1
Colombia					
Croatia				3	
Czech Republic		7		6	–1
Denmark		6		4	–2
Dominican Rep.					
Egypt					
El Salvador					
Estonia		2		1	–1
Finland		7		9	2
France		3		2	–1
Georgia					
Germany (East)		5		2	–3
Germany (West)		4		3	–1
Great Britain		4		3	–1
Greece				5	
Hungary		4		2	–2
Iceland		5		3	–2
India				8	
Indonesia					
Iran					
Iraq					
Ireland		3		4	1
Israel					
Italy		3		5	2
Japan		1		3	2
Jordan					
Korea Republic		15		10	–5

	1981	1990	1995	2000	Change
Kyrgyzstan				4	
Latvia		2		1	–1
Lithuania		1		2	1
Luxembourg				7	
Macedonia				8	
Malta		0		1	1
Mexico		2		6	4
Moldova				3	
Montenegro				2	
Morocco				1	
Netherlands		20		9	–11
New Zealand					
Nigeria					
Northern Ireland		3		4	1
Norway		12			
Pakistan					
Peru				5	
Philippines				9	
Poland		1		1	0
Portugal		3		2	–1
Puerto Rico				5	
Romania		0		1	1
Russian Fed.		1		1	0
Saudi Arabia					
Serbia				1	
Singapore				4	
Slovakia		6		4	–2
Slovenia		1		3	2
South Africa				6	
Spain		1		2	1
Sweden		2		7	5
Switzerland					
Taiwan					
Tanzania				19	
Turkey				0	
Uganda				12	
Ukraine				1	
Uruguay					
USA		8		17	9
Venezuela				10	
Vietnam				15	
Zimbabwe				5	

BELONG OTHER GROUPS

(A079) *Please look carefully at the following list of voluntary organizations and activities and say... which, if any, do you belong to? Other groups*

Belong to (%)

	1981	1990	1995	2000	Change
Albania				5	
Algeria					
Argentina		3		4	1
Armenia					
Australia					
Austria		6		9	3
Azerbaijan					
Bangladesh				2	
Belarus				1	
Belgium		5		11	6
Bosnia and Herz.				3	
Brazil		0			
Bulgaria		3		2	–1
Canada		13		11	–2
Chile		4		1	–3
China		2			
Colombia					
Croatia				4	
Czech Republic		7		9	2
Denmark		11		14	3
Dominican Rep.					
Egypt					
El Salvador					
Estonia		4		5	1
Finland		9		12	3
France		5		7	2
Georgia					
Germany (East)		8		4	–4
Germany (West)		9		4	–5
Great Britain		8		5	–3
Greece				7	
Hungary		2		3	1
Iceland		10		3	–7
India				7	
Indonesia					
Iran					
Iraq					
Ireland		2		5	3
Israel					
Italy		2		3	1
Japan		5		7	2
Jordan					
Korea Republic		4			
Kyrgyzstan				6	
Latvia		4		5	1
Lithuania		2		2	0
Luxembourg				4	
Macedonia				8	
Malta		4		3	–1
Mexico		2		1	–1
Moldova				3	
Montenegro				4	
Morocco				1	
Netherlands		10		9	–1
New Zealand					
Nigeria					
Northern Ireland		7		7	0
Norway		19			
Pakistan					
Peru				0	
Philippines				4	
Poland		3		3	0
Portugal		2		3	1
Puerto Rico				5	
Romania		2		2	0
Russian Fed.		2		1	–1
Saudi Arabia					
Serbia				4	
Singapore				4	
Slovakia		4		8	4
Slovenia		5		10	5
South Africa				9	
Spain		4		2	–2
Sweden		19		25	6
Switzerland					
Taiwan					
Tanzania				18	
Turkey				2	
Uganda				7	
Ukraine				2	
Uruguay					
USA		10		22	12
Venezuela				1	
Vietnam				4	
Zimbabwe				1	

Belong None

(A080) *Please look carefully at the following list of voluntary organizations and activities and say…which, if any, do you belong to? None*

Belong to (%)

	1981	1990	1995	2000	Change
Albania					
Algeria					
Argentina		76			
Armenia					
Australia					
Austria		45		33	–12
Azerbaijan					
Bangladesh					
Belarus				54	
Belgium	58	42		32	–26
Bosnia and Herz.					
Brazil		58			
Bulgaria		59		80	21
Canada	42	36			–6
Chile		55			
China		33			
Colombia					
Croatia				60	
Czech Republic		38		41	3
Denmark	38	19		16	–22
Dominican Rep.					
Egypt					
El Salvador					
Estonia		27		67	40
Finland		23		20	–3
France	73	62		62	–11
Georgia					
Germany (East)		17		56	39
Germany (West)	50	33		48	–2
Great Britain	48	47		66	18
Greece				44	
Hungary		50		71	21
Iceland	17	10		7	–10
India					
Indonesia					
Iran					
Iraq					
Ireland	48	51		44	–4
Israel					
Italy	74	68		58	–16
Japan		64			
Jordan					
Korea Republic					
Kyrgyzstan					
Latvia		32		69	37
Lithuania		40		83	43
Luxembourg				41	
Macedonia					
Malta	59	63		58	–1
Mexico		64			
Moldova					
Montenegro					
Morocco					
Netherlands	38	16		8	–30
New Zealand					
Nigeria					
Northern Ireland	34	44		53	19
Norway	27	19			–8
Pakistan					
Peru					
Philippines					
Poland		59		74	15
Portugal		64		76	12
Puerto Rico					
Romania		70		79	9
Russian Fed.		26		68	42
Saudi Arabia					
Serbia					
Singapore					
Slovakia		44		35	–9
Slovenia		61		48	–13
South Africa					
Spain	69	77		69	0
Sweden		15		4	–11
Switzerland					
Taiwan					
Tanzania					
Turkey				92	
Uganda					
Ukraine				66	
Uruguay					
USA	28	30			2
Venezuela					
Vietnam					
Zimbabwe					

Unpaid Work Social Welfare Service

(A081) *And for which, if any, are you currently doing unpaid voluntary work? Social welfare services for elderly, handicapped or deprived people*

Belong to (%)

	1981	1990	1995	2000	Change
Albania				11	
Algeria				19	
Argentina		2		3	1
Armenia					
Australia					
Austria		2		2	0
Azerbaijan					
Bangladesh				19	
Belarus				3	
Belgium	4	6		6	2
Bosnia and Herz.				1	
Brazil		6			
Bulgaria		2		1	–1
Canada	10	6		10	0
Chile		4		6	2
China		16		56	40
Colombia					
Croatia				1	
Czech Republic		2		3	1
Denmark	2	2		4	2
Dominican Rep.					
Egypt					
El Salvador					
Estonia		1		3	2
Finland		7		7	0
France	3	5		4	1
Georgia					
Germany (East)		4		1	–3
Germany (West)	6	3		2	–4
Great Britain	6	5		13	7
Greece				8	
Hungary		2		2	0
Iceland	12	10		9	–3
India				6	
Indonesia					
Iran					
Iraq					
Ireland	7	7		4	–3
Israel					
Italy	3	3		5	2
Japan		2		5	3
Jordan					
Korea Republic		7		9	2
Kyrgyzstan				4	
Latvia		4		2	–2
Lithuania		1		1	0
Luxembourg				7	
Macedonia				5	
Malta	1	2		5	4
Mexico		3		5	2
Moldova				7	
Montenegro				3	
Morocco					
Netherlands	9	8		9	0
New Zealand					
Nigeria					
Northern Ireland	8	5		3	–5
Norway	6	4			–2
Pakistan					
Peru				3	
Philippines				10	
Poland		5		2	–3
Portugal		3		1	–2
Puerto Rico				11	
Romania		2		1	–1
Russian Fed.		1		1	0
Saudi Arabia					
Serbia				1	
Singapore				12	
Slovakia		3		6	3
Slovenia		1		5	4
South Africa				7	
Spain	8	2		2	–6
Sweden	2	3		9	7
Switzerland					
Taiwan					
Tanzania				25	
Turkey				0	
Uganda				11	
Ukraine				1	
Uruguay					
USA	7	6		14	7
Venezuela					
Vietnam				29	
Zimbabwe				7	

Unpaid Work Church Organizations

(A082) *And for which, if any, are you currently doing unpaid voluntary work? Religious or church organizations*

Belong to (%)

	1981	1990	1995	2000	Change
Albania				15	
Algeria				13	
Argentina		5		9	4
Armenia					
Australia					
Austria		6		7	1
Azerbaijan					
Bangladesh				40	
Belarus				4	
Belgium	5	7		6	1
Bosnia and Herz.				5	
Brazil		13			
Bulgaria		2		2	0
Canada	16	16		18	2
Chile		12		17	5
China		2		4	2
Colombia					
Croatia				5	
Czech Republic		2		3	1
Denmark	2	2		3	1
Dominican Rep.					
Egypt					
El Salvador					
Estonia		1		3	2
Finland		6		8	2
France	3	5		3	0
Georgia					
Germany (East)		7		2	–5
Germany (West)	7	7		6	–1
Great Britain	7	6		6	–1
Greece				6	
Hungary		3		5	2
Iceland	5	4		5	0
India				14	
Indonesia					
Iran					
Iraq					
Ireland	8	7		8	0
Israel					
Italy	5	6		7	2
Japan		2		3	1
Jordan					
Korea Republic		7		27	20

	1981	1990	1995	2000	Change
Kyrgyzstan				1	
Latvia		3		4	1
Lithuania		3		4	1
Luxembourg				6	
Macedonia				9	
Malta	9	9		13	4
Mexico		9		20	11
Moldova				16	
Montenegro				2	
Morocco					
Netherlands	9	9		11	2
New Zealand					
Nigeria					
Northern Ireland	14	10		9	–5
Norway	6	6			0
Pakistan					
Peru				20	
Philippines				30	
Poland		9		4	–5
Portugal		6		3	–3
Puerto Rico				31	
Romania		4		4	0
Russian Fed.		1		1	0
Saudi Arabia					
Serbia				1	
Singapore				12	
Slovakia		5		13	8
Slovenia		2		4	2
South Africa				37	
Spain	10	4		4	–6
Sweden	9	3		23	14
Switzerland					
Taiwan					
Tanzania				62	
Turkey				1	
Uganda				39	
Ukraine				2	
Uruguay					
USA	22	29		38	16
Venezuela					
Vietnam				10	
Zimbabwe				54	

Unpaid Work Cultural Activities

(A083) *And for which, if any, are you currently doing unpaid voluntary work? Education, arts, music or cultural activities*

Belong to (%)

	1981	1990	1995	2000	Change
Albania				10	
Algeria				12	
Argentina		4		4	0
Armenia					
Australia					
Austria		5		7	2
Azerbaijan					
Bangladesh				28	
Belarus				2	
Belgium	6	7		9	3
Bosnia and Herz.				3	
Brazil		3			
Bulgaria		3		2	–1
Canada	5	9		11	6
Chile		6		7	1
China		8		16	8
Colombia					
Croatia				3	
Czech Republic		2		6	4
Denmark	1	4		5	4
Dominican Rep.					
Egypt					
El Salvador					
Estonia		7		5	–2
Finland		9		5	–4
France	3	5		5	2
Georgia					
Germany (East)		3		3	0
Germany (West)	2	4		3	1
Great Britain	1	3		3	2
Greece				14	
Hungary		2		3	1
Iceland	3	5		6	3
India				12	
Indonesia					
Iran					
Iraq					
Ireland	2	4		4	2
Israel					
Italy	3	3		6	3
Japan		3		4	1
Jordan					
Korea Republic		3		9	6

	1981	1990	1995	2000	Change
Kyrgyzstan				3	
Latvia		5		4	–1
Lithuania		6		2	–4
Luxembourg				8	
Macedonia				7	
Malta	3	4		4	1
Mexico		5		5	0
Moldova				9	
Montenegro				3	
Morocco					
Netherlands	5	9		16	11
New Zealand					
Nigeria					
Northern Ireland	2	3		2	0
Norway	2	5			3
Pakistan					
Peru				10	
Philippines				4	
Poland		2		2	0
Portugal		4		2	–2
Puerto Rico				8	
Romania		1		2	1
Russian Fed.		3		0	–3
Saudi Arabia					
Serbia				1	
Singapore				6	
Slovakia		3		6	3
Slovenia		3		7	4
South Africa				7	
Spain	4	2		3	–1
Sweden	4	3		11	7
Switzerland					
Taiwan					
Tanzania				26	
Turkey				1	
Uganda				16	
Ukraine				2	
Uruguay					
USA	4	10		20	16
Venezuela					
Vietnam				16	
Zimbabwe				4	

Unpaid Work Labor Unions/Trade Unions

(A084) *And for which, if any, are you currently doing unpaid voluntary work? Labor unions/trade unions Belong to (%)*

	1981	1990	1995	2000	Change
Albania				4	
Algeria					
Argentina		0		1	1
Armenia					
Australia					
Austria		2		2	0
Azerbaijan					
Bangladesh				14	
Belarus				5	
Belgium	1	2		2	1
Bosnia and Herz.				2	
Brazil		2			
Bulgaria		5		3	–2
Canada	2	4		3	1
Chile		2		2	0
China		1		7	6
Colombia					
Croatia				4	
Czech Republic		6		3	–3
Denmark	3	3		4	1
Dominican Rep.					
Egypt					
El Salvador					
Estonia		11		0	–11
Finland		8		4	–4
France	3	2		1	–2
Georgia					
Germany (East)		10		1	–9
Germany (West)	2	2		0	0
Great Britain	1	1		2	1
Greece				4	
Hungary		5		1	–4
Iceland	3	3		3	0
India				7	
Indonesia					
Iran					
Iraq					
Ireland	2	1		1	–1
Israel					
Italy	4	3		2	–2
Japan		1		1	0
Jordan					
Korea Republic		1		2	1

	1981	1990	1995	2000	Change
Kyrgyzstan				3	
Latvia		9		2	–7
Lithuania		9		1	–8
Luxembourg				3	
Macedonia				2	
Malta	2	2		2	0
Mexico		2		2	0
Moldova				8	
Montenegro				1	
Morocco					
Netherlands	1	2		2	1
New Zealand					
Nigeria					
Northern Ireland	2	2		1	–1
Norway	6	6			0
Pakistan					
Peru				3	
Philippines				3	
Poland		6		2	–4
Portugal		1		0	–1
Puerto Rico				2	
Romania		14		6	–8
Russian Fed.		9		4	–5
Saudi Arabia					
Serbia				2	
Singapore				1	
Slovakia		5		6	1
Slovenia		2		3	1
South Africa				5	
Spain	2	1		1	–1
Sweden	3	6		10	7
Switzerland					
Taiwan					
Tanzania				21	
Turkey				1	
Uganda				4	
Ukraine				4	
Uruguay					
USA	1	2		3	2
Venezuela					
Vietnam				10	
Zimbabwe				1	

Unpaid Work Political Parties or Groups

(A085) *And for which, if any, are you currently doing unpaid voluntary work? Political parties or groups*

Belong to (%)

	1981	1990	1995	2000	Change
Albania				11	
Algeria				6	
Argentina		1		3	2
Armenia					
Australia					
Austria		3		3	0
Azerbaijan					
Bangladesh				23	
Belarus				1	
Belgium	2	2		3	1
Bosnia and Herz.				3	
Brazil		2			
Bulgaria		5		3	–2
Canada	4	4		3	–1
Chile		2		2	0
China		26		10	–16
Colombia					
Croatia				2	
Czech Republic		2		2	0
Denmark	2	2		3	1
Dominican Rep.					
Egypt					
El Salvador					
Estonia		4		1	–3
Finland		7		3	–4
France	2	2		1	–1
Georgia					
Germany (East)		5		1	–4
Germany (West)	4	3		1	–3
Great Britain	1	2		1	0
Greece				5	
Hungary		1		1	0
Iceland	2	4		3	1
India				8	
Indonesia					
Iran					
Iraq					
Ireland	2	2		2	0
Israel					
Italy	4	3		2	–2
Japan		1		1	0
Jordan					
Korea Republic		2		2	0
Kyrgyzstan				1	
Latvia		6		1	–5
Lithuania		4		1	–3
Luxembourg				3	
Macedonia				8	
Malta	3	4		4	1
Mexico		3		3	0
Moldova				5	
Montenegro				3	
Morocco					
Netherlands	2	2		3	1
New Zealand					
Nigeria					
Northern Ireland	2	1		1	–1
Norway	4	4			0
Pakistan					
Peru				3	
Philippines				4	
Poland		1		1	0
Portugal		3		1	–2
Puerto Rico				4	
Romania		2		2	0
Russian Fed.		5		0	–5
Saudi Arabia					
Serbia				1	
Singapore				0	
Slovakia		1		5	4
Slovenia		1		1	0
South Africa				6	
Spain	2	1		1	–1
Sweden	2	4		4	2
Switzerland					
Taiwan					
Tanzania				21	
Turkey				3	
Uganda				6	
Ukraine				1	
Uruguay					
USA	3	5		7	4
Venezuela					
Vietnam				24	
Zimbabwe				5	

Unpaid Work Local Community Action

(A086) *And for which, if any, are you currently doing unpaid voluntary work? Local community action on issues like poverty, employment, housing, racial equality*

Belong to (%)

	1981	1990	1995	2000	Change
Albania				8	
Algeria				7	
Argentina		1		3	2
Armenia					
Australia					
Austria		2		1	–1
Azerbaijan					
Bangladesh				24	
Belarus				1	
Belgium		3		2	–1
Bosnia and Herz.				1	
Brazil		4			
Bulgaria		2		1	–1
Canada		4		5	1
Chile		3		4	1
China		5		14	9
Colombia					
Croatia				1	
Czech Republic		1		2	1
Denmark		2		3	1
Dominican Rep.					
Egypt					
El Salvador					
Estonia		4		2	–2
Finland		3		2	–1
France		3		1	–2
Georgia					
Germany (East)		1		0	–1
Germany (West)		1		0	0
Great Britain		1		2	1
Greece				7	
Hungary		2		1	–1
Iceland		1		1	0
India				5	
Indonesia					
Iran					
Iraq					
Ireland		3		4	1
Israel					
Italy		1		2	1
Japan		0		0	0
Jordan					
Korea Republic		3		7	4

	1981	1990	1995	2000	Change
Kyrgyzstan				2	
Latvia		8		2	–6
Lithuania		2		1	–1
Luxembourg				3	
Macedonia				3	
Malta		2		4	2
Mexico		3		4	1
Moldova				3	
Montenegro				0	
Morocco					
Netherlands		3		4	1
New Zealand					
Nigeria					
Northern Ireland		2		1	–1
Norway		1			
Pakistan					
Peru				4	
Philippines				6	
Poland		2		1	–1
Portugal		1		1	0
Puerto Rico				4	
Romania		1		1	0
Russian Fed.		2		1	–1
Saudi Arabia					
Serbia				0	
Singapore				2	
Slovakia		2		7	5
Slovenia		3		6	3
South Africa				5	
Spain		1		2	1
Sweden		1		5	4
Switzerland					
Taiwan					
Tanzania				23	
Turkey				0	
Uganda				6	
Ukraine				1	
Uruguay					
USA		3		7	4
Venezuela					
Vietnam				26	
Zimbabwe				2	

Unpaid Work Third World Development/Human Rights

(A087) *And for which, if any, are you currently doing unpaid voluntary work? Third world development or human rights*

Belong to (%)

	1981	1990	1995	2000	Change
Albania				2	
Algeria				6	
Argentina		0		0	0
Armenia					
Australia					
Austria		1		1	0
Azerbaijan					
Bangladesh				11	
Belarus				1	
Belgium	0	3		4	4
Bosnia and Herz.				0	
Brazil		1			
Bulgaria		1		0	–1
Canada	2	3		3	1
Chile		1		2	1
China		0		5	5
Colombia					
Croatia				0	
Czech Republic		0		0	0
Denmark	1	1		1	0
Dominican Rep.					
Egypt					
El Salvador					
Estonia		1		0	–1
Finland		2		3	1
France	0	1		1	1
Georgia					
Germany (East)		0		0	0
Germany (West)	1	1		0	0
Great Britain	1	1		4	3
Greece				6	
Hungary		0		0	0
Iceland	1	0		1	0
India				2	
Indonesia					
Iran					
Iraq					
Ireland	1	1		2	1
Israel					
Italy	1	1		2	1
Japan		0		0	0
Jordan					
Korea Republic		2		1	–1

	1981	1990	1995	2000	Change
Kyrgyzstan				1	
Latvia		4		0	–4
Lithuania		1		0	–1
Luxembourg				5	
Macedonia				2	
Malta	0	1		1	1
Mexico		1		1	0
Moldova				2	
Montenegro				0	
Morocco					
Netherlands	1	3		4	3
New Zealand					
Nigeria					
Northern Ireland		0		1	1
Norway	2	1			–1
Pakistan					
Peru				2	
Philippines				5	
Poland		1		0	–1
Portugal		1		1	0
Puerto Rico				2	
Romania		0		0	0
Russian Fed.		0		0	0
Saudi Arabia					
Serbia				0	
Singapore				1	
Slovakia		0		0	0
Slovenia		0		0	0
South Africa				1	
Spain	1	1		1	0
Sweden	2	3		4	2
Switzerland					
Taiwan					
Tanzania				20	
Turkey				0	
Uganda				3	
Ukraine				0	
Uruguay					
USA	2	1		3	1
Venezuela					
Vietnam				1	
Zimbabwe				1	

Unpaid Work Conservation, the Environment, Ecology, Animal Rights

(A088) *And for which, if any, are you currently doing unpaid voluntary work? Conservation, the environment, ecology, animal rights*

Belong to (%)

	1981	1990	1995	2000	Change
Albania				7	
Algeria				6	
Argentina				1	
Armenia					
Australia					
Austria				2	
Azerbaijan					
Bangladesh				19	
Belarus				2	
Belgium	2			3	1
Bosnia and Herz.				2	
Brazil					
Bulgaria				1	
Canada	2			4	2
Chile				2	
China				28	
Colombia					
Croatia				1	
Czech Republic				3	
Denmark	0			2	2
Dominican Rep.					
Egypt					
El Salvador					
Estonia				1	
Finland				2	
France	1			1	0
Georgia					
Germany (East)				1	
Germany (West)	1			1	0
Great Britain	1			8	7
Greece				9	
Hungary				2	
Iceland	2			1	–1
India				5	
Indonesia					
Iran					
Iraq					
Ireland	1			1	0
Israel					
Italy	1			2	1
Japan				1	
Jordan					
Korea Republic				5	

	1981	1990	1995	2000	Change
Kyrgyzstan				1	
Latvia				0	
Lithuania				0	
Luxembourg				4	
Macedonia				3	
Malta	1			2	1
Mexico				3	
Moldova				4	
Montenegro				2	
Morocco					
Netherlands	1			2	1
New Zealand					
Nigeria					
Northern Ireland	1			1	0
Norway	1				
Pakistan					
Peru				2	
Philippines				9	
Poland				0	
Portugal				0	
Puerto Rico				3	
Romania				1	
Russian Fed.				0	
Saudi Arabia					
Serbia				0	
Singapore				1	
Slovakia				2	
Slovenia				3	
South Africa				1	
Spain	1			1	0
Sweden	4			4	0
Switzerland					
Taiwan					
Tanzania				21	
Turkey				0	
Uganda				8	
Ukraine				0	
Uruguay					
USA	2			8	6
Venezuela					
Vietnam				8	
Zimbabwe				1	

Unpaid Work Professional Associations

(A089) *And for which, if any, are you currently doing unpaid voluntary work? Professional associations*

Belong to (%)

	1981	1990	1995	2000	Change
Albania				7	
Algeria				9	
Argentina		0		1	1
Armenia					
Australia					
Austria		1		2	1
Azerbaijan					
Bangladesh					
Belarus				1	
Belgium	2	2		3	1
Bosnia and Herz.				1	
Brazil		2			
Bulgaria		2		2	0
Canada	4	5		6	2
Chile		1		2	1
China		17		4	–13
Colombia					
Croatia				2	
Czech Republic		2		2	0
Denmark	5	3		4	–1
Dominican Rep.					
Egypt					
El Salvador					
Estonia		2		1	–1
Finland		7		2	–5
France	2	3		1	–1
Georgia					
Germany (East)		2		1	–1
Germany (West)	2	2		1	–1
Great Britain	1	2		8	7
Greece				6	
Hungary		2		2	0
Iceland	2	3		3	1
India				6	
Indonesia					
Iran					
Iraq					
Ireland	1	1		3	2
Israel					
Italy	1	1		3	2
Japan		1		1	0
Jordan					
Korea Republic		2		4	2

	1981	1990	1995	2000	Change
Kyrgyzstan				1	
Latvia		3		0	–3
Lithuania		1		0	–1
Luxembourg				1	
Macedonia				3	
Malta	3	1		2	–1
Mexico		1		1	0
Moldova				4	
Montenegro				2	
Morocco					
Netherlands	2	2		3	1
New Zealand					
Nigeria					
Northern Ireland	1	1		1	0
Norway	4	3			–1
Pakistan					
Peru				3	
Philippines				2	
Poland		2		1	–1
Portugal		1		1	0
Puerto Rico				6	
Romania		1		1	0
Russian Fed.		1		0	–1
Saudi Arabia					
Serbia				1	
Singapore				1	
Slovakia		3		3	0
Slovenia		2		3	1
South Africa				2	
Spain	2	1		1	–1
Sweden	4	3		4	0
Switzerland					
Taiwan					
Tanzania				20	
Turkey				1	
Uganda				5	
Ukraine				1	
Uruguay					
USA	5	5		11	6
Venezuela					
Vietnam				10	
Zimbabwe				2	

Unpaid Work Youth Work

(A090) *And for which, if any, are you currently doing unpaid voluntary work? Youth work (e.g. scouts, guides, youth clubs, etc.)*

Belong to (%)

	1981	1990	1995	2000	Change
Albania				9	
Algeria				10	
Argentina		2		2	0
Armenia					
Australia					
Austria		2		2	0
Azerbaijan					
Bangladesh				14	
Belarus				1	
Belgium	3	5		5	2
Bosnia and Herz.				2	
Brazil		2			
Bulgaria		1		1	0
Canada	8	7		8	0
Chile		4		4	0
China		10		10	0
Colombia					
Croatia				2	
Czech Republic		3		6	3
Denmark	5	3		5	0
Dominican Rep.					
Egypt					
El Salvador					
Estonia		2		2	0
Finland		5		4	–1
France	4	2		1	–3
Georgia					
Germany (East)		2		1	–1
Germany (West)	2	2		2	0
Great Britain	6	3		15	9
Greece				5	
Hungary		1		1	0
Iceland	10	5		3	–7
India				5	
Indonesia					
Iran					
Iraq					
Ireland	7	5		4	–3
Israel					
Italy	1	3		3	2
Japan		1		1	0
Jordan					
Korea Republic		3		3	0
Kyrgyzstan				2	
Latvia		3		1	–2
Lithuania		4		1	–3
Luxembourg				6	
Macedonia				3	
Malta	3	2		3	0
Mexico		2		4	2
Moldova				4	
Montenegro				1	
Morocco					
Netherlands	5	5		5	0
New Zealand					
Nigeria					
Northern Ireland	6	8		3	–3
Norway	6	4			–2
Pakistan					
Peru				5	
Philippines				6	
Poland		2		1	–1
Portugal		2		1	–1
Puerto Rico				4	
Romania		1		1	0
Russian Fed.		3		0	–3
Saudi Arabia					
Serbia				0	
Singapore				8	
Slovakia		1		6	5
Slovenia		1		3	2
South Africa				7	
Spain	3	1		1	–2
Sweden	3	7		5	2
Switzerland					
Taiwan					
Tanzania				20	
Turkey				0	
Uganda				18	
Ukraine				1	
Uruguay					
USA	8	10		22	14
Venezuela					
Vietnam				14	
Zimbabwe				4	

Unpaid Work Sports or Recreation

(A091) *And for which, if any, are you currently doing unpaid voluntary work? Sports or recreation*

Belong to (%)

	1981	1990	1995	2000	Change
Albania				8	
Algeria				15	
Argentina		2		3	1
Armenia					
Australia					
Austria		8		9	1
Azerbaijan					
Bangladesh				25	
Belarus				1	
Belgium		6		8	2
Bosnia and Herz.				7	
Brazil		4			
Bulgaria		4		4	0
Canada		12		13	1
Chile		7		12	5
China		6		13	7
Colombia					
Croatia				7	
Czech Republic		8		10	2
Denmark		11		14	3
Dominican Rep.					
Egypt					
El Salvador					
Estonia		8		3	–5
Finland		16		12	–4
France		6		9	3
Georgia					
Germany (East)		11		4	–7
Germany (West)		11		7	–4
Great Britain		4		4	0
Greece				9	
Hungary		2		3	1
Iceland		14		11	–3
India				9	
Indonesia					
Iran					
Iraq					
Ireland		7		13	6
Israel					
Italy		6		6	0
Japan		3		3	0
Jordan					
Korea Republic		3		12	9
Kyrgyzstan				2	
Latvia		9		6	–3
Lithuania		7		2	–5
Luxembourg				9	
Macedonia				9	
Malta		3		6	3
Mexico		5		7	2
Moldova				4	
Montenegro				5	
Morocco					
Netherlands		10		17	7
New Zealand					
Nigeria					
Northern Ireland		6		4	–2
Norway		14			
Pakistan					
Peru				8	
Philippines				12	
Poland		3		2	–1
Portugal		6		4	–2
Puerto Rico				5	
Romania		3		1	–2
Russian Fed.		3		1	–2
Saudi Arabia					
Serbia				4	
Singapore				6	
Slovakia		6		13	7
Slovenia		3		8	5
South Africa				15	
Spain		2		3	1
Sweden		17		18	1
Switzerland					
Taiwan					
Tanzania				30	
Turkey				1	
Uganda				20	
Ukraine				1	
Uruguay					
USA		8		19	11
Venezuela					
Vietnam				18	
Zimbabwe				4	

UNPAID WORK WOMEN'S GROUPS

(A092) *And for which, if any, are you currently doing unpaid voluntary work? Women's Groups Belong to (%)*

	1981	1990	1995	2000	Change
Albania				9	
Algeria				6	
Argentina		0		1	1
Armenia					
Australia					
Austria		2		2	0
Azerbaijan					
Bangladesh				13	
Belarus				1	
Belgium		3		3	0
Bosnia and Herz.				2	
Brazil		1			
Bulgaria		1		1	0
Canada		5		5	0
Chile		2		5	3
China		3		15	12
Colombia					
Croatia				2	
Czech Republic		1		1	0
Denmark		0		1	1
Dominican Rep.					
Egypt					
El Salvador					
Estonia		2		1	–1
Finland		3		2	–1
France		1		0	–1
Georgia					
Germany (East)		2		2	0
Germany (West)		3		2	–1
Great Britain		2		1	–1
Greece				3	
Hungary		1		0	–1
Iceland		3		2	–1
India				6	
Indonesia					
Iran					
Iraq					
Ireland		2		3	1
Israel					
Italy		0		0	0
Japan		1		1	0
Jordan					
Korea Republic		2		4	2

	1981	1990	1995	2000	Change
Kyrgyzstan				2	
Latvia		2		0	–2
Lithuania		2		0	–2
Luxembourg				2	
Macedonia				4	
Malta		1		1	0
Mexico		1		3	2
Moldova				3	
Montenegro				1	
Morocco					
Netherlands		2		2	0
New Zealand					
Nigeria					
Northern Ireland		2		1	–1
Norway		1			
Pakistan					
Peru				5	
Philippines				9	
Poland		3		0	–3
Portugal				0	
Puerto Rico				2	
Romania		0		0	0
Russian Fed.		1		0	–1
Saudi Arabia					
Serbia				0	
Singapore				0	
Slovakia		2		5	3
Slovenia		0		1	1
South Africa				8	
Spain		0		1	1
Sweden		2		2	0
Switzerland					
Taiwan					
Tanzania				23	
Turkey				0	
Uganda				12	
Ukraine				0	
Uruguay					
USA		4		8	4
Venezuela					
Vietnam				27	
Zimbabwe				7	

Unpaid Work Peace Movement

(A093) *And for which, if any, are you currently doing unpaid voluntary work? Peace movement*

Belong to (%)

	1981	1990	1995	2000	Change
Albania				3	
Algeria					
Argentina		0		0	0
Armenia					
Australia					
Austria		0		0	0
Azerbaijan					
Bangladesh				27	
Belarus				1	
Belgium		1		1	0
Bosnia and Herz.				0	
Brazil		1			
Bulgaria		1		0	–1
Canada		2		1	–1
Chile		1		2	1
China		0		16	16
Colombia					
Croatia				1	
Czech Republic		0		0	0
Denmark		0		0	0
Dominican Rep.					
Egypt					
El Salvador					
Estonia		1		0	–1
Finland		1		1	0
France		0		0	0
Georgia					
Germany (East)		0		0	0
Germany (West)		1		0	0
Great Britain		1		4	3
Greece				5	
Hungary		0		0	0
Iceland		0		0	0
India				4	
Indonesia					
Iran					
Iraq					
Ireland		0		1	1
Israel					
Italy		1		1	0
Japan		1		1	0
Jordan					
Korea Republic		2		2	0
Kyrgyzstan				1	
Latvia		1		0	–1
Lithuania		1		0	–1
Luxembourg				1	
Macedonia				3	
Malta		0		0	0
Mexico		1		3	2
Moldova				2	
Montenegro				1	
Morocco					
Netherlands		1		1	0
New Zealand					
Nigeria					
Northern Ireland		0		1	1
Norway		0			
Pakistan					
Peru				0	
Philippines				10	
Poland		0		0	0
Portugal		0		0	0
Puerto Rico				1	
Romania		0			
Russian Fed.		1		0	–1
Saudi Arabia					
Serbia				0	
Singapore				1	
Slovakia		0		0	0
Slovenia		0		1	1
South Africa				4	
Spain		1		1	0
Sweden		2		0	–2
Switzerland					
Taiwan					
Tanzania				4	
Turkey				0	
Uganda				6	
Ukraine					
Uruguay					
USA		1		2	1
Venezuela					
Vietnam				7	
Zimbabwe				1	

Unpaid Work Organizations Concerned with Health

(A094) *And for which, if any, are you currently doing unpaid voluntary work? Voluntary organizations concerned with health*

Belong to (%)

	1981	1990	1995	2000	Change
Albania				8	
Algeria					
Argentina		2		2	0
Armenia					
Australia					
Austria		2		3	1
Azerbaijan					
Bangladesh				22	
Belarus				2	
Belgium		2		5	3
Bosnia and Herz.				2	
Brazil		2			
Bulgaria		2		1	–1
Canada		7		8	1
Chile		2		3	1
China		2		24	22
Colombia					
Croatia				2	
Czech Republic		3		3	0
Denmark		1		1	0
Dominican Rep.					
Egypt					
El Salvador					
Estonia		1		1	0
Finland		4		4	0
France		2		2	0
Georgia					
Germany (East)		2		1	–1
Germany (West)		1		1	0
Great Britain		3		10	7
Greece				5	
Hungary		2		1	–1
Iceland		4		2	–2
India				7	
Indonesia					
Iran					
Iraq					
Ireland		2		3	1
Israel					
Italy		2		3	1
Japan		1		2	1
Jordan					
Korea Republic		3			

	1981	1990	1995	2000	Change
Kyrgyzstan				2	
Latvia		2		0	–2
Lithuania		1		0	–1
Luxembourg				3	
Macedonia				5	
Malta		0		2	2
Mexico		1		5	4
Moldova				4	
Montenegro				3	
Morocco					
Netherlands		3		7	4
New Zealand					
Nigeria					
Northern Ireland		2		3	1
Norway		3			
Pakistan					
Peru				4	
Philippines				9	
Poland		2		1	–1
Portugal		2		1	–1
Puerto Rico				3	
Romania		0		1	1
Russian Fed.		1		0	–1
Saudi Arabia					
Serbia				1	
Singapore				4	
Slovakia		3		4	1
Slovenia		1		2	1
South Africa				5	
Spain		1		1	0
Sweden		1		3	2
Switzerland					
Taiwan					
Tanzania				21	
Turkey				0	
Uganda				9	
Ukraine				1	
Uruguay					
USA		5		11	6
Venezuela					
Vietnam				15	
Zimbabwe				3	

Unpaid Work Other Groups

(A096) *And for which, if any, are you currently doing unpaid voluntary work? Other groups*

Belong to (%)

	1981	1990	1995	2000	Change
Albania					
Algeria					
Argentina		2		2	0
Armenia					
Australia					
Austria		4		4	0
Azerbaijan					
Bangladesh				2	
Belarus				1	
Belgium		3		7	4
Bosnia and Herz.					
Brazil		0			
Bulgaria		2		2	0
Canada		9		8	–1
Chile		3			
China		2		2	0
Colombia					
Croatia				3	
Czech Republic		4		4	0
Denmark		3		7	4
Dominican Rep.					
Egypt					
El Salvador					
Estonia		2		3	1
Finland		7		6	–1
France		4		6	2
Georgia					
Germany (East)		4		3	–1
Germany (West)		4		2	–2
Great Britain		4			
Greece				4	
Hungary		1		2	1
Iceland		4		2	–2
India				5	
Indonesia					
Iran					
Iraq					
Ireland		2		4	2
Israel					
Italy		2		2	0
Japan		4			
Jordan					
Korea Republic		3			

	1981	1990	1995	2000	Change
Kyrgyzstan					
Latvia		2		5	3
Lithuania		2		2	0
Luxembourg				2	
Macedonia					
Malta		1		2	1
Mexico		1			
Moldova					
Montenegro					
Morocco					
Netherlands		4		6	2
New Zealand					
Nigeria					
Northern Ireland		2		4	2
Norway		7			
Pakistan					
Peru				0	
Philippines					
Poland		3		2	–1
Portugal		1		2	1
Puerto Rico				3	
Romania		2		1	–1
Russian Fed.		2		1	–1
Saudi Arabia					
Serbia					
Singapore					
Slovakia		2		6	4
Slovenia		3		6	3
South Africa					
Spain		1		2	1
Sweden		9		10	1
Switzerland					
Taiwan					
Tanzania					
Turkey				1	
Uganda					
Ukraine				1	
Uruguay					
USA		6		15	9
Venezuela					
Vietnam					
Zimbabwe					

Unpaid Work None

(A097) *And for which, if any, are you currently doing unpaid voluntary work? None*

Belong to (%)

	1981	1990	1995	2000	Change
Albania					
Algeria					
Argentina		84			
Armenia					
Australia					
Austria		74		69	–5
Azerbaijan					
Bangladesh					
Belarus				81	
Belgium	79	72		64	–15
Bosnia and Herz.					
Brazil		58			
Bulgaria		80		84	4
Canada	67	57			–10
Chile		69			
China		30			
Colombia					
Croatia				78	
Czech Republic		71		67	–4
Denmark	45	74		63	18
Dominican Rep.					
Egypt					
El Salvador					
Estonia		66		82	16
Finland		55		62	7
France	84	77		74	–10
Georgia					
Germany (East)		62		83	21
Germany (West)	29	69		78	49
Great Britain	78	77		57	–21
Greece				60	
Hungary		84		85	1
Iceland	68	64		67	–1
India					
Indonesia					
Iran					
Iraq					
Ireland	77	74		69	–8
Israel					
Italy	82	78		74	–8
Japan		73			
Jordan					
Korea Republic					
Kyrgyzstan					
Latvia		64		78	14
Lithuania		70		86	16
Luxembourg				69	
Macedonia					
Malta	65	77		72	7
Mexico		73			
Moldova					
Montenegro					
Morocco					
Netherlands	73	65		50	–23
New Zealand					
Nigeria					
Northern Ireland	61	74		78	17
Norway		63			
Pakistan					
Peru					
Philippines					
Poland		72		86	14
Portugal		81		86	5
Puerto Rico					
Romania		75		84	9
Russian Fed.		69		92	23
Saudi Arabia					
Serbia					
Singapore					
Slovakia		73		49	–24
Slovenia		85		71	–14
South Africa					
Spain	77	88		82	5
Sweden		61		44	–17
Switzerland					
Taiwan					
Tanzania					
Turkey				94	
Uganda					
Ukraine				87	
Uruguay					
USA	68	55			–13
Venezuela					
Vietnam					
Zimbabwe					

Neighbours: People with a Criminal Record

(A124) *On this list are various groups of people. Could you please sort out any that you would not like to have as neighbours?*

People with a criminal record (%)

	1981	1990	1995	2000	Change
Albania			94	97	3
Algeria				70	
Argentina	35	41	45	43	8
Armenia			78		
Australia	42		45		3
Austria		31		27	–4
Azerbaijan			69		
Bangladesh			87	4	–83
Belarus		72	67	72	0
Belgium	22	28		30	8
Bosnia and Herz.			78	88	10
Brazil		52	45		–7
Bulgaria		70	70	75	5
Canada	37	42		45	8
Chile		46	50	63	17
China		41	62	71	30
Colombia			64		
Croatia			42	74	32
Czech Republic		70	71	64	–6
Denmark	17	28		31	14
Dominican Rep.			62		
Egypt				3	
El Salvador			78		
Estonia		63	74	69	6
Finland		34	42	39	5
France	11	19		21	10
Georgia			50		
Germany (East)		36	28	22	–14
Germany (West)	28	28	20	26	–2
Great Britain	39	41		48	9
Greece				67	
Hungary	74	77	63		–11
Iceland	12	24		26	14
India		93	67	48	–45
Indonesia				55	
Iran				1	
Iraq				84	
Ireland	44	52		56	12
Israel					
Italy	39	48		47	8
Japan	41	50			9
Jordan				96	
Korea Republic	50	31	18	81	31
Kyrgyzstan				68	
Latvia		63	70	57	–6
Lithuania		69	78	66	–3
Luxembourg				29	
Macedonia			78	76	–2
Malta	76	78		80	4
Mexico		69	57	70	1
Moldova			81	83	2
Montenegro			47	29	–18
Morocco				64	
Netherlands	17	29		32	15
New Zealand			57		
Nigeria		80	93	79	–1
Northern Ireland	39	46		47	8
Norway	35	37	44		9
Pakistan				58	
Peru			64	53	–11
Philippines			82	72	–10
Poland		75	78	68	–7
Portugal		59		44	–15
Puerto Rico			63	36	–27
Romania		67	66	69	2
Russian Fed.		63	64	58	–5
Saudi Arabia				88	
Serbia			49	29	–20
Singapore				30	
Slovakia		74	78	82	8
Slovenia		38	55	40	2
South Africa			68	54	–14
Spain	35	37	37	32	–3
Sweden	27	35	35	33	6
Switzerland		6	20		14
Taiwan			51		
Tanzania				89	
Turkey		81	74	80	–1
Uganda				88	
Ukraine			72	72	0
Uruguay			70		
USA	48	50	61	54	6
Venezuela			68	77	9
Vietnam				48	
Zimbabwe				75	

Neighbours: People of a Different Race

(A125) *On this list are various groups of people. Could you please sort out any that you would not like to have as neighbours?*

People of a different race (%)

	1981	1990	1995	2000	Change
Albania			8	30	22
Algeria				28	
Argentina	3	3	5	5	2
Armenia			19		
Australia	6		5		–1
Austria		8		7	–1
Azerbaijan			12		
Bangladesh			17	72	55
Belarus		17	5	17	0
Belgium	12	17		16	4
Bosnia and Herz.			25	13	–12
Brazil		5	3		–2
Bulgaria		39	17	28	–11
Canada	3	5		3	0
Chile		11	12	9	–2
China		12	23	15	3
Colombia			2		
Croatia			8	20	12
Czech Republic		26	10	10	–16
Denmark	4	7		7	3
Dominican Rep.			18		
Egypt				66	
El Salvador					
Estonia		19	8	15	–4
Finland		25	12	12	–13
France	5	9		9	4
Georgia			9		
Germany (East)		13	4	7	–6
Germany (West)	11	10	2	4	–7
Great Britain	10	9		9	–1
Greece				14	
Hungary		23	19		–4
Iceland	4	8		3	–1
India		35	36	42	7
Indonesia				35	
Iran				24	
Iraq					
Ireland	7	6		12	5
Israel					
Italy	7	13		16	9
Japan	9	11			2
Jordan				20	
Korea Republic	14	58		35	21

	1981	1990	1995	2000	Change
Kyrgyzstan				18	
Latvia		13	5	5	–8
Lithuania		20	14	10	–10
Luxembourg				6	
Macedonia			26	19	–7
Malta	9	10		19	10
Mexico		16	26	15	–1
Moldova			8	11	3
Montenegro			17	19	2
Morocco				11	
Netherlands	10	8		5	–5
New Zealand			3		
Nigeria		31	20	30	–1
Northern Ireland	9	7		11	2
Norway	9	12	8		–1
Pakistan				7	
Peru			12	11	–1
Philippines			24	21	–3
Poland		17	20	17	0
Portugal		15		8	–7
Puerto Rico			7	4	–3
Romania		28	30	24	–4
Russian Fed.		11	8	8	–3
Saudi Arabia				38	
Serbia			15	7	–8
Singapore				5	
Slovakia		30	14	17	–13
Slovenia		40	17	12	–28
South Africa			11	24	13
Spain	9	10	8	11	2
Sweden	6	6	3	2	–4
Switzerland		2	9		7
Taiwan			17		
Tanzania				17	
Turkey		34	41	32	–2
Uganda				18	
Ukraine			9	10	1
Uruguay			7		
USA	8	9	7	8	0
Venezuela			20	16	–4
Vietnam				32	
Zimbabwe				20	

Neighbours: Heavy Drinkers

(A126) *On this list are various groups of people. Could you please sort out any that you would not like to have as neighbours?*

Heavy drinkers (%)

	1981	1990	1995	2000	Change
Albania			83	81	–2
Algeria				69	
Argentina	38	45	44	37	–1
Armenia			86		
Australia	56		60		4
Austria		58		53	–5
Azerbaijan			85		
Bangladesh			90	4	–86
Belarus		82	74	83	1
Belgium	39	50		44	5
Bosnia and Herz.			65	77	12
Brazil		41	46		5
Bulgaria		73	42	76	3
Canada	58	54		51	–7
Chile		52	54	51	–1
China		58	65	74	16
Colombia			33		
Croatia			64	63	–1
Czech Republic		79	67	75	–4
Denmark	29	34		36	7
Dominican Rep.			55		
Egypt				1	
El Salvador			90		
Estonia		90	86	84	–6
Finland		54	55	51	–3
France	47	50		47	0
Georgia			70		
Germany (East)		72	48	53	–19
Germany (West)	67	64	33	57	–10
Great Britain	48	48	67	51	3
Greece				37	
Hungary	79	81	70		–9
Iceland	52	61		62	10
India		91	58	45	–46
Indonesia				58	
Iran				1	
Iraq					
Ireland	33	34		36	3
Israel					
Italy	44	51		40	–4
Japan	53	58			5
Jordan				94	
Korea Republic	56	17	16	76	20
Kyrgyzstan				71	
Latvia		85	86	75	–10
Lithuania		92	86	82	–10
Luxembourg				32	
Macedonia			70	64	–6
Malta	61	61		74	13
Mexico		56	42	56	0
Moldova			78	85	7
Montenegro			73	63	–10
Morocco				86	
Netherlands	51	59		58	7
New Zealand			66		
Nigeria		72	79	65	–7
Northern Ireland	40	43		51	11
Norway	33	32	32		–1
Pakistan				1	
Peru			53	51	–2
Philippines			68	56	–12
Poland		85	79	78	–7
Portugal		51		38	–13
Puerto Rico			58	41	–17
Romania		79	58	77	–2
Russian Fed.		82	80	73	–9
Saudi Arabia					
Serbia			72	57	–15
Singapore				64	
Slovakia		75	68	80	5
Slovenia		45	79	69	24
South Africa			61	50	–11
Spain	38	40	40	39	1
Sweden	44	45	37	33	–11
Switzerland		23	47		24
Taiwan			81		
Tanzania				79	
Turkey		87	89	87	0
Uganda				70	
Ukraine			77	79	2
Uruguay			59		
USA	56	59	63	56	0
Venezuela			55	57	2
Vietnam				44	
Zimbabwe				56	

Neighbours: Emotionally Unstable People

(A127) *On this list are various groups of people. Could you please sort out any that you would not like to have as neighbours?*

Emotionally unstable people (%)

	1981	1990	1995	2000	Change
Albania			58	61	3
Algeria				44	
Argentina	26	21	28	22	−4
Armenia			75		
Australia	39		39		0
Austria		20		18	−2
Azerbaijan			75		
Bangladesh			66	28	−38
Belarus		63	53	60	−3
Belgium	15	21		22	7
Bosnia and Herz.			47	58	11
Brazil		16	18		2
Bulgaria		53	41	44	−9
Canada	28	30		33	5
Chile		28	31	25	−3
China		46	56	64	18
Colombia			17		
Croatia			37	41	4
Czech Republic		29	22	19	−10
Denmark	9	11		14	5
Dominican Rep.			52		
Egypt				28	
El Salvador			81		
Estonia		37	59	54	17
Finland		24	33	29	5
France	9	17		22	13
Georgia			55		
Germany (East)		21	22	22	1
Germany (West)	28	31	27	22	−6
Great Britain	30	28		39	9
Greece				62	
Hungary	66	23	55		−11
Iceland	23	32		31	8
India		69	45	39	−30
Indonesia				49	
Iran				1	
Iraq					
Ireland	23	30		25	2
Israel					
Italy	29	34		38	9
Japan	54	62			8
Jordan				66	
Korea Republic	36	17	9	89	53

	1981	1990	1995	2000	Change
Kyrgyzstan				50	
Latvia		54	62	35	−19
Lithuania		48	57	61	13
Luxembourg				19	
Macedonia			58	47	−11
Malta	32	34		30	−2
Mexico		38	37	34	−4
Moldova			57	68	11
Montenegro			79	77	−2
Morocco				69	
Netherlands	19	20		25	6
New Zealand			60		
Nigeria		57	60	52	−5
Northern Ireland	29	23		35	6
Norway	19	22	37		18
Pakistan				40	
Peru			32	38	6
Philippines			28	25	−3
Poland		49	55	58	9
Portugal		47		27	−20
Puerto Rico			42	33	−9
Romania		64	43	53	−11
Russian Fed.		51	56	54	3
Saudi Arabia				63	
Serbia			72	58	−14
Singapore				58	
Slovakia		31	27	22	−9
Slovenia		37	49	30	−7
South Africa			37	39	2
Spain	22	25	25	25	3
Sweden	12	17	24	17	5
Switzerland		4	17		13
Taiwan			73		
Tanzania				5	
Turkey		72	76	76	4
Uganda				46	
Ukraine			59	63	4
Uruguay			33		
USA	44	43	51	52	8
Venezuela			46	46	0
Vietnam				38	
Zimbabwe				42	

Neighbours: Muslims

(A128) *On this list are various groups of people. Could you please sort out any that you would not like to have as neighbours? Minority group (1)*

Muslims (%)

	1981	1990	1995	2000	Change
Albania				30	
Algeria					
Argentina		6		6	0
Armenia					
Australia					
Austria		15		15	0
Azerbaijan					
Bangladesh					
Belarus		24		27	3
Belgium		26		22	–4
Bosnia and Herz.				13	
Brazil					
Bulgaria		41		21	–20
Canada		10		7	–3
Chile		12		7	–5
China		12			
Colombia					
Croatia				26	
Czech Republic		30		15	–15
Denmark		15		16	1
Dominican Rep.					
Egypt					
El Salvador					
Estonia		21		22	1
Finland		10	40	19	9
France		17		16	–1
Georgia					
Germany (East)		22		15	–7
Germany (West)		20		10	–10
Great Britain		17		14	–3
Greece				21	
Hungary		18			
Iceland		12		12	0
India		28	33		5
Indonesia					
Iran					
Iraq					
Ireland		13		14	1
Israel					
Italy		15		17	2
Japan		29			
Jordan					
Korea Republic	26	21		57	31

	1981	1990	1995	2000	Change
Kyrgyzstan				15	
Latvia		26		15	–11
Lithuania		34		33	–1
Luxembourg				14	
Macedonia				26	
Malta		12		28	16
Mexico		19		17	–2
Moldova				44	
Montenegro				20	
Morocco					
Netherlands		15		12	–3
New Zealand					
Nigeria		24	17		–7
Northern Ireland		15		16	1
Norway		21	19		–2
Pakistan					
Peru				14	
Philippines			29	26	–3
Poland		20		24	4
Portugal		18		8	–10
Puerto Rico					
Romania		34		31	–3
Russian Fed.		15		14	–1
Saudi Arabia					
Serbia				14	
Singapore					
Slovakia		34		25	–9
Slovenia		38		23	–15
South Africa				24	
Spain		12	12	13	1
Sweden		17	13	9	–8
Switzerland			18		
Taiwan			19		
Tanzania				13	
Turkey		55			
Uganda				14	
Ukraine				24	
Uruguay					
USA		14	12	11	–3
Venezuela					
Vietnam				27	
Zimbabwe				18	

NEIGHBOURS: IMMIGRANTS/FOREIGN WORKERS

(A129) *On this list are various groups of people. Could you please sort out any that you would not like to have as neighbours?*

Immigrants/foreign workers (%)

	1981	1990	1995	2000	Change
Albania			10	17	7
Algeria				23	
Argentina	1	2	6	6	5
Armenia			22		
Australia	6		5		–1
Austria		21		12	–9
Azerbaijan			20		
Bangladesh			30	67	37
Belarus		17	6	17	0
Belgium	15	21		18	3
Bosnia and Herz.			20	25	5
Brazil		4	4		0
Bulgaria		34	16	25	–9
Canada	6	6		4	–2
Chile		12	12	11	–1
China		13	20	16	3
Colombia					
Croatia			7	22	15
Czech Republic		26	28	19	–7
Denmark	9	12		11	2
Dominican Rep.			18		
Egypt				42	
El Salvador					
Estonia		17	19	21	4
Finland		5	13	13	8
France	6	13		12	6
Georgia			11		
Germany (East)		21	10	14	–7
Germany (West)	21	16	4	7	–14
Great Britain	13	12	11	16	3
Greece				14	
Hungary		22	25		3
Iceland	2	8		3	1
India		37	33	38	1
Indonesia				40	
Iran				10	
Iraq					
Ireland	6	5		12	6
Israel					
Italy	3	15		17	14
Japan	7	17			10
Jordan				40	
Korea Republic	4	53	39	47	43
Kyrgyzstan				20	
Latvia		31	18	10	–21
Lithuania		15	29	24	9
Luxembourg				8	
Macedonia			24	19	–5
Malta	3	9		15	12
Mexico		18	26	14	–4
Moldova			13	19	6
Montenegro			31	20	–11
Morocco				18	
Netherlands	17	10		5	–12
New Zealand			5		
Nigeria		26	20	28	2
Northern Ireland	9	7		18	9
Norway	10	16	10		0
Pakistan				29	
Peru			10	11	1
Philippines			20	15	–5
Poland		10	21	24	14
Portugal		9		2	–7
Puerto Rico			13	6	–7
Romania		30	33	21	–9
Russian Fed.		12	12	11	–1
Saudi Arabia				33	
Serbia			25	9	–16
Singapore				26	
Slovakia		27	18	23	–4
Slovenia		41	18	16	–25
South Africa			21	31	10
Spain	2	9	7	10	8
Sweden	4	9	5	3	–1
Switzerland		2	10		8
Taiwan			27		
Tanzania				18	
Turkey		28	44	39	11
Uganda				13	
Ukraine			12	15	3
Uruguay			7		
USA	8	10	10	10	2
Venezuela			22	18	–4
Vietnam				33	
Zimbabwe				20	

NEIGHBOURS: PEOPLE WHO HAVE AIDS

(A130) *On this list are various groups of people. Could you please sort out any that you would not like to have as neighbours?*

People who have AIDS (%)

	1981	1990	1995	2000	Change
Albania			63	70	7
Algeria				68	
Argentina		32	15	12	–20
Armenia			85		
Australia			15		
Austria		32		17	–15
Azerbaijan			89		
Bangladesh			82	6	–76
Belarus		73	58	58	–15
Belgium		24		13	–11
Bosnia and Herz.			53	60	7
Brazil		23	14		–9
Bulgaria		63	43	52	–11
Canada		21		12	–9
Chile		41	21	24	–17
China		76	62	79	3
Colombia			8		
Croatia			43	51	8
Czech Republic		53	23	21	–32
Denmark		9		6	–3
Dominican Rep.			29		
Egypt				2	
El Salvador			67		
Estonia		63	44	42	–21
Finland		24	23	21	–3
France		15		9	–6
Georgia			71		
Germany (East)		22	7	10	–12
Germany (West)		29	6	11	–18
Great Britain		23	14	25	2
Greece				27	
Hungary		66	39		–27
Iceland		18		7	–11
India		93	60	39	–54
Indonesia				52	
Iran				0	
Iraq					
Ireland		35		23	–12
Israel					
Italy		44		31	–13
Japan		77			
Jordan				96	
Korea Republic		4	5	89	85

	1981	1990	1995	2000	Change
Kyrgyzstan				64	
Latvia		65	49	29	–36
Lithuania		78	66	55	–23
Luxembourg				12	
Macedonia			63	52	–11
Malta		47		38	–9
Mexico		57	31	34	–23
Moldova			73	66	–7
Montenegro			83	76	–7
Morocco				81	
Netherlands		16		8	–8
New Zealand			17		
Nigeria		79	89	68	–11
Northern Ireland		28		31	3
Norway		25	14		–11
Pakistan				7	
Peru			39	29	–10
Philippines			74	62	–12
Poland		57	51	44	–13
Portugal		44		27	–17
Puerto Rico			17	12	–5
Romania		66	43	47	–19
Russian Fed.		68	56	52	–16
Saudi Arabia				84	
Serbia			71	51	–20
Singapore				35	
Slovakia		62	44	45	–17
Slovenia		42	50	33	–9
South Africa			44	27	–17
Spain		35	23	21	–14
Sweden		18	8	7	–11
Switzerland			12		
Taiwan			72		
Tanzania				32	
Turkey		89	81	83	–6
Uganda				17	
Ukraine			59	59	0
Uruguay			19		
USA		28	19	17	–11
Venezuela			58	44	–14
Vietnam				33	
Zimbabwe				30	

Neighbours: Drug Addicts

(A131) *On this list are various groups of people. Could you please sort out any that you would not like to have as neighbours?*

Drug addicts (%)

	1981	1990	1995	2000	Change
Albania			83	85	2
Algeria				77	
Argentina		50	39	32	–18
Armenia			93		
Australia			74		
Austria		59		53	–6
Azerbaijan			97		
Bangladesh			90	2	–88
Belarus		82	82	87	5
Belgium		53		51	–2
Bosnia and Herz.			67	82	15
Brazil		58	56		–2
Bulgaria		69	66	72	3
Canada		63		64	1
Chile		55	58	53	–2
China		76	71	90	14
Colombia			30		
Croatia			70	69	–1
Czech Republic		79	74	73	–6
Denmark		53		60	7
Dominican Rep.			71		
Egypt				1	
El Salvador			89		
Estonia		87	87	90	3
Finland		68	79	75	7
France		44		48	4
Georgia			81		
Germany (East)		62	56	52	–10
Germany (West)		60	48	60	0
Great Britain		62		72	10
Greece				45	
Hungary		84	74		–10
Iceland		74		76	2
India		93	66	44	–49
Indonesia				59	
Iran				1	
Iraq					
Ireland		64		66	2
Israel					
Italy		60		55	–5
Japan		91			
Jordan				99	
Korea Republic		4	2	93	89
Kyrgyzstan				81	
Latvia		89	88	75	–14
Lithuania		89	90	86	–3
Luxembourg				43	
Macedonia			79	73	–6
Malta		64		71	7
Mexico		69	52	68	–1
Moldova			86	91	5
Montenegro			87	86	–1
Morocco				92	
Netherlands		72		73	1
New Zealand			79		
Nigeria		77	90	74	–3
Northern Ireland		59		78	19
Norway		55	66		11
Pakistan				59	
Peru			73	66	–7
Philippines			86	82	–4
Poland		76	78	69	–7
Portugal		60		48	–12
Puerto Rico			66	47	–19
Romania		76	61	74	–2
Russian Fed.		86	88	84	–2
Saudi Arabia				87	
Serbia			85	71	–14
Singapore				73	
Slovakia		76	77	79	3
Slovenia		47	75	65	18
South Africa			75	62	–13
Spain		57	53	53	–4
Sweden		65	72	60	–5
Switzerland		32	49		17
Taiwan			89		
Tanzania				81	
Turkey		92	92	94	2
Uganda				87	
Ukraine			88	88	0
Uruguay			44		
USA		79	83	74	–5
Venezuela			75	73	–2
Vietnam				54	
Zimbabwe				64	

Neighbours: Homosexuals

(A132) *On this list are various groups of people. Could you please sort out any that you would not like to have as neighbours?*

Homosexuals (%)

	1981	1990	1995	2000	Change
Albania			70	83	13
Algeria				81	
Argentina		39	27	22	–17
Armenia			83		
Australia			25		
Austria		43		25	–18
Azerbaijan			91		
Bangladesh			84	5	–79
Belarus		79	63	63	–16
Belgium		24		17	–7
Bosnia and Herz.			56	64	8
Brazil		30	26		–4
Bulgaria		68	41	54	–14
Canada		30		17	–13
Chile		57	41	33	–24
China		72	61	73	1
Colombia			15		
Croatia			45	53	8
Czech Republic		51	24	20	–31
Denmark		12		8	–4
Dominican Rep.			49		
Egypt				0	
El Salvador			78		
Estonia		73	64	46	–27
Finland		25	30	21	–4
France		24		16	–8
Georgia			77		
Germany (East)		36	16	13	–23
Germany (West)		34	10	13	–21
Great Britain		31	22	24	–7
Greece				27	
Hungary		75	53		–22
Iceland		20		8	–12
India		91	61	29	–62
Indonesia				55	
Iran				1	
Iraq					
Ireland		33		27	–6
Israel					
Italy		39		29	–10
Japan		69			
Jordan				98	
Korea Republic		4		82	78

	1981	1990	1995	2000	Change
Kyrgyzstan				66	
Latvia		78	59	46	–32
Lithuania		87	77	68	–19
Luxembourg				19	
Macedonia			66	53	–13
Malta		44		40	–4
Mexico		60	37	45	–15
Moldova			77	77	0
Montenegro			82	74	–8
Morocco				93	
Netherlands		12		6	–6
New Zealand			22		
Nigeria		76	90	74	–2
Northern Ireland		48		35	–13
Norway		19	14		–5
Pakistan					
Peru			54	49	–5
Philippines			33	24	–9
Poland		70	66	55	–15
Portugal		50		25	–25
Puerto Rico			32	22	–10
Romania		75	56	65	–10
Russian Fed.		81	71	58	–23
Saudi Arabia					
Serbia			75	49	–26
Singapore				46	
Slovakia		64	46	44	–20
Slovenia		43	61	44	1
South Africa			50	46	–4
Spain		30	20	16	–14
Sweden		18	11	6	–12
Switzerland			19		
Taiwan			73		
Tanzania				74	
Turkey		92	90	90	–2
Uganda				76	
Ukraine			65	66	1
Uruguay			32		
USA		39	29	23	–16
Venezuela			68	57	–11
Vietnam				39	
Zimbabwe				67	

NEIGHBOURS: JEWS

(A133) *On this list are various groups of people. Could you please sort out any that you would not like to have as neighbours? Minority group (2)*

Jews (%)

	1981	1990	1995	2000	Change
Albania				17	
Algeria					
Argentina		5	7	6	1
Armenia					
Australia					
Austria		11		8	–3
Azerbaijan					
Bangladesh				20	
Belarus			7	15	8
Belgium		13		13	0
Bosnia and Herz.				28	
Brazil					
Bulgaria		30		18	–12
Canada		6		4	–2
Chile		15	14	9	–6
China					
Colombia					
Croatia				18	
Czech Republic		14		4	–10
Denmark		3		2	–1
Dominican Rep.					
Egypt				17	
El Salvador					
Estonia		13		11	–2
Finland		5		9	4
France		7		6	–1
Georgia					
Germany (East)		9		8	–1
Germany (West)		7		4	–3
Great Britain		7		6	–1
Greece				19	
Hungary		10			
Iceland		7		4	–3
India		53			
Indonesia					
Iran					
Iraq				83	
Ireland		6		11	5
Israel					
Italy		13		13	0
Japan		28			
Jordan					
Korea Republic				41	
Kyrgyzstan				20	
Latvia		9		5	–4
Lithuania		18		23	5
Luxembourg				8	
Macedonia				20	
Malta		8		21	13
Mexico		19	31		12
Moldova				25	
Montenegro					
Morocco					
Netherlands		4		2	–2
New Zealand					
Nigeria		35			
Northern Ireland		6		12	6
Norway		9			
Pakistan					
Peru					
Philippines					
Poland		18		25	7
Portugal		19		11	–8
Puerto Rico					
Romania		28		23	–5
Russian Fed.		13	10	11	–2
Saudi Arabia					
Serbia					
Singapore					
Slovakia		28		10	–18
Slovenia		38		17	–21
South Africa				24	
Spain		10		22	12
Sweden		6		2	–4
Switzerland					
Taiwan					
Tanzania					
Turkey				62	
Uganda				22	
Ukraine				10	
Uruguay			10		
USA		5		9	4
Venezuela			26		
Vietnam					
Zimbabwe				19	

Neighbours: People of a Different Religion

(A135) *On this list are various groups of people. Could you please sort out any that you would not like to have as neighbours?*

People of a different religion (%)

	1981	1990	1995	2000	Change
Albania			25		
Algeria				32	
Argentina					
Armenia					
Australia					
Austria					
Azerbaijan					
Bangladesh			13	66	53
Belarus					
Belgium					
Bosnia and Herz.			28		
Brazil			13		
Bulgaria			17		
Canada					
Chile					
China					
Colombia					
Croatia			14		
Czech Republic					
Denmark					
Dominican Rep.					
Egypt					
El Salvador			11		
Estonia			23		
Finland					
France					
Georgia			27		
Germany (East)			16		
Germany (West)			9		
Great Britain					
Greece					
Hungary					
Iceland					
India				40	
Indonesia				38	
Iran				20	
Iraq				35	
Ireland					
Israel					
Italy					
Japan					
Jordan				32	
Korea Republic					
Kyrgyzstan					
Latvia			25		
Lithuania					
Luxembourg					
Macedonia					
Malta					
Mexico					
Moldova			16		
Montenegro					
Morocco				34	
Netherlands					
New Zealand					
Nigeria				29	
Northern Ireland					
Norway					
Pakistan				8	
Peru					
Philippines					
Poland					
Portugal					
Puerto Rico					
Romania			30		
Russian Fed.					
Saudi Arabia				40	
Serbia					
Singapore					
Slovakia					
Slovenia			23		
South Africa					
Spain					
Sweden					
Switzerland					
Taiwan					
Tanzania					
Turkey				35	
Uganda					
Ukraine					
Uruguay					
USA					
Venezuela				17	
Vietnam					
Zimbabwe					

Neighbours: Gypsies

(A140) *On this list are various groups of people. Could you please sort out any that you would not like to have as neighbours?*

Gypsies (%)

	1981	1990	1995	2000	Change
Albania					
Algeria					
Argentina					
Armenia					
Australia					
Austria				25	
Azerbaijan					
Bangladesh					
Belarus				51	
Belgium				35	
Bosnia and Herz.					
Brazil					
Bulgaria				54	
Canada					
Chile					
China					
Colombia					
Croatia				39	
Czech Republic			46	40	–6
Denmark				15	
Dominican Rep.					
Egypt					
El Salvador					
Estonia				50	
Finland				44	
France				40	
Georgia					
Germany (East)				32	
Germany (West)				33	
Great Britain				37	
Greece				33	
Hungary			42		
Iceland				9	
India					
Indonesia					
Iran					
Iraq					
Ireland				25	
Israel					
Italy				56	
Japan					
Jordan					
Korea Republic					
Kyrgyzstan					
Latvia				27	
Lithuania				63	
Luxembourg				25	
Macedonia					
Malta				30	
Mexico					
Moldova					
Montenegro			29	24	
Morocco					
Netherlands				19	
New Zealand					
Nigeria					
Northern Ireland				58	
Norway					
Pakistan					
Peru					
Philippines					
Poland				39	
Portugal				37	
Puerto Rico					
Romania				51	
Russian Fed.				46	
Saudi Arabia					
Serbia			28	13	–15
Singapore					
Slovakia			68	77	9
Slovenia				37	
South Africa					
Spain				28	
Sweden				20	
Switzerland					
Taiwan					
Tanzania					
Turkey				72	
Uganda					
Ukraine				53	
Uruguay					
USA					
Venezuela					
Vietnam					
Zimbabwe					

NEIGHBOURS: LEFT WING EXTREMISTS

(A149) *On this list are various groups of people. Could you please sort out any that you would not like to have as neighbours?*

Left-wing extremists (%)

	1981	1990	1995	2000	Change
Albania					
Algeria					
Argentina		49			
Armenia					
Australia					
Austria		43		50	7
Azerbaijan					
Bangladesh					
Belarus				42	
Belgium	20	34		36	16
Bosnia and Herz.					
Brazil		12			
Bulgaria		68		54	–14
Canada	28	27			–1
Chile		46			
China					
Colombia					
Croatia				34	
Czech Republic		34		31	–3
Denmark	6	6		9	3
Dominican Rep.					
Egypt					
El Salvador					
Estonia		66		30	–36
Finland		12		13	1
France	10	23		25	15
Georgia					
Germany (East)		59		46	–13
Germany (West)	51	51		50	–1
Great Britain	27	34		27	0
Greece				23	
Hungary		21			
Iceland	22	30		25	3
India		74			
Indonesia					
Iran					
Iraq					
Ireland	21	29		33	12
Israel					
Italy	37	30		28	–9
Japan		77			
Jordan					
Korea Republic		18			

	1981	1990	1995	2000	Change
Kyrgyzstan					
Latvia		69		26	–43
Lithuania		65		34	–31
Luxembourg				42	
Macedonia					
Malta	45	21		37	–8
Mexico		26			
Moldova					
Montenegro					
Morocco					
Netherlands	38	48		50	12
New Zealand					
Nigeria		48			
Northern Ireland	29	35		36	7
Norway	19	19			0
Pakistan					
Peru					
Philippines					
Poland		17		18	1
Portugal		32		11	–21
Puerto Rico					
Romania		45		35	–10
Russian Fed.		41		23	–18
Saudi Arabia					
Serbia					
Singapore					
Slovakia		29		19	–10
Slovenia		32		36	4
South Africa					
Spain	25	25		25	0
Sweden	21	24		23	2
Switzerland		15			
Taiwan					
Tanzania					
Turkey				67	
Uganda					
Ukraine				35	
Uruguay					
USA	30	31			1
Venezuela					
Vietnam					
Zimbabwe					

Neighbours: Right Wing Extremists

(A150) *On this list are various groups of people. Could you please sort out any that you would not like to have as neighbours?*

Right-wing extremists (%)

	1981	1990	1995	2000	Change
Albania					
Algeria					
Argentina		46			
Armenia					
Australia					
Austria		42		60	18
Azerbaijan					
Bangladesh					
Belarus				40	
Belgium	17	38		46	29
Bosnia and Herz.					
Brazil		8			
Bulgaria		65		53	–12
Canada	21	24			3
Chile		46			
China					
Colombia					
Croatia				35	
Czech Republic		32		29	–3
Denmark	3	7		20	17
Dominican Rep.					
Egypt					
El Salvador					
Estonia				23	
Finland		7		18	11
France	14	33		43	29
Georgia					
Germany (East)		70		72	2
Germany (West)	45	62		78	33
Great Britain	22	28		30	8
Greece				31	
Hungary		20			
Iceland	20	29		29	9
India		65			
Indonesia					
Iran					
Iraq					
Ireland	17	21		32	15
Israel					
Italy	40	34		30	–10
Japan		79			
Jordan					
Korea Republic		27			

	1981	1990	1995	2000	Change
Kyrgyzstan					
Latvia				21	
Lithuania				32	
Luxembourg				57	
Macedonia					
Malta	42	21		40	–2
Mexico		27			
Moldova					
Montenegro					
Morocco					
Netherlands	34	53		69	35
New Zealand					
Nigeria		36			
Northern Ireland	23	29		34	11
Norway	18	22			4
Pakistan					
Peru					
Philippines					
Poland		14		15	1
Portugal		29		12	–17
Puerto Rico					
Romania		42		34	–8
Russian Fed.		40		22	–18
Saudi Arabia					
Serbia					
Singapore					
Slovakia		30		17	–13
Slovenia		33		37	4
South Africa					
Spain	24	28		29	5
Sweden	17	29		48	31
Switzerland		18			
Taiwan					
Tanzania					
Turkey				67	
Uganda					
Ukraine				36	
Uruguay					
USA	23	31			8
Venezuela					
Vietnam					
Zimbabwe					

Neighbours: People with Large Families

(A151) *On this list are various groups of people. Could you please sort out any that you would not like to have as neighbours?*

People with large families (%)

	1981	1990	1995	2000	Change
Albania					
Algeria					
Argentina		5			
Armenia					
Australia					
Austria		6		4	–2
Azerbaijan					
Bangladesh					
Belarus				10	
Belgium	4	8		9	5
Bosnia and Herz.					
Brazil		6			
Bulgaria		24		12	–12
Canada	5	6			1
Chile		13			
China		19			
Colombia					
Croatia				15	
Czech Republic		13		9	–4
Denmark	5	3		4	–1
Dominican Rep.					
Egypt					
El Salvador					
Estonia		11		14	3
Finland		4		7	3
France	4	8		10	6
Georgia					
Germany (East)		8		7	–1
Germany (West)	10	8		6	–4
Great Britain	11	11		14	3
Greece				11	
Hungary		7			
Iceland	2	2		3	1
India		35			
Indonesia					
Iran					
Iraq					
Ireland	3	3		9	6
Israel					
Italy	13	12		14	1
Japan		6			
Jordan					
Korea Republic		79			

	1981	1990	1995	2000	Change
Kyrgyzstan					
Latvia		12		5	–7
Lithuania		17		11	–6
Luxembourg				8	
Macedonia					
Malta	11	16		15	4
Mexico		23			
Moldova					
Montenegro					
Morocco					
Netherlands	6	8		8	2
New Zealand					
Nigeria		33			
Northern Ireland	9	9		14	5
Norway	4	6			2
Pakistan					
Peru					
Philippines					
Poland		9		11	2
Portugal		15		5	–10
Puerto Rico					
Romania		22		14	–8
Russian Fed.		12		6	–6
Saudi Arabia					
Serbia					
Singapore					
Slovakia		18		10	–8
Slovenia		41		9	–32
South Africa					
Spain	4	8		6	2
Sweden	5	5		4	–1
Switzerland		1			
Taiwan					
Tanzania					
Turkey				41	
Uganda					
Ukraine				9	
Uruguay					
USA	7	8			1
Venezuela					
Vietnam					
Zimbabwe					

NEIGHBOURS: HINDUS

(A152) *On this list are various groups of people. Could you please sort out any that you would not like to have as neighbours?*

Hindus (%)

	1981	1990	1995	2000	Change
Albania					
Algeria					
Argentina		3			
Armenia					
Australia					
Austria		11			
Azerbaijan					
Bangladesh					
Belarus				21	
Belgium		16			
Bosnia and Herz.					
Brazil					
Bulgaria		21			
Canada		10			
Chile		13			
China					
Colombia					
Croatia					
Czech Republic		73			
Denmark		6			
Dominican Rep.					
Egypt					
El Salvador					
Estonia					
Finland		6			
France		8			
Georgia					
Germany (East)		14			
Germany (West)					
Great Britain		12		12	0
Greece					
Hungary		14			
Iceland		8			
India		2			
Indonesia					
Iran					
Iraq					
Ireland		10			
Israel					
Italy		13			
Japan		28			
Jordan					
Korea Republic					

	1981	1990	1995	2000	Change
Kyrgyzstan					
Latvia					
Lithuania					
Luxembourg					
Macedonia					
Malta		8			
Mexico		14			
Moldova					
Montenegro					
Morocco					
Netherlands		8			
New Zealand					
Nigeria		22			
Northern Ireland		9			
Norway		14			
Pakistan					
Peru					
Philippines					
Poland		37			
Portugal		17			
Puerto Rico					
Romania		72			
Russian Fed.		6			
Saudi Arabia					
Serbia					
Singapore					
Slovakia		73			
Slovenia		43			
South Africa					
Spain		9			
Sweden		9			
Switzerland					
Taiwan					
Tanzania					
Turkey					
Uganda					
Ukraine					
Uruguay					
USA		7			
Venezuela					
Vietnam					
Zimbabwe					

Most People can be Trusted

(A165) *Generally speaking, would you say that most people can be trusted or that you need to be very careful in dealing with people?*

Most people can be trusted (%)

	1981	1990	1995	2000	Change
Albania			27	24	−3
Algeria				11	
Argentina	27	23	18	15	−12
Armenia			25		
Australia	48		40		−8
Austria		32		34	2
Azerbaijan			21		
Bangladesh			21	24	3
Belarus		25	24	42	17
Belgium	29	33		31	2
Bosnia and Herz.			28	16	−12
Brazil		7	3		−4
Bulgaria		30	29	27	−3
Canada	49	52		39	−10
Chile		23	22	23	0
China		60	52	55	−5
Colombia			11		
Croatia			25	18	−7
Czech Republic		27	29	24	−3
Denmark	51	58		67	16
Dominican Rep.			26		
Egypt				38	
El Salvador			15		
Estonia		28	22	23	−5
Finland		63	49	58	−5
France	24	23		22	−2
Georgia			19		
Germany (East)		23	25	43	20
Germany (West)	31	38	42	33	2
Great Britain	44	44	31	30	−14
Greece				24	
Hungary	33	25	23	22	−11
Iceland	41	44		41	0
India		35	38	41	6
Indonesia				52	
Iran				65	
Iraq				48	
Ireland	42	47		36	−6
Israel				23	
Italy	25	34		33	8
Japan	41	42	46	43	2
Jordan				28	
Korea Republic	38	34	30	27	−11
Kyrgyzstan				17	
Latvia		19	25	17	−2
Lithuania		31	22	25	−6
Luxembourg				26	
Macedonia			8	14	6
Malta	10	24		21	11
Mexico		33	31	21	−12
Moldova			22	15	−7
Montenegro			32	34	2
Morocco				24	
Netherlands	44	53		60	16
New Zealand			49		
Nigeria		23	18	26	3
Northern Ireland	45	44		39	−6
Norway	61	65	65		4
Pakistan			21	31	10
Peru			5	11	6
Philippines			6	8	2
Poland		32	18	19	−13
Portugal		21		10	−11
Puerto Rico			6	23	17
Romania		16	19	10	−6
Russian Fed.		37	24	24	−13
Saudi Arabia				53	
Serbia			30	20	−10
Singapore				17	
Slovakia		22	27	16	−6
Slovenia		17	16	22	5
South Africa		28	18	12	−16
Spain	34	34	30	36	2
Sweden	57	66	60	66	9
Switzerland		43	41		−2
Taiwan			38		
Tanzania				8	
Turkey		10	7	16	6
Uganda				8	
Ukraine			31	27	−4
Uruguay			22		
USA	40	52	36	36	−4
Venezuela			14	16	2
Vietnam				41	
Zimbabwe				12	

Good Human Relationships

(A169) *To build good human relationships, what is most important: to try to understand others' preferences or to express one's own preferences clearly?*

Understand others' preferences (%)

	1981	1990	1995	2000	Change
Albania			53	51	–2
Algeria				54	
Argentina			54	57	3
Armenia			63		
Australia			72		
Austria					
Azerbaijan			54		
Bangladesh			56	54	–2
Belarus			74		
Belgium					
Bosnia and Herz.			72	82	10
Brazil			44		
Bulgaria			46		
Canada				66	
Chile			50	55	5
China			76	73	–3
Colombia					
Croatia			70		
Czech Republic			70		
Denmark					
Dominican Rep.			72		
Egypt				76	
El Salvador			52		
Estonia			65		
Finland			69		
France					
Georgia			54		
Germany (East)			82		
Germany (West)			83		
Great Britain					
Greece					
Hungary			68		
Iceland					
India			43	64	21
Indonesia				79	
Iran				63	
Iraq					
Ireland					
Israel					
Italy					
Japan			80	81	1
Jordan					
Korea Republic			82	79	–3

	1981	1990	1995	2000	Change
Kyrgyzstan				61	
Latvia			77		
Lithuania			78		
Luxembourg					
Macedonia			53	57	4
Malta					
Mexico			44	46	2
Moldova			65	59	–6
Montenegro			47	46	–1
Morocco				83	
Netherlands					
New Zealand			83		
Nigeria			56	65	9
Northern Ireland					
Norway			83		
Pakistan				80	
Peru			43	61	18
Philippines			57	55	–2
Poland					
Portugal					
Puerto Rico			54	72	18
Romania			62		
Russian Fed.			76		
Saudi Arabia					
Serbia			43	41	–2
Singapore					
Slovakia			58		
Slovenia			64		
South Africa			64	65	1
Spain			71	72	1
Sweden			55	68	13
Switzerland					
Taiwan			74		
Tanzania				65	
Turkey			34	54	20
Uganda				66	
Ukraine			73		
Uruguay			55		
USA			74	74	0
Venezuela			19	39	20
Vietnam				86	
Zimbabwe				65	

Life Satisfaction

(A170) *All things considered, how satisfied are you with your life as a whole these days?*

(%) Satisfied (7 thru 10)

	1981	1990	1995	2000	Change
Albania			20	30	10
Algeria				44	
Argentina	60	69	62	69	9
Armenia			19		
Australia	83		77		–6
Austria		79		83	4
Azerbaijan			32		
Bangladesh			49	32	–17
Belarus		33	17	24	–9
Belgium	76	78		78	2
Bosnia and Herz.			33	38	5
Brazil		68	63		–5
Bulgaria		25	23	36	11
Canada	82	83		81	–1
Chile		70	57	63	–7
China		68	59	53	–15
Colombia			85		
Croatia			48	54	6
Czech Republic		58	52	67	9
Denmark	84	86		86	2
Dominican Rep.			68		
Egypt				43	
El Salvador			71		
Estonia		45	26	44	–1
Finland		79	85	84	5
France	58	59		66	8
Georgia			25		
Germany (East)		58	58	70	12
Germany (West)	71	71	70	80	9
Great Britain	76	74	77	73	–3
Greece				61	
Hungary	62	44	38	37	–25
Iceland	86	85		87	1
India		53	56	28	–25
Indonesia				62	
Iran				52	
Iraq				31	
Ireland	81	80		86	5
Israel				65	
Italy	58	71		70	12
Japan	54	53	58	53	–1
Jordan				37	
Korea Republic	26	61		47	21

	1981	1990	1995	2000	Change
Kyrgyzstan				53	
Latvia		40	25	33	–7
Lithuania		44	31	33	–11
Luxembourg				82	
Macedonia			34	31	–3
Malta	78	82		86	8
Mexico		72	73	80	8
Moldova			14	19	5
Montenegro			49	41	–8
Morocco				38	
Netherlands	82	84		90	8
New Zealand			78		
Nigeria		54	56	64	10
Northern Ireland	77	83		85	8
Norway	80	78	79		–1
Pakistan				10	
Peru			47	50	3
Philippines			54	53	–1
Poland		55	50	50	–5
Portugal		63		62	–1
Puerto Rico			79	85	6
Romania		44	27	38	–6
Russian Fed.		31	22	27	–4
Saudi Arabia				65	
Serbia			39	40	1
Singapore				71	
Slovakia		54	47	47	–7
Slovenia		47	50	67	20
South Africa		51	39	42	–9
Spain	57	67	55	65	8
Sweden	86	84	81	80	–6
Switzerland		86	85		–1
Taiwan			49		
Tanzania				21	
Turkey		48	45	39	–9
Uganda				36	
Ukraine			13	24	11
Uruguay			63		
USA	77	81	78	79	2
Venezuela			57	70	13
Vietnam				44	
Zimbabwe				18	

Freedom Feeling

(A173) *Some people feel they have completely free choice and control over their lives, while other people feel that what they do has no real effect on what happens to them. Indicate how much freedom of choice and control you feel you have over the way your life turns out*

(%) A great deal (7 thru 10)

	1981	1990	1995	2000	Change
Albania			22	46	24
Algeria				56	
Argentina	61	68	64	68	7
Armenia			36		
Australia	67		76		9
Austria		71		70	–1
Azerbaijan			40		
Bangladesh			50	33	–17
Belarus			31	37	6
Belgium	48	57		59	11
Bosnia and Herz.			37	47	10
Brazil		63	66		3
Bulgaria		28	31	46	18
Canada	69	77		77	8
Chile		61	61	65	4
China		63	59	64	1
Colombia			78		
Croatia			55	60	5
Czech Republic		53	52	59	6
Denmark	62	64		72	10
Dominican Rep.			70		
Egypt				43	
El Salvador			70		
Estonia		50	46	43	–7
Finland		79	82	78	–1
France	50	45		51	1
Georgia			49		
Germany (East)		53	52	66	13
Germany (West)	64	63	70	74	10
Great Britain	58	65		67	9
Greece				65	
Hungary	60	49	51	44	–16
Iceland	72	70		81	9
India		50	55	22	–28
Indonesia				67	
Iran				55	
Iraq				43	
Ireland	63	65		69	6
Israel					
Italy	36	52		51	15
Japan	33	29	37	39	6
Jordan				65	
Korea Republic	27	72		64	37

	1981	1990	1995	2000	Change
Kyrgyzstan				61	
Latvia		48	40	41	–7
Lithuania		54	45	50	–4
Luxembourg				64	
Macedonia			49	42	–7
Malta	65	65		75	10
Mexico		70	73	79	9
Moldova			40	46	6
Montenegro			52	45	–7
Morocco				46	
Netherlands	45	52		65	20
New Zealand			79		
Nigeria		57	61	67	10
Northern Ireland	49	75		74	25
Norway	56	67	70		14
Pakistan				11	
Peru			57	64	7
Philippines			57	55	–2
Poland		47		48	1
Portugal		52		55	3
Puerto Rico			83	83	0
Romania		49	52	58	9
Russian Fed.		47	33	38	–9
Saudi Arabia				55	
Serbia			47	44	–3
Singapore				69	
Slovakia		54	50	50	–4
Slovenia		44	58	64	20
South Africa		57	48	55	–2
Spain	54	57	45	58	4
Sweden	65	74	72	74	9
Switzerland		66	70		4
Taiwan			68		
Tanzania				41	
Turkey			28	39	11
Uganda				51	
Ukraine			31	34	3
Uruguay			60		
USA	71	77	73	82	11
Venezuela			77	82	5
Vietnam				65	
Zimbabwe				43	

Environment: Income

(B001) *I would give part of my income if I were certain that the money would be used to prevent environmental pollution*

Strongly agree/Agree (%)

	1981	1990	1995	2000	Change
Albania				70	
Algeria					
Argentina		62		67	5
Armenia					
Australia					
Austria		59		49	–10
Azerbaijan					
Bangladesh				79	
Belarus				58	
Belgium		57		58	1
Bosnia and Herz.				76	
Brazil		72			
Bulgaria		83		57	–26
Canada		74		70	–4
Chile		84		70	–14
China		78		82	4
Colombia					
Croatia				79	
Czech Republic		85		78	–7
Denmark		84		79	–5
Dominican Rep.					
Egypt					
El Salvador					
Estonia		77		48	–29
Finland		67		53	–14
France		61		46	–15
Georgia					
Germany (East)		61		30	–31
Germany (West)		52		34	–18
Great Britain		68		49	–19
Greece				82	
Hungary		60		51	–9
Iceland		78		63	–15
India		81		67	–14
Indonesia					
Iran					
Iraq					
Ireland		69		54	–15
Israel					
Italy		68		65	–3
Japan		68		70	2
Jordan					
Korea Republic		84		84	0
Kyrgyzstan				79	
Latvia		77		70	–7
Lithuania		75		26	–49
Luxembourg				64	
Macedonia				79	
Malta		69		61	–8
Mexico		81		78	–3
Moldova				68	
Montenegro				60	
Morocco					
Netherlands		81		75	–6
New Zealand					
Nigeria		78			
Northern Ireland		75		46	–29
Norway		80			
Pakistan					
Peru				81	
Philippines				73	
Poland		75		63	–12
Portugal		84		57	–27
Puerto Rico				82	
Romania				52	
Russian Fed.		78		63	–15
Saudi Arabia					
Serbia				80	
Singapore				60	
Slovakia		76		57	–19
Slovenia		89		82	–7
South Africa				55	
Spain		68		59	–9
Sweden		81		79	–2
Switzerland					
Taiwan					
Tanzania				84	
Turkey				77	
Uganda				46	
Ukraine				62	
Uruguay					
USA		74		69	–5
Venezuela					
Vietnam				96	
Zimbabwe				69	

Environment: Taxes

(B002) *I would agree to an increase in taxes, if the extra money were used to prevent environmental pollution*

Strongly agree/Agree (%)

	1981	1990	1995	2000	Change
Albania			57	63	6
Algeria					
Argentina		50	46	41	–9
Armenia			57		
Australia			69		
Austria		52		39	–13
Azerbaijan			55		
Bangladesh			89	76	–13
Belarus		67	66	46	–21
Belgium		41		44	3
Bosnia and Herz.			66	70	4
Brazil		70	73		3
Bulgaria		70	62	45	–25
Canada		64		58	–6
Chile		76	60	62	–14
China		82	83	74	–8
Colombia			67		
Croatia			67	54	–13
Czech Republic		73	65	65	–8
Denmark		69		65	–4
Dominican Rep.			86		
Egypt					
El Salvador			84		
Estonia		59	59	33	–26
Finland		56	55	50	–6
France		54		37	–17
Georgia			69		
Germany (East)		63	59	26	–37
Germany (West)		49	72	30	–19
Great Britain		70		50	–20
Greece				65	
Hungary		35	41	33	–2
Iceland		60		57	–3
India		66	55	53	–13
Indonesia					
Iran					
Iraq					
Ireland		51		39	–12
Israel					
Italy		54		44	–10
Japan		51	69	62	11
Jordan					
Korea Republic		76	76	57	–19

	1981	1990	1995	2000	Change
Kyrgyzstan				55	
Latvia		64	55	45	–19
Lithuania		65	50	20	–45
Luxembourg				56	
Macedonia			62	64	2
Malta		58		48	–10
Mexico		67	54	57	–10
Moldova			67	38	–29
Montenegro			77	61	–16
Morocco					
Netherlands		68		55	–13
New Zealand			55		
Nigeria		59	60		1
Northern Ireland		65		44	–21
Norway		73	75		2
Pakistan					
Peru			63	56	–7
Philippines			56	64	8
Poland		72	54	51	–21
Portugal		65		43	–22
Puerto Rico			82	71	–11
Romania			66	46	–20
Russian Fed.		66	64	54	–12
Saudi Arabia					
Serbia			72	73	1
Singapore				45	
Slovakia		59	54	39	–20
Slovenia		69	66	61	–8
South Africa			40	45	5
Spain		57	68	49	–8
Sweden		77	84	77	0
Switzerland			43		
Taiwan			86		
Tanzania				75	
Turkey		72	76	56	–16
Uganda				44	
Ukraine			56	50	–6
Uruguay			58		
USA		64	58	61	–3
Venezuela			64		
Vietnam				90	
Zimbabwe				45	

Environment: No Cost

(B003) *The Government should reduce environmental pollution, but it should not cost me any money*

Strongly agree/Agree (%)

	1981	1990	1995	2000	Change
Albania				63	
Algeria					
Argentina		72		86	14
Armenia					
Australia					
Austria		61		63	2
Azerbaijan					
Bangladesh				96	
Belarus				75	
Belgium		62		63	1
Bosnia and Herz.				63	
Brazil		65			
Bulgaria		74		83	9
Canada		52		63	11
Chile		58		74	16
China		46		36	–10
Colombia					
Croatia				82	
Czech Republic		42		55	13
Denmark		29		30	1
Dominican Rep.					
Egypt					
El Salvador					
Estonia		72		88	16
Finland		51		64	13
France		74		84	10
Georgia					
Germany (East)		50		71	21
Germany (West)		57		67	10
Great Britain		56		77	21
Greece				71	
Hungary		75		86	11
Iceland		28		32	4
India		52		55	3
Indonesia					
Iran					
Iraq					
Ireland		60		69	9
Israel					
Italy		80		81	1
Japan		56		56	0
Jordan					
Korea Republic		50		67	17

	1981	1990	1995	2000	Change
Kyrgyzstan				61	
Latvia		71		87	16
Lithuania		69		89	20
Luxembourg				61	
Macedonia				83	
Malta		62		66	4
Mexico		40		73	33
Moldova				68	
Montenegro				78	
Morocco					
Netherlands		20		23	3
New Zealand					
Nigeria		61			
Northern Ireland		63		71	8
Norway		44			
Pakistan					
Peru				72	
Philippines				72	
Poland		48		72	24
Portugal		92		75	–17
Puerto Rico				66	
Romania				76	
Russian Fed.		49		80	31
Saudi Arabia					
Serbia				55	
Singapore				73	
Slovakia		64		79	15
Slovenia		56		63	7
South Africa				76	
Spain		76		88	12
Sweden		36		43	7
Switzerland					
Taiwan					
Tanzania				66	
Turkey				75	
Uganda				60	
Ukraine				81	
Uruguay					
USA		53		57	4
Venezuela					
Vietnam				38	
Zimbabwe				71	

Environmental Protection vs. Economic Growth

(B008) *Which statement comes closer to your own point of view: protecting the environment should be given priority or economic growth and creating jobs?*

Protecting the environment (%)

	1981	1990	1995	2000	Change
Albania			45	48	3
Algeria				34	
Argentina			45	45	0
Armenia			44		
Australia			62		
Austria					
Azerbaijan			50		
Bangladesh			46	55	9
Belarus			58		
Belgium					
Bosnia and Herz.			43	42	–1
Brazil			49		
Bulgaria			43		
Canada				64	
Chile			55	50	–5
China			60	61	1
Colombia					
Croatia			59		
Czech Republic			53		
Denmark					
Dominican Rep.			72		
Egypt				51	
El Salvador			85		
Estonia			45		
Finland			43		
France					
Georgia			64		
Germany (East)			34		
Germany (West)			45		
Great Britain					
Greece					
Hungary			31		
Iceland					
India			29	48	19
Indonesia				35	
Iran				45	
Iraq					
Ireland					
Israel				32	
Italy					
Japan			49	49	0
Jordan				54	
Korea Republic			70	53	–17

	1981	1990	1995	2000	Change
Kyrgyzstan				51	
Latvia			45		
Lithuania			35		
Luxembourg					
Macedonia			51	48	–3
Malta					
Mexico			53	55	2
Moldova			61	58	–3
Montenegro			44	35	–9
Morocco				55	
Netherlands					
New Zealand			50		
Nigeria			35	46	11
Northern Ireland					
Norway			63		
Pakistan			51	7	–44
Peru			45	61	16
Philippines			69	63	–6
Poland			49		
Portugal					
Puerto Rico			67	66	–1
Romania			53		
Russian Fed.			56		
Saudi Arabia				40	
Serbia			46	44	–2
Singapore				35	
Slovakia			47		
Slovenia			47		
South Africa			28	36	8
Spain			55	54	–1
Sweden			65	73	8
Switzerland			47		
Taiwan			64		
Tanzania				62	
Turkey			55	67	12
Uganda				39	
Ukraine			57		
Uruguay			61		
USA			52	61	9
Venezuela			45	70	25
Vietnam				61	
Zimbabwe				34	

Human & Nature

(B009) *Which statement comes closest to your own views: human beings should master nature or humans should coexist with nature?*

Coexist with nature (%)

	1981	1990	1995	2000	Change
Albania			55	66	11
Algeria					
Argentina			92	92	0
Armenia			78		
Australia			93		
Austria					
Azerbaijan			66		
Bangladesh			81	85	4
Belarus			85		
Belgium					
Bosnia and Herz.			80	85	5
Brazil			95		
Bulgaria			85		
Canada				92	
Chile			86	92	6
China			59	68	9
Colombia					
Croatia			94		
Czech Republic			96		
Denmark					
Dominican Rep.			94		
Egypt					
El Salvador			84		
Estonia			93		
Finland			92		
France					
Georgia			85		
Germany (East)			95		
Germany (West)			96		
Great Britain					
Greece					
Hungary			96		
Iceland					
India			78	83	5
Indonesia					
Iran					
Iraq					
Ireland					
Israel					
Italy					
Japan			99	99	0
Jordan				57	
Korea Republic			91	95	4

	1981	1990	1995	2000	Change
Kyrgyzstan				82	
Latvia			94		
Lithuania			91		
Luxembourg					
Macedonia			80	88	8
Malta					
Mexico			80	87	7
Moldova			66	71	5
Montenegro			95	88	–7
Morocco					
Netherlands					
New Zealand			93		
Nigeria			44		
Northern Ireland					
Norway			93		
Pakistan			48		
Peru			84	90	6
Philippines			55	50	–5
Poland					
Portugal					
Puerto Rico			93	94	1
Romania			78		
Russian Fed.			81		
Saudi Arabia				38	
Serbia			88	93	5
Singapore					
Slovakia			93		
Slovenia			96		
South Africa			64	62	–2
Spain			92	92	0
Sweden			97	95	–2
Switzerland					
Taiwan			89		
Tanzania				53	
Turkey			94		
Uganda				74	
Ukraine			88		
Uruguay			90		
USA			88	85	–3
Venezuela			83		
Vietnam				53	
Zimbabwe				61	

Men More Right to a Job

(C001) *Do you agree or disagree with the following statement? When jobs are scarce, men should have more right to a job than women*

Agree (%)

	1981	1990	1995	2000	Change
Albania			49	47	–2
Algeria				67	
Argentina		24	24	26	2
Armenia			60		
Australia			26		
Austria		50		27	–23
Azerbaijan			64		
Bangladesh			56	68	12
Belarus		38	45	25	–13
Belgium		38		25	–13
Bosnia and Herz.			40	27	–13
Brazil		38	36		–2
Bulgaria		46	35	39	–7
Canada		19		15	–4
Chile		37	30	25	–12
China		41	43	45	4
Colombia			29		
Croatia			34	29	–5
Czech Republic		51	32	18	–33
Denmark		11		6	–5
Dominican Rep.			15		
Egypt				90	
El Salvador			27		
Estonia		45	33	14	–31
Finland		15	14	10	–5
France		33		22	–11
Georgia			65		
Germany (East)		34	22	25	–9
Germany (West)		31	22	27	–4
Great Britain		34	24	23	–11
Greece				20	
Hungary		42	44	25	–17
Iceland		6		4	–2
India		49	51	57	8
Indonesia				52	
Iran				73	
Iraq				78	
Ireland		36		15	–21
Israel					
Italy		43		27	–16
Japan		34	29	32	–2
Jordan				80	
Korea Republic		42	43	39	–3
Kyrgyzstan				49	
Latvia		34	25	20	–14
Lithuania		66	32	24	–42
Luxembourg				26	
Macedonia			49	43	–6
Malta		70		47	–23
Mexico		23	25	34	11
Moldova			52	45	–7
Montenegro			32	30	–2
Morocco				83	
Netherlands		25		12	–13
New Zealand			13		
Nigeria		48	57	60	12
Northern Ireland		34		16	–18
Norway		16	14		–2
Pakistan			77	67	–10
Peru			20	15	–5
Philippines			50	69	19
Poland		55	45	35	–20
Portugal		34		29	–5
Puerto Rico			34	21	–13
Romania		42	39	38	–4
Russian Fed.		40	49	36	–4
Saudi Arabia				70	
Serbia			33	31	–2
Singapore				30	
Slovakia		55	39	24	–31
Slovenia		29	26	18	–11
South Africa		45	37	32	–13
Spain		31	27	19	–12
Sweden		8	8	2	–6
Switzerland			27		
Taiwan			57		
Tanzania				27	
Turkey		51	67	60	9
Uganda				41	
Ukraine			38	31	–7
Uruguay			28		
USA		24	19	10	–14
Venezuela			33	31	–2
Vietnam				49	
Zimbabwe				40	

Employers should Give Priority to People of Own Nationality

(C002) *Do you agree or disagree with the following statement? When jobs are scarce, employers should give priority to people of own nationality over immigrants*

Agree (%)

	1981	1990	1995	2000	Change
Albania			98	80	–18
Algeria				87	
Argentina		60	78	74	14
Armenia			66		
Australia			45		
Austria		78		72	–6
Azerbaijan			86		
Bangladesh			89	92	3
Belarus		56	73	85	29
Belgium		65		56	–9
Bosnia and Herz.			34	9	–25
Brazil		82	88		6
Bulgaria		87	84	88	1
Canada		52		47	–5
Chile		83	72	83	0
China		65	78	72	7
Colombia					
Croatia			78	91	13
Czech Republic		85	92	84	–1
Denmark		53		34	–19
Dominican Rep.			46		
Egypt				99	
El Salvador					
Estonia		82	47	47	–35
Finland		71	72	65	–6
France		63		54	–9
Georgia			83		
Germany (East)		73	71	69	–4
Germany (West)		62	43	56	–6
Great Britain		51	52	58	7
Greece				78	
Hungary		87	87	90	3
Iceland		87		70	–17
India		84	89	85	1
Indonesia				88	
Iran				94	
Iraq					
Ireland		69		74	5
Israel					
Italy		74		61	–13
Japan		65	57	61	–4
Jordan				93	
Korea Republic		72	90	84	12
Kyrgyzstan				73	
Latvia		80	41	74	–6
Lithuania		92	93	94	2
Luxembourg				48	
Macedonia			79	78	–1
Malta		92		94	2
Mexico		82	74	80	–2
Moldova			61	65	4
Montenegro			81	85	4
Morocco				94	
Netherlands		35		28	–7
New Zealand			51		
Nigeria		80	84	81	1
Northern Ireland		62		75	13
Norway		59	41		–18
Pakistan				57	
Peru			86	73	–13
Philippines			75	86	11
Poland		64	91	91	27
Portugal		88		63	–25
Puerto Rico			78	77	–1
Romania		75	75	74	–1
Russian Fed.		63	75	73	10
Saudi Arabia				53	
Serbia			81	81	0
Singapore				82	
Slovakia		89	86	88	–1
Slovenia		79	81	76	–3
South Africa		74	83	79	5
Spain		77	72	60	–17
Sweden		35	26	11	–24
Switzerland			60		
Taiwan			91		
Tanzania				71	
Turkey		75	81	66	–9
Uganda				92	
Ukraine			65	70	5
Uruguay			83		
USA		51	61	49	–2
Venezuela			85	81	–4
Vietnam				79	
Zimbabwe				79	

When Jobs Scarce, Older People should be Forced to Retire

(C004) *Do you agree or disagree with the following statement? When jobs are scarce, older people should be forced to retire*

Agree (%)

	1981	1990	1995	2000	Change
Albania			89		
Algeria					
Argentina		24	35		11
Armenia			42		
Australia			26		
Austria		43			
Azerbaijan			38		
Bangladesh			21		
Belarus		60	54		–6
Belgium		49			
Bosnia and Herz.			53		
Brazil		33	67		34
Bulgaria		74	59		–15
Canada		31			
Chile		37	45		8
China		38	64		26
Colombia			47		
Croatia			57		
Czech Republic		54	50		–4
Denmark		24			
Dominican Rep.			21		
Egypt					
El Salvador			39		
Estonia		57	61		4
Finland		59	42		–17
France		49			
Georgia			55		
Germany (East)		66	56		–10
Germany (West)		50	42		–8
Great Britain		43			
Greece					
Hungary		41	71		30
Iceland		37			
India		35	54		19
Indonesia					
Iran					
Iraq					
Ireland		47			
Israel					
Italy		54			
Japan		8	7		–1
Jordan					
Korea Republic		28	35		7

	1981	1990	1995	2000	Change
Kyrgyzstan					
Latvia		48	45		–3
Lithuania		64	66		2
Luxembourg					
Macedonia			89		
Malta		57			
Mexico		22	27		5
Moldova			53		
Montenegro			54		
Morocco					
Netherlands		42			
New Zealand			20		
Nigeria		47	68		21
Northern Ireland		43			
Norway		30	42		12
Pakistan			55		
Peru			35		
Philippines			37		
Poland		54	72		18
Portugal		60			
Puerto Rico			44		
Romania		65	59		–6
Russian Fed.		60	69		9
Saudi Arabia					
Serbia			62		
Singapore					
Slovakia		77	60		–17
Slovenia		60	79		19
South Africa		19	44		25
Spain		57	54		–3
Sweden		9	24		15
Switzerland			53		
Taiwan			44		
Tanzania					
Turkey		56	63		7
Uganda					
Ukraine			51		
Uruguay			30		
USA		15	13		–2
Venezuela			41		
Vietnam					
Zimbabwe					

Satisfaction with the Financial Situation of Household

(C006) *How satisfied are you with the financial situation of your household?*

(%) Satisfied (7 thru 10)

	1981	1990	1995	2000	Change
Albania			20	22	2
Algeria				45	
Argentina	38	36	28	37	–1
Armenia			13		
Australia	61		53		–8
Austria		66			
Azerbaijan			19		
Bangladesh			42	29	–13
Belarus		27	8		–19
Belgium	68	70			2
Bosnia and Herz.			21	25	4
Brazil		37	36		–1
Bulgaria		17	12		–5
Canada	70	68		64	–6
Chile		41	40	36	–5
China		46	45	39	–7
Colombia			81		
Croatia			22		
Czech Republic		34	28		–6
Denmark	69	66			–3
Dominican Rep.			47		
Egypt				40	
El Salvador			50		
Estonia		31	15		–16
Finland		59	62		3
France	46	42			–4
Georgia			9		
Germany (East)		42	38		–4
Germany (West)	64	60	57		–7
Great Britain	63	56			–7
Greece					
Hungary	51	30	22		–29
Iceland	55	53			–2
India		47	47	26	–21
Indonesia				52	
Iran				37	
Iraq				32	
Ireland	64	59			–5
Israel					
Italy	53	67			14
Japan	45	41	50	46	1
Jordan				27	
Korea Republic	25	40	34	40	15

	1981	1990	1995	2000	Change
Kyrgyzstan				39	
Latvia		21	10		–11
Lithuania			15		
Luxembourg					
Macedonia			24	21	–3
Malta	68	68			0
Mexico		51	68	58	7
Moldova			8	14	6
Montenegro			23	20	–3
Morocco				27	
Netherlands	77	76			–1
New Zealand			54		
Nigeria		38	42	54	16
Northern Ireland	63	58			–5
Norway	71	56	60		–11
Pakistan			27	5	–22
Peru			28	31	3
Philippines			42	39	–3
Poland		27	21		–6
Portugal		43			
Puerto Rico			61	70	9
Romania		29	15		–14
Russian Fed.		27	9		–18
Saudi Arabia				65	
Serbia			17	15	–2
Singapore				55	
Slovakia		27	22		–5
Slovenia		23	31		8
South Africa		34	24	25	–9
Spain	43	49	34	48	5
Sweden	69	63	52		–17
Switzerland		82	72		–10
Taiwan			39		
Tanzania				16	
Turkey		21	22	16	–5
Uganda				28	
Ukraine			7		
Uruguay			55		
USA	59	62	55	58	–1
Venezuela			32	47	15
Vietnam				34	
Zimbabwe				13	

Work vs. Leisure

(C008) *Which point on this scale most clearly describes how much weight you place on work (including housework and schoolwork), as compared with leisure or recreation?*

Work is what makes life worth living (%)

	1981	1990	1995	2000	Change
Albania			88	82	–6
Algeria				86	
Argentina			62	72	10
Armenia			41		
Australia			30		
Austria					
Azerbaijan			31		
Bangladesh			74	83	9
Belarus			37		
Belgium					
Bosnia and Herz.			58	60	2
Brazil			65		
Bulgaria			49		
Canada				35	
Chile			42	49	7
China			69	74	5
Colombia			81		
Croatia			21		
Czech Republic			47		
Denmark					
Dominican Rep.			65		
Egypt				68	
El Salvador			81		
Estonia			44		
Finland			30		
France					
Georgia			47		
Germany (East)			32		
Germany (West)			21		
Great Britain					
Greece					
Hungary			51		
Iceland					
India			83	51	–32
Indonesia				53	
Iran				67	
Iraq					
Ireland					
Israel				15	
Italy					
Japan			33	34	1
Jordan				6	
Korea Republic			31	52	21
Kyrgyzstan				65	
Latvia			35		
Lithuania			42		
Luxembourg					
Macedonia			77	68	–9
Malta					
Mexico			45	65	20
Moldova			46	53	7
Montenegro			51	62	11
Morocco				66	
Netherlands					
New Zealand			26		
Nigeria			77	78	1
Northern Ireland					
Norway			27		
Pakistan					
Peru			69	72	3
Philippines			78	79	1
Poland					
Portugal					
Puerto Rico			43	37	–6
Romania			18		
Russian Fed.			39		
Saudi Arabia				85	
Serbia			54	56	2
Singapore				37	
Slovakia			60		
Slovenia			43		
South Africa			72	65	–7
Spain			35	23	–12
Sweden			12		
Switzerland			27		
Taiwan			37		
Tanzania				92	
Turkey			67	60	–7
Uganda				80	
Ukraine			39		
Uruguay			34		
USA			33	31	–2
Venezuela			69	68	–1
Vietnam				67	
Zimbabwe				92	

Important in a Job: Good Pay

(C011) *Here are some more aspects of a job that people say are important. Please tell me which ones you personally think are important in a job?*

Good pay (%)

	1981	1990	1995	2000	Change
Albania			99	95	–4
Algeria				90	
Argentina	86	84	74	75	–11
Armenia			94		
Australia	58		61		3
Austria		62		66	4
Azerbaijan			95		
Bangladesh			87	92	5
Belarus		87	82	88	1
Belgium	67	71		73	6
Bosnia and Herz.			94	91	–3
Brazil		81	56		–25
Bulgaria		90	94	91	1
Canada	72	76		76	4
Chile		77	83	85	8
China		68	76	65	–3
Colombia			66		
Croatia			83	86	3
Czech Republic		74	87	74	0
Denmark	48	55		54	6
Dominican Rep.			85		
Egypt				85	
El Salvador					
Estonia		86	89	89	3
Finland		65	59	65	0
France	53	54		68	15
Georgia			93		
Germany (East)		74	72	75	1
Germany (West)	72	73	65	75	3
Great Britain	60	68		81	21
Greece				90	
Hungary	78	85	88	90	12
Iceland	67	86		86	19
India		87	95	92	5
Indonesia				97	
Iran				80	
Iraq					
Ireland	66	73		89	23
Israel					
Italy	66	72		85	19
Japan	64	78	87	83	19
Jordan				98	
Korea Republic	63	18		96	33

	1981	1990	1995	2000	Change
Kyrgyzstan				88	
Latvia		69	90	75	6
Lithuania		79	95	93	14
Luxembourg				66	
Macedonia			93	89	–4
Malta	78	78		89	11
Mexico		79	84	79	0
Moldova			93	86	–7
Montenegro			91	81	–10
Morocco				98	
Netherlands	54	71		72	18
New Zealand			79		
Nigeria		93	98	97	4
Northern Ireland	67	74		89	22
Norway	63	60	58		–5
Pakistan					
Peru			77	73	–4
Philippines			75	78	3
Poland		80	90	93	13
Portugal		79		80	1
Puerto Rico			74	77	3
Romania		76	98	91	15
Russian Fed.		83	90	90	7
Saudi Arabia				86	
Serbia			90	73	–17
Singapore				79	
Slovakia		78	91	91	13
Slovenia		82	89	87	5
South Africa		84		91	7
Spain	78	77	76	84	6
Sweden	55	73	59	58	3
Switzerland			65		
Taiwan			56		
Tanzania				89	
Turkey		90	91	97	7
Uganda				93	
Ukraine			91	88	–3
Uruguay			90		
USA	80	86	84	89	9
Venezuela			90		
Vietnam				76	
Zimbabwe				88	

IMPORTANT IN A JOB: NOT TOO MUCH PRESSURE

(C012) *Here are some more aspects of a job that people say are important. Please tell me which ones you personally think are important in a job?*

Not too much pressure (%)

	1981	1990	1995	2000	Change
Albania			37	46	9
Algeria				60	
Argentina	37	41	32	33	–4
Armenia			53		
Australia	29		24		–5
Austria		16		18	2
Azerbaijan			56		
Bangladesh			14	39	25
Belarus		60	18	20	–40
Belgium	30	25		32	2
Bosnia and Herz.			44	52	8
Brazil		40	33		–7
Bulgaria		35	32	40	5
Canada	30	28		28	–2
Chile		46	43	41	–5
China		30	36	27	–3
Colombia			24		
Croatia			39	63	24
Czech Republic		42	46	36	–6
Denmark	26	16		14	–12
Dominican Rep.			27		
Egypt				66	
El Salvador					
Estonia		32	21	24	–8
Finland		20	27	31	11
France	10	8		11	1
Georgia			30		
Germany (East)		20	13	20	0
Germany (West)	35	28	19	24	–11
Great Britain	22	19		28	6
Greece				54	
Hungary	31	46	49	57	26
Iceland	35	35		32	–3
India		48	37	54	6
Indonesia				85	
Iran				53	
Iraq					
Ireland	27	26		44	17
Israel					
Italy	17	31		60	43
Japan	38	42	72	69	31
Jordan				81	
Korea Republic	59	8		89	30

	1981	1990	1995	2000	Change
Kyrgyzstan				37	
Latvia		18	34	8	–10
Lithuania		40	51	34	–6
Luxembourg				36	
Macedonia			50	32	–18
Malta	55	44		68	13
Mexico		47	50	30	–17
Moldova			36	49	13
Montenegro			52	36	–16
Morocco				94	
Netherlands	38	41		33	–5
New Zealand			35		
Nigeria		64	58	64	0
Northern Ireland	19	20		40	21
Norway	41	23	24		–17
Pakistan					
Peru			17	17	0
Philippines			34	36	2
Poland		48	19	63	15
Portugal		41		24	–17
Puerto Rico			46	21	–25
Romania		37	45	34	–3
Russian Fed.		19	19	17	–2
Saudi Arabia				56	
Serbia			46	24	–22
Singapore				47	
Slovakia		45	54	18	–27
Slovenia		48	73	71	23
South Africa		29		50	21
Spain	37	37	23	39	2
Sweden	36	48	23	35	–1
Switzerland			30		
Taiwan			62		
Tanzania				55	
Turkey		78	84	91	13
Uganda				60	
Ukraine			24	29	5
Uruguay			57		
USA	38	33	34	38	0
Venezuela			75		
Vietnam				55	
Zimbabwe				27	

Important in a Job: Good Job Security

(C013) *Here are some more aspects of a job that people say are important. Please tell me which ones you personally think are important in a job?*

Good job security (%)

	1981	1990	1995	2000	Change
Albania			85	81	–4
Algeria				86	
Argentina	52	63	60	70	18
Armenia			77		
Australia	68		59		–9
Austria		66		75	9
Azerbaijan			74		
Bangladesh			77	97	20
Belarus		37	54	30	–7
Belgium	52	39		47	–5
Bosnia and Herz.			86	90	4
Brazil		71	55		–16
Bulgaria		57	80	81	24
Canada	65	67		65	0
Chile		69	70	74	5
China		44	68	68	24
Colombia			37		
Croatia			71	81	10
Czech Republic		59	76	52	–7
Denmark	51	52		50	–1
Dominican Rep.			65		
Egypt				81	
El Salvador					
Estonia		40	76	51	11
Finland		53	67	68	15
France	47	35		46	–1
Georgia			65		
Germany (East)		73	76	81	8
Germany (West)	73	73	64	79	6
Great Britain	61	57		65	4
Greece				65	
Hungary	70	72	86	89	19
Iceland	37	57		58	21
India		74	89	91	17
Indonesia				96	
Iran				77	
Iraq					
Ireland	55	61		69	14
Israel					
Italy	58	61		76	18
Japan	48	58	82	80	32
Jordan				97	
Korea Republic	67	35		97	30
Kyrgyzstan				74	
Latvia		22	76	38	16
Lithuania		38	87	75	37
Luxembourg				59	
Macedonia			90	85	–5
Malta	57	42		72	15
Mexico		63	69	65	2
Moldova			83	86	3
Montenegro			71	48	–23
Morocco				98	
Netherlands	41	41		29	–12
New Zealand			72		
Nigeria		88	84	82	–6
Northern Ireland	61	62		76	15
Norway	79	78	69		–10
Pakistan					
Peru			49	47	–2
Philippines			74	76	2
Poland		58	80	80	22
Portugal		73		64	–9
Puerto Rico			73	69	–4
Romania		43	92	87	44
Russian Fed.		38	66	69	31
Saudi Arabia				67	
Serbia			59	39	–20
Singapore				66	
Slovakia		62	76	72	10
Slovenia		73	93	88	15
South Africa		68		84	16
Spain	64	64	63	75	11
Sweden	62	65	53	51	–11
Switzerland			64		
Taiwan			75		
Tanzania				79	
Turkey		83	95	98	15
Uganda				81	
Ukraine			72	72	0
Uruguay			77		
USA	72	72	74	72	0
Venezuela			87		
Vietnam				82	
Zimbabwe				81	

Important in a Job: A Job Respected

(C014) *Here are some more aspects of a job that people say are important. Please tell me which ones you personally think are important in a job?*

A job respected by people in general (%)

	1981	1990	1995	2000	Change
Albania			42	65	23
Algeria				72	
Argentina	26	43	33	32	6
Armenia			70		
Australia	38		27		–11
Austria		35		36	1
Azerbaijan			65		
Bangladesh			70	91	21
Belarus		42	38	30	–12
Belgium	34	40		46	12
Bosnia and Herz.			58	54	–4
Brazil		58	54		–4
Bulgaria		58	55	52	–6
Canada	39	36		36	–3
Chile		59	50	55	–4
China		47	56	58	11
Colombia			29		
Croatia			26	51	25
Czech Republic		41	23	35	–6
Denmark	19	13		11	–8
Dominican Rep.			46		
Egypt				84	
El Salvador					
Estonia		38	37	32	–6
Finland		24	26	30	6
France	13	17		26	13
Georgia			44		
Germany (East)		52	19	44	–8
Germany (West)	46	42	14	43	–3
Great Britain	25	27		25	0
Greece				73	
Hungary	49	16	21	83	34
Iceland	37	45		51	14
India		59	66	77	18
Indonesia				87	
Iran				61	
Iraq					
Ireland	24	29		45	21
Israel					
Italy	19	40		61	42
Japan	21	26	43	37	16
Jordan				94	
Korea Republic	47	7		68	21

	1981	1990	1995	2000	Change
Kyrgyzstan				63	
Latvia		31	41	33	2
Lithuania		28	35	21	–7
Luxembourg				37	
Macedonia			52	43	–9
Malta	58	42		74	16
Mexico		54	54	51	–3
Moldova			59	70	11
Montenegro			71	48	–23
Morocco				92	
Netherlands	40	55		50	10
New Zealand			36		
Nigeria		74	74	71	–3
Northern Ireland	21	20		44	23
Norway	41	30	23		–18
Pakistan					
Peru			52	59	7
Philippines			60	55	–5
Poland		55	62	67	12
Portugal		59		50	–9
Puerto Rico			56	60	4
Romania		55	70	69	14
Russian Fed.		40	52	47	7
Saudi Arabia				63	
Serbia			61	33	–28
Singapore				40	
Slovakia		46	21	22	–24
Slovenia		59	77	75	16
South Africa		22		48	26
Spain	41	38	48	48	7
Sweden	28	43	18	29	1
Switzerland			44		
Taiwan			69		
Tanzania				64	
Turkey		87	86	94	7
Uganda				54	
Ukraine			51	53	2
Uruguay			56		
USA	46	44	40	45	–1
Venezuela			80		
Vietnam				67	
Zimbabwe				38	

Important in a Job: Good Hours

(C015) *Here are some more aspects of a job that people say are important. Please tell me which ones you personally think are important in a job?*

Good hours (%)

	1981	1990	1995	2000	Change
Albania			61	55	–6
Algeria				51	
Argentina	56	44	39	42	–14
Armenia			49		
Australia	44		35		–9
Austria		35		43	8
Azerbaijan			55		
Bangladesh			14	37	23
Belarus		59	33	54	–5
Belgium	39	40		45	6
Bosnia and Herz.			57	59	2
Brazil		46	36		–10
Bulgaria		55	54	62	7
Canada	48	52		47	–1
Chile		48	52	52	4
China		37	46	33	–4
Colombia			11		
Croatia			46	69	23
Czech Republic		44	54	31	–13
Denmark	39	32		32	–7
Dominican Rep.			63		
Egypt				69	
El Salvador					
Estonia		58	25	56	–2
Finland		37	37	48	11
France	27	26		36	9
Georgia			26		
Germany (East)		41	30	31	–10
Germany (West)	53	48	31	41	–12
Great Britain	35	37		55	20
Greece				52	
Hungary	68	59	53	79	11
Iceland	53	64		60	7
India		55	54	66	11
Indonesia				86	
Iran				55	
Iraq					
Ireland	38	46		64	26
Israel					
Italy	36	39		64	28
Japan	45	55	78	72	27
Jordan				92	
Korea Republic	46	11		83	37

	1981	1990	1995	2000	Change
Kyrgyzstan				56	
Latvia		34	46	19	–15
Lithuania		54	67	54	0
Luxembourg				52	
Macedonia			56	48	–8
Malta	63	47		79	16
Mexico		56	60	43	–13
Moldova			49	57	8
Montenegro			64	46	–18
Morocco				92	
Netherlands	37	45		37	0
New Zealand			56		
Nigeria		80	62	67	–13
Northern Ireland	44	42		70	26
Norway	48	32	41		–7
Pakistan					
Peru			29	36	7
Philippines			41	46	5
Poland		35	51	50	15
Portugal		62		44	–18
Puerto Rico			58	57	–1
Romania		36	68	59	23
Russian Fed.		46	45	40	–6
Saudi Arabia				65	
Serbia			59	36	–23
Singapore				47	
Slovakia		45	56	43	–2
Slovenia		39	77	41	2
South Africa				68	
Spain	46	45	37	57	11
Sweden	49	64	38	44	–5
Switzerland			40		
Taiwan			72		
Tanzania				61	
Turkey		88	84	92	4
Uganda				57	
Ukraine			44	50	6
Uruguay			49		
USA	58	55	52	66	8
Venezuela			70		
Vietnam				63	
Zimbabwe				54	

Important in a Job: An Opportunity to Use Initiative

(C016) *Here are some more aspects of a job that people say are important. Please tell me which ones you personally think are important in a job?*

An opportunity to use initiative (%)

	1981	1990	1995	2000	Change
Albania			43	40	–3
Algeria				44	
Argentina	47	55	53	41	–6
Armenia			46		
Australia	62		52		–10
Austria		42		49	7
Azerbaijan			35		
Bangladesh			43	84	41
Belarus		40	22	25	–15
Belgium	33	41		49	16
Bosnia and Herz.			41	46	5
Brazil		51	45		–6
Bulgaria		47	39	50	3
Canada	57	54		50	–7
Chile		55	46	48	–7
China		52	41	34	–18
Colombia			25		
Croatia			43	56	13
Czech Republic		43	44	30	–13
Denmark	47	44		50	3
Dominican Rep.			63		
Egypt				45	
El Salvador					
Estonia		30	36	35	5
Finland		45	49	48	3
France	31	38		43	12
Georgia			20		
Germany (East)		57	53	47	–10
Germany (West)	62	59	66	54	–8
Great Britain	48	46		39	–9
Greece				56	
Hungary	42	37	22	61	19
Iceland	35	55		63	28
India		54	47	64	10
Indonesia				84	
Iran				50	
Iraq					
Ireland	35	50		59	24
Israel					
Italy	36	45		64	28
Japan	25	34	59	50	25
Jordan				88	
Korea Republic	39	15		81	42
Kyrgyzstan				55	
Latvia		17	36	14	–3
Lithuania		29	44	32	3
Luxembourg				49	
Macedonia			47	29	–18
Malta	48	37		69	21
Mexico		60	57	42	–18
Moldova			34	48	14
Montenegro			47	26	–21
Morocco				89	
Netherlands	44	64		62	18
New Zealand			73		
Nigeria		82	71		–11
Northern Ireland	32	38		51	19
Norway	49	45	50		1
Pakistan					
Peru			37	40	3
Philippines			49	31	–18
Poland		38	57	56	18
Portugal		55		35	–20
Puerto Rico			56	53	–3
Romania		38	59	59	21
Russian Fed.		29	28	31	2
Saudi Arabia				38	
Serbia			45	24	–21
Singapore				44	
Slovakia		37	36	31	–6
Slovenia		55	78	78	23
South Africa		28		50	22
Spain	36	33	37	39	3
Sweden	44	71	51	52	8
Switzerland			61		
Taiwan			62		
Tanzania				60	
Turkey		81	83	91	10
Uganda				44	
Ukraine			28	42	14
Uruguay			48		
USA	54	52	52	62	8
Venezuela			73		
Vietnam				58	
Zimbabwe				34	

Important in a Job: Generous Holidays

(C017) *Here are some more aspects of a job that people say are important. Please tell me which ones you personally think are important in a job?*

Generous holidays (%)

	1981	1990	1995	2000	Change
Albania			53	48	–5
Algeria				21	
Argentina	37	30	19	21	–16
Armenia			31		
Australia	22		14		–8
Austria		17		20	3
Azerbaijan			38		
Bangladesh			10	28	18
Belarus		53	28	36	–17
Belgium	28	30		34	6
Bosnia and Herz.			38	42	4
Brazil		18	13		–5
Bulgaria		33	31	34	1
Canada	28	26		26	–2
Chile		23	25	32	9
China		15	15	11	–4
Colombia			5		
Croatia			17	48	31
Czech Republic		24	23	17	–7
Denmark	26	17		16	–10
Dominican Rep.			24		
Egypt				13	
El Salvador					
Estonia		32	35	20	–12
Finland		20	15	21	1
France	17	14		20	3
Georgia			14		
Germany (East)		30	9	18	–12
Germany (West)	38	34	12	25	–13
Great Britain	25	25		39	14
Greece				32	
Hungary	42	37	23	54	12
Iceland	11	17		18	7
India		28	37	56	28
Indonesia				30	
Iran				37	
Iraq					
Ireland	28	29		46	18
Israel					
Italy	15	19		35	20
Japan	36	52	78	71	35
Jordan				35	
Korea Republic		8		85	77
Kyrgyzstan				35	
Latvia		31	30	10	–21
Lithuania		40	44	30	–10
Luxembourg				37	
Macedonia			25	16	–9
Malta	30	25		35	5
Mexico		33	46	14	–19
Moldova			38	39	1
Montenegro			48	30	–18
Morocco				78	
Netherlands	30	35		28	–2
New Zealand			32		
Nigeria		51	47	49	–2
Northern Ireland	30	27		56	26
Norway	18	9	11		–7
Pakistan					
Peru			9	12	3
Philippines			8	11	3
Poland		15	34	30	15
Portugal		47		37	–10
Puerto Rico			12	27	15
Romania		34	53	41	7
Russian Fed.		43	33	29	–14
Saudi Arabia				48	
Serbia			36	19	–17
Singapore				27	
Slovakia		28	27	19	–9
Slovenia		29	47	46	17
South Africa		8		37	29
Spain	36	31	19	37	1
Sweden	21	35	11	19	–2
Switzerland			26		
Taiwan			39		
Tanzania				50	
Turkey		44	35	57	13
Uganda				46	
Ukraine			35	43	8
Uruguay			38		
USA	32	31	26	37	5
Venezuela			63		
Vietnam				42	
Zimbabwe				39	

Important in a Job: Achieving

(C018) *Here are some more aspects of a job that people say are important. Please tell me which ones you personally think are important in a job?*

A job in which you feel you can achieve something (%)

	1981	1990	1995	2000	Change
Albania			52	51	–1
Algeria				60	
Argentina	34	50	54	48	14
Armenia			66		
Australia	74		72		–2
Austria		51		56	5
Azerbaijan			49		
Bangladesh			54	88	34
Belarus		42	31	31	–11
Belgium	32	40		47	15
Bosnia and Herz.			62	66	4
Brazil		53	50		–3
Bulgaria		42	58	65	23
Canada	72	74		73	1
Chile		58	62	63	5
China		38	50	31	–7
Colombia			44		
Croatia			55	66	11
Czech Republic		48	49	38	–10
Denmark	51	55		55	4
Dominican Rep.			67		
Egypt				71	
El Salvador					
Estonia		42	55	45	3
Finland		54	60	56	2
France	30	42		50	20
Georgia			45		
Germany (East)		68	58	54	–14
Germany (West)	62	62	50	51	–11
Great Britain	59	66		58	–1
Greece				60	
Hungary	66	58	59	77	11
Iceland	77	83		81	4
India		61	61	69	8
Indonesia				88	
Iran				53	
Iraq					
Ireland	53	60		71	18
Israel					
Italy	42	51		75	33
Japan	35	47	75	70	35
Jordan				94	
Korea Republic	0	24		92	92
Kyrgyzstan				66	
Latvia		26	42	32	6
Lithuania		44	60	42	–2
Luxembourg				55	
Macedonia			58	50	–8
Malta	48	34		69	21
Mexico		66	60	53	–13
Moldova			51	65	14
Montenegro			78	53	–25
Morocco				93	
Netherlands	27	45		40	13
New Zealand			83		
Nigeria		91	85	82	–9
Northern Ireland	51	62		67	16
Norway	73	69	74		1
Pakistan					
Peru			36	47	11
Philippines			61	54	–7
Poland		48	73	67	19
Portugal		67		48	–19
Puerto Rico			67	53	–14
Romania		63	79	74	11
Russian Fed.		28	40	38	10
Saudi Arabia				59	
Serbia			73	51	–22
Singapore				61	
Slovakia		48	49	36	–12
Slovenia		71	90	90	19
South Africa				75	
Spain	37	37	38	48	11
Sweden	61	85	74	72	11
Switzerland			56		
Taiwan			69		
Tanzania				68	
Turkey		86	87	94	8
Uganda				60	
Ukraine			41	51	10
Uruguay			60		
USA	73	71	72	84	11
Venezuela			80		
Vietnam				68	
Zimbabwe				61	

Important in a Job: A Responsible Job

(C019) *Here are some more aspects of a job that people say are important. Please tell me which ones you personally think are important in a job?*

A responsible job (%)

	1981	1990	1995	2000	Change
Albania			17	25	8
Algeria				46	
Argentina	33	58	46	41	8
Armenia			43		
Australia	52		38		–14
Austria		46		49	3
Azerbaijan			45		
Bangladesh			51	88	37
Belarus		27	16	14	–13
Belgium	31	38		41	10
Bosnia and Herz.			38	46	8
Brazil		59	42		–17
Bulgaria		28	33	40	12
Canada	55	56		43	–12
Chile		52	40	44	–8
China		22	26	22	0
Colombia			20		
Croatia			24	44	20
Czech Republic		42	35	29	–13
Denmark	32	42		48	16
Dominican Rep.			59		
Egypt				73	
El Salvador					
Estonia		17	26	17	0
Finland		30	36	40	10
France	38	53		49	11
Georgia			28		
Germany (East)		48	30	48	0
Germany (West)	55	54	36	57	2
Great Britain	38	42		37	–1
Greece				51	
Hungary	62	51	26	78	16
Iceland	19	36		39	20
India		65	68	73	8
Indonesia				95	
Iran				58	
Iraq					
Ireland	35	41		54	19
Israel					
Italy	25	32		53	28
Japan	43	48	73	67	24
Jordan				92	
Korea Republic	21	22		91	70
Kyrgyzstan				62	
Latvia		12	25	15	3
Lithuania		24	37	18	–6
Luxembourg				55	
Macedonia			49	38	–11
Malta	34	37		60	26
Mexico		57	57	53	–4
Moldova			29	43	14
Montenegro			48	25	–23
Morocco				84	
Netherlands	29	47		42	13
New Zealand			51		
Nigeria		84	85	84	0
Northern Ireland	32	35		49	17
Norway	48	43	42		–6
Pakistan					
Peru			38	48	10
Philippines			59	57	–2
Poland		34	59	53	19
Portugal		54		42	–12
Puerto Rico			63	54	–9
Romania		28	51	57	29
Russian Fed.		21	25	26	5
Saudi Arabia				59	
Serbia			44	19	–25
Singapore				47	
Slovakia		43	39	21	–22
Slovenia		53	65	73	20
South Africa		25		67	42
Spain	36	31	35	39	3
Sweden	51	72	53	55	4
Switzerland			62		
Taiwan			70		
Tanzania				54	
Turkey		78	77	90	12
Uganda				56	
Ukraine			27	35	8
Uruguay			50		
USA	58	56	51	55	–3
Venezuela			78		
Vietnam				67	
Zimbabwe				41	

Important in a Job: Interesting

(C020) *Here are some more aspects of a job that people say are important. Please tell me which ones you personally think are important in a job?*

A job that is interesting (%)

	1981	1990	1995	2000	Change
Albania			46	41	–5
Algeria				57	
Argentina	38	51	43	39	1
Armenia			77		
Australia	76		74		–2
Austria		58		57	–1
Azerbaijan			81		
Bangladesh			62	87	25
Belarus		73	54	58	–15
Belgium	40	47		56	16
Bosnia and Herz.			67	71	4
Brazil		46	28		–18
Bulgaria		51	59	63	12
Canada	73	72		70	–3
Chile		50	52	58	8
China		34	42	18	–16
Colombia			12		
Croatia			68	76	8
Czech Republic		66	63	57	–9
Denmark	52	63		65	13
Dominican Rep.			57		
Egypt				47	
El Salvador					
Estonia		68	77	65	–3
Finland		65	81	76	11
France	53	59		66	13
Georgia			65		
Germany (East)		64	49	68	4
Germany (West)	70	71	62	71	1
Great Britain	77	72		68	–9
Greece				69	
Hungary	61	51	59	77	16
Iceland	56	76		76	20
India		64	47	74	10
Indonesia				81	
Iran				57	
Iraq					
Ireland	57	70		72	15
Israel					
Italy	43	56		76	33
Japan	28	36	68	64	36
Jordan				88	
Korea Republic	26	7		79	53
Kyrgyzstan				80	
Latvia		60	79	48	–12
Lithuania		64	83	63	–1
Luxembourg				64	
Macedonia			70	52	–18
Malta	74	51		85	11
Mexico		60	55	42	–18
Moldova			66	75	9
Montenegro			78	58	–20
Morocco				94	
Netherlands	41	61		56	15
New Zealand			84		
Nigeria		83	79	81	–2
Northern Ireland	64	69		75	11
Norway	66	64	70		4
Pakistan					
Peru			29	33	4
Philippines			42	45	3
Poland		58	81	74	16
Portugal		53		45	–8
Puerto Rico			56	55	–1
Romania		43	67	66	23
Russian Fed.		67	72	69	2
Saudi Arabia				60	
Serbia			70	46	–24
Singapore				60	
Slovakia		59	59	49	–10
Slovenia		76	91	92	16
South Africa				65	
Spain	43	46	48	55	12
Sweden	57	80	71	70	13
Switzerland			72		
Taiwan			77		
Tanzania				49	
Turkey		49	34	49	0
Uganda				53	
Ukraine			66	70	4
Uruguay			50		
USA	72	69	73	81	9
Venezuela			73		
Vietnam				59	
Zimbabwe				57	

Important in a Job: Job that Meets One's Abilities

(C021) *Here are some more aspects of a job that people say are important. Please tell me which ones you personally think are important in a job?*

A job that meets one's abilities (%)

	1981	1990	1995	2000	Change
Albania			89	29	–60
Algeria				70	
Argentina	35	58	58	51	16
Armenia			66		
Australia	57		45		–12
Austria		60		59	–1
Azerbaijan			73		
Bangladesh			59	91	32
Belarus		49	40	39	–10
Belgium	35	50		56	21
Bosnia and Herz.			63	74	11
Brazil		66	48		–18
Bulgaria		52	74	78	26
Canada	61	56		52	–9
Chile		59	67	66	7
China		66	63	59	–7
Colombia			24		
Croatia			63	74	11
Czech Republic		71	70	56	–15
Denmark	50	56		54	4
Dominican Rep.			79		
Egypt				85	
El Salvador					
Estonia		54	67	55	1
Finland		45	51	54	9
France	32	43		50	18
Georgia			47		
Germany (East)		65	63	56	–9
Germany (West)	70	70	68	54	–16
Great Britain	46	42		39	–7
Greece				56	
Hungary	75	66	75	86	11
Iceland	56	72		65	9
India		67	75	77	10
Indonesia				93	
Iran				67	
Iraq					
Ireland	40	50		61	21
Israel					
Italy	48	54		75	27
Japan	68	71	93	90	22
Jordan				96	
Korea Republic	52	31		96	44
Kyrgyzstan				61	
Latvia		44	68	42	–2
Lithuania		56	80	52	–4
Luxembourg				57	
Macedonia			67	42	–25
Malta	76	69		93	17
Mexico		65	60	49	–16
Moldova			67	79	12
Montenegro			72	53	–19
Morocco				96	
Netherlands	48	73		69	21
New Zealand			61		
Nigeria		86	82	79	–7
Northern Ireland	36	41		61	25
Norway	54	42	47		–7
Pakistan					
Peru			53	61	8
Philippines			56	57	1
Poland		53		66	13
Portugal		57		47	–10
Puerto Rico			73	73	0
Romania		52	85	79	27
Russian Fed.		54	57	54	0
Saudi Arabia				73	
Serbia			64	41	–23
Singapore				54	
Slovakia		69	71	55	–14
Slovenia		61	87	86	25
South Africa		31		63	32
Spain	52	48	64	60	8
Sweden	27	53	33	41	14
Switzerland			62		
Taiwan			84		
Tanzania				65	
Turkey		90	90	96	6
Uganda				59	
Ukraine			50	61	11
Uruguay			59		
USA	59	57	55	62	3
Venezuela			78		
Vietnam				82	
Zimbabwe				55	

Important in a Job: Pleasant People to Work With

(C022) *Here are some more aspects of a job that people say are important. Please tell me which ones you personally think are important in a job?*

Pleasant people to work with (%)

	1981	1990	1995	2000	Change
Albania					
Algeria					
Argentina		61			
Armenia					
Australia					
Austria		64		68	4
Azerbaijan					
Bangladesh					
Belarus				69	
Belgium	62	68		75	13
Bosnia and Herz.					
Brazil		58			
Bulgaria		63		64	1
Canada	73	73			0
Chile		56			
China		55			
Colombia					
Croatia				76	
Czech Republic		73		64	–9
Denmark	75	77		78	3
Dominican Rep.					
Egypt					
El Salvador					
Estonia		77		71	–6
Finland		64		74	10
France	50	53		65	15
Georgia					
Germany (East)		73		58	–15
Germany (West)	75	76		67	–8
Great Britain	69	65		72	3
Greece				76	
Hungary		65		85	20
Iceland	79	89		83	4
India		69			
Indonesia					
Iran					
Iraq					
Ireland	60	64		77	17
Israel					
Italy	44	50		72	28
Japan		78			
Jordan					
Korea Republic		14			
Kyrgyzstan					
Latvia		55		32	–23
Lithuania		73		60	–13
Luxembourg				74	
Macedonia					
Malta	75	57		83	8
Mexico		69			
Moldova					
Montenegro					
Morocco					
Netherlands	80	92		89	9
New Zealand					
Nigeria		85			
Northern Ireland	61	68		71	10
Norway	84	80			–4
Pakistan					
Peru					
Philippines					
Poland		66		74	8
Portugal		80		67	–13
Puerto Rico					
Romania		56		75	19
Russian Fed.		71		55	–16
Saudi Arabia					
Serbia					
Singapore					
Slovakia		71		51	–20
Slovenia		82		90	8
South Africa		40			
Spain	61	61		66	5
Sweden	81	91		84	3
Switzerland					
Taiwan					
Tanzania					
Turkey				97	
Uganda					
Ukraine				66	
Uruguay					
USA	79	74			–5
Venezuela					
Vietnam					
Zimbabwe					

Important in a Job: Good Chances for Promotion

(C023) *Here are some more aspects of a job that people say are important. Please tell me which ones you personally think are important in a job?*

Good chances for promotion (%)

	1981	1990	1995	2000	Change
Albania					
Algeria					
Argentina		45			
Armenia					
Australia					
Austria		35		36	1
Azerbaijan					
Bangladesh					
Belarus				26	
Belgium	27	31		33	6
Bosnia and Herz.					
Brazil		53			
Bulgaria		36		45	9
Canada	51	49			–2
Chile		49			
China		27			
Colombia					
Croatia				60	
Czech Republic		26		24	–2
Denmark	16	16		17	1
Dominican Rep.					
Egypt					
El Salvador					
Estonia		12		27	15
Finland		30		20	–10
France	19	25		30	11
Georgia					
Germany (East)		29		24	–5
Germany (West)	47	43		41	–6
Great Britain	36	35		35	–1
Greece				68	
Hungary		42		67	25
Iceland	19	36		44	25
India		72			
Indonesia					
Iran					
Iraq					
Ireland	32	38		52	20
Israel					
Italy	32	28		48	16
Japan		23			
Jordan					
Korea Republic		2			
Kyrgyzstan					
Latvia		9		20	11
Lithuania		16		37	21
Luxembourg				35	
Macedonia					
Malta	49	40		61	12
Mexico		61			
Moldova					
Montenegro					
Morocco					
Netherlands	22	39		32	10
New Zealand					
Nigeria		89			
Northern Ireland	37	41		49	12
Norway	26	19			–7
Pakistan					
Peru					
Philippines					
Poland		24		50	26
Portugal		57		32	–25
Puerto Rico					
Romania		29		61	32
Russian Fed.		17		29	12
Saudi Arabia					
Serbia					
Singapore					
Slovakia		28		25	–3
Slovenia		62		74	12
South Africa		37			
Spain	38	35		44	6
Sweden	21	41		30	9
Switzerland					
Taiwan					
Tanzania					
Turkey				73	
Uganda					
Ukraine				39	
Uruguay					
USA	58	58			0
Venezuela					
Vietnam					
Zimbabwe					

Important in a Job: Useful for Society

(C024) *Here are some more aspects of a job that people say are important. Please tell me which ones you personally think are important in a job?*

A useful for society (%)

	1981	1990	1995	2000	Change
Albania					
Algeria					
Argentina		56			
Armenia					
Australia					
Austria		31		36	5
Azerbaijan					
Bangladesh					
Belarus				26	
Belgium	30	32		41	11
Bosnia and Herz.					
Brazil		55			
Bulgaria		53		57	4
Canada	39	41			2
Chile		55			
China		55			
Colombia					
Croatia				59	
Czech Republic		55		32	–23
Denmark	36	21		26	–10
Dominican Rep.					
Egypt					
El Salvador					
Estonia		36		27	–9
Finland		20		31	11
France	24	28		30	6
Georgia					
Germany (East)		46		34	–12
Germany (West)	39	35		33	–6
Great Britain	30	30		27	–3
Greece				52	
Hungary		49		74	25
Iceland	44	54		47	3
India		60			
Indonesia					
Iran					
Iraq					
Ireland	24	30		42	18
Israel					
Italy	41	47		65	24
Japan		42			
Jordan					
Korea Republic		28			
Kyrgyzstan					
Latvia		32		29	–3
Lithuania		47		29	–18
Luxembourg				44	
Macedonia					
Malta	52	37		72	20
Mexico		56			
Moldova					
Montenegro					
Morocco					
Netherlands	39	48		39	0
New Zealand					
Nigeria		83			
Northern Ireland	24	22		40	16
Norway	45	36			–9
Pakistan					
Peru					
Philippines					
Poland		34		48	14
Portugal		60		51	–9
Puerto Rico					
Romania		48		65	17
Russian Fed.		48		22	–26
Saudi Arabia					
Serbia					
Singapore					
Slovakia		50		24	–26
Slovenia		63		73	10
South Africa		23			
Spain	44	39		44	0
Sweden	26	42		25	–1
Switzerland					
Taiwan					
Tanzania					
Turkey				98	
Uganda					
Ukraine				31	
Uruguay					
USA	43	42			–1
Venezuela					
Vietnam					
Zimbabwe					

Important in a Job: Meeting People

(C025) *Here are some more aspects of a job that people say are important. Please tell me which ones you personally think are important in a job?*

Meeting People (%)

	1981	1990	1995	2000	Change
Albania					
Algeria					
Argentina		50			
Armenia					
Australia					
Austria		39		47	8
Azerbaijan					
Bangladesh					
Belarus				37	
Belgium	39	45		53	14
Bosnia and Herz.					
Brazil		42			
Bulgaria		44		56	12
Canada	51	42			–9
Chile		39			
China		26			
Colombia					
Croatia				62	
Czech Republic		48		34	–14
Denmark	41	43		46	5
Dominican Rep.					
Egypt					
El Salvador					
Estonia		57		44	–13
Finland		30		41	11
France	34	39		44	10
Georgia					
Germany (East)		50		47	–3
Germany (West)	53	55		54	1
Great Britain	42	43		42	0
Greece				53	
Hungary		40		69	29
Iceland	40	59		54	14
India		45			
Indonesia					
Iran					
Iraq					
Ireland	33	35		53	20
Israel					
Italy	36	43		66	30
Japan		47			
Jordan					
Korea Republic		24			
Kyrgyzstan					
Latvia		39		43	4
Lithuania		59		40	–19
Luxembourg				47	
Macedonia					
Malta	48	31		59	11
Mexico		47			
Moldova					
Montenegro					
Morocco					
Netherlands	44	66		61	17
New Zealand					
Nigeria		68			
Northern Ireland	41	16		59	18
Norway	48	41			–7
Pakistan					
Peru					
Philippines					
Poland		31		52	21
Portugal		53		36	–17
Puerto Rico					
Romania		27		55	28
Russian Fed.		27		34	7
Saudi Arabia					
Serbia					
Singapore					
Slovakia		45		23	–22
Slovenia		56		69	13
South Africa					
Spain	37	36		38	1
Sweden	42	64		46	4
Switzerland					
Taiwan					
Tanzania					
Turkey				88	
Uganda					
Ukraine				42	
Uruguay					
USA	52	38			–14
Venezuela					
Vietnam					
Zimbabwe					

Job Satisfaction

(C033) *Overall, how satisfied or dissatisfied are you with your job?*

(%) Satisfied (7 thru 10)

	1981	1990	1995	2000	Change
Albania					
Algeria					
Argentina		72			
Armenia					
Australia					
Austria		83		77	–6
Azerbaijan					
Bangladesh					
Belarus				33	
Belgium	80	80		82	2
Bosnia and Herz.					
Brazil		70			
Bulgaria		47		65	18
Canada	84	82			–2
Chile		70			
China		63			
Colombia					
Croatia				57	
Czech Republic		63		69	6
Denmark	86	88		84	–2
Dominican Rep.					
Egypt					
El Salvador					
Estonia		58		58	0
Finland		77		84	7
France	61	59		70	9
Georgia					
Germany (East)		62		78	16
Germany (West)	67	72		85	18
Great Britain	77	71		70	–7
Greece				63	
Hungary		67		58	–9
Iceland	85	82		84	–1
India		58			
Indonesia					
Iran					
Iraq					
Ireland	80	78		77	–3
Israel					
Italy	69	70		73	4
Japan		68			
Jordan					
Korea Republic		57			
Kyrgyzstan					
Latvia		52		57	5
Lithuania		61		61	0
Luxembourg				78	
Macedonia					
Malta	81	87		88	7
Mexico		78			
Moldova					
Montenegro					
Morocco					
Netherlands	84	80		85	1
New Zealand					
Nigeria		68			
Northern Ireland	82	78		73	–9
Norway	86	81			–5
Pakistan					
Peru					
Philippines					
Poland		73		56	–17
Portugal		66		75	9
Puerto Rico					
Romania		56		60	4
Russian Fed.		49		48	–1
Saudi Arabia					
Serbia					
Singapore					
Slovakia		66		60	–6
Slovenia		67		68	1
South Africa		64			
Spain	61	65		71	10
Sweden	82	83		74	–8
Switzerland		88			
Taiwan					
Tanzania					
Turkey				50	
Uganda					
Ukraine				45	
Uruguay					
USA	76	81			5
Venezuela					
Vietnam					
Zimbabwe					

Freedom Decision Taking in Job

(C034) *How free are you to make decisions in your job?*

(%) A great deal (7 thru 10)

	1981	1990	1995	2000	Change
Albania					
Algeria					
Argentina		70			
Armenia					
Australia					
Austria		64		65	1
Azerbaijan					
Bangladesh					
Belarus		40		33	–7
Belgium	59	65		68	9
Bosnia and Herz.					
Brazil		66			
Bulgaria		37		47	10
Canada	69	68			–1
Chile		61			
China		44			
Colombia					
Croatia				41	
Czech Republic		53		50	–3
Denmark	63	74		80	17
Dominican Rep.					
Egypt					
El Salvador					
Estonia		53		45	–8
Finland		69		71	2
France	51	56		55	4
Georgia					
Germany (East)		46		51	5
Germany (West)	52	51		58	6
Great Britain	59	66		59	0
Greece				60	
Hungary		49		34	–15
Iceland	70	63		78	8
India		52			
Indonesia					
Iran					
Iraq					
Ireland	55	63		61	6
Israel					
Italy	56	59		58	2
Japan		66			
Jordan					
Korea Republic		63			
Kyrgyzstan					
Latvia		51		42	–9
Lithuania		52		39	–13
Luxembourg				56	
Macedonia					
Malta	50	63		69	19
Mexico		62			
Moldova					
Montenegro					
Morocco					
Netherlands	69	73		79	10
New Zealand					
Nigeria		64			
Northern Ireland	59	63		54	–5
Norway	63	63			0
Pakistan					
Peru					
Philippines					
Poland		64		46	–18
Portugal		59		57	–2
Puerto Rico					
Romania		48		55	7
Russian Fed.		40		40	0
Saudi Arabia					
Serbia					
Singapore					
Slovakia		50		40	–10
Slovenia		48		53	5
South Africa		54			
Spain	54	55		56	2
Sweden	66	75		77	11
Switzerland		73			
Taiwan					
Tanzania					
Turkey		31		29	–2
Uganda					
Ukraine				37	
Uruguay					
USA	64	72			8
Venezuela					
Vietnam					
Zimbabwe					

Work: Efficiency is Paid More

(C059) *Imagine two secretaries, of the same age, doing practically the same job. One finds out that the other earns considerably more than she does. The better paid secretary, however, is quicker, more efficient and more reliable at her job. In your opinion, is it fair or not fair that one secretary is paid more?*

Fair (%)

	1981	1990	1995	2000	Change
Albania			93	83	–10
Algeria				82	
Argentina	75	83	72	60	–15
Armenia			94		
Australia			82		
Austria		90		89	–1
Azerbaijan			93		
Bangladesh			94	82	–12
Belarus		92	93	85	–7
Belgium	64	73		70	6
Bosnia and Herz.			85	89	4
Brazil		78	77		–1
Bulgaria		86	82	89	3
Canada	74	82		84	10
Chile		62	68	67	5
China		97	82	93	–4
Colombia			82		
Croatia			88	88	0
Czech Republic		46	96	96	50
Denmark	63	76		82	19
Dominican Rep.			91		
Egypt				97	
El Salvador			70		
Estonia		95	96	84	–11
Finland		74	56	76	2
France	65	78		77	12
Georgia			92		
Germany (East)		96	93	89	–7
Germany (West)	73	85	90	87	14
Great Britain	68	79		73	5
Greece				88	
Hungary	74	90	92	83	9
Iceland	65	75		86	21
India		77	79	63	–14
Indonesia				87	
Iran				79	
Iraq					
Ireland	60	73		64	4
Israel					
Italy	49	79		78	29
Japan	68	59	82	88	20
Jordan				82	
Korea Republic	71	73		87	16
Kyrgyzstan				89	
Latvia		95	93	81	–14
Lithuania		93	89	82	–11
Luxembourg				83	
Macedonia			68	72	4
Malta	62	77		77	15
Mexico		85	73	78	–7
Moldova			87	87	0
Montenegro			88	83	–5
Morocco				95	
Netherlands	62	72		75	13
New Zealand			91		
Nigeria		79	81	77	–2
Northern Ireland	65	71		71	6
Norway	57	54	54		–3
Pakistan					
Peru			81	75	–6
Philippines			70	68	–2
Poland		90		88	–2
Portugal		74		73	–1
Puerto Rico			77	77	0
Romania		88	85	89	1
Russian Fed.		94	93	93	–1
Saudi Arabia				71	
Serbia			82	88	6
Singapore				93	
Slovakia		39	91	91	52
Slovenia		91	88	89	–2
South Africa			54	60	6
Spain	70	74	67	66	–4
Sweden	59	62	57	74	15
Switzerland		69	85		16
Taiwan			92		
Tanzania				76	
Turkey		72	75	78	6
Uganda				76	
Ukraine			90	92	2
Uruguay			72		
USA	80	86	87	91	11
Venezuela			78		
Vietnam				94	
Zimbabwe				59	

Business Management: Owners Alone

(C060) *There is a lot of discussion about how business and industry should be managed. Which of these four statements comes closest to your opinion?*

Owners should run their business (%)

	1981	1990	1995	2000	Change
Albania			48	53	5
Algeria				37	
Argentina	33	31	32	29	–4
Armenia			26		
Australia			50		
Austria		49			
Azerbaijan			30		
Bangladesh			55	43	–12
Belarus		9	20		11
Belgium	44	46			2
Bosnia and Herz.			25	20	–5
Brazil		32	35		3
Bulgaria		38	28		–10
Canada	59	53		51	–8
Chile		24	22	41	17
China		22	15	30	8
Colombia			42		
Croatia			34		
Czech Republic		38	42		4
Denmark	45	47			2
Dominican Rep.			44		
Egypt				33	
El Salvador					
Estonia		42	40		–2
Finland		42	35		–7
France	22	24			2
Georgia			33		
Germany (East)		45	30		–15
Germany (West)	51				
Great Britain	52	44			–8
Greece					
Hungary		24	24		0
Iceland	44	48			4
India		22	27	26	4
Indonesia				43	
Iran				22	
Iraq					
Ireland	51	43			–8
Israel					
Italy	32	43			11
Japan	41	44	40	39	–2
Jordan				35	
Korea Republic	25	23	10	14	–11
Kyrgyzstan				27	
Latvia		31	37		6
Lithuania		38	38		0
Luxembourg					
Macedonia			37	41	4
Malta	35	32			–3
Mexico		47	39	45	–2
Moldova			23	21	–2
Montenegro					
Morocco				49	
Netherlands	34	36			2
New Zealand			64		
Nigeria		53	54	48	–5
Northern Ireland	64	55			–9
Norway	38	32	34		–4
Pakistan					
Peru			31	35	4
Philippines			53	56	3
Poland		15	15		0
Portugal		48			
Puerto Rico			51	48	–3
Romania		35	37		2
Russian Fed.		11	16		5
Saudi Arabia				38	
Serbia			25	26	1
Singapore				49	
Slovakia		27	21		–6
Slovenia		26	22		–4
South Africa		40	37	47	7
Spain	26	31	38	38	12
Sweden	31	30	36		5
Switzerland		51	46		–5
Taiwan			30		
Tanzania				25	
Turkey		27	25	32	5
Uganda				64	
Ukraine			23		
Uruguay			47		
USA	60	57	54	59	–1
Venezuela			55	47	–8
Vietnam				23	
Zimbabwe				51	

Following Instructions at Work

(C061) *People have different ideas about following instructions at work. Some say that one should follow one's superior's instructions even when one does not fully agree with them. Others say that one should follow one's superior's instructions only when one is convinced that they are right. With which opinion do you agree?*

Must be convinced first (%)

	1981	1990	1995	2000	Change
Albania			9	30	21
Algeria				45	
Argentina	40	50	53	47	7
Armenia			62		
Australia			40		
Austria		37		40	3
Azerbaijan			46		
Bangladesh			61	54	–7
Belarus		27	58	38	11
Belgium	36	43		44	8
Bosnia and Herz.			14	38	24
Brazil		78	78		0
Bulgaria		65	34	46	–19
Canada	32	29		31	–1
Chile		49	46	35	–14
China		34	15	67	33
Colombia					
Croatia			61	51	–10
Czech Republic		51	25	34	–17
Denmark	23	54		26	3
Dominican Rep.			54		
Egypt				43	
El Salvador			32		
Estonia		44	57	31	–13
Finland		45	63	59	14
France	58	48		40	–18
Georgia			11		
Germany (East)		35	53	28	–7
Germany (West)	53	24	65	28	–25
Great Britain	35	43		33	–2
Greece				32	
Hungary	7	59	25	34	27
Iceland	43	33		33	–10
India		55	32	39	–16
Indonesia				51	
Iran				59	
Iraq					
Ireland	27	41		37	10
Israel					
Italy	40	46		33	–7
Japan	10	11		9	–1
Jordan				72	
Korea Republic	35	48	35	51	16
Kyrgyzstan				74	
Latvia		42	59	46	4
Lithuania		60	58	47	–13
Luxembourg				32	
Macedonia			27	43	16
Malta	30	36		51	21
Mexico		38	16	41	3
Moldova			57	54	–3
Montenegro			48	40	–8
Morocco				51	
Netherlands	36	47		31	–5
New Zealand			23		
Nigeria		48	39	43	–5
Northern Ireland	26	38		36	10
Norway	33	34	33		0
Pakistan					
Peru			61	54	–7
Philippines			57	49	–8
Poland		60		50	–10
Portugal		39		44	5
Puerto Rico			49	43	–6
Romania		75	29	29	–46
Russian Fed.		56	17	47	–9
Saudi Arabia				38	
Serbia			53	43	–10
Singapore				55	
Slovakia		52	21	32	–20
Slovenia		58	65	48	–10
South Africa			40	44	4
Spain	45	50	52	42	–3
Sweden	33	41	11	33	0
Switzerland			42		
Taiwan			56		
Tanzania				28	
Turkey		19	6	55	36
Uganda				47	
Ukraine			45	42	–3
Uruguay			16		
USA	24	22	32	20	–4
Venezuela			35	56	21
Vietnam				40	
Zimbabwe				47	

Ideal Number of Children

(D017) *What do you think is the ideal size of the family? How many children, if any?*

(%) 3 or less

	1981	1990	1995	2000	Change
Albania			86	80	–6
Algeria				55	
Argentina	76	79	81	81	5
Armenia			68		
Australia	76		79		3
Austria		93			
Azerbaijan			79		
Bangladesh			98	99	1
Belarus		91	96		5
Belgium	88	90			2
Bosnia and Herz.			83	87	4
Brazil		81	87		6
Bulgaria		96	97		1
Canada	77	79		82	5
Chile		73	83	82	9
China		98	97		–1
Colombia			88		
Croatia			80		
Czech Republic		97	99		2
Denmark	92	88			–4
Dominican Rep.			77		
Egypt				85	
El Salvador			87		
Estonia		93	95		2
Finland		86	87		1
France	92	91			–1
Georgia			65		
Germany (East)		97	98		1
Germany (West)	93	94	94		1
Great Britain	91	87	93		2
Greece					
Hungary	96	95	96		0
Iceland	80	78			–2
India		96	96	90	–6
Indonesia				76	
Iran				93	
Iraq				35	
Ireland	34	52			18
Israel					
Italy	95	91			–4
Japan	92	92	92	93	1
Jordan				28	
Korea Republic	91	94	91	91	0
Kyrgyzstan				52	
Latvia		90	94		4
Lithuania		84	92		8
Luxembourg					
Macedonia			93	89	–4
Malta	81	53			–28
Mexico		79	90	81	2
Moldova			80	86	6
Montenegro			59	65	6
Morocco				82	
Netherlands	86	85			–1
New Zealand			66		
Nigeria		19	19	20	1
Northern Ireland	64	65			1
Norway	90	88	90		0
Pakistan			53	76	23
Peru			90	92	2
Philippines			64	66	2
Poland		90	89		–1
Portugal		90			
Puerto Rico			85	89	4
Romania		91	95		4
Russian Fed.		89	94		5
Saudi Arabia				45	
Serbia			85	87	2
Singapore				86	
Slovakia		93	94		1
Slovenia		92	94		2
South Africa		60	68	74	14
Spain	77	88	91	94	17
Sweden	94	86	83	90	–4
Switzerland		80	93		13
Taiwan			88		
Tanzania				38	
Turkey		94	92	87	–7
Uganda				31	
Ukraine			95		
Uruguay			86		
USA	78	80	83	84	6
Venezuela			85	78	–7
Vietnam				95	
Zimbabwe				35	

Child Needs a Home with Father and Mother

(D018) *If someone says a child needs a home with both a father and a mother to grow up happily, would you tend to agree or disagree?*

Tend to agree (%)

	1981	1990	1995	2000	Change
Albania			98	99	1
Algeria				97	
Argentina	88	95	94	91	3
Armenia			98		
Australia	97		71		–26
Austria		94		88	–6
Azerbaijan			92		
Bangladesh			98	99	1
Belarus			98	94	–4
Belgium	88	92		81	–7
Bosnia and Herz.			94	95	1
Brazil		88	87		–1
Bulgaria		95	97	97	2
Canada	67	78		72	5
Chile		93	85	83	–10
China		98	91	95	–3
Colombia			86		
Croatia			86	89	3
Czech Republic		96	96	86	–10
Denmark	60	73		67	7
Dominican Rep.			85		
Egypt				99	
El Salvador			94		
Estonia		99	96	96	–3
Finland		86	72	60	–26
France	87	94		86	–1
Georgia			98		
Germany (East)		97	89	92	–5
Germany (West)	92	94	85	90	–2
Great Britain	69	74		67	–2
Greece				96	
Hungary		99	97	95	–4
Iceland	78	78		71	–7
India		97	85	95	–2
Indonesia				89	
Iran				86	
Iraq					
Ireland	75	83		68	–7
Israel					
Italy	92	97		92	0
Japan	89	95	94	90	1
Jordan				98	
Korea Republic	91		96	97	6

	1981	1990	1995	2000	Change
Kyrgyzstan				98	
Latvia		99	96	93	–6
Lithuania		94	88	80	–14
Luxembourg				85	
Macedonia			96	97	1
Malta	94	95		93	–1
Mexico		88	72	87	–1
Moldova			97	97	0
Montenegro			95	97	2
Morocco				98	
Netherlands	80	80		66	–14
New Zealand			77		
Nigeria		97	93	97	0
Northern Ireland	78	81		70	–8
Norway	79	86	85		6
Pakistan				98	
Peru			92	94	2
Philippines			95	97	2
Poland		99	97	97	–2
Portugal		93		73	–20
Puerto Rico			78	76	–2
Romania		97	96	95	–2
Russian Fed.		97	97	95	–2
Saudi Arabia				95	
Serbia			91	90	–1
Singapore				94	
Slovakia		97	98	95	–2
Slovenia		94	93	88	–6
South Africa		92	90	89	–3
Spain	87	93	89	86	–1
Sweden	71	85	82	60	–11
Switzerland			89		
Taiwan			98		
Tanzania				97	
Turkey		96	97	97	1
Uganda				96	
Ukraine			96	97	1
Uruguay			90		
USA	64	73	74	64	0
Venezuela			83	89	6
Vietnam				97	
Zimbabwe				98	

Women Needs Children

(D019) *Do you think that a woman has to have children in order to be fulfilled or is this not necessary?*

Needs children (%)

	1981	1990	1995	2000	Change
Albania			99	92	–7
Algeria				81	
Argentina	54	60	54	56	2
Armenia			83		
Australia	78		20		–58
Austria		50		34	–16
Azerbaijan			61		
Bangladesh			97	98	1
Belarus		97	85	77	–20
Belgium	47	46		33	–14
Bosnia and Herz.			80	87	7
Brazil		56	53		–3
Bulgaria		92	71	76	–16
Canada	26	24		19	–7
Chile		64	62	65	1
China		46	82	37	–9
Colombia			56		
Croatia			53	59	6
Czech Republic		74	78	44	–30
Denmark	73	82		80	7
Dominican Rep.			65		
Egypt				88	
El Salvador			69		
Estonia		91	80	75	–16
Finland		20	18	12	–8
France	73	75		67	–6
Georgia			81		
Germany (East)		67	57	70	3
Germany (West)	39	44	27	50	11
Great Britain	22	21	18	21	–1
Greece				75	
Hungary	89	96	95	94	5
Iceland	49	42		35	–14
India		89	84	85	–4
Indonesia				93	
Iran				49	
Iraq				88	
Ireland	27	26		16	–11
Israel					
Italy	53	67		56	3
Japan	68	76	68	66	–2
Jordan				91	
Korea Republic	74	76	67	92	18

	1981	1990	1995	2000	Change
Kyrgyzstan				92	
Latvia		96	73	91	–5
Lithuania		88	76	68	–20
Luxembourg				38	
Macedonia			67	70	3
Malta	72	56		44	–28
Mexico		52	43	45	–7
Moldova			85	79	–6
Montenegro			82	78	–4
Morocco				88	
Netherlands	12	12		7	–5
New Zealand			18		
Nigeria		87	82	92	5
Northern Ireland	42	32		18	–24
Norway	20	23	19		–1
Pakistan				98	
Peru			51	40	–11
Philippines			87	87	0
Poland		75	70	70	–5
Portugal		61		68	7
Puerto Rico			28	34	6
Romania		85	73	83	–2
Russian Fed.		92	83	83	–9
Saudi Arabia				68	
Serbia			75	68	–7
Singapore				56	
Slovakia		77	82	45	–32
Slovenia		58	51	38	–20
South Africa		70	57	45	–25
Spain	49	49	45	48	–1
Sweden	16	21	17		1
Switzerland		31	35		4
Taiwan			54		
Tanzania				84	
Turkey		72	78	75	3
Uganda				63	
Ukraine			80	86	6
Uruguay			59		
USA	18	20	16	15	–3
Venezuela			60	54	–6
Vietnam				86	
Zimbabwe				77	

Marriage is an Out-Dated Institution

(D022) *Do you agree or disagree with the following statement: "Marriage is an out-dated institution"*

Agree (%)

	1981	1990	1995	2000	Change
Albania			5	9	4
Algeria				13	
Argentina	24	9	16	19	–5
Armenia			14		
Australia	13		18		5
Austria		12		20	8
Azerbaijan			18		
Bangladesh			92	5	–87
Belarus		16	19	17	1
Belgium	18	22		31	13
Bosnia and Herz.			14	14	0
Brazil		27	30		3
Bulgaria		11	19	18	7
Canada	13	12		22	9
Chile		15	19	31	16
China		15	8	14	–1
Colombia			25		
Croatia			15	8	–7
Czech Republic		8	13	11	3
Denmark	18	18		15	–3
Dominican Rep.			11		
Egypt				4	
El Salvador			15		
Estonia		11	18	16	5
Finland		13	21	18	5
France	31	29		36	5
Georgia			15		
Germany (East)		15	28	18	3
Germany (West)	15	15	30	19	4
Great Britain	14	18		26	12
Greece				16	
Hungary	17	11	15	17	0
Iceland	13	6		8	–5
India		5	25	20	15
Indonesia				3	
Iran				20	
Iraq					
Ireland	13	10		22	9
Israel					
Italy	23	13		17	–6
Japan	24	7	10	10	–14
Jordan				12	
Korea Republic	13		15	16	3
Kyrgyzstan				33	
Latvia		9	21	16	7
Lithuania		9	16	20	11
Luxembourg				33	
Macedonia			17	18	1
Malta	13	6		7	–6
Mexico		17	29	21	4
Moldova			29	32	3
Montenegro			18	12	–6
Morocco				5	
Netherlands	15	21		25	10
New Zealand			16		
Nigeria		13	17	15	2
Northern Ireland	14	14		23	9
Norway	13	10	13		0
Pakistan				1	
Peru			21	20	–1
Philippines			13	17	4
Poland		6	11	9	3
Portugal		23		26	3
Puerto Rico			11	13	2
Romania		9	14	12	3
Russian Fed.		15	17	22	7
Saudi Arabia				17	
Serbia			17	17	0
Singapore				21	
Slovakia		7	12	12	5
Slovenia		18	25	27	9
South Africa		13	22	34	21
Spain	24	15	17	21	–3
Sweden	15	14	16	20	5
Switzerland		13	24		11
Taiwan			16		
Tanzania				8	
Turkey		11	8	8	–3
Uganda				20	
Ukraine			17	18	1
Uruguay			21		
USA	10	8	11	10	0
Venezuela			31	25	–6
Vietnam				9	
Zimbabwe				11	

WOMAN AS A SINGLE PARENT

(D023) *If a woman wants to have a child as a single parent but she doesn't want to have a stable relationship with a man, do you approve or disapprove?*

Approve (%)

	1981	1990	1995	2000	Change
Albania			31	12	–19
Algeria				6	
Argentina	29	58	62	61	32
Armenia			37		
Australia	36		36		0
Austria		39		38	–1
Azerbaijan			24		
Bangladesh				4	
Belarus		47	53	61	14
Belgium	32	32		52	20
Bosnia and Herz.			47	48	1
Brazil		51	52		1
Bulgaria		47	39	46	–1
Canada	35	38		45	10
Chile		60	65	73	13
China		6	7	2	–4
Colombia			76		
Croatia			62	66	4
Czech Republic		27	41	39	12
Denmark	72	67		52	–20
Dominican Rep.			48		
Egypt				5	
El Salvador			28		
Estonia		32	58	29	–3
Finland		56	61	54	–2
France	62	39		49	–13
Georgia			41		
Germany (East)		34	63	30	–4
Germany (West)	25	23	55	31	6
Great Britain	32	36		31	–1
Greece				31	
Hungary	28	39	40	38	10
Iceland	88	84		82	–6
India		3	7	10	7
Indonesia				4	
Iran				3	
Iraq					
Ireland	21	23		32	11
Israel					
Italy	36	39		28	–8
Japan	13	15	26	23	10
Jordan				2	
Korea Republic	31			22	–9
Kyrgyzstan				30	
Latvia		26	60	55	29
Lithuania		55	70	61	6
Luxembourg				46	
Macedonia			43	53	10
Malta	18	16		16	–2
Mexico		43	39	47	4
Moldova			44	37	–7
Montenegro			54	37	–17
Morocco				2	
Netherlands	33	38		50	17
New Zealand			15		
Nigeria		9	6	18	9
Northern Ireland	22	24		31	9
Norway	36	27	23		–13
Pakistan				0	
Peru			42	49	7
Philippines			12	14	2
Poland		13	20	42	29
Portugal		40		37	–3
Puerto Rico			44	57	13
Romania		38	46	49	11
Russian Fed.		42	52	54	12
Saudi Arabia				4	
Serbia			55	53	–2
Singapore				18	
Slovakia		25	36	23	–2
Slovenia		60	68	56	–4
South Africa		19	22	36	17
Spain	38	63	75	72	34
Sweden	41	25	26	32	–9
Switzerland		37	38		1
Taiwan			11		
Tanzania				15	
Turkey		6	11	6	0
Uganda				19	
Ukraine			33	40	7
Uruguay			67		
USA	33	38	43	42	9
Venezuela			63	65	2
Vietnam				16	
Zimbabwe				7	

Enjoy Sexual Freedom

(D024) *If someone said that individuals should have the chance to enjoy complete sexual freedom without being restricted, would you tend to agree or disagree?*

Agree (%)

	1981	1990	1995	2000	Change
Albania			16		
Algeria					
Argentina	34	39	32		–2
Armenia			24		
Australia	28		31		3
Austria		39			
Azerbaijan			16		
Bangladesh					
Belarus		18	27		9
Belgium	19	28			9
Bosnia and Herz.			27		
Brazil		29	42		13
Bulgaria		30	20		–10
Canada	21	24			3
Chile		18	28		10
China		5	8		3
Colombia			34		
Croatia			34		
Czech Republic		15	14		–1
Denmark	7	11			4
Dominican Rep.			38		
Egypt					
El Salvador			11		
Estonia		25	24		–1
Finland		12	28		16
France	31	32			1
Georgia			26		
Germany (East)		49	23		–26
Germany (West)	23	36	25		2
Great Britain	25	31			6
Greece					
Hungary	11	18	16		5
Iceland	25	23			–2
India		7	20		13
Indonesia					
Iran					
Iraq					
Ireland	18	17			–1
Israel					
Italy	27	39			12
Japan	10	13	18		8
Jordan					
Korea Republic	15		17		2

	1981	1990	1995	2000	Change
Kyrgyzstan					
Latvia		17	29		12
Lithuania		27	25		–2
Luxembourg					
Macedonia			29		
Malta	10	7			–3
Mexico		31	23		–8
Moldova			25		
Montenegro			29		
Morocco					
Netherlands	24	33			9
New Zealand			28		
Nigeria		22	14		–8
Northern Ireland	19	22			3
Norway	7	10	11		4
Pakistan					
Peru			29		
Philippines			7		
Poland		27	20		–7
Portugal		24			
Puerto Rico			26		
Romania		17	28		11
Russian Fed.		16	22		6
Saudi Arabia					
Serbia			29		
Singapore					
Slovakia		10	13		3
Slovenia		45	27		–18
South Africa		24	27		3
Spain	29	53	56		27
Sweden	16	22	17		1
Switzerland		44	32		–12
Taiwan			15		
Tanzania					
Turkey		24	29		5
Uganda					
Ukraine			23		
Uruguay			36		
USA	23	25	25		2
Venezuela			34		
Vietnam					
Zimbabwe					

Marriage Success: Faithfulness

(D027) *Here is a list of things which some people think make for a successful marriage. Please tell me, for each one, whether you think it is... Faithfulness*

Very important (%)

	1981	1990	1995	2000	Change
Albania					
Algeria					
Argentina		85			
Armenia					
Australia					
Austria		83		86	3
Azerbaijan					
Bangladesh					
Belarus				70	
Belgium	87	85		89	2
Bosnia and Herz.					
Brazil		76			
Bulgaria		63		74	11
Canada	90	91			1
Chile		92			
China		90			
Colombia					
Croatia				72	
Czech Republic		72		73	1
Denmark	76	81		84	8
Dominican Rep.					
Egypt					
El Salvador					
Estonia		61		61	0
Finland		75		82	7
France	72	74		80	8
Georgia					
Germany (East)		78		83	5
Germany (West)	80	78		85	5
Great Britain	88	90		90	2
Greece				87	
Hungary		84		85	1
Iceland	90	90		96	6
India		94			
Indonesia					
Iran					
Iraq					
Ireland	90	93		95	5
Israel					
Italy	83	84		84	1
Japan		73			
Jordan					
Korea Republic		90			

	1981	1990	1995	2000	Change
Kyrgyzstan					
Latvia		74		78	4
Lithuania		70		64	–6
Luxembourg				88	
Macedonia					
Malta	94	94		97	3
Mexico		81			
Moldova					
Montenegro					
Morocco					
Netherlands	85	88		87	2
New Zealand					
Nigeria		99			
Northern Ireland	90	94		94	4
Norway	89	91			2
Pakistan					
Peru					
Philippines					
Poland		84		87	3
Portugal		77		74	–3
Puerto Rico					
Romania		77		83	6
Russian Fed.		77		72	–5
Saudi Arabia					
Serbia					
Singapore					
Slovakia		86		81	–5
Slovenia		80		81	1
South Africa					
Spain	78	80		79	1
Sweden	80	89		88	8
Switzerland		81			
Taiwan					
Tanzania					
Turkey				96	
Uganda					
Ukraine				79	
Uruguay					
USA	93	94			1
Venezuela					
Vietnam					
Zimbabwe					

Marriage Success: Adequate Income

(D028) *Here is a list of things which some people think make for a successful marriage. Please tell me, for each one, whether you think it is... An adequate income*

Very important (%)

	1981	1990	1995	2000	Change
Albania					
Algeria					
Argentina		44			
Armenia					
Australia					
Austria		31		28	–3
Azerbaijan					
Bangladesh					
Belarus				38	
Belgium	40	45		40	0
Bosnia and Herz.					
Brazil		55			
Bulgaria		45		51	6
Canada	42	40			–2
Chile		67			
China		31			
Colombia					
Croatia				23	
Czech Republic		45		36	–9
Denmark	13	10		5	–8
Dominican Rep.					
Egypt					
El Salvador					
Estonia		30		29	–1
Finland		32		17	–15
France	41	38		36	–5
Georgia					
Germany (East)		30		29	–1
Germany (West)	33	26		26	–7
Great Britain	47	35		34	–13
Greece				54	
Hungary		52		58	6
Iceland	34	39		31	–3
India		59			
Indonesia					
Iran					
Iraq					
Ireland	55	52		46	–9
Israel					
Italy	41	32		29	–12
Japan		55			
Jordan					
Korea Republic		34			
Kyrgyzstan					
Latvia		35		36	1
Lithuania		36		42	6
Luxembourg				26	
Macedonia					
Malta	48	38		39	–9
Mexico		55			
Moldova					
Montenegro					
Morocco					
Netherlands	37	27		23	–14
New Zealand					
Nigeria		75			
Northern Ireland	42	40		34	–8
Norway	23	21			–2
Pakistan					
Peru					
Philippines					
Poland		37		45	8
Portugal		49		36	–13
Puerto Rico					
Romania		45		54	9
Russian Fed.		54		54	0
Saudi Arabia					
Serbia					
Singapore					
Slovakia		54		47	–7
Slovenia		40		30	–10
South Africa					
Spain	38	43		34	–4
Sweden	24	22		19	–5
Switzerland		35			
Taiwan					
Tanzania					
Turkey				84	
Uganda					
Ukraine				66	
Uruguay					
USA	46	45			–1
Venezuela					
Vietnam					
Zimbabwe					

Marriage Success: Same Social Background

(D029) *Here is a list of things which some people think make for a successful marriage. Please tell me, for each one, whether you think it is... Being of the same background*

Very important (%)

	1981	1990	1995	2000	Change
Albania					
Algeria					
Argentina		26			
Armenia					
Australia					
Austria		14		13	–1
Azerbaijan					
Bangladesh					
Belarus				11	
Belgium	25	22		21	–4
Bosnia and Herz.					
Brazil		28			
Bulgaria		18		30	12
Canada	22	20			–2
Chile		34			
China		13			
Colombia					
Croatia				7	
Czech Republic		14		7	–7
Denmark	16	11		6	–10
Dominican Rep.					
Egypt					
El Salvador					
Estonia		8		8	0
Finland		8		9	1
France	26	21		16	–10
Georgia					
Germany (East)		7		11	4
Germany (West)	15	12		15	0
Great Britain	24	21		18	–6
Greece				21	
Hungary		16		15	–1
Iceland	14	14		7	–7
India		47			
Indonesia					
Iran					
Iraq					
Ireland	30	25		26	–4
Israel					
Italy	19	17		13	–6
Japan		23			
Jordan					
Korea Republic		21			

	1981	1990	1995	2000	Change
Kyrgyzstan					
Latvia		11		15	4
Lithuania		8		12	4
Luxembourg				15	
Macedonia					
Malta	56	47		51	–5
Mexico		30			
Moldova					
Montenegro					
Morocco					
Netherlands	28	23		15	–13
New Zealand					
Nigeria		49			
Northern Ireland	20	21		23	3
Norway	15	14			–1
Pakistan					
Peru					
Philippines					
Poland		17		17	0
Portugal		26		14	–12
Puerto Rico					
Romania		25		28	3
Russian Fed.		9		10	1
Saudi Arabia					
Serbia					
Singapore					
Slovakia		18		16	–2
Slovenia		24		15	–9
South Africa					
Spain	27	24		17	–10
Sweden	13	12		7	–6
Switzerland		16			
Taiwan					
Tanzania					
Turkey				65	
Uganda					
Ukraine				15	
Uruguay					
USA	27	29			2
Venezuela					
Vietnam					
Zimbabwe					

Marriage Success: Respect + Appreciation

(D030) *Here is a list of things which some people think make for a successful marriage. Please tell me, for each one, whether you think it is... Mutual respect and appreciation*

Very important (%)

	1981	1990	1995	2000	Change
Albania					
Algeria					
Argentina		90			
Armenia					
Australia					
Austria		82		89	7
Azerbaijan					
Bangladesh					
Belarus				76	
Belgium	83	87		91	8
Bosnia and Herz.					
Brazil		73			
Bulgaria		68		81	13
Canada	92	92			0
Chile		95			
China		82			
Colombia					
Croatia				74	
Czech Republic		92		87	–5
Denmark	77	83		85	8
Dominican Rep.					
Egypt					
El Salvador					
Estonia		74		71	–3
Finland		83		86	3
France	86	84		89	3
Georgia					
Germany (East)		77		71	–6
Germany (West)	79	79		83	4
Great Britain	87	84		81	–6
Greece				94	
Hungary		90		87	–3
Iceland	95	96		96	1
India		80			
Indonesia					
Iran					
Iraq					
Ireland	80	83		87	7
Israel					
Italy	90	90		90	0
Japan		74			
Jordan					
Korea Republic		68			
Kyrgyzstan					
Latvia		74		75	1
Lithuania		65		52	–13
Luxembourg				84	
Macedonia					
Malta	92	92		97	5
Mexico		87			
Moldova					
Montenegro					
Morocco					
Netherlands	90	92		94	4
New Zealand					
Nigeria		97			
Northern Ireland	77	83		84	7
Norway	90	93			3
Pakistan					
Peru					
Philippines					
Poland		85		87	2
Portugal		83		66	–17
Puerto Rico					
Romania		82		76	–6
Russian Fed.		78		68	–10
Saudi Arabia					
Serbia					
Singapore					
Slovakia		90		81	–9
Slovenia		87		89	2
South Africa					
Spain	73	79		79	6
Sweden	81	91		94	13
Switzerland		90			
Taiwan					
Tanzania					
Turkey				95	
Uganda					
Ukraine				84	
Uruguay					
USA	90	92			2
Venezuela					
Vietnam					
Zimbabwe					

Marriage Success: Share Religious Beliefs

(D031) *Here is a list of things which some people think make for a successful marriage. Please tell me, for each one, whether you think it is... Shared religious beliefs*

Very important (%)

	1981	1990	1995	2000	Change
Albania					
Algeria					
Argentina		28			
Armenia					
Australia					
Austria		22		19	–3
Azerbaijan					
Bangladesh					
Belarus				14	
Belgium	28	22		18	–10
Bosnia and Herz.					
Brazil		35			
Bulgaria		14		27	13
Canada	34	28			–6
Chile		52			
China		6			
Colombia					
Croatia				28	
Czech Republic		17		8	–9
Denmark	19	16		13	–6
Dominican Rep.					
Egypt					
El Salvador					
Estonia		8		11	3
Finland		13		15	2
France	19	16		13	–6
Georgia					
Germany (East)		14		8	–6
Germany (West)	20	14		16	–4
Great Britain	21	19		14	–7
Greece				33	
Hungary		22		15	–7
Iceland	19	18		10	–9
India		40			
Indonesia					
Iran					
Iraq					
Ireland	40	33		27	–13
Israel					
Italy	26	26		23	–3
Japan		18			
Jordan					
Korea Republic		21			
Kyrgyzstan					
Latvia		9		11	2
Lithuania		14		16	2
Luxembourg				15	
Macedonia					
Malta	71	62		56	–15
Mexico		50			
Moldova					
Montenegro					
Morocco					
Netherlands	25	19		11	–14
New Zealand					
Nigeria		83			
Northern Ireland	41	37		33	–8
Norway	27	24			–3
Pakistan					
Peru					
Philippines					
Poland		49		40	–9
Portugal		34		20	–14
Puerto Rico					
Romania		31		41	10
Russian Fed.		11		12	1
Saudi Arabia					
Serbia					
Singapore					
Slovakia		34		26	–8
Slovenia		34		20	–14
South Africa					
Spain	31	28		21	–10
Sweden	18	18		13	–5
Switzerland		21			
Taiwan					
Tanzania					
Turkey				73	
Uganda					
Ukraine				24	
Uruguay					
USA	44	44			0
Venezuela					
Vietnam					
Zimbabwe					

Marriage Success: Good Housing

(D032) *Here is a list of things which some people think make for a successful marriage. Please tell me, for each one, whether you think it is... Good housing*

Very important (%)

	1981	1990	1995	2000	Change
Albania					
Algeria					
Argentina		40			
Armenia					
Australia					
Austria		40		33	–7
Azerbaijan					
Bangladesh					
Belarus				48	
Belgium	35	39		41	6
Bosnia and Herz.					
Brazil		47			
Bulgaria		43		45	2
Canada	35	33			–2
Chile		60			
China		25			
Colombia					
Croatia				18	
Czech Republic		49		41	–8
Denmark	39	30		18	–21
Dominican Rep.					
Egypt					
El Salvador					
Estonia		35		26	–9
Finland		22		18	–4
France	44	37		36	–8
Georgia					
Germany (East)		41		30	–11
Germany (West)	32	25		25	–7
Great Britain	50	37		39	–11
Greece				59	
Hungary		51		60	9
Iceland	39	33		26	–13
India		40			
Indonesia					
Iran					
Iraq					
Ireland	53	46		47	–6
Israel					
Italy	26	25		20	–6
Japan		35			
Jordan					
Korea Republic		7			
Kyrgyzstan					
Latvia		45		30	–15
Lithuania		33		27	–6
Luxembourg				28	
Macedonia					
Malta	60	31		38	–22
Mexico		44			
Moldova					
Montenegro					
Morocco					
Netherlands	49	36		26	–23
New Zealand					
Nigeria		74			
Northern Ireland	39	36		36	–3
Norway	34	23			–11
Pakistan					
Peru					
Philippines					
Poland		53		52	–1
Portugal		52		35	–17
Puerto Rico					
Romania		51		51	0
Russian Fed.		51		45	–6
Saudi Arabia					
Serbia					
Singapore					
Slovakia		52		49	–3
Slovenia		39		30	–9
South Africa					
Spain	30	37		31	1
Sweden	36	39		29	–7
Switzerland		34			
Taiwan					
Tanzania					
Turkey				62	
Uganda					
Ukraine				62	
Uruguay					
USA	42	40			–2
Venezuela					
Vietnam					
Zimbabwe					

Marriage Success: Agreement on Politics

(D033) *Here is a list of things which some people think make for a successful marriage. Please tell me, for each one, whether you think it is… Agreement on Politics*

Very important (%)

	1981	1990	1995	2000	Change
Albania					
Algeria					
Argentina		8			
Armenia					
Australia					
Austria		7		6	–1
Azerbaijan					
Bangladesh					
Belarus				5	
Belgium	11	9		7	–4
Bosnia and Herz.					
Brazil		13			
Bulgaria		15		15	0
Canada	8	6			–2
Chile		18			
China		24			
Colombia					
Croatia				4	
Czech Republic		16		6	–10
Denmark	8	4		2	–6
Dominican Rep.					
Egypt					
El Salvador					
Estonia		6		5	–1
Finland		5		4	–1
France	9	7		8	–1
Georgia					
Germany (East)		11		9	–2
Germany (West)	8	7		10	2
Great Britain	8	7		7	–1
Greece				14	
Hungary		11		7	–4
Iceland	3	5		2	–1
India		12			
Indonesia					
Iran					
Iraq					
Ireland	6	4		7	1
Israel					
Italy	11	10		7	–4
Japan		8			
Jordan					
Korea Republic		10			

	1981	1990	1995	2000	Change
Kyrgyzstan					
Latvia		13		7	–6
Lithuania		7		8	1
Luxembourg				7	
Macedonia					
Malta	49	33		24	–25
Mexico		18			
Moldova					
Montenegro					
Morocco					
Netherlands	12	8		4	–8
New Zealand					
Nigeria		20			
Northern Ireland	11	10		12	1
Norway	12	7			–5
Pakistan					
Peru					
Philippines					
Poland		9		13	4
Portugal		15		9	–6
Puerto Rico					
Romania		7		15	8
Russian Fed.		8		3	–5
Saudi Arabia					
Serbia					
Singapore					
Slovakia		12		8	–4
Slovenia		13		6	–7
South Africa					
Spain	18	12		10	–8
Sweden	14	10		6	–8
Switzerland		9			
Taiwan					
Tanzania					
Turkey				49	
Uganda					
Ukraine				10	
Uruguay					
USA	11	12			1
Venezuela					
Vietnam					
Zimbabwe					

Marriage Success: Understanding and Tolerance

(D034) *Here is a list of things which some people think make for a successful marriage. Please tell me, for each one, whether you think it is… Understanding and tolerance*

Very important (%)

	1981	1990	1995	2000	Change
Albania					
Algeria					
Argentina		89			
Armenia					
Australia					
Austria		82		84	2
Azerbaijan					
Bangladesh					
Belarus				74	
Belgium	74	78		82	8
Bosnia and Herz.					
Brazil		70			
Bulgaria		63		75	12
Canada	86	84			−2
Chile		90			
China		70			
Colombia					
Croatia				68	
Czech Republic		90		86	−4
Denmark	78	80		79	1
Dominican Rep.					
Egypt					
El Salvador					
Estonia		57		61	4
Finland		70		69	−1
France	73	74		79	6
Georgia					
Germany (East)		72		71	−1
Germany (West)	79	77		84	5
Great Britain	85	86		81	−4
Greece				90	
Hungary		76		80	4
Iceland	90	86		88	−2
India		81			
Indonesia					
Iran					
Iraq					
Ireland	77	81		85	8
Israel					
Italy	83	80		81	−2
Japan		77			
Jordan					
Korea Republic		73			
Kyrgyzstan					
Latvia		62		66	4
Lithuania		33		42	9
Luxembourg				80	
Macedonia					
Malta	90	86		94	4
Mexico		81			
Moldova					
Montenegro					
Morocco					
Netherlands	89	86		87	−2
New Zealand					
Nigeria		99			
Northern Ireland	85	81		82	−3
Norway	80	84			4
Pakistan					
Peru					
Philippines					
Poland		72		77	5
Portugal		75		59	−16
Puerto Rico					
Romania		72		72	0
Russian Fed.		67		62	−5
Saudi Arabia					
Serbia					
Singapore					
Slovakia		88		79	−9
Slovenia		78		83	5
South Africa					
Spain	70	74		76	6
Sweden	81	89		87	6
Switzerland		86			
Taiwan					
Tanzania					
Turkey				92	
Uganda					
Ukraine				81	
Uruguay					
USA	84	83			−1
Venezuela					
Vietnam					
Zimbabwe					

Marriage Success: Apart from In-Laws

(D035) *Here is a list of things which some people think make for a successful marriage. Please tell me, for each one, whether you think it is... Living apart fom your in-laws*

Very important (%)

	1981	1990	1995	2000	Change
Albania					
Algeria					
Argentina		41			
Armenia					
Australia					
Austria		37		44	7
Azerbaijan					
Bangladesh					
Belarus				45	
Belgium	53	57		60	7
Bosnia and Herz.					
Brazil		48			
Bulgaria		43		58	15
Canada	53	51			–2
Chile		53			
China		8			
Colombia					
Croatia				26	
Czech Republic		52		40	–12
Denmark	58	54		55	–3
Dominican Rep.					
Egypt					
El Salvador					
Estonia		42		39	–3
Finland		23		24	1
France	71	64		69	–2
Georgia					
Germany (East)		45		26	–19
Germany (West)	37	37		32	–5
Great Britain	62	54		51	–11
Greece				51	
Hungary		48		49	1
Iceland	48	43		40	–8
India		20			
Indonesia					
Iran					
Iraq					
Ireland	46	46		45	–1
Israel					
Italy	46	46		47	1
Japan		7			
Jordan					
Korea Republic		5			

	1981	1990	1995	2000	Change
Kyrgyzstan					
Latvia		42		32	–10
Lithuania		35		34	–1
Luxembourg				54	
Macedonia					
Malta	51	44		57	6
Mexico		40			
Moldova					
Montenegro					
Morocco					
Netherlands	58	60		56	–2
New Zealand					
Nigeria		57			
Northern Ireland	49	54		47	–2
Norway	41	41			0
Pakistan					
Peru					
Philippines					
Poland		64		61	–3
Portugal		54		31	–23
Puerto Rico					
Romania		40		38	–2
Russian Fed.		36		37	1
Saudi Arabia					
Serbia					
Singapore					
Slovakia		46		18	–28
Slovenia		31		30	–1
South Africa					
Spain	33	34		32	–1
Sweden	13	53		42	29
Switzerland		59			
Taiwan					
Tanzania					
Turkey				60	
Uganda					
Ukraine				52	
Uruguay					
USA	49	47			–2
Venezuela					
Vietnam					
Zimbabwe					

MARRIAGE SUCCESS: HAPPY SEXUAL RELATIONSHIP

(D036) *Here is a list of things which some people think make for a successful marriage. Please tell me, for each one, whether you think it is... Happy sexual relationship*

Very important (%)

	1981	1990	1995	2000	Change
Albania					
Algeria					
Argentina		81			
Armenia					
Australia					
Austria		57		64	7
Azerbaijan					
Bangladesh					
Belarus				54	
Belgium	66	65		66	0
Bosnia and Herz.					
Brazil		72			
Bulgaria		48		61	13
Canada	75	72			–3
Chile		74			
China		37			
Colombia					
Croatia				37	
Czech Republic		70		56	–14
Denmark	60	65		56	–4
Dominican Rep.					
Egypt					
El Salvador					
Estonia		53		52	–1
Finland		61		52	–9
France	71	68		73	2
Georgia					
Germany (East)		54		51	–3
Germany (West)	54	51		47	–7
Great Britain	74	66		64	–10
Greece				82	
Hungary		69		70	1
Iceland	83	73		71	–12
India		78			
Indonesia					
Iran					
Iraq					
Ireland	67	68		71	4
Israel					
Italy	71	67		67	–4
Japan		28			
Jordan					
Korea Republic					

	1981	1990	1995	2000	Change
Kyrgyzstan					
Latvia		59		53	–6
Lithuania		37		37	0
Luxembourg				61	
Macedonia					
Malta	79	59		82	3
Mexico		77			
Moldova					
Montenegro					
Morocco					
Netherlands	68	62		51	–17
New Zealand					
Nigeria		91			
Northern Ireland	69	69		67	–2
Norway	66	62			–4
Pakistan					
Peru					
Philippines					
Poland		61		66	5
Portugal		69		41	–28
Puerto Rico					
Romania		59		49	–10
Russian Fed.		46		50	4
Saudi Arabia					
Serbia					
Singapore					
Slovakia		70		59	–11
Slovenia		61		64	3
South Africa					
Spain	57	63		60	3
Sweden	59	67		60	1
Switzerland		68			
Taiwan					
Tanzania					
Turkey				84	
Uganda					
Ukraine				67	
Uruguay					
USA	76	71			–5
Venezuela					
Vietnam					
Zimbabwe					

Marriage Success: Household Chores

(D037) *Here is a list of things which some people think make for a successful marriage. Please tell me, for each one, whether you think it is... Sharing household chores*

Very important (%)

	1981	1990	1995	2000	Change
Albania					
Algeria					
Argentina		53			
Armenia					
Australia					
Austria		29		29	0
Azerbaijan					
Bangladesh					
Belarus				45	
Belgium	34	38		42	8
Bosnia and Herz.					
Brazil		37			
Bulgaria		42		34	–8
Canada	46	53			7
Chile		62			
China		35			
Colombia					
Croatia				23	
Czech Republic		43		24	–19
Denmark	46	48		41	–5
Dominican Rep.					
Egypt					
El Salvador					
Estonia		19		18	–1
Finland		25		29	4
France	33	35		40	7
Georgia					
Germany (East)		30		27	–3
Germany (West)	20	21		19	–1
Great Britain	42	44		50	8
Greece				44	
Hungary		40		41	1
Iceland	43	42		45	2
India		58			
Indonesia					
Iran					
Iraq					
Ireland	31	38		53	22
Israel					
Italy	30	30		29	–1
Japan		10			
Jordan					
Korea Republic					

	1981	1990	1995	2000	Change
Kyrgyzstan					
Latvia		31		26	–5
Lithuania		25		26	1
Luxembourg				37	
Macedonia					
Malta	45	39		55	10
Mexico		47			
Moldova					
Montenegro					
Morocco					
Netherlands	30	34		33	3
New Zealand					
Nigeria		67			
Northern Ireland	25	45		47	22
Norway	26	33			7
Pakistan					
Peru					
Philippines					
Poland		52		55	3
Portugal		50		23	–27
Puerto Rico					
Romania		42		43	1
Russian Fed.		38		28	–10
Saudi Arabia					
Serbia					
Singapore					
Slovakia		47		31	–16
Slovenia		35		36	1
South Africa					
Spain	26	36		36	10
Sweden	34	48		52	18
Switzerland		33			
Taiwan					
Tanzania					
Turkey				60	
Uganda					
Ukraine				45	
Uruguay					
USA	45	47			2
Venezuela					
Vietnam					
Zimbabwe					

Marriage Success: Children

(D038) *Here is a list of things which some people think make for a successful marriage. Please tell me, for each one, whether you think it is... Children*

Very important (%)

	1981	1990	1995	2000	Change
Albania					
Algeria					
Argentina		88			
Armenia					
Australia					
Austria		63		60	–3
Azerbaijan					
Bangladesh					
Belarus				76	
Belgium	46	55		58	12
Bosnia and Herz.					
Brazil		60			
Bulgaria		84		78	–6
Canada	60	66			6
Chile		92			
China		55			
Colombia					
Croatia				63	
Czech Republic		86		77	–9
Denmark	37	42		36	–1
Dominican Rep.					
Egypt					
El Salvador					
Estonia		74		64	–10
Finland		60		55	–5
France	65	65		63	–2
Georgia					
Germany (East)		64		52	–12
Germany (West)	42	44		47	5
Great Britain	58	58		48	–10
Greece				72	
Hungary		85		83	–2
Iceland	69	66		51	–18
India		79			
Indonesia					
Iran					
Iraq					
Ireland	53	62		59	6
Israel					
Italy	55	64		58	3
Japan		52			
Jordan					
Korea Republic					
Kyrgyzstan					
Latvia		78		73	–5
Lithuania		66		51	–15
Luxembourg				43	
Macedonia					
Malta	80	69		70	–10
Mexico		75			
Moldova					
Montenegro					
Morocco					
Netherlands	50	54		47	–3
New Zealand					
Nigeria		94			
Northern Ireland	63	69		55	–8
Norway	54	61			7
Pakistan					
Peru					
Philippines					
Poland		78		73	–5
Portugal		65		43	–22
Puerto Rico					
Romania		68		70	2
Russian Fed.		80		74	–6
Saudi Arabia					
Serbia					
Singapore					
Slovakia		88		70	–18
Slovenia		73		71	–2
South Africa					
Spain	67	71		65	–2
Sweden	47	61		59	12
Switzerland		54			
Taiwan					
Tanzania					
Turkey				78	
Uganda					
Ukraine				84	
Uruguay					
USA	60	65			5
Venezuela					
Vietnam					
Zimbabwe					

Make My Parents Proud

(D054) *Do you agree strongly, agree, disagree, or disagree strongly with the following statement? "One of my main goals in life has been to make my parents proud"*

Agree strongly/Agree (%)

	1981	1990	1995	2000	Change
Albania			79	94	15
Algeria				92	
Argentina			76	85	9
Armenia			84		
Australia			69		
Austria					
Azerbaijan			86		
Bangladesh			93	96	3
Belarus			64		
Belgium					
Bosnia and Herz.			82	88	6
Brazil			88		
Bulgaria			77		
Canada				81	
Chile			70	84	14
China			73	61	–12
Colombia			93		
Croatia			70		
Czech Republic			65		
Denmark					
Dominican Rep.			89		
Egypt				99	
El Salvador			96		
Estonia			65		
Finland			35		
France					
Georgia			85		
Germany (East)			69		
Germany (West)			47		
Great Britain					
Greece					
Hungary			61		
Iceland					
India			92	89	–3
Indonesia				92	
Iran				92	
Iraq				96	
Ireland					
Israel					
Italy					
Japan			37	73	36
Jordan				99	
Korea Republic			60	75	15
Kyrgyzstan				89	
Latvia			56		
Lithuania			56		
Luxembourg					
Macedonia			80	84	4
Malta					
Mexico			79	93	14
Moldova			78	93	15
Montenegro			86	74	–12
Morocco				97	
Netherlands					
New Zealand			58		
Nigeria			95	98	3
Northern Ireland					
Norway			54		
Pakistan				97	
Peru			93	96	3
Philippines			90	96	6
Poland			85		
Portugal					
Puerto Rico			94	96	2
Romania			76		
Russian Fed.			64		
Saudi Arabia				96	
Serbia			77	75	–2
Singapore				91	
Slovakia			69		
Slovenia			65		
South Africa			93	94	1
Spain			80	85	5
Sweden			51	38	–13
Switzerland			44		
Taiwan			64		
Tanzania				88	
Turkey			94	97	3
Uganda				94	
Ukraine			65		
Uruguay			68		
USA			77	83	6
Venezuela			95	97	2
Vietnam				97	
Zimbabwe				97	

Live Up to What My Friends Expect

(D055) *Do you agree strongly, agree, disagree, or disagree strongly with the following statement? "I make a lot of effort to live up to what my friends expect"*

Agree strongly/Agree (%)

	1981	1990	1995	2000	Change
Albania			59	51	–8
Algeria				71	
Argentina			27	25	–2
Armenia			73		
Australia			34		
Austria					
Azerbaijan			74		
Bangladesh			64	59	–5
Belarus			57		
Belgium					
Bosnia and Herz.			65	31	–34
Brazil			75		
Bulgaria			74		
Canada				44	
Chile			26	35	9
China			87	76	–11
Colombia			41		
Croatia			42		
Czech Republic			54		
Denmark					
Dominican Rep.			70		
Egypt				72	
El Salvador					
Estonia			42		
Finland			38		
France					
Georgia			89		
Germany (East)			32		
Germany (West)			20		
Great Britain					
Greece					
Hungary			40		
Iceland					
India			67	55	–12
Indonesia				58	
Iran				53	
Iraq					
Ireland					
Israel					
Italy					
Japan			50	65	15
Jordan				87	
Korea Republic			64	72	8
Kyrgyzstan				75	
Latvia			51		
Lithuania			41		
Luxembourg					
Macedonia			39	35	–4
Malta					
Mexico			29	54	25
Moldova			54	70	16
Montenegro			76	69	–7
Morocco				73	
Netherlands					
New Zealand			30		
Nigeria			72	77	5
Northern Ireland					
Norway			19		
Pakistan				48	
Peru			67	57	–10
Philippines			71	55	–16
Poland			59		
Portugal					
Puerto Rico			66	52	–14
Romania			49		
Russian Fed.			52		
Saudi Arabia				68	
Serbia			64	63	–1
Singapore				43	
Slovakia			66		
Slovenia			57		
South Africa			41	38	–3
Spain			48	58	10
Sweden			38		
Switzerland			47		
Taiwan			59		
Tanzania				40	
Turkey			75		
Uganda				80	
Ukraine			53		
Uruguay			29		
USA			40	33	–7
Venezuela			49	37	–12
Vietnam				77	
Zimbabwe				50	

A Working Mother Relationship

(D056) *Do you agree strongly, agree, disagree, or disagree strongly with the following statement? "A working mother can establish just as warm and secure a relationship with her children as a mother who does not work"*

Agree strongly/Agree (%)

	1981	1990	1995	2000	Change
Albania			58	76	18
Algeria				65	
Argentina		74	68	76	2
Armenia			82		
Australia			69		
Austria		51			
Azerbaijan			80		
Bangladesh			47	60	13
Belarus		65	78	82	17
Belgium		74		79	5
Bosnia and Herz.			82	82	0
Brazil		64	68		4
Bulgaria		61	79	79	18
Canada		70		78	8
Chile		72	69	78	6
China		91	84	94	3
Colombia			61		
Croatia			75	66	–9
Czech Republic		62	81	81	19
Denmark		83		86	3
Dominican Rep.			61		
Egypt				46	
El Salvador			47		
Estonia		82	83	71	–11
Finland		94	94	95	1
France		73		77	4
Georgia			79		
Germany (East)		55	83	90	35
Germany (West)		41	69	62	21
Great Britain		70		73	3
Greece				76	
Hungary		70	73	78	8
Iceland		82		86	4
India		57	65	62	5
Indonesia				64	
Iran				77	
Iraq				55	
Ireland		63			
Israel					
Italy		63		64	1
Japan		89	92	95	6
Jordan				47	
Korea Republic		43	84	83	40
Kyrgyzstan				83	
Latvia		47	73	76	29
Lithuania		42	74	76	34
Luxembourg				76	
Macedonia			67	74	7
Malta		41		61	20
Mexico		64	53	69	5
Moldova			79	85	6
Montenegro			72	77	5
Morocco				60	
Netherlands		69		81	12
New Zealand			69		
Nigeria		65	64	74	9
Northern Ireland		71			
Norway		69	70		1
Pakistan			43	18	–25
Peru			61	70	9
Philippines			71	73	2
Poland		38	49	54	16
Portugal		76		67	–9
Puerto Rico			50	78	28
Romania		84	84	83	–1
Russian Fed.		64	77	83	19
Saudi Arabia				63	
Serbia			77	79	2
Singapore				74	
Slovakia		58	80	81	23
Slovenia		74	77	82	8
South Africa			71	80	9
Spain		66	65	79	13
Sweden		73	78	84	11
Switzerland					
Taiwan			92		
Tanzania				74	
Turkey		57	44	70	13
Uganda				58	
Ukraine			78	83	5
Uruguay			70		
USA		72	76	79	7
Venezuela			64	72	8
Vietnam				84	
Zimbabwe				73	

Being a Housewife Fulfilling

(D057) *Do you agree strongly, agree, disagree, or disagree strongly with the following statement? "Being a housewife is just as fulfilling as working for pay"*

Agree strongly/Agree (%)

	1981	1990	1995	2000	Change
Albania			15	46	31
Algeria				66	
Argentina		62	61	75	13
Armenia			75		
Australia			70		
Austria		63			
Azerbaijan			73		
Bangladesh			21	29	8
Belarus		81	62	64	–17
Belgium		67		64	–3
Bosnia and Herz.			87	71	–16
Brazil		61	61		0
Bulgaria		87	75	49	–38
Canada		71		82	11
Chile		73	66	69	–4
China		88	69	90	2
Colombia			66		
Croatia			72	56	–16
Czech Republic		70	41	76	6
Denmark		55		54	–1
Dominican Rep.			49		
Egypt				74	
El Salvador			70		
Estonia		71	66	59	–12
Finland		54	82	81	27
France		60		62	2
Georgia			79		
Germany (East)		36	29	25	–11
Germany (West)		54	47	46	–8
Great Britain		60		61	1
Greece				42	
Hungary		76	80	61	–15
Iceland		71		64	–7
India		46	65	64	18
Indonesia				23	
Iran				75	
Iraq				82	
Ireland		72			
Israel					
Italy		56		55	–1
Japan		83	89	89	6
Jordan				76	
Korea Republic		67	89	88	21

	1981	1990	1995	2000	Change
Kyrgyzstan				73	
Latvia		66	63	40	–26
Lithuania		85	83	79	–6
Luxembourg				64	
Macedonia			42	52	10
Malta		87		87	0
Mexico		68	60	73	5
Moldova			65	72	7
Montenegro			64	65	1
Morocco				65	
Netherlands		56		51	–5
New Zealand			67		
Nigeria		49	40	44	–5
Northern Ireland		70			
Norway		53	61		8
Pakistan			59	76	17
Peru			62	73	11
Philippines			85	86	1
Poland		63	56	60	–3
Portugal		49		51	2
Puerto Rico			72	81	9
Romania		48	47	48	0
Russian Fed.		86	70	64	–22
Saudi Arabia				69	
Serbia			69	69	0
Singapore				72	
Slovakia		46	45	71	25
Slovenia		63	68	54	–9
South Africa			55	56	1
Spain		60	60	60	0
Sweden		62	66	51	–11
Switzerland					
Taiwan			86		
Tanzania				43	
Turkey		79	80	78	–1
Uganda				37	
Ukraine			67	58	–9
Uruguay			69		
USA		75	80	80	5
Venezuela			61	65	4
Vietnam				86	
Zimbabwe				66	

HUSBAND AND WIFE SHOULD CONTRIBUTE

(D058) *Do you agree strongly, agree, disagree, or disagree strongly with the following statement? "Both the husband and wife should contribute to household income"*

Agree strongly/Agree (%)

	1981	1990	1995	2000	Change
Albania			98	96	–2
Algeria				71	
Argentina		77	88	90	13
Armenia			80		
Australia			67		
Austria		74			
Azerbaijan			82		
Bangladesh			85	87	2
Belarus			86	85	–1
Belgium		67		70	3
Bosnia and Herz.			92	94	2
Brazil		93	96		3
Bulgaria		83	93	92	9
Canada		69		75	6
Chile		88	87	87	–1
China		95	89	98	3
Colombia			94		
Croatia			89	94	5
Czech Republic		90	94	93	3
Denmark		71		68	–3
Dominican Rep.			92		
Egypt				76	
El Salvador			94		
Estonia		81	92	82	1
Finland		78	79	71	–7
France		80		81	1
Georgia			88		
Germany (East)		87	94	93	6
Germany (West)		64	76	69	5
Great Britain		70		70	0
Greece				88	
Hungary		83	86	89	6
Iceland		68		64	–4
India		82	77	84	2
Indonesia				85	
Iran				70	
Iraq				72	
Ireland		70			
Israel					
Italy		80		81	1
Japan		46	58	57	11
Jordan				77	
Korea Republic		59	79	75	16
Kyrgyzstan				75	
Latvia		77	87	89	12
Lithuania		75	82	90	15
Luxembourg				54	
Macedonia			94	93	–1
Malta		74		73	–1
Mexico		82	75	89	7
Moldova			89	91	2
Montenegro			96	94	–2
Morocco				74	
Netherlands		30		38	8
New Zealand			62		
Nigeria		94	92	90	–4
Northern Ireland		82			
Norway		74	80		6
Pakistan			60	70	10
Peru			95	94	–1
Philippines			85	92	7
Poland		81	93	87	6
Portugal		98		88	–10
Puerto Rico			93	95	2
Romania		91	92	85	–6
Russian Fed.		80	87	83	3
Saudi Arabia				67	
Serbia			95	89	–6
Singapore				81	
Slovakia		85	95	89	4
Slovenia		93	93	91	–2
South Africa			87	88	1
Spain		84	91	87	3
Sweden		87	91	89	2
Switzerland					
Taiwan			89		
Tanzania				89	
Turkey			88	88	0
Uganda				92	
Ukraine			86	86	0
Uruguay			94		
USA		67	78	69	2
Venezuela			95	95	0
Vietnam				97	
Zimbabwe				92	

Men make better Political Leaders

(D059) *Do you agree strongly, agree, disagree, or disagree strongly with the following statement? "On the whole, men make better political leaders than women do"*

Agree strongly/Agree (%)

	1981	1990	1995	2000	Change
Albania			53	51	–2
Algeria				70	
Argentina			36	32	–4
Armenia			83		
Australia			24		
Austria					
Azerbaijan			72		
Bangladesh			56	67	11
Belarus			70		
Belgium					
Bosnia and Herz.			60	33	–27
Brazil			47		
Bulgaria			61		
Canada				21	
Chile			42	39	–3
China			54	50	–4
Colombia			33		
Croatia			54		
Czech Republic			51		
Denmark					
Dominican Rep.			41		
Egypt				84	
El Salvador			37		
Estonia			69		
Finland			21		
France					
Georgia			80		
Germany (East)			18		
Germany (West)			13		
Great Britain					
Greece					
Hungary			52		
Iceland					
India			49	58	9
Indonesia				61	
Iran				66	
Iraq				90	
Ireland					
Israel					
Italy					
Japan			57	43	–14
Jordan				87	
Korea Republic			63	48	–15
Kyrgyzstan				57	
Latvia			66		
Lithuania			56		
Luxembourg					
Macedonia			46	41	–5
Malta					
Mexico			44	42	–2
Moldova			67	61	–6
Montenegro			65	55	–10
Morocco				73	
Netherlands					
New Zealand			18		
Nigeria			74	80	6
Northern Ireland					
Norway			16		
Pakistan			66	49	–17
Peru			30	24	–6
Philippines			58	63	5
Poland			61		
Portugal					
Puerto Rico			30	19	–11
Romania			67		
Russian Fed.			60		
Saudi Arabia				75	
Serbia			57	48	–9
Singapore				50	
Slovakia			68		
Slovenia			45		
South Africa			54	44	–10
Spain			26	19	–7
Sweden			18	19	1
Switzerland					
Taiwan			48		
Tanzania				44	
Turkey			66	62	–4
Uganda				68	
Ukraine			63		
Uruguay			38		
USA			31	23	–8
Venezuela			41	40	–1
Vietnam				56	
Zimbabwe				52	

University is More Important for a Boy

(D060) *Do you agree strongly, agree, disagree, or disagree strongly with the following statement? "A university education is more important for a boy than for a girl"*

Agree strongly/Agree (%)

	1981	1990	1995	2000	Change
Albania			20	15	–5
Algeria				28	
Argentina			19	15	–4
Armenia			42		
Australia			11		
Austria					
Azerbaijan			37		
Bangladesh			41	63	22
Belarus			41		
Belgium					
Bosnia and Herz.			31	18	–13
Brazil			24		
Bulgaria			19		
Canada				5	
Chile			24	30	6
China			24	9	–15
Colombia			11		
Croatia			25		
Czech Republic			33		
Denmark					
Dominican Rep.			20		
Egypt				31	
El Salvador			14		
Estonia			34		
Finland			14		
France					
Georgia			34		
Germany (East)			12		
Germany (West)			10		
Great Britain					
Greece					
Hungary			20		
Iceland					
India			31	42	11
Indonesia				17	
Iran				38	
Iraq				46	
Ireland					
Israel					
Italy					
Japan			33	23	–10
Jordan				39	
Korea Republic			37	24	–13
Kyrgyzstan				28	
Latvia			27		
Lithuania			23		
Luxembourg					
Macedonia			13	12	–1
Malta					
Mexico			32	33	1
Moldova			32	24	–8
Montenegro			25	24	–1
Morocco				42	
Netherlands					
New Zealand			8		
Nigeria			36	44	8
Northern Ireland					
Norway			11		
Pakistan			42	23	–19
Peru			28	20	–8
Philippines			37	37	0
Poland			35		
Portugal					
Puerto Rico			13	11	–2
Romania			32		
Russian Fed.			34		
Saudi Arabia				62	
Serbia			27	21	–6
Singapore				15	
Slovakia			37		
Slovenia			23		
South Africa			17	19	2
Spain			17	12	–5
Sweden			9	7	–2
Switzerland					
Taiwan			24		
Tanzania				16	
Turkey			34	29	–5
Uganda				23	
Ukraine			36		
Uruguay			13		
USA			15	7	–8
Venezuela			21	15	–6
Vietnam				24	
Zimbabwe				18	

Children Suffer with Working Mother

(D061) *Do you agree strongly, agree, disagree, or disagree strongly with the following statement? "A pre-school child is likely to suffer if his or her mother works"*

Agree strongly/Agree (%)

	1981	1990	1995	2000	Change
Albania					
Algeria					
Argentina		78			
Armenia					
Australia					
Austria		83			
Azerbaijan					
Bangladesh					
Belarus				60	
Belgium		61		51	–10
Bosnia and Herz.					
Brazil		75			
Bulgaria		76		61	–15
Canada		53			
Chile		82			
China		61			
Colombia					
Croatia				64	
Czech Republic		71		47	–24
Denmark		32		18	–14
Dominican Rep.					
Egypt					
El Salvador					
Estonia		91		65	–26
Finland		52		41	–11
France		65		56	–9
Georgia					
Germany (East)		80		36	–44
Germany (West)		84		73	–11
Great Britain		55		46	–9
Greece				78	
Hungary		70		63	–7
Iceland		52		33	–19
India		92			
Indonesia					
Iran					
Iraq					
Ireland		53			
Israel					
Italy		78		81	3
Japan		70			
Jordan					
Korea Republic		72			

	1981	1990	1995	2000	Change
Kyrgyzstan					
Latvia		92		75	–17
Lithuania		90		71	–19
Luxembourg				68	
Macedonia					
Malta		89		87	–2
Mexico		78			
Moldova					
Montenegro					
Morocco					
Netherlands		63		46	–17
New Zealand					
Nigeria		54			
Northern Ireland		44			
Norway		46			
Pakistan					
Peru					
Philippines					
Poland		94		77	–17
Portugal		84		72	–12
Puerto Rico					
Romania		58		47	–11
Russian Fed.		70		73	3
Saudi Arabia					
Serbia					
Singapore					
Slovakia		76		63	–13
Slovenia		67		47	–20
South Africa					
Spain		56		46	–10
Sweden		74		38	–36
Switzerland					
Taiwan					
Tanzania					
Turkey					
Uganda					
Ukraine				73	
Uruguay					
USA		51			
Venezuela					
Vietnam					
Zimbabwe					

WOMEN WANT HOME AND CHILDREN

(D062) *Do you agree strongly, agree, disagree, or disagree strongly with the following statement? "A job is alright but what most women really want is a home and children"*

Agree strongly/Agree (%)

	1981	1990	1995	2000	Change
Albania					
Algeria					
Argentina		73			
Armenia					
Australia					
Austria		62			
Azerbaijan					
Bangladesh					
Belarus				68	
Belgium		61		54	–7
Bosnia and Herz.					
Brazil		72			
Bulgaria		90		76	–14
Canada		43			
Chile		77			
China		78			
Colombia					
Croatia				66	
Czech Republic		87		72	–15
Denmark		25		18	–7
Dominican Rep.					
Egypt					
El Salvador					
Estonia		85		68	–17
Finland		42		50	8
France		68		65	–3
Georgia					
Germany (East)		52		30	–22
Germany (West)		51		47	–4
Great Britain		45		44	–1
Greece				65	
Hungary		76		70	–6
Iceland		71		62	–9
India		91			
Indonesia					
Iran					
Iraq					
Ireland		58			
Israel					
Italy		72		68	–4
Japan		81			
Jordan					
Korea Republic		70			

	1981	1990	1995	2000	Change
Kyrgyzstan					
Latvia		90		67	–23
Lithuania		97		94	–3
Luxembourg				56	
Macedonia					
Malta		70		70	0
Mexico		61			
Moldova					
Montenegro					
Morocco					
Netherlands		41		34	–7
New Zealand					
Nigeria		87			
Northern Ireland		53			
Norway		51			
Pakistan					
Peru					
Philippines					
Poland		88		74	–14
Portugal		62		52	–10
Puerto Rico					
Romania		82		85	3
Russian Fed.		91		86	–5
Saudi Arabia					
Serbia					
Singapore					
Slovakia		87		61	–26
Slovenia		76		65	–11
South Africa					
Spain		56		47	–9
Sweden				40	
Switzerland					
Taiwan					
Tanzania					
Turkey					
Uganda					
Ukraine				80	
Uruguay					
USA		56			
Venezuela					
Vietnam					
Zimbabwe					

Job Independence Women

(D063) *Do you agree strongly, agree, disagree, or disagree strongly with the following statement? "Having a job is the best way for a woman to be an independent person"*

Agree strongly/Agree (%)

	1981	1990	1995	2000	Change
Albania					
Algeria					
Argentina		63			
Armenia					
Australia					
Austria		74			
Azerbaijan					
Bangladesh					
Belarus				58	
Belgium		70		77	7
Bosnia and Herz.					
Brazil		74			
Bulgaria		63		79	16
Canada		55			
Chile		72			
China		75			
Colombia					
Croatia				79	
Czech Republic		59		76	17
Denmark		80		84	4
Dominican Rep.					
Egypt					
El Salvador					
Estonia		56		79	23
Finland		77		63	–14
France		79		84	5
Georgia					
Germany (East)		75		87	12
Germany (West)		75		80	5
Great Britain		68		65	–3
Greece				83	
Hungary		48		72	24
Iceland		43		46	3
India		58			
Indonesia					
Iran					
Iraq					
Ireland		61			
Israel					
Italy		74		77	3
Japan		78			
Jordan					
Korea Republic		34			
Kyrgyzstan					
Latvia		62		85	23
Lithuania		41		77	36
Luxembourg				84	
Macedonia					
Malta		39		45	6
Mexico		62			
Moldova					
Montenegro					
Morocco					
Netherlands		55		61	6
New Zealand					
Nigeria		61			
Northern Ireland		70			
Norway		75			
Pakistan					
Peru					
Philippines					
Poland		64		76	12
Portugal		80		79	–1
Puerto Rico					
Romania		68		81	13
Russian Fed.		58		70	12
Saudi Arabia					
Serbia					
Singapore					
Slovakia		60		75	15
Slovenia		73		79	6
South Africa					
Spain		78		81	3
Sweden		74		84	10
Switzerland					
Taiwan					
Tanzania					
Turkey					
Uganda					
Ukraine				73	
Uruguay					
USA		60			
Venezuela					
Vietnam					
Zimbabwe					

Be Willing to Fight in War for your Country

(E012) *Of course, we all hope that there will not be another war, but if it were to come to that, would you be willing to fight for your country?*

Yes (%)

	1981	1990	1995	2000	Change
Albania			81	72	–9
Algeria					
Argentina	60	63	66	65	5
Armenia			80		
Australia	75		75		0
Austria		67		55	–12
Azerbaijan			97		
Bangladesh			89	96	7
Belarus		92	88	84	–8
Belgium	34	41			7
Bosnia and Herz.			82	74	–8
Brazil		36	72		36
Bulgaria		91	74		–17
Canada	64	68		67	3
Chile		83	74	60	–23
China		97	93	97	0
Colombia					
Croatia			80	84	4
Czech Republic		81	54		–27
Denmark	73	89			16
Dominican Rep.			79		
Egypt					
El Salvador			69		
Estonia		92	75		–17
Finland		88	84	87	–1
France	48	66		58	10
Georgia			72		
Germany (East)		54	50	41	–13
Germany (West)	46	42	49	48	2
Great Britain	70	75			5
Greece					
Hungary	87	77	69		–18
Iceland	74	77			3
India		92	94	82	–10
Indonesia					
Iran					
Iraq				37	
Ireland	62	61			–1
Israel				80	
Italy	33	31		60	27
Japan	34	20	23	25	–9
Jordan					
Korea Republic	92	87	82	75	–17
Kyrgyzstan				87	
Latvia		97	68		–29
Lithuania		84	68	72	–12
Luxembourg				54	
Macedonia			83	80	–3
Malta	80	63			–17
Mexico		74	71	74	0
Moldova			80	85	5
Montenegro			90	65	–25
Morocco				94	
Netherlands	56	68			12
New Zealand			65		
Nigeria		80	67		–13
Northern Ireland	58	61			3
Norway	90	91	89		–1
Pakistan					
Peru			90	81	–9
Philippines			88	87	–1
Poland		91	83		–8
Portugal		68			
Puerto Rico			67	76	9
Romania		92	86	84	–8
Russian Fed.		84	82	77	–7
Saudi Arabia					
Serbia			84	72	–12
Singapore				85	
Slovakia		75	64		–11
Slovenia		95	90	85	–10
South Africa		70	69	68	–2
Spain	66	60	59	43	–23
Sweden	87	89	92		5
Switzerland		78	69		–9
Taiwan			86		
Tanzania				93	
Turkey		93	96		3
Uganda				65	
Ukraine			84	74	–10
Uruguay			57		
USA	75	79	77	73	–2
Venezuela			86	82	–4
Vietnam				98	
Zimbabwe				54	

Less Emphasis on Money

(E014) *I'm going to read out a list of various changes in our way of life that might take place in the near future. If it were to happen, do you think it would be a good thing, a bad thing, or don't you mind? Less emphasis on money*

Good (%)

	1981	1990	1995	2000	Change
Albania			21	37	16
Algeria				40	
Argentina	78	71	69	64	–14
Armenia			59		
Australia	64		69		5
Austria		54		50	–4
Azerbaijan			64		
Bangladesh			30	36	6
Belarus		60	45	48	–12
Belgium	64	65		67	3
Bosnia and Herz.			47	54	7
Brazil		62	65		3
Bulgaria		61	43	58	–3
Canada	66	62		65	–1
Chile		60	59	65	5
China		67	46	47	–20
Colombia			59		
Croatia			46	77	31
Czech Republic		44	68	49	5
Denmark	71	78		70	–1
Dominican Rep.			52		
Egypt				56	
El Salvador			42		
Estonia			46	54	8
Finland		71	55	66	–5
France	73	71		71	–2
Georgia			70		
Germany (East)		47	63	53	6
Germany (West)	57	51	58	54	–3
Great Britain	62	64	65	66	4
Greece				78	
Hungary	39	44	72	45	6
Iceland	62	59		61	–1
India		43	35	43	0
Indonesia				27	
Iran				56	
Iraq					
Ireland	74	73		70	–4
Israel				75	
Italy	69	72		71	2
Japan	34	41	48	39	5
Jordan				59	
Korea Republic	68	63	46	53	–15
Kyrgyzstan				61	
Latvia			48	32	–16
Lithuania		33	37	46	13
Luxembourg				71	
Macedonia			55	52	–3
Malta	65	76		81	16
Mexico		68	59	58	–10
Moldova			34	46	12
Montenegro			52	52	0
Morocco				66	
Netherlands	63	62		60	–3
New Zealand			56		
Nigeria		64	53	63	–1
Northern Ireland	67	60		72	5
Norway	64	60	61		–3
Pakistan				70	
Peru			43	49	6
Philippines			39	49	10
Poland		61	59	60	–1
Portugal		64		57	–7
Puerto Rico			51	62	11
Romania			51	65	14
Russian Fed.		41	49	45	4
Saudi Arabia				56	
Serbia			47	51	4
Singapore				38	
Slovakia		25	59	61	36
Slovenia		50	49	63	13
South Africa		45	29	35	–10
Spain	78	81	74	76	–2
Sweden	65	66	74	67	2
Switzerland		82	68		–14
Taiwan			52		
Tanzania				60	
Turkey		56	64	70	14
Uganda				25	
Ukraine			49	44	–5
Uruguay			75		
USA	68	71	69	65	–3
Venezuela			52	48	–4
Vietnam				58	
Zimbabwe				28	

Less Importance Placed on Work

(E015) *I'm going to read out a list of various changes in our way of life that might take place in the near future. If it were to happen, do you think it would be a good thing, a bad thing, or don't you mind? Less importance placed on work in our lives*

Good (%)

	1981	1990	1995	2000	Change
Albania			6	10	4
Algeria				9	
Argentina	40	20	22	20	–20
Armenia			22		
Australia	29		32		3
Austria		23		30	7
Azerbaijan			30		
Bangladesh			2	7	5
Belarus		28	18	20	–8
Belgium	30	42		46	16
Bosnia and Herz.			16	14	–2
Brazil		19	22		3
Bulgaria		41	19	36	–5
Canada	25	31		33	8
Chile		18	23	35	17
China		8	19	17	9
Colombia			12		
Croatia			10	33	23
Czech Republic		8	7	10	2
Denmark	27	27		33	6
Dominican Rep.			10		
Egypt				2	
El Salvador			18		
Estonia			14	13	–1
Finland		24	19	25	1
France	61	35		65	4
Georgia			38		
Germany (East)		14	25	31	17
Germany (West)	30	35	32	42	12
Great Britain	26	32		53	27
Greece				30	
Hungary	11	25	39	20	9
Iceland	31	33		43	12
India		7	10	14	7
Indonesia				5	
Iran				16	
Iraq					
Ireland	22	22		37	15
Israel				34	
Italy	23	25		25	2
Japan	4	6	7	5	1
Jordan				27	
Korea Republic	11	16	17	11	0

	1981	1990	1995	2000	Change
Kyrgyzstan				15	
Latvia			14	9	–5
Lithuania		12	15	13	1
Luxembourg				47	
Macedonia			19	24	5
Malta	21	44		31	10
Mexico		28	18	29	1
Moldova			14	24	10
Montenegro			18	20	2
Morocco				43	
Netherlands	26	35		38	12
New Zealand			28		
Nigeria		14	23	34	20
Northern Ireland	19	22		42	23
Norway	12	16	26		14
Pakistan				10	
Peru			18	13	–5
Philippines			24	33	9
Poland		22	21	16	–6
Portugal		38		20	–18
Puerto Rico			23	32	9
Romania			20	19	–1
Russian Fed.		26	15	16	–10
Saudi Arabia				31	
Serbia			12	14	2
Singapore				29	
Slovakia		5	8	8	3
Slovenia		12	16	20	8
South Africa		14	19	21	7
Spain	39	52	37	45	6
Sweden	15	27	38	51	36
Switzerland		46	39		–7
Taiwan			12		
Tanzania				6	
Turkey		16	14	26	10
Uganda				9	
Ukraine			22	21	–1
Uruguay			15		
USA	22	23	28	33	11
Venezuela			16	21	5
Vietnam				28	
Zimbabwe				11	

More Emphasis on Technology

(E016) *I'm going to read out a list of various changes in our way of life that might take place in the near future. If it were to happen, do you think it would be a good thing, a bad thing, or don't you mind? More emphasis on the development of technology*

Good (%)

	1981	1990	1995	2000	Change
Albania			80	61	–19
Algeria				87	
Argentina	67	78	67	68	1
Armenia			83		
Australia	58		58		0
Austria		43		57	14
Azerbaijan			77		
Bangladesh			92	89	–3
Belarus		84	83	82	–2
Belgium	50	55		56	6
Bosnia and Herz.			73	70	–3
Brazil		78	70		–8
Bulgaria		81	67	84	3
Canada	59	63		58	–1
Chile		73	51	56	–17
China		95	92	97	2
Colombia			83		
Croatia			63	79	16
Czech Republic		84	68	76	–8
Denmark	36	59		62	26
Dominican Rep.			51		
Egypt				89	
El Salvador			72		
Estonia		84	77	75	–9
Finland		68	45	55	–13
France	67	76		58	–9
Georgia			82		
Germany (East)		83	61	63	–20
Germany (West)	56	52	51	63	7
Great Britain	62	64	71	70	8
Greece				52	
Hungary	84	75	70	59	–25
Iceland	75	69		85	10
India		85	55	57	–28
Indonesia				63	
Iran				80	
Iraq					
Ireland	63	61		70	7
Israel				78	
Italy	62	60		65	3
Japan	66	65	66	61	–5
Jordan				95	
Korea Republic	88	90	67	69	–19

	1981	1990	1995	2000	Change
Kyrgyzstan				79	
Latvia		81	71	87	6
Lithuania		88	72	79	–9
Luxembourg				65	
Macedonia			71	65	–6
Malta	73	75		88	15
Mexico		78	64	76	–2
Moldova			80	77	–3
Montenegro			76	76	0
Morocco				93	
Netherlands	34	49		48	14
New Zealand			38		
Nigeria		96	82	86	–10
Northern Ireland	60	60		62	2
Norway	41	47	46		5
Pakistan				77	
Peru			79	78	–1
Philippines			82	68	–14
Poland		90	81	79	–11
Portugal		74		71	–3
Puerto Rico			75	80	5
Romania			76	85	9
Russian Fed.		84	89	88	4
Saudi Arabia				77	
Serbia			82	81	–1
Singapore				67	
Slovakia		75	65	79	4
Slovenia		87	75	79	–8
South Africa		82	68	62	–20
Spain	62	62	57	60	–2
Sweden	34	35	34	35	1
Switzerland		56	34		–22
Taiwan			93		
Tanzania				90	
Turkey		90	94	90	0
Uganda				69	
Ukraine			76	90	14
Uruguay			63		
USA	67	70	53	57	–10
Venezuela			86	87	1
Vietnam				78	
Zimbabwe				76	

More Emphasis on Individual

(E017) *Here is a list of various changes in our way of life that might take place in the near future. If it were to happen, do you think it would be a good thing, a bad thing, or don't you mind? Greater emphasis on the development of the individual*

Good (%)

	1981	1990	1995	2000	Change
Albania					
Algeria					
Argentina		95			
Armenia					
Australia					
Austria		76		89	13
Azerbaijan					
Bangladesh					
Belarus				87	
Belgium	76	81		86	10
Bosnia and Herz.					
Brazil		92			
Bulgaria		87		92	5
Canada	83	85			2
Chile		90			
China		40			
Colombia					
Croatia				75	
Czech Republic		88		88	0
Denmark	87	93		93	6
Dominican Rep.					
Egypt					
El Salvador					
Estonia		85		83	–2
Finland		93		90	–3
France	88	88		87	–1
Georgia					
Germany (East)		88		87	–1
Germany (West)	77	85		90	13
Great Britain	71	77		75	4
Greece				93	
Hungary		72		71	–1
Iceland	97	94		96	–1
India		71			
Indonesia					
Iran					
Iraq					
Ireland	83	89		91	8
Israel					
Italy	91	93		92	1
Japan		70			
Jordan					
Korea Republic		84			
Kyrgyzstan					
Latvia		86		90	4
Lithuania		91		87	–4
Luxembourg				78	
Macedonia					
Malta	82	87		96	14
Mexico		88			
Moldova					
Montenegro					
Morocco					
Netherlands	75	83		86	11
New Zealand					
Nigeria		93			
Northern Ireland	73	81		83	10
Norway	89	88			–1
Pakistan					
Peru					
Philippines					
Poland		90		87	–3
Portugal		76		79	3
Puerto Rico					
Romania				90	
Russian Fed.		89		92	3
Saudi Arabia					
Serbia					
Singapore					
Slovakia		80		86	6
Slovenia		81			
South Africa		90			
Spain	84	89		86	2
Sweden	83	88		90	7
Switzerland		91			
Taiwan					
Tanzania					
Turkey				95	
Uganda					
Ukraine				94	
Uruguay					
USA	87	87			0
Venezuela					
Vietnam					
Zimbabwe					

Greater respect for Authority

(E018) *I'm going to read out a list of various changes in our way of life that might take place in the near future. If it were to happen, do you think it would be a good thing, a bad thing, or don't you mind? Greater respect for authority*

Good (%)

	1981	1990	1995	2000	Change
Albania			41	34	–7
Algeria				63	
Argentina	61	69	64	72	11
Armenia			63		
Australia	68		73		5
Austria		47		39	–8
Azerbaijan			61		
Bangladesh			87	92	5
Belarus		71	68	72	1
Belgium	61	50		63	2
Bosnia and Herz.			43	26	–17
Brazil		81	83		2
Bulgaria		78	57	69	–9
Canada	77	64		66	–11
Chile		80	53	56	–24
China		24	41	64	40
Colombia			89		
Croatia			23	56	33
Czech Republic		62	47	52	–10
Denmark	40	35		38	–2
Dominican Rep.			56		
Egypt				86	
El Salvador			86		
Estonia			45	44	–1
Finland		26	27	39	13
France	60	59		69	9
Georgia			75		
Germany (East)		59	39	58	–1
Germany (West)	44	30	24	43	–1
Great Britain	74	72	81	71	–3
Greece				17	
Hungary	72	61	58	69	–3
Iceland	49	42		47	–2
India		54	33	43	–11
Indonesia				37	
Iran				71	
Iraq					
Ireland	85	82		77	–8
Israel				59	
Italy	64	49		51	–13
Japan	7	5	5	4	–3
Jordan				90	
Korea Republic	10	14	16	19	9
Kyrgyzstan				51	
Latvia			30	49	19
Lithuania		53	39	44	–9
Luxembourg				53	
Macedonia			44	48	4
Malta	93	95		92	–1
Mexico		65	62	76	11
Moldova			60	48	–12
Montenegro			62	45	–17
Morocco				89	
Netherlands	60	53		67	7
New Zealand			53		
Nigeria		91	79	83	–8
Northern Ireland	87	82		77	–10
Norway	38	32	32		–6
Pakistan				62	
Peru			71	80	9
Philippines			76	70	–6
Poland		73	58	55	–18
Portugal		74		78	4
Puerto Rico			93	94	1
Romania			58	84	26
Russian Fed.		68	63	56	–12
Saudi Arabia				73	
Serbia			53	54	1
Singapore				52	
Slovakia		54	42	68	14
Slovenia		66	36	43	–23
South Africa		88	80	73	–15
Spain	76	68	72	59	–17
Sweden	31	22	21	22	–9
Switzerland		46	31		–15
Taiwan			45		
Tanzania				82	
Turkey		64	72	68	4
Uganda				73	
Ukraine			62	64	2
Uruguay			58		
USA	86	78	76	70	–16
Venezuela			89	91	2
Vietnam				80	
Zimbabwe				90	

More Emphasis on Family Life

(E019) *I'm going to read out a list of various changes in our way of life that might take place in the near future. If it were to happen, do you think it would be a good thing, a bad thing, or don't you mind? More emphasis on family life*

Good (%)

	1981	1990	1995	2000	Change
Albania			97	96	–1
Algeria				96	
Argentina	88	96	96	97	9
Armenia			92		
Australia	90		95		5
Austria		92		92	0
Azerbaijan			95		
Bangladesh			89	92	3
Belarus		95	93	91	–4
Belgium	84	85		90	6
Bosnia and Herz.			84	82	–2
Brazil		98	98		0
Bulgaria		90	87	95	5
Canada	91	94		94	3
Chile		97	85	92	–5
China		74	85	92	18
Colombia			99		
Croatia			85	93	8
Czech Republic		94	92	93	–1
Denmark	90	94		95	5
Dominican Rep.			75		
Egypt				99	
El Salvador			95		
Estonia		86	96	89	3
Finland		96	93	95	–1
France	90	90		91	1
Georgia			94		
Germany (East)		92	91	86	–6
Germany (West)	85	87	83	91	6
Great Britain	84	88		90	6
Greece				91	
Hungary	96	94	98	92	–4
Iceland	95	96		96	1
India		75	54	75	0
Indonesia				83	
Iran				91	
Iraq					
Ireland	91	94		95	4
Israel				93	
Italy	89	93		92	3
Japan	80	85	90	89	9
Jordan				98	
Korea Republic	91	89	86	93	2
Kyrgyzstan				93	
Latvia		85	87	92	7
Lithuania		96	92	97	1
Luxembourg				88	
Macedonia			76	82	6
Malta	95	90		99	4
Mexico		91	80	91	0
Moldova			92	87	–5
Montenegro			95	95	0
Morocco				99	
Netherlands	72	67		68	–4
New Zealand			90		
Nigeria		92	87	94	2
Northern Ireland	89	92		91	2
Norway	93	95	95		2
Pakistan				89	
Peru			94	95	1
Philippines			95	92	–3
Poland		97	94	95	–2
Portugal		95		91	–4
Puerto Rico			98	95	–3
Romania			93	95	2
Russian Fed.		95	96	93	–2
Saudi Arabia				90	
Serbia			93	95	2
Singapore				93	
Slovakia		91	92	95	4
Slovenia		91	90	96	5
South Africa		94	89	79	–15
Spain	84	89	91	88	4
Sweden	84	85	87	78	–6
Switzerland		91	89		–2
Taiwan			96		
Tanzania				95	
Turkey		95	97	97	2
Uganda				80	
Ukraine			90	91	1
Uruguay			94		
USA	95	95	93	94	–1
Venezuela			98	97	–1
Vietnam				88	
Zimbabwe				96	

A Simple and More Natural Lifestyle

(E020) *Here is a list of various changes in our way of life that might take place in the near future. If it were to happen, do you think it would be a good thing, a bad thing, or don't you mind? A simple and more natural lifestyle*

Good (%)

	1981	1990	1995	2000	Change
Albania					
Algeria					
Argentina		92			
Armenia					
Australia					
Austria		84		82	–2
Azerbaijan					
Bangladesh					
Belarus				80	
Belgium	83	84		85	2
Bosnia and Herz.					
Brazil		93			
Bulgaria		82		79	–3
Canada	84	84			0
Chile		93			
China		51			
Colombia					
Croatia				97	
Czech Republic		84		82	–2
Denmark	82	85		81	–1
Dominican Rep.					
Egypt					
El Salvador					
Estonia		84		86	2
Finland		91		80	–11
France	95	92		94	–1
Georgia					
Germany (East)		64		67	3
Germany (West)	69	63		72	3
Great Britain	76	79		75	–1
Greece				94	
Hungary		85		84	–1
Iceland	79	79		78	–1
India		80			
Indonesia					
Iran					
Iraq					
Ireland	87	87		82	–5
Israel					
Italy	92	93		89	–3
Japan		76			
Jordan					
Korea Republic		66			

	1981	1990	1995	2000	Change
Kyrgyzstan					
Latvia		80		81	1
Lithuania		89		90	1
Luxembourg				85	
Macedonia					
Malta	90	87		96	6
Mexico		83			
Moldova					
Montenegro					
Morocco					
Netherlands	78	76		67	–11
New Zealand					
Nigeria		90			
Northern Ireland	73	86		75	2
Norway	80	80			0
Pakistan					
Peru					
Philippines					
Poland		89		86	–3
Portugal		92		81	–11
Puerto Rico					
Romania				84	
Russian Fed.		89		59	–30
Saudi Arabia					
Serbia					
Singapore					
Slovakia		82		88	6
Slovenia		90		92	2
South Africa		86			
Spain	87	92		90	3
Sweden	92	90		84	–8
Switzerland		90			
Taiwan					
Tanzania					
Turkey				67	
Uganda					
Ukraine				64	
Uruguay					
USA	83	85			2
Venezuela					
Vietnam					
Zimbabwe					

Opinion about Scientific Advance

(E022) *In the long run, do you think the scientific advances we are making will help or harm mankind?*

Will help (%)

	1981	1990	1995	2000	Change
Albania			65	55	–10
Algeria				55	
Argentina	41	47	49	51	10
Armenia			74		
Australia	47		57		10
Austria		31		35	4
Azerbaijan			61		
Bangladesh			77	70	–7
Belarus		38	66	56	18
Belgium	29	34			5
Bosnia and Herz.			60	54	–6
Brazil		64	66		2
Bulgaria		62	64		2
Canada	46	55		52	6
Chile		43	35	42	–1
China		58	80	80	22
Colombia			67		
Croatia			50	38	–12
Czech Republic		45	48		3
Denmark	34	43			9
Dominican Rep.			45		
Egypt				80	
El Salvador			49		
Estonia		52	69		17
Finland		42	51		9
France	39	42			3
Georgia			70		
Germany (East)		54	50	48	–6
Germany (West)	35	39	53	52	17
Great Britain	50	48		40	–10
Greece					
Hungary	65	55	53		–12
Iceland	55	54		66	11
India		51	50	59	8
Indonesia				50	
Iran				73	
Iraq					
Ireland	42	40		40	–2
Israel					
Italy	40	37		31	–9
Japan	25	26	27	24	–1
Jordan				68	
Korea Republic	57	40	30	49	–8
Kyrgyzstan				58	
Latvia		34	59		25
Lithuania		61	70	62	1
Luxembourg					
Macedonia			68	65	–3
Malta	42	58			16
Mexico		44	39	50	6
Moldova			75	55	–20
Montenegro			47	44	–3
Morocco				78	
Netherlands	25	37			12
New Zealand			27		
Nigeria		79	74	87	8
Northern Ireland	39	46		38	–1
Norway	35	36	39		4
Pakistan				41	
Peru			48	54	6
Philippines			45	68	23
Poland		70	72		2
Portugal		47			
Puerto Rico			43	47	4
Romania		57	50		–7
Russian Fed.		60	67		7
Saudi Arabia				65	
Serbia			58	45	–13
Singapore				39	
Slovakia		45	55		10
Slovenia		41	41	34	–7
South Africa		57	61	57	0
Spain	47	45	48	66	19
Sweden	36	47	47	44	8
Switzerland			40		
Taiwan			36		
Tanzania				49	
Turkey		72	82	86	14
Uganda				58	
Ukraine			55		
Uruguay			42		
USA	57	63	62	56	–1
Venezuela			72	63	–9
Vietnam				78	
Zimbabwe				72	

INTERESTED IN POLITICS

(E023) *How interested would you say you are in politics?*

Very/Somewhat interested (%)

	1981	1990	1995	2000	Change
Albania			37	40	3
Algeria				24	
Argentina	43	30	26	18	–25
Armenia			52		
Australia			56		
Austria		54		67	13
Azerbaijan			43		
Bangladesh			51	41	–10
Belarus			56	46	–10
Belgium		30		39	9
Bosnia and Herz.			49	39	–10
Brazil		46	31		–15
Bulgaria		73	43	49	–24
Canada		58		48	–10
Chile		37	21	25	–12
China		67		71	4
Colombia			29		
Croatia			42		
Czech Republic		82	56	70	–12
Denmark		54		60	6
Dominican Rep.			46		
Egypt				43	
El Salvador			15		
Estonia		60	49		–11
Finland		47	39	28	–19
France		38		37	–1
Georgia			50		
Germany (East)		84	76	67	–17
Germany (West)		69	78	59	–10
Great Britain		49		37	–12
Greece				42	
Hungary	66	52	50		–16
Iceland		47		50	3
India		47	39	45	–2
Indonesia				37	
Iran				56	
Iraq				53	
Ireland		37		43	6
Israel				70	
Italy		29		32	3
Japan	56	62	55	64	8
Jordan				51	
Korea Republic	48	73	62	50	2

	1981	1990	1995	2000	Change
Kyrgyzstan				48	
Latvia		79	52		–27
Lithuania		74	44	46	–28
Luxembourg				47	
Macedonia			34	46	12
Malta		37			
Mexico		38	44	34	–4
Moldova			35	48	13
Montenegro			39	45	6
Morocco				20	
Netherlands		63		66	3
New Zealand			60		
Nigeria		35	37	53	18
Northern Ireland		34		40	6
Norway		72	69		–3
Pakistan				30	
Peru			33	48	15
Philippines			49	50	1
Poland		49	42	42	–7
Portugal		31		29	–2
Puerto Rico			40	42	2
Romania		18	40		22
Russian Fed.		53	35	39	–14
Saudi Arabia				66	
Serbia			37	39	2
Singapore				36	
Slovakia		63	58		–5
Slovenia		57	44	42	–15
South Africa		56	50	51	–5
Spain		26	26	28	2
Sweden		47	51		4
Switzerland		66	43		–23
Taiwan			41		
Tanzania				72	
Turkey		48	59	40	–8
Uganda				50	
Ukraine			41	42	1
Uruguay			37		
USA		61	63	65	4
Venezuela			20	24	4
Vietnam				80	
Zimbabwe				31	

POLITICAL ACTION: SIGNING A PETITION

(E025) *I'd like you to tell me, for each one, whether you have actually done any of these things, whether you might do it or would never, under any circumstances, do it. Signing a petition*

Might do (%)

	1981	1990	1995	2000	Change
Albania			33	43	10
Algeria				29	
Argentina	38	33	38	31	–7
Armenia			39		
Australia	25		16		–9
Austria		31		24	–7
Azerbaijan			16		
Bangladesh			39	42	3
Belarus		52	28	28	–24
Belgium	38	27		20	–18
Bosnia and Herz.			53	50	–3
Brazil		30	35		5
Bulgaria		39	42	37	–2
Canada	26	15		19	–7
Chile		34	39	27	–7
China					
Colombia			49		
Croatia			42	59	17
Czech Republic		32	54	27	–5
Denmark	29	25		27	–2
Dominican Rep.			58		
Egypt				37	
El Salvador			41		
Estonia		38	42	33	–5
Finland		46	38	37	–9
France	31	29		22	–9
Georgia			15		
Germany (East)		26	36	30	4
Germany (West)	37	31	30	36	–1
Great Britain	27	17	34	15	–12
Greece				38	
Hungary		30	50	32	2
Iceland	47	37		37	–10
India		45	44	29	–16
Indonesia				21	
Iran					
Iraq					
Ireland	47	40		27	–20
Israel				30	
Italy	32	35		30	–2
Japan	34	25	31	30	–4
Jordan				9	
Korea Republic	51	42	43	37	–14

	1981	1990	1995	2000	Change
Kyrgyzstan				25	
Latvia		23	40	33	10
Lithuania		29	34	39	10
Luxembourg				32	
Macedonia			56	40	–16
Malta	34	26		36	2
Mexico		44	48	38	–6
Moldova			34	22	–12
Montenegro			40	51	11
Morocco				34	
Netherlands	40	31		30	–10
New Zealand			8		
Nigeria		32	32	27	–5
Northern Ireland	43	27		21	–22
Norway	27	28	26		–1
Pakistan				24	
Peru			43	59	16
Philippines			19	23	4
Poland		42	41	28	–14
Portugal		46		39	–7
Puerto Rico			44	44	0
Romania			46	36	–10
Russian Fed.		44	37	32	–12
Saudi Arabia					
Serbia			39	37	–2
Singapore				40	
Slovakia		38	42	23	–15
Slovenia		34	48	44	10
South Africa		47	41	43	–4
Spain	44	38	36	37	–7
Sweden	37	24	23	10	–27
Switzerland		17	18		1
Taiwan			36		
Tanzania				47	
Turkey		41	41	42	1
Uganda				43	
Ukraine			34	35	1
Uruguay			30		
USA	24	20	19	16	–8
Venezuela			33	68	35
Vietnam				46	
Zimbabwe				34	

Political Action: Joining in Boycotts

(E026) *I'd like you to tell me, for each one, whether you have actually done any of these things, whether you might do it or would never, under any circumstances, do it. Joining in boycotts*

Might do (%)

	1981	1990	1995	2000	Change
Albania			19	23	4
Algeria				30	
Argentina	20	9	11	7	–13
Armenia			22		
Australia	39		43		4
Austria		25		34	9
Azerbaijan			12		
Bangladesh			30	40	10
Belarus		38	19	21	–17
Belgium	24	28		30	6
Bosnia and Herz.			52	45	–7
Brazil		36	29		–7
Bulgaria		33	23	27	–6
Canada	44	43		42	–2
Chile		11	13	13	2
China					
Colombia			29		
Croatia			55	57	2
Czech Republic		30	53	30	0
Denmark	28	32		37	9
Dominican Rep.			26		
Egypt				30	
El Salvador					
Estonia		40	34	27	–13
Finland		69	52	54	–15
France	35	40		43	8
Georgia			9		
Germany (East)		31	46	40	9
Germany (West)	31	37	56	42	11
Great Britain	30	34		44	14
Greece				22	
Hungary		14	39	18	4
Iceland	57	53		59	2
India		44	48	27	–17
Indonesia				20	
Iran					
Iraq					
Ireland	33	33		35	2
Israel				32	
Italy	28	46		44	16
Japan	54	53	66	64	10
Jordan				6	
Korea Republic	48	50	59	62	14
Kyrgyzstan				17	
Latvia		37	42	27	–10
Lithuania		60	37	37	–23
Luxembourg				39	
Macedonia			52	40	–12
Malta	17	21		28	11
Mexico		35	32	18	–17
Moldova			14	13	–1
Montenegro			36	56	20
Morocco				28	
Netherlands	29	33		38	9
New Zealand			57		
Nigeria		25	27	23	–2
Northern Ireland	36	29		26	–10
Norway	38	52	56		18
Pakistan				5	
Peru			14	41	27
Philippines			13	12	–1
Poland		28	22	24	–4
Portugal		31		33	2
Puerto Rico			25	27	2
Romania			17	17	0
Russian Fed.		36	22	22	–14
Saudi Arabia					
Serbia			35	34	–1
Singapore				18	
Slovakia		37	42	29	–8
Slovenia		46	49	54	8
South Africa		36	34	29	–7
Spain	28	25	22	23	–5
Sweden	52	62	49	55	3
Switzerland			34		
Taiwan			33		
Tanzania				23	
Turkey		23	19	28	5
Uganda				37	
Ukraine			19	25	6
Uruguay			18		
USA	35	45	44	51	16
Venezuela			15	6	–9
Vietnam				16	
Zimbabwe				29	

Political Action: Attending Lawful Demonstrations

(E027) *I'd like you to tell me, for each one, whether you have actually done any of these things, whether you might do it or would never, under any circumstances, do it. Attending lawful demonstrations*

Might do (%)

	1981	1990	1995	2000	Change
Albania			60	52	–8
Algeria				30	
Argentina	33	21	26	23	–10
Armenia			28		
Australia	34		42		8
Austria		34		36	2
Azerbaijan			22		
Bangladesh			38	40	2
Belarus		55	31	29	–26
Belgium	32	29		31	–1
Bosnia and Herz.			58	49	–9
Brazil		40	38		–2
Bulgaria		48	41	38	–10
Canada	44	43		41	–3
Chile		24	29	23	–1
China					
Colombia			42		
Croatia			57	64	7
Czech Republic		46	53	42	–4
Denmark	35	32		39	4
Dominican Rep.			53		
Egypt				15	
El Salvador			14		
Estonia		42	40	31	–11
Finland		53	44	44	–9
France	28	32		34	6
Georgia			15		
Germany (East)		35	56	33	–2
Germany (West)	34	42	49	44	10
Great Britain	32	35		39	7
Greece				38	
Hungary		27	41	29	2
Iceland	63	52		59	–4
India		43	46	29	–14
Indonesia				25	
Iran					
Iraq					
Ireland	40	42		44	4
Israel				31	
Italy	22	37		39	17
Japan	28	25	40	37	9
Jordan				6	
Korea Republic	36	33	37	45	9
Kyrgyzstan				37	
Latvia		42	42	37	–5
Lithuania		51	45	48	–3
Luxembourg				43	
Macedonia			51	43	–8
Malta	20	17		22	2
Mexico		43	47	10	–33
Moldova			43	27	–16
Montenegro			46	47	1
Morocco				29	
Netherlands	32	39		37	5
New Zealand			53		
Nigeria		30	32	35	5
Northern Ireland	28	31		30	2
Norway	44	56	52		8
Pakistan				7	
Peru			33	51	18
Philippines			18	14	–4
Poland		43	34	31	–12
Portugal		49		39	–10
Puerto Rico			42	38	–4
Romania			50	41	–9
Russian Fed.		42	33	33	–9
Saudi Arabia					
Serbia			40	33	–7
Singapore				23	
Slovakia		54	44	43	–11
Slovenia		50	53	58	8
South Africa		41	38	32	–9
Spain	36	38	35	37	1
Sweden	51	59	48	53	2
Switzerland		20	33		13
Taiwan			36		
Tanzania				56	
Turkey		32	29	35	3
Uganda				36	
Ukraine			34	34	0
Uruguay			16		
USA	38	44	43	54	16
Venezuela			26	34	8
Vietnam				38	
Zimbabwe				37	

Political Action: Joining Unofficial Strikes

(E028) *I'd like you to tell me, for each one, whether you have actually done any of these things, whether you might do it or would never, under any circumstances, do it. Joining unofficial strikes*

Might do (%)

	1981	1990	1995	2000	Change
Albania			3	5	2
Algeria				8	
Argentina	15	11	10	10	–5
Armenia			19		
Australia	23		33		10
Austria		9		18	9
Azerbaijan			11		
Bangladesh			26	24	–2
Belarus		29	13	16	–13
Belgium	14	18		19	5
Bosnia and Herz.			47	31	–16
Brazil		19	15		–4
Bulgaria		25	32	21	–4
Canada	17	28		26	9
Chile		16	18	15	–1
China					
Colombia			18		
Croatia			41	37	–4
Czech Republic		32	31	29	–3
Denmark	23	23		31	8
Dominican Rep.			12		
Egypt				3	
El Salvador			6		
Estonia		19	20	12	–7
Finland		35	22	25	–10
France	23	25		32	9
Georgia			6		
Germany (East)		14	17	16	2
Germany (West)	12	14	26	16	4
Great Britain	16	19		28	12
Greece				33	
Hungary		27	21	10	–17
Iceland	25	20		30	5
India		16	20	18	2
Indonesia				6	
Iran					
Iraq					
Ireland	23	23		32	9
Israel				24	
Italy	9	18		16	7
Japan	14	13	21	19	5
Jordan				3	
Korea Republic	15		37	55	40

	1981	1990	1995	2000	Change
Kyrgyzstan				8	
Latvia		30	17	14	–16
Lithuania		50	28	24	–26
Luxembourg				23	
Macedonia			24	28	4
Malta	13	14		16	3
Mexico		36	33	12	–24
Moldova			11	23	12
Montenegro			29	31	2
Morocco				2	
Netherlands	13	21		28	15
New Zealand			35		
Nigeria		14	17	19	5
Northern Ireland	20	17		20	0
Norway	11	58	28		17
Pakistan				1	
Peru			15	15	0
Philippines			6	6	0
Poland		19	15	16	–3
Portugal		19		21	2
Puerto Rico			15	11	–4
Romania			22	8	–14
Russian Fed.		30	16	16	–14
Saudi Arabia					
Serbia			26	30	4
Singapore					
Slovakia		38	24	21	–17
Slovenia		8	30	33	25
South Africa		24	17	14	–10
Spain	20	19	15	21	1
Sweden	25	41	35	47	22
Switzerland		22	16		–6
Taiwan			12		
Tanzania				7	
Turkey		6	6	13	7
Uganda				22	
Ukraine			10	16	6
Uruguay			20		
USA	16	30	27	38	22
Venezuela			7	6	–1
Vietnam				10	
Zimbabwe				11	

Political Action: Occupying Buildings or Factories

(E029) *I'd like you to tell me, for each one, whether you have actually done any of these things, whether you might do it or would never, under any circumstances, do it. Occupying buildings or factories*

Might do (%)

	1981	1990	1995	2000	Change
Albania			2	2	0
Algeria				4	
Argentina	9	8	9	9	0
Armenia			12		
Australia	15		17		2
Austria		7		10	3
Azerbaijan			3		
Bangladesh			2	6	4
Belarus		12	5	4	–8
Belgium	17	21		26	9
Bosnia and Herz.			21	12	–9
Brazil		12	16		4
Bulgaria		14	20	14	0
Canada	15	21		18	3
Chile		11	12	10	–1
China					
Colombia			11		
Croatia			18	18	0
Czech Republic		17	13	10	–7
Denmark	9	7		12	3
Dominican Rep.			28		
Egypt				2	
El Salvador			5		
Estonia		7	7	5	–2
Finland		20	11	15	–5
France	22	25		35	13
Georgia			2		
Germany (East)		13	22	14	1
Germany (West)	11	10	25	14	3
Great Britain	10	10		16	6
Greece				27	
Hungary		4	9	4	0
Iceland	8	9		12	4
India		6	15	13	7
Indonesia				10	
Iran					
Iraq					
Ireland	15	19		17	2
Israel				7	
Italy	11	20		18	7
Japan	6	7	9	8	2
Jordan				1	
Korea Republic	10	37	21		11
Kyrgyzstan				6	
Latvia		5	7	4	–1
Lithuania		21	12	12	–9
Luxembourg				18	
Macedonia			15	16	1
Malta	6	11		13	7
Mexico		29	31	7	–22
Moldova			4	11	7
Montenegro			13	16	3
Morocco				5	
Netherlands	20	22		23	3
New Zealand			19		
Nigeria		11	24	33	22
Northern Ireland	8	8		10	2
Norway	4	10	10		6
Pakistan				0	
Peru			11	12	1
Philippines			11	6	–5
Poland		15	13	16	1
Portugal		11		22	11
Puerto Rico			5	7	2
Romania			10	6	–4
Russian Fed.		12	6	8	–4
Saudi Arabia					
Serbia			11	17	6
Singapore					
Slovakia		18	14	15	–3
Slovenia		12	26	24	12
South Africa		24	16	20	–4
Spain	13	19	14	16	3
Sweden	11	19	15	19	8
Switzerland			13		
Taiwan			5		
Tanzania				4	
Turkey		3	2	5	2
Uganda				45	
Ukraine			4	5	1
Uruguay			16		
USA	9	17	15	25	16
Venezuela			9	8	–1
Vietnam				22	
Zimbabwe				4	

Freedom or Equality

(E032) *Which of these two statements comes closest to your own opinion? A. personal freedom more important, or B. equality more important*

Freedom above equality (%)

	1981	1990	1995	2000	Change
Albania					
Algeria					
Argentina		58			
Armenia					
Australia					
Austria		65		56	–9
Azerbaijan					
Bangladesh					
Belarus				62	
Belgium	55	52		46	–9
Bosnia and Herz.					
Brazil		41			
Bulgaria		48		60	12
Canada	65	61			–4
Chile		53			
China		21			
Colombia					
Croatia				42	
Czech Republic		56		59	3
Denmark	58	62		69	11
Dominican Rep.					
Egypt					
El Salvador					
Estonia		71		55	–16
Finland		74		53	–21
France	58	53		50	–8
Georgia					
Germany (East)		50		47	–3
Germany (West)	39	66		65	26
Great Britain	72	65		60	–12
Greece					
Hungary		51		45	–6
Iceland	51	45		46	–5
India		45			
Indonesia					
Iran					
Iraq					
Ireland	51	45		48	–3
Israel					
Italy	46	46		40	–6
Japan		46			
Jordan					
Korea Republic		51			

	1981	1990	1995	2000	Change
Kyrgyzstan					
Latvia		58			
Lithuania		73		58	–15
Luxembourg				49	
Macedonia					
Malta	62	48		58	–4
Mexico		61			
Moldova					
Montenegro					
Morocco					
Netherlands	60	57		56	–4
New Zealand					
Nigeria		62			
Northern Ireland	68	64		47	–21
Norway	65	67			2
Pakistan					
Peru					
Philippines					
Poland		55		55	0
Portugal		42		49	7
Puerto Rico					
Romania		54			
Russian Fed.		45		47	2
Saudi Arabia					
Serbia					
Singapore					
Slovakia		50		63	13
Slovenia		42		46	4
South Africa		48			
Spain	41	45		49	8
Sweden	60	67		62	2
Switzerland		58			
Taiwan					
Tanzania					
Turkey				41	
Uganda					
Ukraine				53	
Uruguay					
USA	72	71			–1
Venezuela					
Vietnam					
Zimbabwe					

Self Positioning in Political Scale: Left

(E033) *In political matters, people talk of "the left" and "the right". How would you place your views on this scale, generally speaking?*

(%) Left (1 thru 4)

	1981	1990	1995	2000	Change
Albania			44	39	–5
Algeria				19	
Argentina	25	17	15	13	–12
Armenia			29		
Australia	19		23		4
Austria		18		20	2
Azerbaijan			25		
Bangladesh			17	8	–9
Belarus		60	22	15	–45
Belgium	19	27		25	6
Bosnia and Herz.			30	24	–6
Brazil		30	27		–3
Bulgaria		31	23	25	–6
Canada	12	16		21	9
Chile		30	24	31	1
China					
Colombia			10		
Croatia			27	19	–8
Czech Republic		19	24	21	2
Denmark	17	24		26	9
Dominican Rep.			19		
Egypt					
El Salvador			17		
Estonia			19	11	–8
Finland		21	25	24	3
France	37	42		39	2
Georgia			20		
Germany (East)		30	38	29	–1
Germany (West)	26				
Great Britain	21	24		26	5
Greece				34	
Hungary		18	29	23	5
Iceland	26	30		28	2
India		30	21	22	–8
Indonesia				9	
Iran				39	
Iraq					
Ireland	13	12		14	1
Israel				42	
Italy	46	41		32	–14
Japan	17	16	17	19	2
Jordan				17	
Korea Republic	21	13	34	32	11
Kyrgyzstan				20	
Latvia			22	13	–9
Lithuania			20	25	5
Luxembourg				26	
Macedonia			33	27	–6
Malta	19	8		13	–6
Mexico		21	22	16	–5
Moldova			33	31	–2
Montenegro					
Morocco				26	
Netherlands	32	31		36	4
New Zealand			23		
Nigeria		22	34	33	11
Northern Ireland	15	10		19	4
Norway	22	27	24		2
Pakistan				4	
Peru			14	21	7
Philippines			11	10	–1
Poland		16	23	27	11
Portugal		23		35	12
Puerto Rico			14	13	–1
Romania		18	29	18	0
Russian Fed.		33	26	30	–3
Saudi Arabia					
Serbia			37	26	–11
Singapore					
Slovakia		25	29	33	8
Slovenia		23	21	25	2
South Africa		39	33	26	–13
Spain	41	47	42	40	–1
Sweden	35	28	38	34	–1
Switzerland		23	28		5
Taiwan			4		
Tanzania				24	
Turkey		25	22	21	–4
Uganda				34	
Ukraine			26	27	1
Uruguay			28		
USA	19	17	17	18	–1
Venezuela			21	17	–4
Vietnam				2	
Zimbabwe				59	

Social Change: Radical

(E034) *On this card are three basic kinds of attitudes concerning the society we live in. Please choose the one which best describes your own opinion*

Our society must be radically changed by revolutionary action (%)

	1981	1990	1995	2000	Change
Albania			12	11	–1
Algeria				7	
Argentina	13	8	5	4	–9
Armenia			16		
Australia	5		6		1
Austria		2		2	0
Azerbaijan			24		
Bangladesh			11	13	2
Belarus		26	4	5	–21
Belgium	7	3			–4
Bosnia and Herz.			15	12	–3
Brazil		16	18		2
Bulgaria		22	7		–15
Canada	5	5		7	2
Chile		5	6	8	3
China		5			
Colombia			7		
Croatia			5		
Czech Republic		18	5	6	–12
Denmark	4	2			–2
Dominican Rep.			13		
Egypt				5	
El Salvador			6		
Estonia		22	3		–19
Finland		3	2		–1
France	8	4			–4
Georgia			10		
Germany (East)		4	3		–1
Germany (West)	2				
Great Britain	5	5			0
Greece					
Hungary		6	2		–4
Iceland	2	3			1
India		14	15	14	0
Indonesia				5	
Iran					
Iraq					
Ireland	4	4			0
Israel					
Italy	7	7		4	–3
Japan	3	2	4	5	2
Jordan				9	
Korea Republic	22	7	13	10	–12
Kyrgyzstan				15	
Latvia		31	11		–20
Lithuania		32	10	23	–9
Luxembourg					
Macedonia			12	15	3
Malta	1	15			14
Mexico		17	14	16	–1
Moldova			10	28	18
Montenegro					
Morocco				6	
Netherlands	3	2			–1
New Zealand			5		
Nigeria		28	29	31	3
Northern Ireland	1	5			4
Norway	2	2	3		1
Pakistan			27	20	–7
Peru			8	6	–2
Philippines			23	21	–2
Poland		19	9		–10
Portugal		4			
Puerto Rico			4	4	0
Romania			8		
Russian Fed.		17	11	15	–2
Saudi Arabia				23	
Serbia			12	9	–3
Singapore					
Slovakia		17	3		–14
Slovenia		14	7	7	–7
South Africa		19	13	20	1
Spain	8	4	5	6	–2
Sweden	4	6	4		0
Switzerland			7		
Taiwan			3		
Tanzania				27	
Turkey		14	20	23	9
Uganda				9	
Ukraine			9	10	1
Uruguay			9		
USA	5	7	5	9	4
Venezuela			11	12	1
Vietnam				54	
Zimbabwe				13	

Income: Larger Income Differences

(E035) *Now I'd like you to tell me your views on various issues. How would you place your views on this scale?*

% We need larger income differences as incentives for individual effort (7 thru 10)

	1981	1990	1995	2000	Change
Albania			25	49	24
Algeria				77	
Argentina		65	49	35	–30
Armenia			53		
Australia			41		
Austria		43		26	–17
Azerbaijan			43		
Bangladesh			64	67	3
Belarus		71	55	36	–35
Belgium		50		42	–8
Bosnia and Herz.			38	46	8
Brazil		48	47		–1
Bulgaria		61	40	48	–13
Canada		63		40	–23
Chile		47	34	22	–25
China		80	36	56	–24
Colombia			52		
Croatia			34	22	–12
Czech Republic		66	54	42	–24
Denmark		57			
Dominican Rep.			75		
Egypt				87	
El Salvador			63		
Estonia		77	36	62	–15
Finland		61	18	28	–33
France		40		33	–7
Georgia			72		
Germany (East)		73	25		–48
Germany (West)		51	37		–14
Great Britain		58	33	39	–19
Greece					
Hungary		49	20		–29
Iceland		47		44	–3
India		47	22	30	–17
Indonesia				65	
Iran				33	
Iraq				43	
Ireland		58		50	–8
Israel				12	
Italy		47		49	2
Japan		34	30	35	1
Jordan				72	
Korea Republic		39	62	60	21
Kyrgyzstan				38	
Latvia		68	55		–13
Lithuania		73	38	34	–39
Luxembourg				62	
Macedonia			35	35	0
Malta		78			
Mexico		50	44	39	–11
Moldova			62	58	–4
Montenegro			47	40	–7
Morocco				73	
Netherlands		52		51	–1
New Zealand			37		
Nigeria		73	61	55	–18
Northern Ireland		67		44	–23
Norway		47	34		–13
Pakistan			86	11	–75
Peru			58	70	12
Philippines			44	51	7
Poland		77	61	51	–26
Portugal		25			
Puerto Rico			52	70	18
Romania		55	52	20	–35
Russian Fed.		63	53	65	2
Saudi Arabia				54	
Serbia			39	47	8
Singapore				63	
Slovakia		56	44		–12
Slovenia		48	24	20	–28
South Africa		37	35	39	2
Spain		33	42	35	2
Sweden		58	45		–13
Switzerland			34		
Taiwan			46		
Tanzania				38	
Turkey		31	41	25	–6
Uganda				67	
Ukraine			54	66	12
Uruguay			36		
USA		62	38	43	–19
Venezuela			38	44	6
Vietnam				50	
Zimbabwe				63	

Government Ownership of Business

(E036) *Now I'd like you to tell me your views on various issues. How would you place your views on this scale?*

% Government ownership of business and industry should be increased (7 thru 10)

	1981	1990	1995	2000	Change
Albania			9	16	7
Algeria				32	
Argentina		18	32	40	22
Armenia			47		
Australia			12		
Austria		7		7	0
Azerbaijan			37		
Bangladesh			30	34	4
Belarus		42	46	30	–12
Belgium		14			
Bosnia and Herz.			23	21	–2
Brazil		37	35		–2
Bulgaria		20	31		11
Canada		10		11	1
Chile		41	38	39	–2
China		61	52	61	0
Colombia			57		
Croatia			7	28	21
Czech Republic		14	33	23	9
Denmark		10			
Dominican Rep.			50		
Egypt				57	
El Salvador			52		
Estonia		19	35	40	21
Finland		6	13	14	8
France		18		12	–6
Georgia			39		
Germany (East)		8	26	26	18
Germany (West)		9	10	9	0
Great Britain		22	23	21	–1
Greece					
Hungary		17	30		13
Iceland		11		9	–2
India		31	32	51	20
Indonesia				37	
Iran				35	
Iraq				65	
Ireland		15		14	–1
Israel					
Italy		18		13	–5
Japan		17	10	9	–8
Jordan				43	
Korea Republic		28	23	22	–6
Kyrgyzstan				44	
Latvia		22	33		11
Lithuania		28	30	27	–1
Luxembourg					
Macedonia			20	18	–2
Malta		22			
Mexico		24	25	41	17
Moldova			56	52	–4
Montenegro			34	25	–9
Morocco				32	
Netherlands		10		13	3
New Zealand			16		
Nigeria		49	42		–7
Northern Ireland		20		17	–3
Norway		14	13		–1
Pakistan			47	17	–30
Peru			40	49	9
Philippines			39	48	9
Poland		45	44	38	–7
Portugal		17		20	3
Puerto Rico			33	22	–11
Romania		31	23	27	–4
Russian Fed.		40	58	44	4
Saudi Arabia				36	
Serbia			34	27	–7
Singapore				19	
Slovakia		28	51		23
Slovenia		17	19		2
South Africa		25	32	36	11
Spain		30	31	34	4
Sweden		14	15		1
Switzerland			8		
Taiwan			21		
Tanzania				38	
Turkey		42	41	34	–8
Uganda				21	
Ukraine			41	37	–4
Uruguay			36		
USA		7	7	10	3
Venezuela			29	41	12
Vietnam				30	
Zimbabwe				27	

Government more Responsibility

(E037) *Now I'd like you to tell me your views on various issues. How would you place your views on this scale?*

% The government should take more responsibility to ensure that everyone is provided for (1 thru 4)

	1981	1990	1995	2000	Change
Albania			65	50	–15
Algeria				43	
Argentina		33	38	53	20
Armenia			66		
Australia			27		
Austria		13		18	5
Azerbaijan			64		
Bangladesh			48	36	–12
Belarus		43	60	39	–4
Belgium		29		33	4
Bosnia and Herz.			59	47	–12
Brazil		41	39		–2
Bulgaria		35	53	32	–3
Canada		19		24	5
Chile		55	51	60	5
China		33	44	35	2
Colombia			45		
Croatia			71	36	–35
Czech Republic		26	57	28	2
Denmark		16		17	1
Dominican Rep.			41		
Egypt				54	
El Salvador			37		
Estonia		35	64	43	8
Finland		20	31	26	6
France		19		16	–3
Georgia			65		
Germany (East)		23	60	42	19
Germany (West)		22	34	16	–6
Great Britain		33		20	–13
Greece				39	
Hungary		50	66	48	–2
Iceland		26		24	–2
India		20	52	51	31
Indonesia				36	
Iran				38	
Iraq				69	
Ireland		30		23	–7
Israel				79	
Italy		39		37	–2
Japan		55	56	51	–4
Jordan				56	
Korea Republic		25	78	76	51

	1981	1990	1995	2000	Change
Kyrgyzstan				55	
Latvia		55	61	54	–1
Lithuania		44	51	34	–10
Luxembourg				18	
Macedonia			67	70	3
Malta		41		33	–8
Mexico		35	45	45	10
Moldova			70	56	–14
Montenegro			68	77	9
Morocco				50	
Netherlands		22		23	1
New Zealand			27		
Nigeria		54	58	68	14
Northern Ireland		36		25	–11
Norway		21	30		9
Pakistan			40	57	17
Peru			39	34	–5
Philippines			41	34	–7
Poland		36	42	35	–1
Portugal		28		26	–2
Puerto Rico			32	20	–12
Romania		36	48	33	–3
Russian Fed.		32	58	40	8
Saudi Arabia				30	
Serbia			67	63	–4
Singapore				40	
Slovakia		45	68	50	5
Slovenia		44	53	50	6
South Africa		39	53	50	11
Spain		45	51	48	3
Sweden		11	13	17	6
Switzerland			13		
Taiwan			32		
Tanzania				65	
Turkey		50	46	51	1
Uganda				45	
Ukraine			68	47	–21
Uruguay			62		
USA		13	17	20	7
Venezuela			40	41	1
Vietnam				21	
Zimbabwe				60	

Competition is Good

(E039) *Now I'd like you to tell me your views on various issues. How would you place your views on this scale?*

% Competition is good. It stimulates people to work hard and develop new ideas (1 thru 4)

	1981	1990	1995	2000	Change
Albania			82	80	–2
Algeria					
Argentina		68	61	59	–9
Armenia			56		
Australia			76		
Austria		74		74	0
Azerbaijan			64		
Bangladesh			92	71	–21
Belarus		68	63	65	–3
Belgium		60		48	–12
Bosnia and Herz.			79	74	–5
Brazil		68	69		1
Bulgaria		80	67	66	–14
Canada		76		70	–6
Chile		60	46	46	–14
China		84	77	80	–4
Colombia					
Croatia			79	75	–4
Czech Republic		89	72	77	–12
Denmark		62		61	–1
Dominican Rep.			72		
Egypt					
El Salvador			66		
Estonia		81	76	52	–29
Finland		77	67	59	–18
France		61		46	–15
Georgia			73		
Germany (East)		78	72	66	–12
Germany (West)		75	72	66	–9
Great Britain		65		59	–6
Greece				55	
Hungary		68	67	61	–7
Iceland		80		84	4
India		74	79	64	–10
Indonesia					
Iran					
Iraq					
Ireland		68		64	–4
Israel					
Italy		61		57	–4
Japan		48	47	56	8
Jordan					
Korea Republic		81	60	58	–23

	1981	1990	1995	2000	Change
Kyrgyzstan				66	
Latvia		80	74	68	–12
Lithuania		78	69	60	–18
Luxembourg				52	
Macedonia			75	77	2
Malta		65		76	11
Mexico		65	57	59	–6
Moldova			60	61	1
Montenegro			71	73	2
Morocco				83	
Netherlands		59		50	–9
New Zealand			72		
Nigeria		81	77		–4
Northern Ireland		65		64	–1
Norway		78	70		–8
Pakistan			75		
Peru			69	67	–2
Philippines			55	55	0
Poland		69	53	59	–10
Portugal		56		49	–7
Puerto Rico			63	73	10
Romania		81	78	79	–2
Russian Fed.		72	59	58	–14
Saudi Arabia					
Serbia			78	71	–7
Singapore				75	
Slovakia		77	70	68	–9
Slovenia		72	70	73	1
South Africa		73	71	65	–8
Spain		55	54	52	–3
Sweden		78	78	74	–4
Switzerland			75		
Taiwan			60		
Tanzania				75	
Turkey		60	68	65	5
Uganda				78	
Ukraine			62	62	0
Uruguay			49		
USA		76	75	71	–5
Venezuela			66	65	–1
Vietnam				58	
Zimbabwe				82	

HARD WORK

(E040) *Where would you place your views on this scale?*

% In the long run, hard work usually brings a better life (1 thru 4)

	1981	1990	1995	2000	Change
Albania			87		
Algeria					
Argentina		48	43		–5
Armenia			38		
Australia			61		
Austria		60			
Azerbaijan			57		
Bangladesh			86		
Belarus		54	52		–2
Belgium		47			
Bosnia and Herz.			60		
Brazil		26	25		–1
Bulgaria		62	51		–11
Canada		67			
Chile		50	41		–9
China		46	69		23
Colombia					
Croatia			54		
Czech Republic		64	43		–21
Denmark		22			
Dominican Rep.			69		
Egypt					
El Salvador			55		
Estonia		57	57		0
Finland		67	57		–10
France		51			
Georgia			56		
Germany (East)		73	33		–40
Germany (West)		57	25		–32
Great Britain		49			
Greece					
Hungary		53	43		–10
Iceland		65			
India		71	83		12
Indonesia					
Iran					
Iraq					
Ireland		55			
Israel					
Italy		48			
Japan		53	58		5
Jordan					
Korea Republic		74	60		–14

	1981	1990	1995	2000	Change
Kyrgyzstan					
Latvia		44	52		8
Lithuania		41	33		–8
Luxembourg					
Macedonia			35		
Malta		57			
Mexico		54	45		–9
Moldova			54		
Montenegro			32		
Morocco					
Netherlands		37			
New Zealand			61		
Nigeria		70	68		–2
Northern Ireland		56			
Norway		47	42		–5
Pakistan			74		
Peru			67		
Philippines			59		
Poland		43	32		–11
Portugal		34			
Puerto Rico			56		
Romania		65	63		–2
Russian Fed.		58	48		–10
Saudi Arabia					
Serbia			46		
Singapore					
Slovakia		54	45		–9
Slovenia		59	58		–1
South Africa		78	78		0
Spain		41	55		14
Sweden		48	49		1
Switzerland			59		
Taiwan			52		
Tanzania					
Turkey		55	63		8
Uganda					
Ukraine			43		
Uruguay			42		
USA		71	68		–3
Venezuela			51		
Vietnam					
Zimbabwe					

Wealth Accumulation

(E041) *Where would you place your views on this scale?*

% Wealth can grow so there's enough for everyone (7 thru 10)

	1981	1990	1995	2000	Change
Albania			48		
Algeria					
Argentina		63	56		–7
Armenia			54		
Australia			46		
Austria		64			
Azerbaijan			63		
Bangladesh			65		
Belarus		61	63		2
Belgium		52			
Bosnia and Herz.			35		
Brazil		63	67		4
Bulgaria		54	39		–15
Canada		62			
Chile		68	60		–8
China		72	78		6
Colombia					
Croatia			43		
Czech Republic		49	33		–16
Denmark		47			
Dominican Rep.			70		
Egypt					
El Salvador					
Estonia		55	70		15
Finland		49	55		6
France		42			
Georgia			64		
Germany (East)		73	55		–18
Germany (West)		55	53		–2
Great Britain		46			
Greece					
Hungary		60	44		–16
Iceland		61			
India		50	25		–25
Indonesia					
Iran					
Iraq					
Ireland		50			
Israel					
Italy		64			
Japan		38	38		0
Jordan					
Korea Republic		54	54		0

	1981	1990	1995	2000	Change
Kyrgyzstan					
Latvia		47	72		25
Lithuania		63	49		–14
Luxembourg					
Macedonia			36		
Malta		73			
Mexico		50	46		–4
Moldova			60		
Montenegro			40		
Morocco					
Netherlands		66			
New Zealand			48		
Nigeria		47	42		–5
Northern Ireland		47			
Norway		48	47		–1
Pakistan			18		
Peru			58		
Philippines			56		
Poland		77	51		–26
Portugal		34			
Puerto Rico			67		
Romania		48	36		–12
Russian Fed.		51	66		15
Saudi Arabia					
Serbia			42		
Singapore					
Slovakia		47	30		–17
Slovenia		39	34		–5
South Africa		72	46		–26
Spain		40	52		12
Sweden		43	34		–9
Switzerland			49		
Taiwan			79		
Tanzania					
Turkey		46	57		11
Uganda					
Ukraine			63		
Uruguay			49		
USA		46	60		14
Venezuela			56		
Vietnam					
Zimbabwe					

Major Changes in Life

(E045) *Where would you place your views on this scale?*

% Cautious major changes in life (1 thru 4)

	1981	1990	1995	2000	Change
Albania			41		
Algeria					
Argentina		45	39		–6
Armenia			36		
Australia			28		
Austria		36		28	–8
Azerbaijan			56		
Bangladesh			43		
Belarus		38	45	17	–21
Belgium		34			
Bosnia and Herz.			34		
Brazil		62	59		–3
Bulgaria		39	38		–1
Canada		42			
Chile		53	33		–20
China		60	52		–8
Colombia					
Croatia			28		
Czech Republic		39	54		15
Denmark		19			
Dominican Rep.			51		
Egypt					
El Salvador					
Estonia		29	29	16	–13
Finland		7	24	33	26
France		37			
Georgia			38		
Germany (East)		26	11		–15
Germany (West)		28	10		–18
Great Britain		31			
Greece					
Hungary		38	35		–3
Iceland		15		15	0
India		35	55		20
Indonesia					
Iran					
Iraq					
Ireland		42			
Israel					
Italy		25		33	8
Japan		34	25		–9
Jordan					
Korea Republic		50	73		23
Kyrgyzstan					
Latvia		37	35		–2
Lithuania		34	41	47	13
Luxembourg				57	
Macedonia			55		
Malta		28			
Mexico		51	37		–14
Moldova			38		
Montenegro			52		
Morocco					
Netherlands		15			
New Zealand			22		
Nigeria		48	43		–5
Northern Ireland		43			
Norway		20	13		–7
Pakistan			72		
Peru			45		
Philippines			41		
Poland		29	15		–14
Portugal		45			
Puerto Rico			57		
Romania		46	33	48	2
Russian Fed.		37	42	38	1
Saudi Arabia					
Serbia			57		
Singapore					
Slovakia		52	58		6
Slovenia		48	44		–4
South Africa		39	44		5
Spain		45	34		–11
Sweden		8	6		–2
Switzerland			29		
Taiwan			66		
Tanzania					
Turkey		41	60		19
Uganda					
Ukraine			44	31	–13
Uruguay			52		
USA		39	27		–12
Venezuela			34		
Vietnam					
Zimbabwe					

OLD IDEAS ARE BETTER THAN NEW ONES

(E046) *Now I'd like you to tell me your views on various issues. How would you place your views on this scale?*

% Ideas that have stood the test of time are generally better (1 thru 4)

	1981	1990	1995	2000	Change
Albania			46	33	–13
Algeria					
Argentina		31	31	32	1
Armenia			38		
Australia			30		
Austria		39			
Azerbaijan			62		
Bangladesh			11	3	–8
Belarus		41	50		9
Belgium		34			
Bosnia and Herz.			23	14	–9
Brazil		41	36		–5
Bulgaria		34	37		3
Canada		30		24	–6
Chile		29	24	33	4
China		67	45		–22
Colombia			8		
Croatia			30		
Czech Republic		39	47		8
Denmark		22			
Dominican Rep.			24		
Egypt					
El Salvador			34		
Estonia		33	37		4
Finland		37	41		4
France		32			
Georgia			51		
Germany (East)		39	23		–16
Germany (West)					
Great Britain		32			
Greece					
Hungary		46	43		–3
Iceland		34			
India		51	59	61	10
Indonesia					
Iran					
Iraq					
Ireland		41			
Israel					
Italy		37			
Japan		50	49		–1
Jordan					
Korea Republic		62	34		–28
Kyrgyzstan					
Latvia		43	42		–1
Lithuania		42	49		7
Luxembourg					
Macedonia			28	34	6
Malta		26			
Mexico		35	26	34	–1
Moldova			45	31	–14
Montenegro					
Morocco					
Netherlands		18			
New Zealand			28		
Nigeria		43	52		9
Northern Ireland		39			
Norway		21	22		1
Pakistan			58		
Peru			31		
Philippines			31		
Poland		34	38		4
Portugal		26			
Puerto Rico			25	17	–8
Romania		45	37		–8
Russian Fed.		45	54		9
Saudi Arabia					
Serbia			49		
Singapore					
Slovakia		40	48		8
Slovenia		45	42		–3
South Africa		27	35	30	3
Spain		32	26		–6
Sweden		18	22		4
Switzerland			38		
Taiwan			55		
Tanzania					
Turkey		35	41		6
Uganda				27	
Ukraine			51		
Uruguay			30		
USA		40	35	23	–17
Venezuela			35	25	–10
Vietnam					
Zimbabwe				36	

Confidence: Churches

(E069) *I am going to name a number of organizations. For each one, could you tell me how much confidence you have in them: is it a great deal of confidence, quite a lot of confidence, not very much confidence or none at all? The churches*

A great deal/ Quite a lot (%)

	1981	1990	1995	2000	Change
Albania			54	66	12
Algeria				89	
Argentina	46	45	50	60	14
Armenia			68		
Australia	56		42		–14
Austria		49		39	–10
Azerbaijan			72		
Bangladesh			99	99	0
Belarus		53	74	70	17
Belgium	65	49		40	–25
Bosnia and Herz.			72	50	–22
Brazil		75	74		–1
Bulgaria		30	58	35	5
Canada	70	64		59	–11
Chile		76	80	78	2
China		5			
Colombia			82		
Croatia			57	64	7
Czech Republic		31	33	20	–11
Denmark	50	47		59	9
Dominican Rep.			72		
Egypt				84	
El Salvador			63		
Estonia		54	60	44	–10
Finland		32	56	58	26
France	56	50		46	–10
Georgia			80		
Germany (East)		44	20	25	–19
Germany (West)	47	40	35	43	–4
Great Britain	49	43		34	–15
Greece				55	
Hungary	39	56	44	48	9
Iceland	71	68		65	–6
India		85	73	82	–3
Indonesia				97	
Iran				86	
Iraq				77	
Ireland	78	72		54	–24
Israel					
Italy	61	63		67	6
Japan	16	11	13	10	–6
Jordan				91	
Korea Republic	63	58	42	49	–14

	1981	1990	1995	2000	Change
Kyrgyzstan				67	
Latvia		64	64	67	3
Lithuania		73	69	71	–2
Luxembourg				48	
Macedonia			31	46	15
Malta	86	82		82	–4
Mexico		76	75	82	6
Moldova			77	82	5
Montenegro			38	48	10
Morocco				97	
Netherlands	41	32		29	–12
New Zealand			40		
Nigeria		88	83	95	7
Northern Ireland	71	80		64	–7
Norway	50	45	54		4
Pakistan			79	88	9
Peru			71	71	0
Philippines			94	92	–2
Poland		84	67	69	–15
Portugal		57		80	23
Puerto Rico			86	84	–2
Romania		72	80	83	11
Russian Fed.		65	66	61	–4
Saudi Arabia				97	
Serbia			38	53	15
Singapore					
Slovakia		50	59	69	19
Slovenia		39	38	35	–4
South Africa		83	85	83	0
Spain	51	50	49	42	–9
Sweden	39	37	49	45	6
Switzerland			39		
Taiwan			62		
Tanzania				93	
Turkey		66	70	71	5
Uganda				89	
Ukraine			67	66	–1
Uruguay			56		
USA	77	68	76	75	–2
Venezuela			74	77	3
Vietnam				23	
Zimbabwe				84	

Confidence: Armed Forces

(E070) *I am going to name a number of organizations. For each one, could you tell me how much confidence you have in them: is it a great deal of confidence, quite a lot of confidence, not very much confidence or none at all? The armed forces*

A great deal/ Quite a lot (%)

	1981	1990	1995	2000	Change
Albania			58	57	–1
Algeria				67	
Argentina	19	28	23	27	8
Armenia			72		
Australia	67		68		1
Austria		28		39	11
Azerbaijan			56		
Bangladesh			57	74	17
Belarus		61	73	70	9
Belgium	44	33		37	–7
Bosnia and Herz.			88	61	–27
Brazil		67	71		4
Bulgaria		69	81	58	–11
Canada	60	57		63	3
Chile		40	56	48	8
China		90		97	7
Colombia			61		
Croatia			79	66	–13
Czech Republic		40	44	25	–15
Denmark	41	46		61	20
Dominican Rep.			30		
Egypt				57	
El Salvador			45		
Estonia		23	48	35	12
Finland		57	82	84	27
France	57	56		63	6
Georgia			52		
Germany (East)		14	39	46	32
Germany (West)	54	40	52	57	3
Great Britain	82	81		83	1
Greece				68	
Hungary		52	58	46	–6
Iceland		24		40	16
India		93	84	92	–1
Indonesia				74	
Iran					
Iraq				57	
Ireland	76	61		60	–16
Israel					
Italy	58	48		52	–6
Japan	37	24	62	67	30
Jordan				92	
Korea Republic	87	80	71	64	–23

	1981	1990	1995	2000	Change
Kyrgyzstan				57	
Latvia		25	31	48	23
Lithuania		21	41	50	29
Luxembourg				54	
Macedonia			39	55	16
Malta	37	43		72	35
Mexico		47	59	54	7
Moldova			57	57	0
Montenegro			61	51	–10
Morocco				71	
Netherlands	44	31		40	–4
New Zealand			62		
Nigeria		61	45	47	–14
Northern Ireland	77	78		56	–21
Norway	68	65	73		5
Pakistan			97	86	–11
Peru			42	22	–20
Philippines			69	74	5
Poland		65	80	67	2
Portugal		47		71	24
Puerto Rico			64	53	–11
Romania		82	82	83	1
Russian Fed.		69	69	67	–2
Saudi Arabia					
Serbia			62	73	11
Singapore					
Slovakia		50	68	77	27
Slovenia		45	45	42	–3
South Africa		60	57	55	–5
Spain	63	40	43	42	–21
Sweden	61	49	54	44	–17
Switzerland			50		
Taiwan			76		
Tanzania				91	
Turkey		91	94	86	–5
Uganda				76	
Ukraine			68	69	1
Uruguay			38		
USA	80	48	86	82	2
Venezuela			60	64	4
Vietnam				96	
Zimbabwe				62	

Confidence: Education System

(E071) *I am going to name a number of organizations. For each one, could you tell me how much confidence you have in them: is it a great deal of confidence, quite a lot of confidence, not very much confidence or none at all? The education system*

A great deal/ Quite a lot (%)

	1981	1990	1995	2000	Change
Albania					
Algeria					
Argentina		38			
Armenia					
Australia					
Austria		65		86	21
Azerbaijan					
Bangladesh					
Belarus				84	
Belgium	79	73		80	1
Bosnia and Herz.					
Brazil		67			
Bulgaria		53		57	4
Canada	67	73			6
Chile		73			
China		92			
Colombia					
Croatia				64	
Czech Republic		62		55	–7
Denmark	65	81		75	10
Dominican Rep.					
Egypt					
El Salvador					
Estonia		48		74	26
Finland		78		89	11
France	57	66		68	11
Georgia					
Germany (East)		42		78	36
Germany (West)	43	54		71	28
Great Britain	62	47		66	4
Greece				29	
Hungary		61		64	3
Iceland	69	80		82	13
India		73			
Indonesia					
Iran					
Iraq					
Ireland	68	73		87	19
Israel					
Italy	56	48		53	–3
Japan		46			
Jordan					
Korea Republic		64			

	1981	1990	1995	2000	Change
Kyrgyzstan					
Latvia		53		74	21
Lithuania		57		67	10
Luxembourg				68	
Macedonia					
Malta	68	79		84	16
Mexico		76			
Moldova					
Montenegro					
Morocco					
Netherlands	73	65		73	0
New Zealand					
Nigeria		84			
Northern Ireland	74	66		83	9
Norway	80	79			–1
Pakistan					
Peru					
Philippines					
Poland		77		81	4
Portugal		51		60	9
Puerto Rico					
Romania		79		79	0
Russian Fed.		55		71	16
Saudi Arabia					
Serbia					
Singapore					
Slovakia		67		76	9
Slovenia		67		80	13
South Africa		77			
Spain	51	64		68	17
Sweden	62	70		68	6
Switzerland					
Taiwan					
Tanzania					
Turkey				57	
Uganda					
Ukraine				72	
Uruguay					
USA	67	55			–12
Venezuela					
Vietnam					
Zimbabwe					

Confidence: The Press

(E072) *I am going to name a number of organizations. For each one, could you tell me how much confidence you have in them: is it a great deal of confidence, quite a lot of confidence, not very much confidence or none at all? The press*

A great deal/Quite a lot (%)

	1981	1990	1995	2000	Change
Albania			17	35	18
Algeria				48	
Argentina	46	27	33	38	–8
Armenia			34		
Australia	29		17		–12
Austria		17		32	15
Azerbaijan			32		
Bangladesh			71	93	22
Belarus		25	41	41	16
Belgium	36	44		37	1
Bosnia and Herz.			54	25	–29
Brazil		55	61		6
Bulgaria		35	47	26	–9
Canada	45	46		35	–10
Chile		43	52	48	5
China		55		69	14
Colombia			45		
Croatia			22	18	–4
Czech Republic		36	43	38	2
Denmark	30	31		33	3
Dominican Rep.			33		
Egypt				69	
El Salvador			46		
Estonia		63	55	42	–21
Finland		38	30	36	–2
France	32	38		36	4
Georgia			60		
Germany (East)		22	11	37	15
Germany (West)	33	34	24	36	3
Great Britain	30	14		16	–14
Greece				31	
Hungary	81	40	31	31	–50
Iceland	16	20		39	23
India		66	63	70	4
Indonesia				55	
Iran				36	
Iraq					
Ireland	44	36		34	–10
Israel					
Italy	30	39		35	5
Japan	54	55	74	73	19
Jordan				59	
Korea Republic	69	66	65	66	–3
Kyrgyzstan				44	
Latvia		60	50	45	–15
Lithuania		68	71	77	9
Luxembourg				46	
Macedonia			18	20	2
Malta	35	27		36	1
Mexico		49	51	42	–7
Moldova			35	44	9
Montenegro			33	24	–9
Morocco				37	
Netherlands	28	36		56	28
New Zealand			34		
Nigeria		71	56	64	–7
Northern Ireland	32	16		18	–14
Norway	41	43	33		–8
Pakistan			54	52	–2
Peru			30	23	–7
Philippines			72	67	–5
Poland		48	46	47	–1
Portugal		36		66	30
Puerto Rico			50	41	–9
Romania		28	36	38	10
Russian Fed.		44	40	30	–14
Saudi Arabia				63	
Serbia			24	29	5
Singapore					
Slovakia		39	42	49	10
Slovenia		50	43	61	11
South Africa		58	54	65	7
Spain	47	49	43	41	–6
Sweden	27	33	29	46	19
Switzerland			22		
Taiwan			41		
Tanzania				76	
Turkey		42	49	34	–8
Uganda				67	
Ukraine			44	47	3
Uruguay			61		
USA	49	56	27	27	–22
Venezuela			59	65	6
Vietnam				84	
Zimbabwe				54	

Confidence: Labour Unions

(E073) *I am going to name a number of organizations. For each one, could you tell me how much confidence you have in them: is it a great deal of confidence, quite a lot of confidence, not very much confidence or none at all? Labour unions*

A great deal/Quite a lot (%)

	1981	1990	1995	2000	Change
Albania			16	33	17
Algeria				29	
Argentina	31	8	10	12	–19
Armenia			19		
Australia	24		26		2
Austria		35		31	–4
Azerbaijan			30		
Bangladesh			46	72	26
Belarus		25	45	28	3
Belgium	33	37		37	4
Bosnia and Herz.			57	23	–34
Brazil		48	55		7
Bulgaria		32	34	15	–17
Canada	33	35		36	3
Chile		47	46	45	–2
China		42		73	31
Colombia			35		
Croatia			24	29	5
Czech Republic		26	42	22	–4
Denmark	51	46		48	–3
Dominican Rep.			19		
Egypt				68	
El Salvador			18		
Estonia		27	45	32	5
Finland		32	51	54	22
France	39	32		35	–4
Georgia			28		
Germany (East)		29	38	36	7
Germany (West)	37	36	38	38	1
Great Britain	27	26		28	1
Greece				14	
Hungary	67	30	27	24	–43
Iceland	46	51		49	3
India		52	54	48	–4
Indonesia				38	
Iran				37	
Iraq					
Ireland	37	43		47	10
Israel					
Italy	27	34		29	2
Japan	31	26	47	43	12
Jordan				51	
Korea Republic	60	67	56	52	–8

	1981	1990	1995	2000	Change
Kyrgyzstan				39	
Latvia		24	37	32	8
Lithuania		27	28	40	13
Luxembourg				52	
Macedonia			15	13	–2
Malta	40	35		49	9
Mexico		38	37	29	–9
Moldova			35	33	–2
Montenegro			35	20	–15
Morocco				22	
Netherlands	40	53		58	18
New Zealand			23		
Nigeria		66	48	65	–1
Northern Ireland	23	24		38	15
Norway	56	59	66		10
Pakistan				26	
Peru			16	22	6
Philippines			55	54	–1
Poland		23	30	34	11
Portugal		29		47	18
Puerto Rico			41	42	1
Romania		30	32	27	–3
Russian Fed.		47	43	30	–17
Saudi Arabia					
Serbia			26	23	–3
Singapore					
Slovakia		31	35	43	12
Slovenia		27	25	31	4
South Africa		61	44	52	–9
Spain	33	40	32	30	–3
Sweden	49	40	44	42	–7
Switzerland			37		
Taiwan			58		
Tanzania				70	
Turkey		40	54	53	13
Uganda				58	
Ukraine			39	38	–1
Uruguay			39		
USA	38	33	34	38	0
Venezuela			27	23	–4
Vietnam				80	
Zimbabwe				63	

Confidence: The Police

(E074) *I am going to name a number of organizations. For each one, could you tell me how much confidence you have in them: is it a great deal of confidence, quite a lot of confidence, not very much confidence or none at all? The police*

A great deal/Quite a lot (%)

	1981	1990	1995	2000	Change
Albania			73	65	–8
Algeria				67	
Argentina	25	26	23	24	–1
Armenia			32		
Australia	80		76		–4
Austria		67		76	9
Azerbaijan			41		
Bangladesh			38	53	15
Belarus		21	38	40	19
Belgium	64	51		56	–8
Bosnia and Herz.			80	64	–16
Brazil		38	45		7
Bulgaria		46	51	47	1
Canada	85	84		79	–6
Chile		59	51	55	–4
China		68		73	5
Colombia			50		
Croatia			61	53	–8
Czech Republic		38	44	33	–5
Denmark	86	89		91	5
Dominican Rep.			13		
Egypt				87	
El Salvador			49		
Estonia		19	51	34	15
Finland		76	86	90	14
France	66	67		66	0
Georgia			38		
Germany (East)		40	52	65	25
Germany (West)	71	70	71	75	4
Great Britain	87	77		70	–17
Greece				28	
Hungary		51	55	45	–6
Iceland	76	85		83	7
India		39	41	38	–1
Indonesia				52	
Iran				61	
Iraq					
Ireland	86	86		83	–3
Israel					
Italy	68	67		67	–1
Japan	69	59	79	50	–19
Jordan				91	
Korea Republic	73	53	47	50	–23

	1981	1990	1995	2000	Change
Kyrgyzstan				23	
Latvia		20	31	40	20
Lithuania		28	21	26	–2
Luxembourg				72	
Macedonia			27	51	24
Malta	55	52		67	12
Mexico		32	33	30	–2
Moldova			34	35	1
Montenegro			55	40	–15
Morocco				53	
Netherlands	73	73		64	–9
New Zealand			81		
Nigeria		44	29	35	–9
Northern Ireland	84	80		63	–21
Norway	89	88	86		–3
Pakistan			16	29	13
Peru			22	16	–6
Philippines			55	61	6
Poland		32	53	55	23
Portugal		44		66	22
Puerto Rico			56	57	1
Romania		45	39	45	0
Russian Fed.		35	30	29	–6
Saudi Arabia					
Serbia			45	47	2
Singapore					
Slovakia		36	40	44	8
Slovenia		51	47	50	–1
South Africa		64	75	56	–8
Spain	64	45	62	59	–5
Sweden	80	74	81	76	–4
Switzerland			69		
Taiwan			59		
Tanzania				67	
Turkey		63	72	71	8
Uganda				55	
Ukraine			37	33	–4
Uruguay			53		
USA	74	75	71	71	–3
Venezuela			30	41	11
Vietnam				93	
Zimbabwe				64	

Confidence: Parliament

(E075) *I am going to name a number of organizations. For each one, could you tell me how much confidence you have in them: is it a great deal of confidence, quite a lot of confidence, not very much confidence or none at all? Parliament*

A great deal/Quite a lot (%)

	1981	1990	1995	2000	Change
Albania			61	45	–16
Algeria				33	
Argentina	73	17	16	11	–62
Armenia			30		
Australia	55		31		–24
Austria		41		41	0
Azerbaijan			74		
Bangladesh			84	89	5
Belarus		29	30	37	8
Belgium	38	43		36	–2
Bosnia and Herz.			57	20	–37
Brazil		24	34		10
Bulgaria		49	45	27	–22
Canada	44	38		41	–3
Chile		63	39	35	–28
China		81		95	14
Colombia			25		
Croatia			42	23	–19
Czech Republic		41	20	12	–29
Denmark	37	42		49	12
Dominican Rep.			12		
Egypt				68	
El Salvador			31		
Estonia			44	27	–17
Finland		34	31	44	10
France	56	48		41	–15
Georgia			41		
Germany (East)		41	17	40	–1
Germany (West)	53	51	29	35	–18
Great Britain	41	46		36	–5
Greece				24	
Hungary	92	40	39	34	–58
Iceland	58	53		72	14
India		67	65	55	–12
Indonesia				43	
Iran				70	
Iraq					
Ireland	52	50		31	–21
Israel					
Italy	30	32		34	4
Japan	29	29	25	22	–7
Jordan				65	
Korea Republic	68	34	31	11	–57
Kyrgyzstan				36	
Latvia			25	27	2
Lithuania			27	11	–16
Luxembourg				63	
Macedonia			16	7	–9
Malta	46	42		52	6
Mexico		35	45	23	–12
Moldova			41	35	–6
Montenegro			45	33	–12
Morocco				22	
Netherlands	45	54		55	10
New Zealand			15		
Nigeria		54	27	45	–9
Northern Ireland	47	46		40	–7
Norway	78	59	69		–9
Pakistan				76	
Peru			15	10	–5
Philippines			60	61	1
Poland		73	35	33	–40
Portugal		34		49	15
Puerto Rico			30	28	–2
Romania		21	19	19	–2
Russian Fed.		47	23	19	–28
Saudi Arabia					
Serbia			33	24	–9
Singapore					
Slovakia		31	31	43	12
Slovenia		36	25	25	–11
South Africa		66	69	60	–6
Spain	49	38	37	48	–1
Sweden	47	47	45	51	4
Switzerland			44		
Taiwan			46		
Tanzania				79	
Turkey		58	53	43	–15
Uganda				77	
Ukraine			38	27	–11
Uruguay			42		
USA	53	46	30	38	–15
Venezuela			23	34	11
Vietnam				97	
Zimbabwe				50	

CONFIDENCE: THE CIVIL SERVICES

(E076) *I am going to name a number of organizations. For each one, could you tell me how much confidence you have in them: is it a great deal of confidence, quite a lot of confidence, not very much confidence or none at all? The Civil Service*

A great deal/Quite a lot (%)

	1981	1990	1995	2000	Change
Albania			23	40	17
Algeria				58	
Argentina	50	7	8	7	–43
Armenia			37		
Australia	47		38		–9
Austria		41		42	1
Azerbaijan			44		
Bangladesh			80	96	16
Belarus		20	51	23	3
Belgium	47	42		45	–2
Bosnia and Herz.			62	30	–32
Brazil		49	59		10
Bulgaria		30	48	24	–6
Canada	52	50		50	–2
Chile		49	46	40	–9
China		59		66	7
Colombia			32		
Croatia			38	35	–3
Czech Republic		33	39	22	–11
Denmark	47	51		55	8
Dominican Rep.			10		
Egypt				63	
El Salvador					
Estonia			61	40	–21
Finland		33	34	41	8
France	53	49		46	–7
Georgia			56		
Germany (East)		18	41	36	18
Germany (West)	36	39	48	39	3
Great Britain	49	44		46	–3
Greece				14	
Hungary	74	50	52	50	–24
Iceland	48	46		56	8
India		74	70	49	–25
Indonesia				59	
Iran				44	
Iraq					
Ireland	55	59		61	6
Israel					
Italy	28	27		33	5
Japan	32	34	37	32	0
Jordan				66	
Korea Republic	88	61	78	67	–21

	1981	1990	1995	2000	Change
Kyrgyzstan				45	
Latvia			44	49	5
Lithuania			41	21	–20
Luxembourg				60	
Macedonia			19	17	–2
Malta	57	39		49	–8
Mexico		28	43	22	–6
Moldova			54	47	–7
Montenegro			48	29	–19
Morocco				41	
Netherlands	45	46		37	–8
New Zealand			29		
Nigeria		76	59	71	–5
Northern Ireland	60	57		52	–8
Norway	58	44	51		–7
Pakistan			47	50	3
Peru			11	9	–2
Philippines			68	71	3
Poland		57	35	33	–24
Portugal		32		54	22
Puerto Rico			57	27	–30
Romania		31	28	27	–4
Russian Fed.		48	49	38	–10
Saudi Arabia				70	
Serbia			34	29	–5
Singapore					
Slovakia		34	40	39	5
Slovenia		40	29	25	–15
South Africa		60	59	58	–2
Spain	40	35	42	41	1
Sweden	46	44	45	49	3
Switzerland			46		
Taiwan			60		
Tanzania				71	
Turkey		50	68	60	10
Uganda				69	
Ukraine			43	39	–4
Uruguay			45		
USA	57	59	52	55	–2
Venezuela			31	38	7
Vietnam				79	
Zimbabwe				59	

Confidence: Social Security System

(E077) *I am going to name a number of organizations. For each one, could you tell me how much confidence you have in them: is it a great deal of confidence, quite a lot of confidence, not very much confidence or none at all? The social security system*

A great deal/Quite a lot (%)

	1981	1990	1995	2000	Change
Albania					
Algeria					
Argentina		20			
Armenia					
Australia					
Austria		67		67	0
Azerbaijan					
Bangladesh					
Belarus				56	
Belgium		67		69	2
Bosnia and Herz.					
Brazil		32			
Bulgaria		36		26	–10
Canada		61			
Chile		53			
China		80			
Colombia					
Croatia				32	
Czech Republic		46		33	–13
Denmark		69		67	–2
Dominican Rep.					
Egypt					
El Salvador					
Estonia		46		51	5
Finland		74		71	–3
France		70		67	–3
Georgia					
Germany (East)		59		49	–10
Germany (West)		70		43	–27
Great Britain		33		36	3
Greece				19	
Hungary		50		42	–8
Iceland		69		50	–19
India		67			
Indonesia					
Iran					
Iraq					
Ireland		59		57	–2
Israel					
Italy		38		34	–4
Japan		44			
Jordan					
Korea Republic		98			
Kyrgyzstan					
Latvia		37		57	20
Lithuania		52		32	–20
Luxembourg				79	
Macedonia					
Malta		71		76	5
Mexico		48			
Moldova					
Montenegro					
Morocco					
Netherlands		69		65	–4
New Zealand					
Nigeria		65			
Northern Ireland		48		54	6
Norway		48			
Pakistan					
Peru					
Philippines					
Poland		42		39	–3
Portugal		47		51	4
Puerto Rico					
Romania		36		30	–6
Russian Fed.		67		45	–22
Saudi Arabia					
Serbia					
Singapore					
Slovakia		42		37	–5
Slovenia		40		47	7
South Africa		60			
Spain		44		63	19
Sweden		46		51	5
Switzerland					
Taiwan					
Tanzania					
Turkey				65	
Uganda					
Ukraine				44	
Uruguay					
USA		53			
Venezuela					
Vietnam					
Zimbabwe					

Confidence: Television

(E078) *I am going to name a number of organizations. For each one, could you tell me how much confidence you have in them: is it a great deal of confidence, quite a lot of confidence, not very much confidence or none at all? Television*

A great deal/Quite a lot (%)

	1981	1990	1995	2000	Change
Albania			24	54	30
Algeria				45	
Argentina			27	33	6
Armenia			45		
Australia			26		
Austria					
Azerbaijan			42		
Bangladesh			67	84	17
Belarus			48		
Belgium					
Bosnia and Herz.			60	35	–25
Brazil		38	57		19
Bulgaria			69		
Canada				38	
Chile			59	53	–6
China				74	
Colombia			50		
Croatia			22		
Czech Republic		71	50		–21
Denmark					
Dominican Rep.			38		
Egypt				68	
El Salvador			49		
Estonia			68		
Finland			50		
France					
Georgia			61		
Germany (East)			21		
Germany (West)			23		
Great Britain					
Greece					
Hungary			41		
Iceland					
India		33	57	72	39
Indonesia				61	
Iran				49	
Iraq				56	
Ireland					
Israel					
Italy					
Japan		27	68	68	41
Jordan				58	
Korea Republic			61	63	2
Kyrgyzstan				52	
Latvia			58		
Lithuania			76		
Luxembourg					
Macedonia			22	22	0
Malta					
Mexico			49	47	–2
Moldova			45	49	4
Montenegro			41	37	–4
Morocco				30	
Netherlands					
New Zealand			38		
Nigeria		69	59	72	3
Northern Ireland					
Norway			49		
Pakistan			63	57	–6
Peru			35	25	–10
Philippines			70	71	1
Poland			47		
Portugal					
Puerto Rico			39	27	–12
Romania			49		
Russian Fed.		55	47		–8
Saudi Arabia				67	
Serbia			26	30	4
Singapore					
Slovakia		54	50		–4
Slovenia			53		
South Africa			67	77	10
Spain			39	39	0
Sweden			49		
Switzerland			31		
Taiwan			51		
Tanzania				79	
Turkey			50	37	–13
Uganda				67	
Ukraine			48		
Uruguay			57		
USA			29	25	–4
Venezuela			53	64	11
Vietnam				93	
Zimbabwe				59	

CONFIDENCE: THE GOVERNMENT

(E079) *I am going to name a number of organizations. For each one, could you tell me how much confidence you have in them: is it a great deal of confidence, quite a lot of confidence, not very much confidence or none at all? The government*

A great deal/Quite a lot (%)

	1981	1990	1995	2000	Change
Albania			41	58	17
Algeria				54	
Argentina			27	19	–8
Armenia			42		
Australia			26		
Austria					
Azerbaijan			92		
Bangladesh			81	87	6
Belarus			51		
Belgium					
Bosnia and Herz.			71	30	–41
Brazil			49		
Bulgaria			60		
Canada				42	
Chile		59	53	58	–1
China				97	
Colombia			36		
Croatia			52		
Czech Republic		48	31		–17
Denmark					
Dominican Rep.			13		
Egypt				61	
El Salvador			41		
Estonia			50		
Finland			32		
France					
Georgia			51		
Germany (East)			17		
Germany (West)			24		
Great Britain					
Greece					
Hungary			44		
Iceland					
India		43	58	56	13
Indonesia				52	
Iran				69	
Iraq				40	
Ireland					
Israel					
Italy					
Japan			30	27	–3
Jordan				83	
Korea Republic			44	30	–14
Kyrgyzstan				35	
Latvia			38		
Lithuania			36		
Luxembourg					
Macedonia			20	11	–9
Malta					
Mexico		24	42	37	13
Moldova			44	37	–7
Montenegro			48	34	–14
Morocco				59	
Netherlands					
New Zealand			16		
Nigeria		26	28	48	22
Northern Ireland					
Norway			66		
Pakistan				39	
Peru			39	19	–20
Philippines			59	51	–8
Poland			39		
Portugal					
Puerto Rico			53	45	–8
Romania			22		
Russian Fed.			26		
Saudi Arabia					
Serbia			36	31	–5
Singapore					
Slovakia		35	43		8
Slovenia			41		
South Africa			69	61	–8
Spain		28	31	44	16
Sweden			42		
Switzerland			52		
Taiwan			70		
Tanzania				83	
Turkey		49	52	46	–3
Uganda				78	
Ukraine			44		
Uruguay			42		
USA			31	38	7
Venezuela			27	56	29
Vietnam				98	
Zimbabwe				51	

Confidence: The Political Parties

(E080) *I am going to name a number of organizations. For each one, could you tell me how much confidence you have in them: is it a great deal of confidence, quite a lot of confidence, not very much confidence or none at all? Political parties*

A great deal/Quite a lot (%)

	1981	1990	1995	2000	Change
Albania			23	29	6
Algeria				19	
Argentina			8	7	–1
Armenia			16		
Australia			16		
Austria					
Azerbaijan			54		
Bangladesh			71	79	8
Belarus		23	16		–7
Belgium					
Bosnia and Herz.			47	15	–32
Brazil			32		
Bulgaria			29		
Canada				23	
Chile		50	25	28	–22
China		80		93	13
Colombia			17		
Croatia			22		
Czech Republic		48	15		–33
Denmark					
Dominican Rep.			9		
Egypt				51	
El Salvador			17		
Estonia			23		
Finland			13		
France					
Georgia			34		
Germany (East)			10		
Germany (West)			14		
Great Britain					
Greece					
Hungary			20		
Iceland					
India		55	47	34	–21
Indonesia				33	
Iran				34	
Iraq					
Ireland					
Israel					
Italy					
Japan			16	18	2
Jordan				26	
Korea Republic			25	11	–14

	1981	1990	1995	2000	Change
Kyrgyzstan				26	
Latvia			10		
Lithuania			14		
Luxembourg					
Macedonia			11	9	–2
Malta					
Mexico		30	35	25	–5
Moldova			18	24	6
Montenegro			24	26	2
Morocco				19	
Netherlands					
New Zealand			6		
Nigeria		38	26	44	6
Northern Ireland					
Norway			33		
Pakistan			33	28	–5
Peru			6	8	2
Philippines			45	46	1
Poland			13		
Portugal					
Puerto Rico			21	20	–1
Romania			14		
Russian Fed.		46	19		–27
Saudi Arabia					
Serbia			18	15	–3
Singapore					
Slovakia		35	23		–12
Slovenia			14		
South Africa		58	47	44	–14
Spain		61	19	27	–34
Sweden			28		
Switzerland			27		
Taiwan			36		
Tanzania				59	
Turkey			29	29	0
Uganda				41	
Ukraine			20		
Uruguay			36		
USA			21	23	2
Venezuela			15	20	5
Vietnam				92	
Zimbabwe				29	

Confidence: Major Companies

(E081) *I am going to name a number of organizations. For each one, could you tell me how much confidence you have in them: is it a great deal of confidence, quite a lot of confidence, not very much confidence or none at all? Major companies*

A great deal/Quite a lot (%)

	1981	1990	1995	2000	Change
Albania			24	49	25
Algeria				43	
Argentina	35	24	30	26	–9
Armenia			50		
Australia	79		59		–20
Austria		41		41	0
Azerbaijan			42		
Bangladesh			65	90	25
Belarus		37	68	59	22
Belgium	43	50			7
Bosnia and Herz.			61	34	–27
Brazil		58	68		10
Bulgaria		34	34		0
Canada	57	51		56	–1
Chile		53	57	50	–3
China		36	61	55	19
Colombia			59		
Croatia			29	30	1
Czech Republic		24	38	20	–4
Denmark	35	38			3
Dominican Rep.			47		
Egypt				32	
El Salvador			40		
Estonia		15	61		46
Finland		41	51	43	2
France	50	67		48	–2
Georgia			55		
Germany (East)		47	25	44	–3
Germany (West)	34	38	26	34	0
Great Britain	50	48		40	–10
Greece				20	
Hungary		34	37		3
Iceland	33	40		42	9
India		61	66	46	–15
Indonesia				47	
Iran				31	
Iraq					
Ireland	50	52			2
Israel					
Italy	34	62		50	16
Japan	25	28	36	29	4
Jordan				54	
Korea Republic	54	35	35	30	–24

	1981	1990	1995	2000	Change
Kyrgyzstan				41	
Latvia		11	46		35
Lithuania		16	32	17	1
Luxembourg				40	
Macedonia			27	23	–4
Malta	62	68			6
Mexico		46	50	46	0
Moldova			51	50	–1
Montenegro			46	29	–17
Morocco				41	
Netherlands	36	48			12
New Zealand			46		
Nigeria		76	64	70	–6
Northern Ireland	54	47			–7
Norway	45	53	60		15
Pakistan				37	
Peru			31	26	–5
Philippines			64	58	–6
Poland		59	53		–6
Portugal		45		53	8
Puerto Rico			61	45	–16
Romania		35	37		2
Russian Fed.		46	23	21	–25
Saudi Arabia				59	
Serbia			34	32	–2
Singapore					
Slovakia		31	31		0
Slovenia		33	40		7
South Africa		76	74	74	–2
Spain	38	46	47	39	1
Sweden	42	53	65		23
Switzerland			40		
Taiwan			55		
Tanzania				66	
Turkey		29	62	51	22
Uganda				70	
Ukraine			58	21	–37
Uruguay			45		
USA	50	51	54	54	4
Venezuela			55	64	9
Vietnam				47	
Zimbabwe				77	

Confidence: The Environmental Protection Movement

(E082) *I am going to name a number of organizations. For each one, could you tell me how much confidence you have in them: is it a great deal of confidence, quite a lot of confidence, not very much confidence or none at all? Environmental Protection*

A great deal/Quite a lot (%)

	1981	1990	1995	2000	Change
Albania			17	38	21
Algeria					
Argentina			72	67	–5
Armenia			47		
Australia			56		
Austria					
Azerbaijan			14		
Bangladesh			79	83	4
Belarus			78		
Belgium					
Bosnia and Herz.			62	52	–10
Brazil			80		
Bulgaria			45		
Canada				68	
Chile			78	65	–13
China			69	88	19
Colombia			70		
Croatia			53		
Czech Republic			57		
Denmark					
Dominican Rep.			64		
Egypt				77	
El Salvador			38		
Estonia			76		
Finland			41		
France					
Georgia			42		
Germany (East)			64		
Germany (West)			71		
Great Britain					
Greece					
Hungary			45		
Iceland					
India			64	52	–12
Indonesia				55	
Iran				55	
Iraq					
Ireland					
Israel					
Italy					
Japan			64	57	–7
Jordan				69	
Korea Republic			85	74	–11
Kyrgyzstan				48	
Latvia			62		
Lithuania			63		
Luxembourg					
Macedonia			40	42	2
Malta					
Mexico			55	54	–1
Moldova			52	52	0
Montenegro			45	34	–11
Morocco				66	
Netherlands					
New Zealand			48		
Nigeria			52	61	9
Northern Ireland					
Norway			63		
Pakistan				36	
Peru			52	48	–4
Philippines			74	74	0
Poland			79		
Portugal					
Puerto Rico			77	70	–7
Romania			48		
Russian Fed.			79		
Saudi Arabia				58	
Serbia			49	43	–6
Singapore					
Slovakia			55		
Slovenia			58		
South Africa			56	61	5
Spain			64	61	–3
Sweden			74		
Switzerland			43		
Taiwan			79		
Tanzania				61	
Turkey			85	70	–15
Uganda				76	
Ukraine			66		
Uruguay			69		
USA			54	60	6
Venezuela			55	68	13
Vietnam				79	
Zimbabwe				69	

Confidence: The Women's Movement

(E083) *I am going to name a number of organizations. For each one, could you tell me how much confidence you have in them: is it a great deal of confidence, quite a lot of confidence, not very much confidence or none at all? The women's movement*

A great deal/Quite a lot (%)

	1981	1990	1995	2000	Change
Albania			37	38	1
Algeria				30	
Argentina			41	36	–5
Armenia			29		
Australia			43		
Austria					
Azerbaijan			20		
Bangladesh			77	80	3
Belarus			70		
Belgium					
Bosnia and Herz.			58	45	–13
Brazil			69		
Bulgaria			47		
Canada				63	
Chile			51	47	–4
China			73	92	19
Colombia			52		
Croatia			29		
Czech Republic			41		
Denmark					
Dominican Rep.			52		
Egypt				74	
El Salvador					
Estonia			63		
Finland			29		
France					
Georgia			41		
Germany (East)			54		
Germany (West)			52		
Great Britain					
Greece					
Hungary			35		
Iceland					
India			59	53	–6
Indonesia				51	
Iran				43	
Iraq					
Ireland					
Israel					
Italy					
Japan			44	45	1
Jordan				53	
Korea Republic			77	70	–7

	1981	1990	1995	2000	Change
Kyrgyzstan				51	
Latvia			49		
Lithuania			41		
Luxembourg					
Macedonia			29	45	16
Malta					
Mexico			44	39	–5
Moldova			49	47	–2
Montenegro			37	29	–8
Morocco				41	
Netherlands					
New Zealand			38		
Nigeria			53	54	1
Northern Ireland					
Norway			43		
Pakistan				29	
Peru			37	36	–1
Philippines			74	77	3
Poland			54		
Portugal					
Puerto Rico			57	56	–1
Romania			42		
Russian Fed.			70		
Saudi Arabia				44	
Serbia			35	39	4
Singapore					
Slovakia			50		
Slovenia			44		
South Africa			57	63	6
Spain			44	48	4
Sweden			51		
Switzerland			39		
Taiwan			76		
Tanzania				80	
Turkey			76	65	–11
Uganda				75	
Ukraine			62		
Uruguay			49		
USA			53	59	6
Venezuela			43	50	7
Vietnam				85	
Zimbabwe				61	

Confidence: Justice System

(E085) *I am going to name a number of organizations. For each one, could you tell me how much confidence you have in them: is it a great deal of confidence, quite a lot of confidence, not very much confidence or none at all? The justice system*

A great deal/Quite a lot (%)

	1981	1990	1995	2000	Change
Albania			58		
Algeria					
Argentina	59	23	27		–32
Armenia			31		
Australia	60		35		–25
Austria		59		69	10
Azerbaijan			47		
Bangladesh			75		
Belarus		26	49	46	20
Belgium	58	45		34	–24
Bosnia and Herz.			71		
Brazil		44	55		11
Bulgaria		45	39	28	–17
Canada	65	54			–11
Chile		45	45		0
China		76			
Colombia			48		
Croatia			51	35	–16
Czech Republic		45	29	23	–22
Denmark	80	79		78	–2
Dominican Rep.			15		
Egypt					
El Salvador			41		
Estonia		33	62	32	–1
Finland		66	69	66	0
France	56	58		46	–10
Georgia			46		
Germany (East)		41	33	50	9
Germany (West)	67	65	54	64	–3
Great Britain	67	54		49	–18
Greece				44	
Hungary	89	60	52	45	–44
Iceland	70	67		74	4
India		64	78		14
Indonesia					
Iran					
Iraq					
Ireland	58	47		55	–3
Israel					
Italy	43	32		32	–11
Japan	71	62	80		9
Jordan					
Korea Republic	81	67	59		–22

	1981	1990	1995	2000	Change
Kyrgyzstan					
Latvia		36	38	47	11
Lithuania		39	22	19	–20
Luxembourg				59	
Macedonia			24		
Malta	48	39		45	–3
Mexico		53	41		–12
Moldova			50		
Montenegro			60		
Morocco					
Netherlands	65	63		49	–16
New Zealand			47		
Nigeria		64	48		–16
Northern Ireland	69	56		48	–21
Norway	84	75	70		–14
Pakistan			50		
Peru			17		
Philippines			66		
Poland		51	53	42	–9
Portugal		41		41	0
Puerto Rico			48		
Romania		48	45	40	–8
Russian Fed.		38	39	36	–2
Saudi Arabia					
Serbia			46		
Singapore					
Slovakia		43	42	36	–7
Slovenia		51	36	44	–7
South Africa		74	64		–10
Spain	50	47	47	42	–8
Sweden	73	56	63	61	–12
Switzerland			66		
Taiwan			59		
Tanzania					
Turkey		64	71	57	–7
Uganda					
Ukraine			44	32	–12
Uruguay			60		
USA	53	58	36		–17
Venezuela			37		
Vietnam					
Zimbabwe					

CONFIDENCE: THE EUROPEAN UNION

(E086) *I am going to name a number of organizations. For each one, could you tell me how much confidence you have in them: is it a great deal of confidence, quite a lot of confidence, not very much confidence or none at all? The European Union*

A great deal/Quite a lot (%)

	1981	1990	1995	2000	Change
Albania			86	84	–2
Algeria				16	
Argentina					
Armenia			59		
Australia					
Austria				37	
Azerbaijan			28		
Bangladesh					
Belarus			67	47	–20
Belgium		66		47	–19
Bosnia and Herz.			64	48	–16
Brazil					
Bulgaria		50	72	43	–7
Canada					
Chile		32			
China		17		39	22
Colombia					
Croatia			33	44	11
Czech Republic		63	49	43	–20
Denmark		39		27	–12
Dominican Rep.					
Egypt					
El Salvador					
Estonia			65	31	–34
Finland		47	32	25	–22
France		73		48	–25
Georgia			60		
Germany (East)		64	25	34	–30
Germany (West)		48	34	38	–10
Great Britain		47		26	–21
Greece				25	
Hungary		63	65	59	–4
Iceland		36		45	9
India					
Indonesia					
Iran					
Iraq					
Ireland		71		59	–12
Israel					
Italy		74		69	–5
Japan					
Jordan					
Korea Republic					

	1981	1990	1995	2000	Change
Kyrgyzstan				56	
Latvia			59	35	–24
Lithuania			52	31	–21
Luxembourg				58	
Macedonia			38	33	–5
Malta		58		56	–2
Mexico		27			
Moldova			72	75	3
Montenegro			40	51	11
Morocco				24	
Netherlands		55		33	–22
New Zealand					
Nigeria					
Northern Ireland		49		40	–9
Norway		40	29		–11
Pakistan					
Peru					
Philippines					
Poland		59	61	43	–16
Portugal		57		69	12
Puerto Rico					
Romania		48	50	39	–9
Russian Fed.			53	26	–27
Saudi Arabia					
Serbia			24	27	3
Singapore					
Slovakia		45	56	55	10
Slovenia		46	42	37	–9
South Africa					
Spain		51	53	53	2
Sweden		58	25	29	–29
Switzerland			43		
Taiwan			64		
Tanzania					
Turkey		37	49	40	3
Uganda					
Ukraine			64	45	–19
Uruguay					
USA					
Venezuela					
Vietnam					
Zimbabwe					

CONFIDENCE: NATO

(E087) *I am going to name a number of organizations. For each one, could you tell me how much confidence you have in them: is it a great deal of confidence, quite a lot of confidence, not very much confidence or none at all? NATO (North Atlantic Treaty Organization)*

A great deal/Quite a lot (%)

	1981	1990	1995	2000	Change
Albania				86	
Algeria				6	
Argentina					
Armenia					
Australia					
Austria				28	
Azerbaijan					
Bangladesh				89	
Belarus				21	
Belgium		46		44	–2
Bosnia and Herz.				38	
Brazil					
Bulgaria		28			
Canada		50		57	7
Chile		29		50	21
China		22		26	4
Colombia					
Croatia				56	
Czech Republic		39		44	5
Denmark		52		59	7
Dominican Rep.					
Egypt					
El Salvador					
Estonia				37	
Finland		29			
France		60			
Georgia					
Germany (East)		19		40	21
Germany (West)		42		54	12
Great Britain		59		59	0
Greece				7	
Hungary		42			
Iceland		35		47	12
India		35			
Indonesia					
Iran					
Iraq					
Ireland		59			
Israel					
Italy		54		56	2
Japan		27			
Jordan					
Korea Republic					

	1981	1990	1995	2000	Change
Kyrgyzstan				40	
Latvia				36	
Lithuania				36	
Luxembourg				62	
Macedonia				27	
Malta				52	
Mexico		27		32	5
Moldova				66	
Montenegro				19	
Morocco				11	
Netherlands		47		52	5
New Zealand					
Nigeria		55			
Northern Ireland		53			
Norway		67			
Pakistan					
Peru					
Philippines				63	
Poland		38		57	19
Portugal		35		68	33
Puerto Rico					
Romania		47		35	–12
Russian Fed.		68		8	–60
Saudi Arabia					
Serbia				6	
Singapore					
Slovakia		23		36	13
Slovenia		25		37	12
South Africa				60	
Spain		21		33	12
Sweden		36		41	5
Switzerland					
Taiwan					
Tanzania					
Turkey				39	
Uganda				53	
Ukraine				32	
Uruguay					
USA		52		53	1
Venezuela				49	
Vietnam					
Zimbabwe				38	

Confidence: The United Nations

(E088) *I am going to name a number of organizations. For each one, could you tell me how much confidence you have in them: is it a great deal of confidence, quite a lot of confidence, not very much confidence or none at all? United Nations*

A great deal/Quite a lot (%)

	1981	1990	1995	2000	Change
Albania			86	86	0
Algeria				15	
Argentina			39	42	3
Armenia			70		
Australia			50		
Austria				42	
Azerbaijan			33		
Bangladesh			83	93	10
Belarus			71	53	–18
Belgium				45	
Bosnia and Herz.			63	39	–24
Brazil			70		
Bulgaria			73	40	–33
Canada				65	
Chile			63	58	–5
China			56	69	13
Colombia					
Croatia			27	47	20
Czech Republic			62	48	–14
Denmark				64	
Dominican Rep.			44		
Egypt				32	
El Salvador			51		
Estonia			70	43	–27
Finland			55	44	–11
France				54	
Georgia			61		
Germany (East)			34	47	13
Germany (West)			47	53	6
Great Britain				60	
Greece				19	
Hungary			67	59	–8
Iceland				72	
India			55	53	–2
Indonesia				48	
Iran				36	
Iraq				16	
Ireland				62	
Israel					
Italy				68	
Japan			63	61	–2
Jordan				36	
Korea Republic			81	62	–19
Kyrgyzstan				59	
Latvia			65	48	–17
Lithuania			58	47	–11
Luxembourg				65	
Macedonia			43	37	–6
Malta				63	
Mexico			51	45	–6
Moldova			76	74	–2
Montenegro			47	44	–3
Morocco				13	
Netherlands				55	
New Zealand			56		
Nigeria			72	70	–2
Northern Ireland				53	
Norway			73		
Pakistan				22	
Peru			52	44	–8
Philippines			75	76	1
Poland			68	58	–10
Portugal				71	
Puerto Rico			72	67	–5
Romania			53	44	–9
Russian Fed.			61	27	–34
Saudi Arabia				33	
Serbia			23	17	–6
Singapore					
Slovakia			58	52	–6
Slovenia			39	49	10
South Africa			59	67	8
Spain			50	49	–1
Sweden			66	74	8
Switzerland			43		
Taiwan			49		
Tanzania				82	
Turkey			47	46	–1
Uganda				87	
Ukraine			68	55	–13
Uruguay			56		
USA			51	57	6
Venezuela			43	52	9
Vietnam				61	
Zimbabwe				70	

Rate System for Governing Country Today

(E111) *People have different views about the system for governing this country. Here is a scale for rating how well things are going. (1 = very bad; 10 = very good)*

% (very) Bad (1 thru 4)

	1981	1990	1995	2000	Change
Albania			25	51	26
Algeria				52	
Argentina			43	37	–6
Armenia			62		
Australia			50		
Austria				21	
Azerbaijan			2		
Bangladesh					
Belarus			67	55	–12
Belgium				36	
Bosnia and Herz.			48	60	12
Brazil			52		
Bulgaria			43	49	6
Canada					
Chile			29		
China					
Colombia					
Croatia			34	67	33
Czech Republic			48	53	5
Denmark				36	
Dominican Rep.			61		
Egypt					
El Salvador			44		
Estonia			47	43	–4
Finland			46	22	–24
France				40	
Georgia			55		
Germany (East)			44	23	–21
Germany (West)					
Great Britain				32	
Greece				43	
Hungary			44	56	12
Iceland				18	
India			47	24	–23
Indonesia				37	
Iran				23	
Iraq					
Ireland				23	
Israel					
Italy				51	
Japan			54		
Jordan				17	
Korea Republic					

	1981	1990	1995	2000	Change
Kyrgyzstan					
Latvia			58	46	–12
Lithuania			51	73	22
Luxembourg				12	
Macedonia			64	76	12
Malta				12	
Mexico			65		
Moldova			70	54	–16
Montenegro					
Morocco				30	
Netherlands				11	
New Zealand			74		
Nigeria			81		
Northern Ireland				33	
Norway			13		
Pakistan				63	
Peru			21	27	6
Philippines			32		
Poland			42	55	13
Portugal				16	
Puerto Rico			38	26	–12
Romania			78	65	–13
Russian Fed.			82	83	1
Saudi Arabia				14	
Serbia			63		
Singapore					
Slovakia			46	64	18
Slovenia			43	48	5
South Africa			26	34	8
Spain			42	23	–19
Sweden			53	37	–16
Switzerland			33		
Taiwan			25		
Tanzania				23	
Turkey			58	76	18
Uganda					
Ukraine			71	70	–1
Uruguay			63		
USA			43		
Venezuela			83		
Vietnam				1	
Zimbabwe					

Rate System for Governing Country Ten Years Ago

(E112) *Where on this scale would you put the political system as it was ten years ago (1 = very bad; 10 = very good)*

% (very) Bad (1 thru 4)

	1981	1990	1995	2000	Change
Albania			81	74	–7
Algeria					
Argentina			72	62	–10
Armenia			26		
Australia			27		
Austria				17	
Azerbaijan			25		
Bangladesh			11	29	18
Belarus			36	38	2
Belgium				30	
Bosnia and Herz.			37	23	–14
Brazil			48		
Bulgaria			50	47	–3
Canada				28	
Chile			42	37	–5
China				12	
Colombia					
Croatia			64	56	–8
Czech Republic			57	65	8
Denmark				30	
Dominican Rep.			73		
Egypt				10	
El Salvador			34		
Estonia			53	52	–1
Finland			12	24	12
France				30	
Georgia			36		
Germany (East)			21	23	2
Germany (West)					
Great Britain				34	
Greece				38	
Hungary			38	31	–7
Iceland				29	
India			9		
Indonesia					
Iran					
Iraq					
Ireland				40	
Israel					
Italy				49	
Japan			25	53	28
Jordan					
Korea Republic			20	69	49
Kyrgyzstan				12	
Latvia			57	52	–5
Lithuania			49	38	–11
Luxembourg				11	
Macedonia			38	30	–8
Malta				18	
Mexico			35	36	1
Moldova			28	51	23
Montenegro					
Morocco					
Netherlands				10	
New Zealand			31		
Nigeria			29		
Northern Ireland				43	
Norway			18		
Pakistan					
Peru			30		
Philippines			39	30	–9
Poland			58	53	–5
Portugal				36	
Puerto Rico			23		
Romania			81	51	–30
Russian Fed.			31	30	–1
Saudi Arabia					
Serbia			29	72	43
Singapore					
Slovakia			38	37	–1
Slovenia			45	44	–1
South Africa			71	69	–2
Spain			62	32	–30
Sweden			17	22	5
Switzerland			12		
Taiwan			25		
Tanzania				27	
Turkey			32	28	–4
Uganda				46	
Ukraine			43	44	1
Uruguay			43		
USA			25	25	0
Venezuela			42	53	11
Vietnam				6	
Zimbabwe				33	

Having a Strong Leader

(E114) *I'm going to describe various types of political systems and ask what you think about each as a way of governing this country. "Having a strong leader who does not have to bother with parliament and elections"*

Very good/Fairly good (%)

	1981	1990	1995	2000	Change
Albania			43	17	–26
Algeria				39	
Argentina			29	42	13
Armenia			53		
Australia			25		
Austria				16	
Azerbaijan			7		
Bangladesh			7	12	5
Belarus			55	40	–15
Belgium				33	
Bosnia and Herz.			53	37	–16
Brazil			61		
Bulgaria			63	48	–15
Canada				23	
Chile			35	43	8
China				19	
Colombia			53		
Croatia			30	12	–18
Czech Republic			16	17	1
Denmark				14	
Dominican Rep.			28		
Egypt				8	
El Salvador			59		
Estonia			38	18	–20
Finland			27	27	0
France				35	
Georgia			66		
Germany (East)			18	23	5
Germany (West)			10	15	5
Great Britain			27	25	–2
Greece				9	
Hungary			19	22	3
Iceland				11	
India			68	59	–9
Indonesia				19	
Iran				39	
Iraq				20	
Ireland				27	
Israel					
Italy				16	
Japan			32	28	–4
Jordan				42	
Korea Republic			32	28	–4
Kyrgyzstan				61	
Latvia			46	58	12
Lithuania			64	56	–8
Luxembourg				45	
Macedonia			62	74	12
Malta				19	
Mexico			46	56	10
Moldova			57	62	5
Montenegro			25	15	–10
Morocco				18	
Netherlands				27	
New Zealand			20		
Nigeria			36	43	7
Northern Ireland				19	
Norway			14		
Pakistan			64	34	–30
Peru			35	39	4
Philippines			65	63	–2
Poland				22	
Portugal				36	
Puerto Rico			27	33	6
Romania			47	67	20
Russian Fed.			50	49	–1
Saudi Arabia					
Serbia			31	19	–12
Singapore				23	
Slovakia			19	20	1
Slovenia			25	24	–1
South Africa			34	34	0
Spain			30	21	–9
Sweden			26	21	–5
Switzerland			31		
Taiwan			41		
Tanzania				3	
Turkey			41	71	30
Uganda				30	
Ukraine			54	60	6
Uruguay			27		
USA			25	30	5
Venezuela			30	48	18
Vietnam				99	
Zimbabwe				27	

Having Experts Make Decisions

(E115) *I'm going to describe various types of political systems and ask what you think about each as a way of governing this country. "Having experts, not government, make decisions according to what they think is best for the country"*

Very good/Fairly good (%)

	1981	1990	1995	2000	Change
Albania			90	88	–2
Algeria				81	
Argentina			53	54	1
Armenia			55		
Australia			42		
Austria				61	
Azerbaijan			2		
Bangladesh			85	77	–8
Belarus			57	79	22
Belgium				58	
Bosnia and Herz.			78	74	–4
Brazil			83		
Bulgaria			67	82	15
Canada				44	
Chile			44	58	14
China				30	
Colombia			71		
Croatia			82	88	6
Czech Republic			82	63	–19
Denmark				30	
Dominican Rep.			49		
Egypt				67	
El Salvador			69		
Estonia			45	57	12
Finland			65	58	–7
France				51	
Georgia			58		
Germany (East)			68	65	–3
Germany (West)			57	54	–3
Great Britain			56	47	–9
Greece				13	
Hungary			85	85	0
Iceland				42	
India			67	68	1
Indonesia				48	
Iran				27	
Iraq				78	
Ireland				37	
Israel					
Italy				51	
Japan			57	58	1
Jordan				88	
Korea Republic			66	53	–13

	1981	1990	1995	2000	Change
Kyrgyzstan				66	
Latvia			56	61	5
Lithuania			50	57	7
Luxembourg				46	
Macedonia			76	84	8
Malta				34	
Mexico			62	66	4
Moldova			59	51	–8
Montenegro			86	89	3
Morocco				70	
Netherlands				40	
New Zealand			44		
Nigeria			67	73	6
Northern Ireland				38	
Norway			34		
Pakistan				19	
Peru			56	63	7
Philippines			63	62	–1
Poland				88	
Portugal				47	
Puerto Rico			48	43	–5
Romania			49	85	36
Russian Fed.			59	52	–7
Saudi Arabia					
Serbia			85	88	3
Singapore				40	
Slovakia			84	86	2
Slovenia			80	81	1
South Africa			49	52	3
Spain			59	44	–15
Sweden			39	41	2
Switzerland			46		
Taiwan			60		
Tanzania				30	
Turkey			55	74	19
Uganda				36	
Ukraine			61	50	–11
Uruguay			40		
USA			37	44	7
Venezuela			50	69	19
Vietnam				98	
Zimbabwe				69	

Having the Army Rule

(E116) *I'm going to describe various types of political systems and ask what you think about each as a way of governing this country. "Having the army rule"*

Very good/Fairly good (%)

	1981	1990	1995	2000	Change
Albania			82	12	–70
Algeria				19	
Argentina			13	18	5
Armenia			19		
Australia			7		
Austria				2	
Azerbaijan			2		
Bangladesh			7	19	12
Belarus			14	20	6
Belgium				4	
Bosnia and Herz.			24	9	–15
Brazil			45		
Bulgaria			17	12	–5
Canada				6	
Chile			31	24	–7
China				45	
Colombia			34		
Croatia			14	6	–8
Czech Republic			5	2	–3
Denmark				1	
Dominican Rep.			6		
Egypt					
El Salvador			39		
Estonia			5	3	–2
Finland			11	6	–5
France				4	
Georgia			11		
Germany (East)			2	2	0
Germany (West)			1	2	1
Great Britain			6	7	1
Greece				10	
Hungary			5	3	–2
Iceland				1	
India			37	20	–17
Indonesia				96	
Iran				84	
Iraq				17	
Ireland				5	
Israel					
Italy				4	
Japan			3	2	–1
Jordan				58	
Korea Republic			5	4	–1
Kyrgyzstan				34	
Latvia			5	5	0
Lithuania			6	4	–2
Luxembourg				7	
Macedonia			10	26	16
Malta				4	
Mexico			26	35	9
Moldova			11	14	3
Montenegro			10	7	–3
Morocco				15	
Netherlands				1	
New Zealand			2		
Nigeria			31	26	–5
Northern Ireland				2	
Norway			5		
Pakistan			41	4	–37
Peru			18	15	–3
Philippines			53	49	–4
Poland				17	
Portugal				9	
Puerto Rico			9	11	2
Romania			25	28	3
Russian Fed.			21	19	–2
Saudi Arabia					
Serbia			10	10	0
Singapore				13	
Slovakia			5	7	2
Slovenia			6	5	–1
South Africa			25	22	–3
Spain			9	7	–2
Sweden			4	7	3
Switzerland			5		
Taiwan			16		
Tanzania				14	
Turkey			32	29	–3
Uganda				34	
Ukraine			12	13	1
Uruguay			8		
USA			7	9	2
Venezuela			26	23	–3
Vietnam				99	
Zimbabwe				12	

Having a Democratic Political System

(E117) *I'm going to describe various types of political systems and ask what you think about each as a way of governing this country. "Having a democratic political system"*

Very good/Fairly good (%)

	1981	1990	1995	2000	Change
Albania			99	98	–1
Algeria				93	
Argentina			93	91	–2
Armenia			85		
Australia			87		
Austria				96	
Azerbaijan			97		
Bangladesh			98	98	0
Belarus			80	88	8
Belgium				89	
Bosnia and Herz.			93	92	–1
Brazil			85		
Bulgaria			86	86	0
Canada				88	
Chile			85	85	0
China				96	
Colombia			85		
Croatia			98	98	0
Czech Republic			91	93	2
Denmark				98	
Dominican Rep.			91		
Egypt				99	
El Salvador			85		
Estonia			89	87	–2
Finland			77	87	10
France				89	
Georgia			91		
Germany (East)			95	92	–3
Germany (West)			96	95	–1
Great Britain				88	
Greece				98	
Hungary			91	87	–4
Iceland				98	
India			92	93	1
Indonesia				96	
Iran				86	
Iraq				91	
Ireland				90	
Israel					
Italy				97	
Japan			92	92	0
Jordan				94	
Korea Republic			85	85	0
Kyrgyzstan				82	
Latvia			87	88	1
Lithuania			88	86	–2
Luxembourg				92	
Macedonia			84	91	7
Malta				94	
Mexico			77	86	9
Moldova			85	75	–10
Montenegro			95	95	0
Morocco				96	
Netherlands				96	
New Zealand			91		
Nigeria			92	95	3
Northern Ireland				92	
Norway			96		
Pakistan			68	88	20
Peru			91	93	2
Philippines			84	82	–2
Poland				84	
Portugal				91	
Puerto Rico			91	92	1
Romania			91	89	–2
Russian Fed.			58	63	5
Saudi Arabia					
Serbia			91	94	3
Singapore				94	
Slovakia			92	84	–8
Slovenia			86	89	3
South Africa			91	90	–1
Spain			95	95	0
Sweden			96	97	1
Switzerland			93		
Taiwan			93		
Tanzania				93	
Turkey			89	92	3
Uganda				93	
Ukraine			80	85	5
Uruguay			96		
USA			90	89	–1
Venezuela			87	93	6
Vietnam				95	
Zimbabwe				88	

In Democracy, the Economic System runs Badly

(E120) *I'm going to read off some things that people sometimes say about a democratic political system. "In democracy, the economic system runs badly"*

Disagree/Strongly disagree (%)

	1981	1990	1995	2000	Change
Albania			86	79	–7
Algeria				69	
Argentina			63	55	–8
Armenia			58		
Australia			70		
Austria				87	
Azerbaijan			84		
Bangladesh			88	90	2
Belarus			62	68	6
Belgium				67	
Bosnia and Herz.			70	75	5
Brazil			30		
Bulgaria			55	60	5
Canada				72	
Chile			73	63	–10
China				74	
Colombia					
Croatia			75	71	–4
Czech Republic			59	63	4
Denmark				85	
Dominican Rep.			73		
Egypt				82	
El Salvador					
Estonia			77	69	–8
Finland			55	80	25
France				50	
Georgia			69		
Germany (East)			77	79	2
Germany (West)			88	90	2
Great Britain				71	
Greece				58	
Hungary			74	61	–13
Iceland				88	
India			41	57	16
Indonesia				79	
Iran				67	
Iraq				70	
Ireland				80	
Israel					
Italy				67	
Japan			83	79	–4
Jordan				67	
Korea Republic			78	82	4
Kyrgyzstan				49	
Latvia			72	52	–20
Lithuania			58	60	2
Luxembourg				79	
Macedonia			62	55	–7
Malta				88	
Mexico			52	45	–7
Moldova			48	58	10
Montenegro			70	80	10
Morocco				65	
Netherlands				92	
New Zealand			77		
Nigeria			74	63	–11
Northern Ireland				79	
Norway			66		
Pakistan				61	
Peru			65	45	–20
Philippines			55	48	–7
Poland			53	53	0
Portugal				61	
Puerto Rico			52	51	–1
Romania			61	44	–17
Russian Fed.			40	45	5
Saudi Arabia				63	
Serbia			71	70	–1
Singapore					
Slovakia			66	52	–14
Slovenia			51	53	2
South Africa			62	56	–6
Spain			74	76	2
Sweden			69	90	21
Switzerland			77		
Taiwan			74		
Tanzania				73	
Turkey			76	69	–7
Uganda				80	
Ukraine			57	64	7
Uruguay			81		
USA			75	78	3
Venezuela			18	56	38
Vietnam				82	
Zimbabwe				70	

Democracies are Indecisive

(E121) *I'm going to read off some things that people sometimes say about a democratic political system. "Democracies are indecisive and have too much quibbling"*

Disagree/Strongly disagree (%)

	1981	1990	1995	2000	Change
Albania			67	72	5
Algeria				37	
Argentina			34	33	–1
Armenia			42		
Australia			50		
Austria				60	
Azerbaijan			81		
Bangladesh			69	87	18
Belarus			41	60	19
Belgium				40	
Bosnia and Herz.			59	55	–4
Brazil			16		
Bulgaria			40	58	18
Canada				50	
Chile			50	56	6
China				65	
Colombia					
Croatia			57	74	17
Czech Republic			42	49	7
Denmark				57	
Dominican Rep.			61		
Egypt				71	
El Salvador					
Estonia			57	54	–3
Finland			39	53	14
France				26	
Georgia			52		
Germany (East)			63	62	–1
Germany (West)			69	67	–2
Great Britain				55	
Greece				49	
Hungary			51	38	–13
Iceland				81	
India			32	34	2
Indonesia				75	
Iran				72	
Iraq				42	
Ireland				60	
Israel					
Italy				48	
Japan			59	57	–2
Jordan				56	
Korea Republic			62	62	0
Kyrgyzstan				36	
Latvia			41	30	–11
Lithuania			40	37	–3
Luxembourg				47	
Macedonia			52	59	7
Malta				80	
Mexico			47	38	–9
Moldova			44	58	14
Montenegro			54	73	19
Morocco				29	
Netherlands				58	
New Zealand			57		
Nigeria			63	45	–18
Northern Ireland				67	
Norway			42		
Pakistan				71	
Peru			46	42	–4
Philippines			49	43	–6
Poland			17	20	3
Portugal				40	
Puerto Rico			36	44	8
Romania			56	27	–29
Russian Fed.			22	28	6
Saudi Arabia				54	
Serbia			54	53	–1
Singapore					
Slovakia			46	45	–1
Slovenia			29	31	2
South Africa			53	48	–5
Spain			58	64	6
Sweden			38	52	14
Switzerland			25		
Taiwan			39		
Tanzania				51	
Turkey			35	43	8
Uganda				55	
Ukraine			39	46	7
Uruguay			58		
USA			58	61	3
Venezuela			22	45	23
Vietnam				69	
Zimbabwe				63	

Democracies aren't Good at Maintaining Order

(E122) *I'm going to read off some things that people sometimes say about a democratic political system. "Democracies aren't good at maintaining order"*

Disagree/Strongly disagree (%)

	1981	1990	1995	2000	Change
Albania			74	71	–3
Algeria				68	
Argentina			73	65	–8
Armenia			49		
Australia			71		
Austria				87	
Azerbaijan			79		
Bangladesh			83	88	5
Belarus			48	59	11
Belgium				62	
Bosnia and Herz.			71	82	11
Brazil			43		
Bulgaria			55	65	10
Canada				71	
Chile			64	64	0
China				82	
Colombia					
Croatia			74	81	7
Czech Republic			56	46	–10
Denmark				84	
Dominican Rep.			64		
Egypt				80	
El Salvador			85		
Estonia			68	69	1
Finland			66	81	15
France				45	
Georgia			55		
Germany (East)			77	78	1
Germany (West)			88	86	–2
Great Britain				66	
Greece				67	
Hungary			67	61	–6
Iceland				89	
India			59	59	0
Indonesia				77	
Iran				68	
Iraq				61	
Ireland				77	
Israel					
Italy				80	
Japan			80	80	0
Jordan				66	
Korea Republic			77	77	0

	1981	1990	1995	2000	Change
Kyrgyzstan				38	
Latvia			50	56	6
Lithuania			62	50	–12
Luxembourg				79	
Macedonia			60	59	–1
Malta				87	
Mexico			57	49	–8
Moldova			48	57	9
Montenegro			66	81	15
Morocco				59	
Netherlands				78	
New Zealand			75		
Nigeria			65	55	–10
Northern Ireland				75	
Norway			67		
Pakistan				47	
Peru			57	52	–5
Philippines			51	50	–1
Poland			24	32	8
Portugal				59	
Puerto Rico			74	56	–18
Romania			62	49	–13
Russian Fed.			29	35	6
Saudi Arabia				58	
Serbia			66	69	3
Singapore					
Slovakia			64	58	–6
Slovenia			48	54	6
South Africa			60	61	1
Spain			71	81	10
Sweden			73	85	12
Switzerland			73		
Taiwan			66		
Tanzania				79	
Turkey			70	65	–5
Uganda				79	
Ukraine			45	50	5
Uruguay			79		
USA			77	78	1
Venezuela			43	64	21
Vietnam				75	
Zimbabwe				68	

Democracy may have Problems but is Better

(E123) *I'm going to read off some things that people sometimes say about a democratic political system. "Democracy may have problems but it's better than any other form of government"*

Agree strongly/Agree (%)

	1981	1990	1995	2000	Change
Albania			97	95	–2
Algeria				88	
Argentina			92	91	–1
Armenia			73		
Australia			87		
Austria				97	
Azerbaijan			96		
Bangladesh			97	98	1
Belarus			81	87	6
Belgium				92	
Bosnia and Herz.			89	92	3
Brazil			83		
Bulgaria			81	84	3
Canada				87	
Chile			82	82	0
China				90	
Colombia					
Croatia			94	96	2
Czech Republic			91	93	2
Denmark				99	
Dominican Rep.			93		
Egypt				98	
El Salvador					
Estonia			90	90	0
Finland			85	91	6
France				93	
Georgia			86		
Germany (East)			92	93	1
Germany (West)			94	97	3
Great Britain				78	
Greece				97	
Hungary			85	81	–4
Iceland				97	
India			90	92	2
Indonesia				71	
Iran				69	
Iraq				85	
Ireland				92	
Israel					
Italy				94	
Japan			93	92	–1
Jordan				89	
Korea Republic			92	91	–1
Kyrgyzstan				78	
Latvia			83	89	6
Lithuania			90	88	–2
Luxembourg				96	
Macedonia			75	81	6
Malta				94	
Mexico			78	80	2
Moldova			73	78	5
Montenegro			94	92	–2
Morocco				96	
Netherlands				96	
New Zealand			87		
Nigeria			85	45	–40
Northern Ireland				93	
Norway			95		
Pakistan				82	
Peru			86	89	3
Philippines			77	80	3
Poland			88	90	2
Portugal				93	
Puerto Rico			88	91	3
Romania			87	78	–9
Russian Fed.			59	63	4
Saudi Arabia				74	
Serbia			89	89	0
Singapore					
Slovakia			89	84	–5
Slovenia			88	90	2
South Africa			90	84	–6
Spain			93	93	0
Sweden			94	94	0
Switzerland			91		
Taiwan			84		
Tanzania				88	
Turkey			92	88	–4
Uganda				92	
Ukraine			77	82	5
Uruguay			96		
USA			91	87	–4
Venezuela			86	93	7
Vietnam				72	
Zimbabwe				88	

Satisfaction with the People in National Office

(E125) *How satisfied are you with the way the people now in national office are handling the country's affairs? Would you say you are very satisfied, fairly satisfied, fairly dissatisfied or very dissatisfied?*

Very satisfied/Fairly satisfied (%)

	1981	1990	1995	2000	Change
Albania			25	19	–6
Algeria				28	
Argentina			28	27	–1
Armenia			15		
Australia			45		
Austria					
Azerbaijan			26		
Bangladesh			92	76	–16
Belarus			7		
Belgium					
Bosnia and Herz.			49	24	–25
Brazil			57		
Bulgaria			28		
Canada				65	
Chile			59	66	7
China				73	
Colombia			28		
Croatia			42		
Czech Republic			25		
Denmark					
Dominican Rep.			6		
Egypt				92	
El Salvador					
Estonia			13		
Finland			39		
France					
Georgia			23		
Germany (East)			30		
Germany (West)			33		
Great Britain					
Greece					
Hungary			34		
Iceland					
India			43	60	17
Indonesia				23	
Iran				71	
Iraq					
Ireland					
Israel					
Italy					
Japan			9	8	–1
Jordan				77	
Korea Republic			39	31	–8
Kyrgyzstan				32	
Latvia			19		
Lithuania			12		
Luxembourg					
Macedonia			26	19	–7
Malta					
Mexico			28	48	20
Moldova			13	21	8
Montenegro			49	28	–21
Morocco				48	
Netherlands					
New Zealand			27		
Nigeria			31	72	41
Northern Ireland					
Norway			86		
Pakistan				43	
Peru			55	35	–20
Philippines			53	51	–2
Poland			34		
Portugal					
Puerto Rico			52	42	–10
Romania			17		
Russian Fed.			4		
Saudi Arabia					
Serbia			30	37	7
Singapore				91	
Slovakia			36		
Slovenia			36		
South Africa			53	57	4
Spain			21	46	25
Sweden			45	44	–1
Switzerland			65		
Taiwan			38		
Tanzania				60	
Turkey			33	28	–5
Uganda				68	
Ukraine			7		
Uruguay			31		
USA			48	67	19
Venezuela			14	62	48
Vietnam				94	
Zimbabwe				31	

Country is Run by Big Interest

(E128) *Generally speaking, would you say that this country is run by a few big interests looking out for themselves, or that it is run for the benefit of all the people?*

Run by few big interests (%)

	1981	1990	1995	2000	Change
Albania			79	65	–14
Algeria				87	
Argentina			88	90	2
Armenia			96		
Australia			68		
Austria					
Azerbaijan			78		
Bangladesh			40	56	16
Belarus			83		
Belgium					
Bosnia and Herz.			57	81	24
Brazil			75		
Bulgaria			73		
Canada				52	
Chile		45	68	65	20
China		8		17	9
Colombia			79		
Croatia			66		
Czech Republic		65	82		17
Denmark					
Dominican Rep.			92		
Egypt				69	
El Salvador			74		
Estonia			85		
Finland			72		
France					
Georgia			94		
Germany (East)			78		
Germany (West)			64		
Great Britain					
Greece					
Hungary			82		
Iceland					
India		55	71	66	11
Indonesia				70	
Iran				49	
Iraq				70	
Ireland					
Israel					
Italy					
Japan			80	84	4
Jordan				69	
Korea Republic			83	88	5
Kyrgyzstan				83	
Latvia			96		
Lithuania			90		
Luxembourg					
Macedonia			74	93	19
Malta					
Mexico		81	71	71	–10
Moldova			83	91	8
Montenegro			57	74	17
Morocco				76	
Netherlands					
New Zealand			78		
Nigeria		78	83	72	–6
Northern Ireland					
Norway			28		
Pakistan				89	
Peru			43	57	14
Philippines			59	60	1
Poland			80		
Portugal					
Puerto Rico			61	52	–9
Romania			80		
Russian Fed.			93		
Saudi Arabia				59	
Serbia			70	70	0
Singapore				22	
Slovakia		72	66		–6
Slovenia			78		
South Africa			39	60	21
Spain		51	66	60	9
Sweden			59		
Switzerland			61		
Taiwan			52		
Tanzania				48	
Turkey		53	76	82	29
Uganda				51	
Ukraine			88		
Uruguay			76		
USA			74	63	–11
Venezuela			84	37	–47
Vietnam				9	
Zimbabwe				82	

ECONOMIC AID

(E129) *Some people favor, and others are against, having this country provide economic aid to poorer countries. Do you think that this country should provide more or less economic aid to poorer countries? Would you say we should give…*

Provide a lot more that we do/Somewhat more than we do (%)

	1981	1990	1995	2000	Change
Albania			84	43	–41
Algeria				39	
Argentina			44	4	–40
Armenia			63		
Australia			75		
Austria					
Azerbaijan			57		
Bangladesh				63	
Belarus			60		
Belgium					
Bosnia and Herz.			77	49	–28
Brazil			65		
Bulgaria			42		
Canada				56	
Chile			57	50	–7
China			85	69	–16
Colombia					
Croatia			95		
Czech Republic			64		
Denmark					
Dominican Rep.			68		
Egypt					
El Salvador					
Estonia			57		
Finland			75		
France					
Georgia			56		
Germany (East)			76		
Germany (West)			83		
Great Britain					
Greece					
Hungary			68		
Iceland					
India			63	55	–8
Indonesia					
Iran					
Iraq					
Ireland					
Israel					
Italy					
Japan			90	45	–45
Jordan					
Korea Republic					
Kyrgyzstan				35	
Latvia			33		
Lithuania			31		
Luxembourg					
Macedonia			57	20	–37
Malta					
Mexico			45	68	23
Moldova			64	63	–1
Montenegro			74	48	–26
Morocco				62	
Netherlands					
New Zealand			69		
Nigeria			59		
Northern Ireland					
Norway			82		
Pakistan					
Peru			89	94	5
Philippines			64	36	–28
Poland					
Portugal					
Puerto Rico			87	85	–2
Romania			65		
Russian Fed.			35		
Saudi Arabia					
Serbia			62	27	–35
Singapore				68	
Slovakia			59		
Slovenia			72		
South Africa			52	45	–7
Spain			85	83	–2
Sweden			84	39	–45
Switzerland					
Taiwan			76		
Tanzania				40	
Turkey					
Uganda				37	
Ukraine			45		
Uruguay			62		
USA			55	44	–11
Venezuela			34	66	32
Vietnam				73	
Zimbabwe				54	

Immigrant Policy

(E143) *How about people from other countries coming here to work. Which one of the following do you think the government should do?*

Let people come as long as there are jobs available (%)

	1981	1990	1995	2000	Change
Albania			60	45	–15
Algeria				45	
Argentina			51	45	–6
Armenia			50		
Australia			52		
Austria				52	
Azerbaijan			59		
Bangladesh				50	
Belarus			54	35	–19
Belgium				31	
Bosnia and Herz.			34	55	21
Brazil			37		
Bulgaria			51	31	–20
Canada				49	
Chile			51	48	–3
China			37	48	11
Colombia					
Croatia			50	28	–22
Czech Republic			36	30	–6
Denmark				24	
Dominican Rep.			37		
Egypt				43	
El Salvador					
Estonia			45	37	–8
Finland			31	35	4
France				34	
Georgia			53		
Germany (East)			32	32	0
Germany (West)			57	33	–24
Great Britain				34	
Greece				45	
Hungary			25	12	–13
Iceland				59	
India			22	19	–3
Indonesia				23	
Iran				28	
Iraq					
Ireland				47	
Israel					
Italy				47	
Japan			50	52	2
Jordan				31	
Korea Republic			50	58	8
Kyrgyzstan				46	
Latvia			45	27	–18
Lithuania			40	36	–4
Luxembourg				52	
Macedonia			17	20	3
Malta				30	
Mexico			46	42	–4
Moldova			43	54	11
Montenegro			35	27	–8
Morocco				38	
Netherlands				35	
New Zealand			57		
Nigeria			37	41	4
Northern Ireland				35	
Norway			42		
Pakistan				43	
Peru			39	42	3
Philippines			16	18	2
Poland			28	18	–10
Portugal				61	
Puerto Rico			25	31	6
Romania			53	39	–14
Russian Fed.			48	46	–2
Saudi Arabia				45	
Serbia			39	36	–3
Singapore				24	
Slovakia			31	27	–4
Slovenia			59	48	–11
South Africa			26	26	0
Spain			57	58	1
Sweden			33	54	21
Switzerland			55		
Taiwan			32		
Tanzania				19	
Turkey			34	38	4
Uganda				45	
Ukraine			53	44	–9
Uruguay			55		
USA			32	45	13
Venezuela			39	49	10
Vietnam				54	
Zimbabwe				53	

Watch TV

(E188) *Do you ever watch television? If yes: How much time do you usually spend watching television on an average weekday (NOT WEEKENDS)?*

Less than 4 hours per day (%)

	1981	1990	1995	2000	Change
Albania			95		
Algeria				70	
Argentina			81	77	–4
Armenia			42		
Australia			70		
Austria					
Azerbaijan			48		
Bangladesh			96	94	–2
Belarus			66		
Belgium	81				
Bosnia and Herz.			70		
Brazil			70		
Bulgaria			64		
Canada	65				
Chile			77		
China			86		
Colombia			85		
Croatia			79		
Czech Republic			76		
Denmark	89				
Dominican Rep.			85		
Egypt				78	
El Salvador			81		
Estonia			75		
Finland			84		
France	82				
Georgia			100		
Germany (East)			80		
Germany (West)	86		88		2
Great Britain	58				
Greece					
Hungary			81		
Iceland	93				
India			99		
Indonesia				76	
Iran					
Iraq				73	
Ireland	60				
Israel					
Italy	82				
Japan			76		
Jordan				73	
Korea Republic					
Kyrgyzstan					
Latvia			79		
Lithuania			72		
Luxembourg					
Macedonia			52		
Malta	81				
Mexico			90		
Moldova			80		
Montenegro			76		
Morocco				78	
Netherlands	85				
New Zealand			80		
Nigeria			82	75	–7
Northern Ireland	63				
Norway	90		87		–3
Pakistan			90	93	3
Peru			80	80	0
Philippines			86		
Poland			80		
Portugal					
Puerto Rico			72	79	7
Romania			71		
Russian Fed.			67		
Saudi Arabia				75	
Serbia			77		
Singapore					
Slovakia			83		
Slovenia			91		
South Africa			84	68	–16
Spain	79		81	79	0
Sweden	90		92		2
Switzerland			93		
Taiwan			76		
Tanzania					
Turkey					
Uganda				88	
Ukraine			85		
Uruguay			70		
USA	59		74		15
Venezuela			71		
Vietnam					
Zimbabwe				88	

Thinking about Meaning and Purpose of Life

(F001) *How often, if at all, do you think about the meaning and purpose of life?*

Often (%)

	1981	1990	1995	2000	Change
Albania			42	53	11
Algeria				50	
Argentina	30	57	51	51	21
Armenia			60		
Australia	34		44		10
Austria		27		34	7
Azerbaijan			42		
Bangladesh			41	47	6
Belarus		35	47	36	1
Belgium	22	29			7
Bosnia and Herz.			33	41	8
Brazil		43	37		–6
Bulgaria		44	33	46	2
Canada	37	43		52	15
Chile		53	50	50	–3
China		31	26	32	1
Colombia			70		
Croatia			26	41	15
Czech Republic		30	26		–4
Denmark	29	29		37	8
Dominican Rep.			56		
Egypt				52	
El Salvador			53		
Estonia		35	39	40	5
Finland		38	40	42	4
France	35	39			4
Georgia			73		
Germany (East)		38	46	24	–14
Germany (West)	30	30	41	21	–9
Great Britain	34	36		24	–10
Greece					
Hungary	44	45	45		1
Iceland	39	36			–3
India		34	25	36	2
Indonesia				58	
Iran				46	
Iraq				50	
Ireland	26	34			8
Israel					
Italy	36	47		50	14
Japan	21	21	26	26	5
Jordan				60	
Korea Republic	29	39		41	12
Kyrgyzstan				72	
Latvia		36	43		7
Lithuania		41	41	40	–1
Luxembourg				36	
Macedonia			51	50	–1
Malta	31	23			–8
Mexico		40	35	44	4
Moldova			49	57	8
Montenegro			39	37	–2
Morocco				75	
Netherlands	24	31			7
New Zealand			44		
Nigeria		59	51	56	–3
Northern Ireland	29	33			4
Norway	26	31	32		6
Pakistan				35	
Peru			41	54	13
Philippines			43	64	21
Poland		38			
Portugal		43			
Puerto Rico			68	76	8
Romania		45	53		8
Russian Fed.		41	45	49	8
Saudi Arabia				26	
Serbia			43	38	–5
Singapore				32	
Slovakia		34	28		–6
Slovenia		37	33		–4
South Africa		57	46	56	–1
Spain	24	27	24	22	–2
Sweden	20	24	28	37	17
Switzerland		44	43		–1
Taiwan			28		
Tanzania				84	
Turkey		38	47		9
Uganda				59	
Ukraine			43	51	8
Uruguay			42		
USA	49	48	46	58	9
Venezuela			51	66	15
Vietnam				58	
Zimbabwe				69	

ABSOLUTE STANDARDS OF GOOD AND EVIL

(F022) *Here are two statements which people sometimes make when discussing good and evil. Which one comes closest to your own point of view?*

There are absolutely clear guidelines about what is good and evil (%)

	1981	1990	1995	2000	Change
Albania			46	49	3
Algeria					
Argentina	25	33	38	39	14
Armenia			41		
Australia			42		
Austria		27		20	–7
Azerbaijan			57		
Bangladesh			37	48	11
Belarus		26	37	25	–1
Belgium	38	33		31	–7
Bosnia and Herz.			52	54	2
Brazil		46	49		3
Bulgaria		47	33	33	–14
Canada	32	31		42	10
Chile		35	46	53	18
China		35	41	36	1
Colombia			38		
Croatia			41	35	–6
Czech Republic		17	23	23	6
Denmark	11	10		10	–1
Dominican Rep.			36		
Egypt					
El Salvador			49		
Estonia		23	32	30	7
Finland		25	34	29	4
France	22	24		25	3
Georgia			60		
Germany (East)		22	15	38	16
Germany (West)	24	26	17	34	10
Great Britain	29	36		41	12
Greece				16	
Hungary	12	17	22	15	3
Iceland	10	11		9	–1
India		45	38	30	–15
Indonesia					
Iran					
Iraq					
Ireland	37	42		41	4
Israel					
Italy	35	45		36	1
Japan	16	15	17	19	3
Jordan					
Korea Republic	28	23		37	9
Kyrgyzstan				56	
Latvia		27	32	41	14
Lithuania		23	37	35	12
Luxembourg				23	
Macedonia			51	55	4
Malta	41	44		48	7
Mexico		38	30	41	3
Moldova			40	39	–1
Montenegro			31	49	18
Morocco				78	
Netherlands	27	26		27	0
New Zealand			42		
Nigeria		60	58		–2
Northern Ireland	46	51		47	1
Norway	31	32	29		–2
Pakistan					
Peru			44	53	9
Philippines			60	55	–5
Poland		47	37	51	4
Portugal		31		39	8
Puerto Rico			39	45	6
Romania		23	57	40	17
Russian Fed.		31	45	39	8
Saudi Arabia					
Serbia			40	47	7
Singapore				38	
Slovakia		26	25	36	10
Slovenia		21	31	22	1
South Africa		51	61	63	12
Spain	26	31	42	39	13
Sweden	21	19	25	16	–5
Switzerland		22	28		6
Taiwan			28		
Tanzania				69	
Turkey		34	29	35	1
Uganda				59	
Ukraine			48	43	–5
Uruguay			34		
USA	39	50	48	49	10
Venezuela			38	41	3
Vietnam				58	
Zimbabwe				57	

BELONG TO RELIGIOUS DENOMINATION

(F024) *Do you belong to a religious denomination?*

Yes (%)

	1981	1990	1995	2000	Change
Albania			99	87	–12
Algeria					
Argentina	87	84	86	87	0
Armenia			87		
Australia	97		81		–16
Austria		85		88	3
Azerbaijan			94		
Bangladesh			100	100	0
Belarus			65	52	–13
Belgium	84	68		64	–20
Bosnia and Herz.			71	75	4
Brazil		88	88		0
Bulgaria		34	67	70	36
Canada	89	74		69	–20
Chile		83	88	66	–17
China		3		6	3
Colombia			92		
Croatia			87	89	2
Czech Republic		41	44	34	–7
Denmark	94	92		90	–4
Dominican Rep.			76		
Egypt				100	
El Salvador			84		
Estonia		13	27	25	12
Finland		89	88	88	–1
France	74	61		57	–17
Georgia			94		
Germany (East)		38	25	34	–4
Germany (West)	91	89	77	87	–4
Great Britain	91	58		83	–8
Greece				96	
Hungary	98	58	78	57	–41
Iceland	99	98		96	–3
India		99	97	93	–6
Indonesia				100	
Iran				99	
Iraq				100	
Ireland	99	96		91	–8
Israel				100	
Italy	94	85		82	–12
Japan	96	33	35	44	–52
Jordan				100	
Korea Republic	53	70	61	63	10
Kyrgyzstan				85	
Latvia		37	60	59	22
Lithuania		63	86	81	18
Luxembourg				72	
Macedonia			72	86	14
Malta	100	97		99	–1
Mexico		85	78	81	–4
Moldova			85	100	15
Montenegro			94	97	3
Morocco				100	
Netherlands	63	51		45	–18
New Zealand			83		
Nigeria		95	98	99	4
Northern Ireland	97	90		86	–11
Norway	96	90	91		–5
Pakistan			98	71	–27
Peru			93	95	2
Philippines			100	90	–10
Poland		96	97	96	0
Portugal		72		89	17
Puerto Rico			81	89	8
Romania		94	100	98	4
Russian Fed.		34	54	51	17
Saudi Arabia				100	
Serbia			83	94	11
Singapore				80	
Slovakia		74	87	77	3
Slovenia		74	77	70	–4
South Africa		91	89	86	–5
Spain	91	86	86	83	–8
Sweden	93	82	92	76	–17
Switzerland		92	100		8
Taiwan			79		
Tanzania				98	
Turkey		100	98	98	–2
Uganda				99	
Ukraine			66	56	–10
Uruguay			52		
USA	94	77	79	78	–16
Venezuela			92	73	–19
Vietnam				54	
Zimbabwe				86	

How Often Do You Attend Religious Services

(F028) *Apart from weddings, funerals and christenings, about how often do you attend religious services these days?*

Once month or more (%)

	1981	1990	1995	2000	Change
Albania			35	29	–6
Algeria				50	
Argentina	56	55	41	43	–13
Armenia			30		
Australia	40		25		–15
Austria		44		42	–2
Azerbaijan			14		
Bangladesh			90	67	–23
Belarus		6	14	15	9
Belgium	38	31		27	–11
Bosnia and Herz.			46	45	–1
Brazil		50	75		25
Bulgaria		9	16	20	11
Canada	47	40		36	–11
Chile		46	44	45	–1
China		1		3	2
Colombia			67		
Croatia			36	53	17
Czech Republic		11	14	12	1
Denmark	13	11		12	–1
Dominican Rep.			55		
Egypt				45	
El Salvador			69		
Estonia			9	11	2
Finland		11	11	14	3
France	18	17		12	–6
Georgia			27		
Germany (East)		17	9	12	–5
Germany (West)	37	34	25	34	–3
Great Britain	22	23		19	–3
Greece				34	
Hungary	34	23	17	18	–16
Iceland	11	9		12	1
India		71	55	51	–20
Indonesia				76	
Iran				46	
Iraq				36	
Ireland	88	88		70	–18
Israel					
Italy	52	53		54	2
Japan	15	14	11	12	–3
Jordan				47	
Korea Republic	45	64	27	38	–7

	1981	1990	1995	2000	Change
Kyrgyzstan				24	
Latvia		9	16	15	6
Lithuania			31	31	0
Luxembourg				32	
Macedonia			18	33	15
Malta	94	90		87	–7
Mexico		63	65	75	12
Moldova			23	29	6
Montenegro			10	17	7
Morocco				48	
Netherlands	40	30		25	–15
New Zealand			22		
Nigeria		88	89	95	7
Northern Ireland	68	69		63	–5
Norway	15	13	12		–3
Pakistan				91	
Peru			64	71	7
Philippines			90	79	–11
Poland		84	74	78	–6
Portugal		41		51	10
Puerto Rico			65	70	5
Romania		31	40	46	15
Russian Fed.		6	8	9	3
Saudi Arabia				44	
Serbia			14	20	6
Singapore				44	
Slovakia		40	46	50	10
Slovenia		35	33	31	–4
South Africa			70	68	–2
Spain	54	41	37	36	–18
Sweden	14	10	11	9	–5
Switzerland		42	25		–17
Taiwan			14		
Tanzania				87	
Turkey		38	53	40	2
Uganda				88	
Ukraine			18	17	–1
Uruguay			23		
USA	60	58	55	60	0
Venezuela			49	48	–1
Vietnam				13	
Zimbabwe				81	

Religious Service Birth

(F031) *Do you personally think it is important to hold a religious service for any of the following events? Birth*

Yes (%)

	1981	1990	1995	2000	Change
Albania					
Algeria					
Argentina		67			
Armenia					
Australia					
Austria		87		81	–6
Azerbaijan					
Bangladesh					
Belarus				84	
Belgium		74		70	–4
Bosnia and Herz.					
Brazil		81			
Bulgaria		78		78	0
Canada		68			
Chile		77			
China		4			
Colombia					
Croatia				91	
Czech Republic		45		42	–3
Denmark		69		65	–4
Dominican Rep.					
Egypt					
El Salvador					
Estonia		66		64	–2
Finland		58		84	26
France		65		61	–4
Georgia					
Germany (East)		38		26	–12
Germany (West)		72		73	1
Great Britain		66		59	–7
Greece				67	
Hungary		79		75	–4
Iceland		67		74	7
India		74			
Indonesia					
Iran					
Iraq					
Ireland		94		91	–3
Israel					
Italy		86		89	3
Japan		36			
Jordan					
Korea Republic					

	1981	1990	1995	2000	Change
Kyrgyzstan					
Latvia		84		65	–19
Lithuania		87		93	6
Luxembourg				70	
Macedonia					
Malta		97		96	–1
Mexico		76			
Moldova					
Montenegro					
Morocco					
Netherlands		47		40	–7
New Zealand					
Nigeria		92			
Northern Ireland		83		81	–2
Norway		66			
Pakistan					
Peru					
Philippines					
Poland		96		96	0
Portugal		75		90	15
Puerto Rico					
Romania		86		98	12
Russian Fed.		78		75	–3
Saudi Arabia					
Serbia					
Singapore					
Slovakia		80		83	3
Slovenia		79		73	–6
South Africa		77			
Spain		76		78	2
Sweden		56		60	4
Switzerland					
Taiwan					
Tanzania					
Turkey				42	
Uganda					
Ukraine				86	
Uruguay					
USA		57			
Venezuela					
Vietnam					
Zimbabwe					

Religious Service Marriage

(F032) *Do you personally think it is important to hold a religious service for any of the following events? Marriage*

Yes (%)

	1981	1990	1995	2000	Change
Albania					
Algeria					
Argentina		73			
Armenia					
Australia					
Austria		85		76	–9
Azerbaijan					
Bangladesh					
Belarus				61	
Belgium		76		70	–6
Bosnia and Herz.					
Brazil		82			
Bulgaria		81		83	2
Canada		82			
Chile		87			
China		13			
Colombia					
Croatia				95	
Czech Republic		44		40	–4
Denmark		64		63	–1
Dominican Rep.					
Egypt					
El Salvador					
Estonia		64		65	1
Finland		64		83	19
France		68		66	–2
Georgia					
Germany (East)		47		34	–13
Germany (West)		75		76	1
Great Britain		80		69	–11
Greece				83	
Hungary		76		75	–1
Iceland		66		67	1
India		79			
Indonesia					
Iran					
Iraq					
Ireland		94		93	–1
Israel					
Italy		83		85	2
Japan		56			
Jordan					
Korea Republic					

	1981	1990	1995	2000	Change
Kyrgyzstan					
Latvia		79		78	–1
Lithuania		84		89	5
Luxembourg				66	
Macedonia					
Malta		96		96	0
Mexico		82			
Moldova					
Montenegro					
Morocco					
Netherlands		52		46	–6
New Zealand					
Nigeria		95			
Northern Ireland		93		90	–3
Norway		70			
Pakistan					
Peru					
Philippines					
Poland		96		95	–1
Portugal		79		89	10
Puerto Rico					
Romania		92		98	6
Russian Fed.		62		54	–8
Saudi Arabia					
Serbia					
Singapore					
Slovakia		76		80	4
Slovenia		76		70	–6
South Africa		93			
Spain		76		75	–1
Sweden		59		62	3
Switzerland					
Taiwan					
Tanzania					
Turkey				82	
Uganda					
Ukraine				69	
Uruguay					
USA		86			
Venezuela					
Vietnam					
Zimbabwe					

Religious Service Death

(F033) *Do you personally think it is important to hold a religious service for any of the following events? Death*

Yes (%)

	1981	1990	1995	2000	Change
Albania					
Algeria					
Argentina		66			
Armenia					
Australia					
Austria		88		85	–3
Azerbaijan					
Bangladesh					
Belarus				88	
Belgium		79		74	–5
Bosnia and Herz.					
Brazil		76			
Bulgaria		86		89	3
Canada		83			
Chile		82			
China		11			
Colombia					
Croatia				96	
Czech Republic		55		50	–5
Denmark		80		80	0
Dominican Rep.					
Egypt					
El Salvador					
Estonia		72		76	4
Finland		83		90	7
France		73		73	0
Georgia					
Germany (East)		62		39	–23
Germany (West)		83		81	–2
Great Britain		86		78	–8
Greece				87	
Hungary		86		82	–4
Iceland		93		91	–2
India		75			
Indonesia					
Iran					
Iraq					
Ireland		97		96	–1
Israel					
Italy		87		89	2
Japan		87			
Jordan					
Korea Republic					
Kyrgyzstan					
Latvia		85		88	3
Lithuania		89		95	6
Luxembourg				77	
Macedonia					
Malta		97		97	0
Mexico		81			
Moldova					
Montenegro					
Morocco					
Netherlands		60		56	–4
New Zealand					
Nigeria		90			
Northern Ireland		96		93	–3
Norway		81			
Pakistan					
Peru					
Philippines					
Poland		95		96	1
Portugal		79		92	13
Puerto Rico					
Romania		89		98	9
Russian Fed.		74		79	5
Saudi Arabia					
Serbia					
Singapore					
Slovakia		83		85	2
Slovenia		80		77	–3
South Africa		86			
Spain		77		80	3
Sweden		80		78	–2
Switzerland					
Taiwan					
Tanzania					
Turkey				95	
Uganda					
Ukraine				85	
Uruguay					
USA		87			
Venezuela					
Vietnam					
Zimbabwe					

RELIGIOUS PERSON

(F034) *Independently of whether you go to church or not, would you say you are…*

A religious person (%)

	1981	1990	1995	2000	Change
Albania			45	68	23
Algeria				59	
Argentina	67	73	81	84	17
Armenia			75		
Australia	57		59		2
Austria		80		79	–1
Azerbaijan			88		
Bangladesh			84	97	13
Belarus		41	70	28	–13
Belgium	81	68		67	–14
Bosnia and Herz.			70	74	4
Brazil		88	85		–3
Bulgaria		36	53	52	16
Canada	77	71		73	–4
Chile		77	75	71	–6
China		5		15	10
Colombia			85		
Croatia			71	85	14
Czech Republic		40	43	43	3
Denmark	74	73		77	3
Dominican Rep.			76		
Egypt				99	
El Salvador			70		
Estonia		21	36	42	21
Finland		59	57	67	8
France	56	51		47	–9
Georgia			89		
Germany (East)		37	28	29	–8
Germany (West)	69	65	65	62	–7
Great Britain	59	56		42	–17
Greece				80	
Hungary	45	57	55	59	14
Iceland	68	75		74	6
India		83	80	79	–4
Indonesia				85	
Iran				95	
Iraq				87	
Ireland	66	72		74	8
Israel					
Italy	86	86		86	0
Japan	27	26	22	26	–1
Jordan				86	
Korea Republic				31	

	1981	1990	1995	2000	Change
Kyrgyzstan				75	
Latvia		54	64	77	23
Lithuania		55	84	84	29
Luxembourg				63	
Macedonia			66	84	18
Malta	96	74		75	–21
Mexico		75	62	77	2
Moldova			82	91	9
Montenegro			49	73	24
Morocco				95	
Netherlands	70	60		62	–8
New Zealand			52		
Nigeria		93	94	97	4
Northern Ireland	63	72		62	–1
Norway	48	48	47		–1
Pakistan				91	
Peru			82	88	6
Philippines			84	79	–5
Poland		96	94	94	–2
Portugal		69		88	19
Puerto Rico			86	83	–3
Romania		74	84	85	11
Russian Fed.		56	64	66	10
Saudi Arabia				70	
Serbia			59	74	15
Singapore					
Slovakia		74	78	82	8
Slovenia		73	69	70	–3
South Africa		83	80	79	–4
Spain	65	68	69	61	–4
Sweden	34	31	33	39	5
Switzerland		74	57		–17
Taiwan			75		
Tanzania				94	
Turkey		75	78	80	5
Uganda				94	
Ukraine			64	75	11
Uruguay			55		
USA	84	84	81	83	–1
Venezuela			86	79	–7
Vietnam				38	
Zimbabwe				89	

Churches give Answers: Moral Problems

(F035) *Generally speaking, do you think that the churches in your country are giving adequate answers to… The moral problems and needs of the individual*

Yes (%)

	1981	1990	1995	2000	Change
Albania				64	
Algeria				91	
Argentina		42		54	12
Armenia					
Australia					
Austria		46		37	–9
Azerbaijan					
Bangladesh				62	
Belarus				56	
Belgium	49	42		33	–16
Bosnia and Herz.				48	
Brazil		44			
Bulgaria		49		44	–5
Canada	64	55		51	–13
Chile		77		65	–12
China					
Colombia					
Croatia				60	
Czech Republic		67		35	–32
Denmark	25	20		20	–5
Dominican Rep.					
Egypt				92	
El Salvador					
Estonia				45	
Finland		25		44	19
France	48	38		36	–12
Georgia					
Germany (East)		58		33	–25
Germany (West)	45	41		52	7
Great Britain	40	34		33	–7
Greece				43	
Hungary		78		46	–32
Iceland	40	37		40	0
India		38		33	–5
Indonesia				80	
Iran				79	
Iraq				76	
Ireland	56	42		31	–25
Israel					
Italy	51	54		62	11
Japan		28		20	–8
Jordan				64	
Korea Republic				47	
Kyrgyzstan				61	
Latvia		88		58	–30
Lithuania				82	
Luxembourg				33	
Macedonia				47	
Malta	84	86		66	–18
Mexico		65		73	8
Moldova				73	
Montenegro				52	
Morocco				97	
Netherlands	41	37		36	–5
New Zealand					
Nigeria		86		79	–7
Northern Ireland	56	55		49	–7
Norway	47	41			–6
Pakistan				62	
Peru				68	
Philippines				64	
Poland		80		64	–16
Portugal		57		57	0
Puerto Rico				65	
Romania		62		81	19
Russian Fed.		88		71	–17
Saudi Arabia				82	
Serbia				50	
Singapore					
Slovakia		64		68	4
Slovenia		64		45	–19
South Africa				69	
Spain	47	44		40	–7
Sweden	23	19		26	3
Switzerland					
Taiwan					
Tanzania				80	
Turkey				76	
Uganda				89	
Ukraine				80	
Uruguay					
USA	72	67		57	–15
Venezuela					
Vietnam				45	
Zimbabwe				87	

Churches give Answers: The Problems of Family Life

(F036) *Generally speaking, do you think that the churches in your country are giving adequate answers to… The problems of family life*

Yes (%)

	1981	1990	1995	2000	Change
Albania				53	
Algeria				90	
Argentina		49		59	10
Armenia					
Australia					
Austria		33		29	–4
Azerbaijan					
Bangladesh				54	
Belarus				36	
Belgium	43	36		30	–13
Bosnia and Herz.				34	
Brazil		51			
Bulgaria		38		29	–9
Canada	64	56		48	–16
Chile		83		68	–15
China					
Colombia					
Croatia				59	
Czech Republic		58		30	–28
Denmark	16	13		15	–1
Dominican Rep.					
Egypt				87	
El Salvador					
Estonia				30	
Finland		27		42	15
France	40	28		28	–12
Georgia					
Germany (East)		42		27	–15
Germany (West)	42	35		42	0
Great Britain	41	36		30	–11
Greece				31	
Hungary		70		41	–29
Iceland	39	39		45	6
India		28		27	–1
Indonesia				78	
Iran				73	
Iraq				71	
Ireland	52	36		27	–25
Israel					
Italy	51	47		48	–3
Japan		22		16	–6
Jordan				61	
Korea Republic				39	

	1981	1990	1995	2000	Change
Kyrgyzstan				55	
Latvia		63		48	–15
Lithuania				81	
Luxembourg				24	
Macedonia				31	
Malta	89	90		74	–15
Mexico		64		74	10
Moldova				67	
Montenegro				34	
Morocco				97	
Netherlands	40	33		31	–9
New Zealand					
Nigeria		86		79	–7
Northern Ireland	57	59		48	–9
Norway	36	29			–7
Pakistan				49	
Peru				76	
Philippines				63	
Poland		81		64	–17
Portugal		57		46	–11
Puerto Rico				72	
Romania		53		78	25
Russian Fed.		74		55	–19
Saudi Arabia				74	
Serbia				38	
Singapore					
Slovakia		59		64	5
Slovenia		54		43	–11
South Africa				73	
Spain	41	44		37	–4
Sweden	18	14		18	0
Switzerland					
Taiwan					
Tanzania				81	
Turkey				67	
Uganda				84	
Ukraine				63	
Uruguay					
USA	74	69		61	–13
Venezuela					
Vietnam				30	
Zimbabwe				88	

(F037) *Generally speaking, do you think that the churches in your country are giving adequate answers to… People's spiritual needs*

Yes (%)

	1981	1990	1995	2000	Change
Albania				79	
Algeria				98	
Argentina		59		68	9
Armenia					
Australia					
Austria		68		60	–8
Azerbaijan					
Bangladesh				78	
Belarus				70	
Belgium	59	58		49	–10
Bosnia and Herz.				66	
Brazil		57			
Bulgaria		56		55	–1
Canada	78	75		72	–6
Chile		86		83	–3
China					
Colombia					
Croatia				87	
Czech Republic		80		69	–11
Denmark	36	48		51	15
Dominican Rep.					
Egypt				93	
El Salvador					
Estonia				73	
Finland		51		68	17
France	56	59		55	–1
Georgia					
Germany (East)		64		41	–23
Germany (West)	59	68		59	0
Great Britain	57	63		58	1
Greece				62	
Hungary		90		67	–23
Iceland	55	58		54	–1
India		59		43	–16
Indonesia				84	
Iran				75	
Iraq				79	
Ireland	73	71		64	–9
Israel					
Italy	60	71		72	12
Japan		41		34	–7
Jordan				64	
Korea Republic				59	
Kyrgyzstan				76	
Latvia		87		81	–6
Lithuania				87	
Luxembourg				46	
Macedonia				75	
Malta	96	91		85	–11
Mexico		80		83	3
Moldova				82	
Montenegro				75	
Morocco				97	
Netherlands	54	53		49	–5
New Zealand					
Nigeria		89		85	–4
Northern Ireland	71	80		77	6
Norway	64	55			–9
Pakistan				65	
Peru				80	
Philippines				80	
Poland		89		83	–6
Portugal		62		73	11
Puerto Rico				76	
Romania		78		89	11
Russian Fed.		92		74	–18
Saudi Arabia				78	
Serbia				73	
Singapore					
Slovakia		79		83	4
Slovenia		77		70	–7
South Africa				82	
Spain	55	58		55	0
Sweden	52	51		57	5
Switzerland					
Taiwan					
Tanzania				90	
Turkey				83	
Uganda				93	
Ukraine				82	
Uruguay					
USA	84	84		74	–10
Venezuela					
Vietnam				60	
Zimbabwe				91	

(F038) *Generally speaking, do you think that the churches in your country are giving adequate answers to… The social problems facing our country today*

Yes (%)

	1981	1990	1995	2000	Change
Albania				33	
Algeria				77	
Argentina		37		50	13
Armenia					
Australia					
Austria		37		30	–7
Azerbaijan					
Bangladesh				58	
Belarus				23	
Belgium		28		27	–1
Bosnia and Herz.				27	
Brazil		42			
Bulgaria		22		15	–7
Canada		44		35	–9
Chile		76		50	–26
China					
Colombia					
Croatia				44	
Czech Republic		38		15	–23
Denmark		8		11	3
Dominican Rep.					
Egypt				83	
El Salvador					
Estonia				14	
Finland		12		31	19
France		24		21	–3
Georgia					
Germany (East)		58		14	–44
Germany (West)		33		36	3
Great Britain		29		27	–2
Greece				31	
Hungary		55		25	–30
Iceland		24		28	4
India		24		28	4
Indonesia				64	
Iran				62	
Iraq				77	
Ireland		33		27	–6
Israel					
Italy		43		43	0
Japan		7		7	0
Jordan				65	
Korea Republic				23	

	1981	1990	1995	2000	Change
Kyrgyzstan				27	
Latvia		42		26	–16
Lithuania				61	
Luxembourg				24	
Macedonia				21	
Malta		77		56	–21
Mexico		47		54	7
Moldova				39	
Montenegro				22	
Morocco				91	
Netherlands		31		37	6
New Zealand					
Nigeria		83		73	–10
Northern Ireland		52		36	–16
Norway		19			
Pakistan				45	
Peru				64	
Philippines				52	
Poland		52		39	–13
Portugal		44		36	–8
Puerto Rico				66	
Romania		32		52	20
Russian Fed.		60		25	–35
Saudi Arabia				77	
Serbia				28	
Singapore					
Slovakia		31		30	–1
Slovenia		49		34	–15
South Africa				62	
Spain		35		31	–4
Sweden		12		17	5
Switzerland					
Taiwan					
Tanzania				74	
Turkey				44	
Uganda				70	
Ukraine				30	
Uruguay					
USA		57		46	–11
Venezuela					
Vietnam				18	
Zimbabwe				72	

Believe in God

(F050) *Which, if any, of the following do you believe in? Believe in God*

Yes (%)

	1981	1990	1995	2000	Change
Albania			94	92	–2
Algeria				100	
Argentina	89	92	95	96	7
Armenia			86		
Australia	85		80		–5
Austria		86		87	1
Azerbaijan			98		
Bangladesh			99	99	0
Belarus		43	78	83	40
Belgium	87	69		71	–16
Bosnia and Herz.			85	88	3
Brazil		99	99		0
Bulgaria		40	67	66	26
Canada	94	89		89	–5
Chile		95	98	97	2
China					
Colombia			99		
Croatia			81	93	12
Czech Republic		35	42	39	4
Denmark	68	64		69	1
Dominican Rep.			93		
Egypt				100	
El Salvador			99		
Estonia			52	51	–1
Finland		76	81	83	7
France	68	62		62	–6
Georgia			93		
Germany (East)		36	29	30	–6
Germany (West)	82	78	74	77	–5
Great Britain	83	78		72	–11
Greece				91	
Hungary	57	65	66	68	11
Iceland	81	85		84	3
India		94	94	95	1
Indonesia				100	
Iran				99	
Iraq				100	
Ireland	97	98		96	–1
Israel					
Italy	90	91		93	3
Japan	62	65	57	53	–9
Jordan				100	
Korea Republic	60				
Kyrgyzstan				95	
Latvia		58	74	80	22
Lithuania			86	87	1
Luxembourg				73	
Macedonia			84	90	6
Malta	100	100		99	–1
Mexico		93	94	98	5
Moldova			91	96	5
Montenegro			65	83	18
Morocco				100	
Netherlands	72	65		60	–12
New Zealand			79		
Nigeria		100	99	100	0
Northern Ireland	97	97		93	–4
Norway	76	65	69		–7
Pakistan			100	100	0
Peru			98	98	0
Philippines			100	99	–1
Poland		97		97	0
Portugal		86		96	10
Puerto Rico			99	99	0
Romania		94	97	96	2
Russian Fed.		44	69	70	26
Saudi Arabia				100	
Serbia			69	83	14
Singapore				87	
Slovakia		73	82	83	10
Slovenia		63	64	65	2
South Africa		98	99	99	1
Spain	92	86	91	85	–7
Sweden	60	45	56	53	–7
Switzerland			83		
Taiwan			76		
Tanzania				99	
Turkey			98	98	0
Uganda				99	
Ukraine			77	80	3
Uruguay			87		
USA	98	96	96	96	–2
Venezuela			99		
Vietnam				19	
Zimbabwe				99	

Believe in Life After Death

(F051) *Which, if any, of the following do you believe in? Believe in life after death*

Yes (%)

	1981	1990	1995	2000	Change
Albania			31	47	16
Algeria				100	
Argentina	54	65	69	63	9
Armenia			36		
Australia	59		64		5
Austria		56		59	3
Azerbaijan			56		
Bangladesh			57	56	–1
Belarus		18	50	41	23
Belgium	48	44		44	–4
Bosnia and Herz.			54	60	6
Brazil		74	71		–3
Bulgaria		18	30	36	18
Canada	71	69		72	1
Chile		70	76	82	12
China					
Colombia			70		
Croatia			53	68	15
Czech Republic		22	32	36	14
Denmark	32	34		38	6
Dominican Rep.			72		
Egypt				100	
El Salvador			83		
Estonia			29	36	7
Finland		60	60	57	–3
France	41	44		45	4
Georgia			58		
Germany (East)		17	18	15	–2
Germany (West)	49	50	55	45	–4
Great Britain	56	52		58	2
Greece				61	
Hungary	18	26	39	33	15
Iceland	82	81		78	–4
India		41	50	66	25
Indonesia				99	
Iran				98	
Iraq				97	
Ireland	85	83		80	–5
Israel					
Italy	59	68		73	14
Japan	56	54	49	51	–5
Jordan				97	
Korea Republic	52				

	1981	1990	1995	2000	Change
Kyrgyzstan				68	
Latvia		30	43	45	15
Lithuania			73	79	6
Luxembourg				54	
Macedonia			40	47	7
Malta	90	91		86	–4
Mexico		61	66	76	15
Moldova			47	59	12
Montenegro			24	23	–1
Morocco				100	
Netherlands	51	46		51	0
New Zealand			66		
Nigeria		82	85	87	5
Northern Ireland	84	78		75	–9
Norway	51	45	47		–4
Pakistan			100	100	0
Peru			74	72	–2
Philippines			94	86	–8
Poland		73		80	7
Portugal		39		47	8
Puerto Rico			80	78	–2
Romania		58	72	68	10
Russian Fed.		21	33	37	16
Saudi Arabia				99	
Serbia			26	27	1
Singapore				74	
Slovakia		51	61	68	17
Slovenia		28	37	32	4
South Africa		78	79	73	–5
Spain	68	52	66	53	–15
Sweden	35	38	49	46	11
Switzerland		64	64		0
Taiwan			61		
Tanzania				87	
Turkey		80	89	90	10
Uganda				85	
Ukraine			44	40	–4
Uruguay			45		
USA	80	78	80	81	1
Venezuela			62		
Vietnam				16	
Zimbabwe				74	

Believe in People have a Soul

(F052) *Which, if any, of the following do you believe in? Do you believe people have a soul?*

Yes (%)

	1981	1990	1995	2000	Change
Albania			51	75	24
Algeria				99	
Argentina	71	81	85	85	14
Armenia			65		
Australia	73		85		12
Austria		73			
Azerbaijan			69		
Bangladesh			98	99	1
Belarus		45	73		28
Belgium	66	60			–6
Bosnia and Herz.			75	85	10
Brazil		84	82		–2
Bulgaria		38	45		7
Canada	87	84		91	4
Chile		81	82	89	8
China					
Colombia			87		
Croatia			81		
Czech Republic		34	54		20
Denmark	42	47			5
Dominican Rep.			89		
Egypt				100	
El Salvador			94		
Estonia			63		
Finland		73	83		10
France	52	55			3
Georgia			76		
Germany (East)		36	66		30
Germany (West)	71	75	88		17
Great Britain	68	70			2
Greece					
Hungary	45	14	83		38
Iceland	87	88			1
India		75	74	81	6
Indonesia				99	
Iran				99	
Iraq				96	
Ireland	88	88			0
Israel					
Italy	74	77			3
Japan	80	75	64	71	–9
Jordan				100	
Korea Republic	73				

	1981	1990	1995	2000	Change
Kyrgyzstan				86	
Latvia		78	74		–4
Lithuania			85		
Luxembourg					
Macedonia			79	80	1
Malta	95	94			–1
Mexico		72	73	93	21
Moldova			72	81	9
Montenegro			42	34	–8
Morocco				100	
Netherlands	70	72			2
New Zealand			87		
Nigeria		92	95	97	5
Northern Ireland	89	92			3
Norway	59	54	60		1
Pakistan			100	100	0
Peru			90	89	–1
Philippines			97	96	–1
Poland		82			
Portugal		66			
Puerto Rico			95	96	1
Romania		76	89		13
Russian Fed.		54	67		13
Saudi Arabia				99	
Serbia			40	34	–6
Singapore				91	
Slovakia		58	76		18
Slovenia		46	71		25
South Africa		91	94	94	3
Spain	74	68	79	72	–2
Sweden	50	58	69		19
Switzerland		81	89		8
Taiwan			77		
Tanzania				98	
Turkey		87	92	92	5
Uganda				92	
Ukraine			68		
Uruguay			61		
USA	92	93	94	96	4
Venezuela			90		
Vietnam				38	
Zimbabwe				93	

Believe in Hell

(F053) *Which, if any, of the following do you believe in? Believe in hell*

Yes (%)

	1981	1990	1995	2000	Change
Albania			39	41	2
Algeria				99	
Argentina	37	41	46	44	7
Armenia			36		
Australia	40		41		1
Austria		21		18	–3
Azerbaijan			59		
Bangladesh			97	95	–2
Belarus		9	42	35	26
Belgium	22	17		16	–6
Bosnia and Herz.			56	60	4
Brazil		39	49		10
Bulgaria		11	25	30	19
Canada	43	42		50	7
Chile		45	55	65	20
China					
Colombia			40		
Croatia			42	57	15
Czech Republic		11	12	13	2
Denmark	9	8		9	0
Dominican Rep.			68		
Egypt				100	
El Salvador			76		
Estonia			17	16	–1
Finland		27	36	31	4
France	16	17		20	4
Georgia			59		
Germany (East)		7	5	10	3
Germany (West)	16	15	17	22	6
Great Britain	29	28		35	6
Greece				41	
Hungary	12	16	22	20	8
Iceland	13	12		18	5
India		39	55	68	29
Indonesia				100	
Iran				98	
Iraq				99	
Ireland	61	53		54	–7
Israel					
Italy	37	42		49	12
Japan	28	31	23	30	2
Jordan				99	
Korea Republic	49				

	1981	1990	1995	2000	Change
Kyrgyzstan				70	
Latvia		7	28	28	21
Lithuania			58	68	10
Luxembourg				22	
Macedonia			40	47	7
Malta	85	84		81	–4
Mexico		48	59	75	27
Moldova			45	65	20
Montenegro			18	21	3
Morocco				100	
Netherlands	17	15		14	–3
New Zealand			35		
Nigeria		51	88	94	43
Northern Ireland	76	73		74	–2
Norway	24	19	20		–4
Pakistan			100	100	0
Peru			64	65	1
Philippines			91	92	1
Poland		41		66	25
Portugal		25		38	13
Puerto Rico			73	73	0
Romania		43	68	71	28
Russian Fed.		16	32	36	20
Saudi Arabia				100	
Serbia			20	18	–2
Singapore				79	
Slovakia		32	41	46	14
Slovenia		17	26	20	3
South Africa		52	64	60	8
Spain	39	30	37	37	–2
Sweden	11	8	12	9	–2
Switzerland		24	21		–3
Taiwan			62		
Tanzania				96	
Turkey		85	92	94	9
Uganda				76	
Ukraine			41	38	–3
Uruguay			25		
USA	72	71	75	75	3
Venezuela			55		
Vietnam				17	
Zimbabwe				79	

Believe in Heaven

(F054) *Which, if any, of the following do you believe in? Believe in heaven*

Yes (%)

	1981	1990	1995	2000	Change
Albania			41	48	7
Algeria				100	
Argentina	51	69	75	81	30
Armenia			41		
Australia	64		63		–1
Austria		47		41	–6
Azerbaijan			61		
Bangladesh			98	100	2
Belarus		12	45	37	25
Belgium	42	34		31	–11
Bosnia and Herz.			60	62	2
Brazil		76	82		6
Bulgaria		16	28	33	17
Canada	76	72		74	–2
Chile		77	79	80	3
China					
Colombia			82		
Croatia			53	64	11
Czech Republic		23	24	21	–2
Denmark	20	19		18	–2
Dominican Rep.			81		
Egypt				100	
El Salvador			86		
Estonia			21	19	–2
Finland		55	63	61	6
France	29	32		31	2
Georgia			63		
Germany (East)		23	17	14	–9
Germany (West)	37	38	43	35	–2
Great Britain	64	59		56	–8
Greece				47	
Hungary	21	27	35	29	8
Iceland	58	57		59	1
India		43	57	72	29
Indonesia				100	
Iran				98	
Iraq				100	
Ireland	89	90		86	–3
Israel					
Italy	48	54		59	11
Japan	37	43	36	38	1
Jordan				100	
Korea Republic	53				
Kyrgyzstan				70	
Latvia		12	29	33	21
Lithuania			70	71	1
Luxembourg				33	
Macedonia			46	50	4
Malta	92	92		88	–4
Mexico		70	73	88	18
Moldova			53	68	15
Montenegro			22	18	–4
Morocco				100	
Netherlands	45	38		38	–7
New Zealand			63		
Nigeria		96	98	99	3
Northern Ireland	89	90		87	–2
Norway	52	44	47		–5
Pakistan			100	100	0
Peru			86	85	–1
Philippines			98	96	–2
Poland		75		80	5
Portugal		56		60	4
Puerto Rico			92	91	–1
Romania		57	76	75	18
Russian Fed.		18	33	36	18
Saudi Arabia				100	
Serbia			23	17	–6
Singapore				81	
Slovakia		47	60	55	8
Slovenia		30	35	28	–2
South Africa		91	94	91	0
Spain	57	53	60	51	–6
Sweden	31	31	36	31	0
Switzerland		44	45		1
Taiwan			62		
Tanzania				92	
Turkey		87	92	94	7
Uganda				92	
Ukraine			44	40	–4
Uruguay			51		
USA	90	87	86	87	–3
Venezuela			88		
Vietnam				16	
Zimbabwe				93	

Believe in Sin

(F055) *Which, if any, of the following do you believe in? Sin*

Yes (%)

	1981	1990	1995	2000	Change
Albania			62		
Algeria					
Argentina	56	72	77		21
Armenia			65		
Australia	69		74		5
Austria		67		61	–6
Azerbaijan			75		
Bangladesh			88		
Belarus		47	78	59	12
Belgium	55	45		43	–12
Bosnia and Herz.			81		
Brazil		82	89		7
Bulgaria		30	51	53	23
Canada	76	74			–2
Chile		88	86		–2
China					
Colombia			85		
Croatia			85	76	–9
Czech Republic		55	45	59	4
Denmark	37	24		21	–16
Dominican Rep.			83		
Egypt					
El Salvador			95		
Estonia			57	52	–5
Finland		66	73	67	1
France	45	43		40	–5
Georgia			84		
Germany (East)		34	27	20	–14
Germany (West)	67	63	54	46	–21
Great Britain	73	71		67	–6
Greece				74	
Hungary	46	39	58	45	–1
Iceland	69	70		64	–5
India		67	75		8
Indonesia					
Iran					
Iraq					
Ireland	90	87		86	–4
Israel					
Italy	69	73		73	4
Japan	32	28	28		–4
Jordan					
Korea Republic	58				
Kyrgyzstan					
Latvia		50	70	74	24
Lithuania			88	91	3
Luxembourg				47	
Macedonia			84		
Malta	95	94		93	–2
Mexico		74	76		2
Moldova			84		
Montenegro			53		
Morocco					
Netherlands	55	46		40	–15
New Zealand			69		
Nigeria		62	87		25
Northern Ireland	95	91		90	–5
Norway	59	44	45		–14
Pakistan			100		
Peru			94		
Philippines			100		
Poland		89		90	1
Portugal		68		71	3
Puerto Rico			97		
Romania		77	89	91	14
Russian Fed.		47	71	68	21
Saudi Arabia					
Serbia			43		
Singapore					
Slovakia		68	76	76	8
Slovenia		47	60	43	–4
South Africa		69	79		10
Spain	65	60	65	51	–14
Sweden	40	31	34	26	–14
Switzerland		64	57		–7
Taiwan			46		
Tanzania					
Turkey		91	95	96	5
Uganda					
Ukraine			73	74	1
Uruguay			52		
USA	91	89	90		–1
Venezuela			94		
Vietnam					
Zimbabwe					

Believe in Re-Incarnation

(F057) *Do you believe in re-incarnation, that is, that we are born into this world again?*

Yes (%)

	1981	1990	1995	2000	Change
Albania					
Algeria					
Argentina		39			
Armenia					
Australia					
Austria		30		23	–7
Azerbaijan					
Bangladesh					
Belarus				33	
Belgium	18	16		17	–1
Bosnia and Herz.					
Brazil		57			
Bulgaria		25		30	5
Canada	34	31			–3
Chile		49			
China					
Colombia					
Croatia				23	
Czech Republic		11		23	12
Denmark	13	17		17	4
Dominican Rep.					
Egypt					
El Salvador					
Estonia				37	
Finland		34		18	–16
France	25	28		29	4
Georgia					
Germany (East)		12		11	–1
Germany (West)	24	26		21	–3
Great Britain	33	29			–4
Greece				26	
Hungary		23		20	–3
Iceland	31	39		41	10
India		91			
Indonesia					
Iran					
Iraq					
Ireland	32	20		24	–8
Israel					
Italy	27	27		18	–9
Japan		50			
Jordan					
Korea Republic					

	1981	1990	1995	2000	Change
Kyrgyzstan					
Latvia		45		33	–12
Lithuania				44	
Luxembourg				24	
Macedonia					
Malta	31	18		12	–19
Mexico		43			
Moldova					
Montenegro					
Morocco					
Netherlands	13	17		22	9
New Zealand					
Nigeria		39			
Northern Ireland	24	33		17	–7
Norway	38	15			–23
Pakistan					
Peru					
Philippines					
Poland		42		25	–17
Portugal		29		29	0
Puerto Rico					
Romania		24		28	4
Russian Fed.		22		32	10
Saudi Arabia					
Serbia					
Singapore					
Slovakia		21		20	–1
Slovenia		17		17	0
South Africa		43			
Spain	33	27		20	–13
Sweden	17	20		22	5
Switzerland		36			
Taiwan					
Tanzania					
Turkey				33	
Uganda					
Ukraine				28	
Uruguay					
USA	29	26			–3
Venezuela					
Vietnam					
Zimbabwe					

Believe in Devil

(F059) *Which, if any, of the following do you believe in? Devil*

Yes (%)

	1981	1990	1995	2000	Change
Albania			39		
Algeria					
Argentina	39	47	53		14
Armenia			40		
Australia	42		47		5
Austria		23			
Azerbaijan			47		
Bangladesh			96		
Belarus		10	47		37
Belgium	25	19			–6
Bosnia and Herz.			51		
Brazil		44	57		13
Bulgaria		10	25		15
Canada	44	43			–1
Chile		50	60		10
China					
Colombia			41		
Croatia			40		
Czech Republic		13	14		1
Denmark	13	10			–3
Dominican Rep.			76		
Egypt					
El Salvador			74		
Estonia			26		
Finland		31	47		16
France	18	20			2
Georgia			60		
Germany (East)		7	7		0
Germany (West)	20	18	21		1
Great Britain	33	33			0
Greece					
Hungary	9	19	25		16
Iceland	15	19			4
India		27	39		12
Indonesia					
Iran					
Iraq					
Ireland	63	55			–8
Israel					
Italy	36	42			6
Japan	21	19	18		–3
Jordan					
Korea Republic	47				
Kyrgyzstan					
Latvia		9	42		33
Lithuania			58		
Luxembourg					
Macedonia			38		
Malta	83	84			1
Mexico		44	58		14
Moldova			45		
Montenegro			15		
Morocco					
Netherlands	24	18			–6
New Zealand			40		
Nigeria		45	96		51
Northern Ireland	75	76			1
Norway	30	24	28		–2
Pakistan			100		
Peru			69		
Philippines			92		
Poland		33			
Portugal		28			
Puerto Rico			79		
Romania		42	71		29
Russian Fed.		15	40		25
Saudi Arabia					
Serbia			19		
Singapore					
Slovakia		30	41		11
Slovenia		16	27		11
South Africa		51	78		27
Spain	39	32	41		2
Sweden	13	12	17		4
Switzerland		28	31		3
Taiwan			68		
Tanzania					
Turkey		69	88		19
Uganda					
Ukraine			47		
Uruguay			27		
USA	70	70	76		6
Venezuela			58		
Vietnam					
Zimbabwe					

Believe in a Personal God

(F062) *Which of these statements comes closest to your beliefs?*

Personal God (%)

	1981	1990	1995	2000	Change
Albania					
Algeria					
Argentina		58			
Armenia					
Australia					
Austria		29		32	3
Azerbaijan					
Bangladesh					
Belarus				64	
Belgium	45	31		29	–16
Bosnia and Herz.					
Brazil		56			
Bulgaria		10		36	26
Canada	52	44			–8
Chile		52			
China		3			
Colombia					
Croatia				41	
Czech Republic		12		7	–5
Denmark	27	20		25	–2
Dominican Rep.					
Egypt					
El Salvador					
Estonia		7		16	9
Finland		29		50	21
France	28	22		22	–6
Georgia					
Germany (East)		14		20	6
Germany (West)	27	25		39	12
Great Britain	32	33		31	–1
Greece				66	
Hungary		40		45	5
Iceland	18	51		51	33
India		30			
Indonesia					
Iran					
Iraq					
Ireland	76	67		65	–11
Israel					
Italy	28	67		71	43
Japan		5			
Jordan					
Korea Republic					

	1981	1990	1995	2000	Change
Kyrgyzstan					
Latvia		10		8	–2
Lithuania		21		51	30
Luxembourg				33	
Macedonia					
Malta	79	72		78	–1
Mexico		56			
Moldova					
Montenegro					
Morocco					
Netherlands	37	28		24	–13
New Zealand					
Nigeria		68			
Northern Ireland	72	66		61	–11
Norway	39	30			–9
Pakistan					
Peru					
Philippines					
Poland		79		83	4
Portugal		62		79	17
Puerto Rico					
Romania		36		37	1
Russian Fed.		8		32	24
Saudi Arabia					
Serbia					
Singapore					
Slovakia		36		35	–1
Slovenia		22		24	2
South Africa					
Spain	57	51		49	–8
Sweden	20	16		16	–4
Switzerland		23			
Taiwan					
Tanzania					
Turkey					
Uganda					
Ukraine				42	
Uruguay					
USA	67	69			2
Venezuela					
Vietnam					
Zimbabwe					

How Important is God in your Life

(F063) *How important is God in your life? (10 = very important; 1 = not at all important)*

% (very) Important (7 thru 10)

	1981	1990	1995	2000	Change
Albania			67	70	3
Algeria				98	
Argentina	64	74	81	83	19
Armenia			59		
Australia	49		45		–4
Austria		51		54	3
Azerbaijan			86		
Bangladesh			95	95	0
Belarus		22	43	44	22
Belgium	47	38		37	–10
Bosnia and Herz.			65	68	3
Brazil		94	96		2
Bulgaria		20	32	37	17
Canada	67	62		67	0
Chile		84	84	85	1
China		3			
Colombia			97		
Croatia			53	66	13
Czech Republic		21	25	20	–1
Denmark	27	18		20	–7
Dominican Rep.			94		
Egypt				98	
El Salvador			98		
Estonia			25	22	–3
Finland		42	46	49	7
France	32	27		27	–5
Georgia			72		
Germany (East)		24	16	20	–4
Germany (West)	43	39	46	44	1
Great Britain	43	36	37	34	–9
Greece				68	
Hungary	35	40	40	39	4
Iceland	53	47		51	–2
India		68	80	93	25
Indonesia				100	
Iran				96	
Iraq				99	
Ireland	78	74		67	–11
Israel				72	
Italy	63	65		68	5
Japan	23	20	24	28	5
Jordan				100	
Korea Republic				37	
Kyrgyzstan				73	
Latvia			46	40	–6
Lithuania			53	58	5
Luxembourg				40	
Macedonia			53	70	17
Malta	96	94		93	–3
Mexico		82	75	94	12
Moldova			62	70	8
Montenegro			44	55	11
Morocco				99	
Netherlands	42	36		36	–6
New Zealand			45		
Nigeria		98	96	97	–1
Northern Ireland	67	73		63	–4
Norway	34	27	30		–4
Pakistan			99	100	1
Peru			90	92	2
Philippines			96	95	–1
Poland		84		82	–2
Portugal		57		74	17
Puerto Rico			97	98	1
Romania		67	77	86	19
Russian Fed.		21	38	38	17
Saudi Arabia				98	
Serbia			38	49	11
Singapore				60	
Slovakia		47	58	58	11
Slovenia		30	37	35	5
South Africa		88	90	89	1
Spain	53	49	60	46	–7
Sweden	23	19	21	23	0
Switzerland		56	49		–7
Taiwan			31		
Tanzania				96	
Turkey		86	92	92	6
Uganda				93	
Ukraine			46	49	3
Uruguay			58		
USA	83	77	78	83	0
Venezuela			93	96	3
Vietnam				38	
Zimbabwe				94	

Comfort and Strength from Religion

(F064) *Do you find that you get comfort and strength from religion?*

Yes (%)

	1981	1990	1995	2000	Change
Albania			59	73	14
Algeria				99	
Argentina	58	66	74	77	19
Armenia			70		
Australia			49		
Austria		59		62	3
Azerbaijan			88		
Bangladesh			99	99	0
Belarus		31	82	54	23
Belgium	59	46		49	–10
Bosnia and Herz.			65	72	7
Brazil		86	89		3
Bulgaria		33	59	45	12
Canada	67	62		63	–4
Chile		83	79	75	–8
China		4			
Colombia			91		
Croatia			61	82	21
Czech Republic		27	30	26	–1
Denmark	32	27		33	1
Dominican Rep.			81		
Egypt				100	
El Salvador			89		
Estonia			84	36	–48
Finland		49	53	59	10
France	40	36		35	–5
Georgia			83		
Germany (East)		29	29	28	–1
Germany (West)	53	45	55	55	2
Great Britain	48	45		37	–11
Greece				76	
Hungary	44	49	49	49	5
Iceland	76	75		75	–1
India		81	86	85	4
Indonesia				100	
Iran				96	
Iraq				98	
Ireland	82	83		76	–6
Israel					
Italy	67	71		72	5
Japan	47	42	32	35	–12
Jordan				100	
Korea Republic				67	

	1981	1990	1995	2000	Change
Kyrgyzstan				75	
Latvia		37	89	63	26
Lithuania			68	72	4
Luxembourg				49	
Macedonia			58	71	13
Malta	98	95		93	–5
Mexico		77	79	89	12
Moldova			92	92	0
Montenegro			49	66	17
Morocco				100	
Netherlands	50	45		43	–7
New Zealand			51		
Nigeria		96		98	2
Northern Ireland	76	77		69	–7
Norway	49	36	39		–10
Pakistan			97	96	–1
Peru			92	91	–1
Philippines			93	91	–2
Poland		86	81	82	–4
Portugal		67		80	13
Puerto Rico			89	87	–2
Romania		76	84	87	11
Russian Fed.		35	57	57	22
Saudi Arabia				99	
Serbia			50	63	13
Singapore				77	
Slovakia		54	62	64	10
Slovenia		51	57	48	–3
South Africa		89	93	89	0
Spain	63	57	62	54	–9
Sweden	31	27	34	33	2
Switzerland			55		
Taiwan			68		
Tanzania				96	
Turkey		88	93	93	5
Uganda				95	
Ukraine			89	65	–24
Uruguay			55		
USA	84	80	81	80	–4
Venezuela			89		
Vietnam				27	
Zimbabwe				93	

Moments of Prayer, Meditation

(F065) *Do you take some moments of prayer, meditation or contemplation or something like that?*

Yes (%)

	1981	1990	1995	2000	Change
Albania				81	
Algeria					
Argentina		75		78	3
Armenia					
Australia					
Austria		70		69	–1
Azerbaijan					
Bangladesh				95	
Belarus				71	
Belgium	63	55		62	–1
Bosnia and Herz.				80	
Brazil		89			
Bulgaria		36		34	–2
Canada	74	73		80	6
Chile		85		82	–3
China		20			
Colombia					
Croatia				75	
Czech Republic		33		37	4
Denmark	49	43		51	2
Dominican Rep.					
Egypt					
El Salvador					
Estonia				51	
Finland		22		75	53
France	45	46		41	–4
Georgia					
Germany (East)		52		30	–22
Germany (West)	67	70		60	–7
Great Britain	49	54		50	1
Greece				61	
Hungary		58		61	3
Iceland	44	46		54	10
India		85		88	3
Indonesia					
Iran					
Iraq					
Ireland	82	84		82	0
Israel					
Italy	73	76		79	6
Japan		41		40	–1
Jordan					
Korea Republic				59	

	1981	1990	1995	2000	Change
Kyrgyzstan				60	
Latvia		66		65	–1
Lithuania				62	
Luxembourg				58	
Macedonia				62	
Malta	91	88		91	0
Mexico		82		87	5
Moldova				88	
Montenegro				58	
Morocco					
Netherlands	61	68		69	8
New Zealand					
Nigeria		98			
Northern Ireland	75	76		73	–2
Norway	62	64			2
Pakistan					
Peru				80	
Philippines				97	
Poland		90		87	–3
Portugal		62		73	11
Puerto Rico				91	
Romania		86		94	8
Russian Fed.		37		33	–4
Saudi Arabia					
Serbia				59	
Singapore				70	
Slovakia		62		66	4
Slovenia		45		46	1
South Africa		86		89	3
Spain	72	62		55	–17
Sweden	34	34		44	10
Switzerland					
Taiwan					
Tanzania				97	
Turkey				93	
Uganda				95	
Ukraine				49	
Uruguay					
USA	86	84		89	3
Venezuela					
Vietnam				30	
Zimbabwe				91	

Justifiable: Claiming Government Benefits

(F114) *Please tell me for each of the following statements whether you think it can always be justified, never be justified, or something in between. Claiming government benefits to which you have no right.*

Never justifiable (%)

	1981	1990	1995	2000	Change
Albania			5	58	53
Algeria				51	
Argentina	69	77	69	64	–5
Armenia			44		
Australia	73		73		0
Austria		67		58	–9
Azerbaijan			62		
Bangladesh			80	92	12
Belarus		55	49	35	–20
Belgium	68	51		57	–11
Bosnia and Herz.			54	76	22
Brazil		65	55		–10
Bulgaria		68	74	70	2
Canada	63	69		71	8
Chile		43	48	47	4
China		75	58	62	–13
Colombia			72		
Croatia			39	78	39
Czech Republic		50	45	64	14
Denmark	92	81		83	–9
Dominican Rep.			70		
Egypt				73	
El Salvador			74		
Estonia		61	64	36	–25
Finland		13	63	51	38
France	42	38		41	–1
Georgia			47		
Germany (East)		74	66	63	–11
Germany (West)	66	57	57	63	–3
Great Britain	78	69		67	–11
Greece				24	
Hungary	82	61	55	74	–8
Iceland	77	72		68	–9
India		76	74	75	–1
Indonesia				42	
Iran				67	
Iraq					
Ireland	73	68		67	–6
Israel					
Italy	84	67		65	–19
Japan	70	67	62	64	–6
Jordan				80	
Korea Republic	63	77			14

	1981	1990	1995	2000	Change
Kyrgyzstan				56	
Latvia		73	41	62	–11
Lithuania		61	54	54	–7
Luxembourg				46	
Macedonia			47	47	0
Malta	88	92		85	–3
Mexico		22	49	45	23
Moldova			49	28	–21
Montenegro			50	42	–8
Morocco				86	
Netherlands	82	73		77	–5
New Zealand			70		
Nigeria		67	68	62	–5
Northern Ireland	77	77		66	–11
Norway	80	79	71		–9
Pakistan				77	
Peru			48	44	–4
Philippines			32	28	–4
Poland		63	55	53	–10
Portugal		55		59	4
Puerto Rico			76	71	–5
Romania		71	63	70	–1
Russian Fed.		65	62	58	–7
Saudi Arabia				55	
Serbia			56	61	5
Singapore				48	
Slovakia		43	34	37	–6
Slovenia		49	41	49	0
South Africa		72	63	50	–22
Spain	61	62	67	56	–5
Sweden	81	74	58	55	–26
Switzerland		74	66		–8
Taiwan			54		
Tanzania				87	
Turkey		83		90	7
Uganda				72	
Ukraine			43	48	5
Uruguay			79		
USA	78	68	75	64	–14
Venezuela			69	54	–15
Vietnam				73	
Zimbabwe				80	

Justifiable: Avoiding a fare on Public Transport

(F115) *Please tell me for each of the following statements whether you think it can always be justified, never be justified, or something in between. Avoiding a fare on public transport*

Never justifiable (%)

	1981	1990	1995	2000	Change
Albania			41	47	6
Algeria				64	
Argentina	62	71	62	67	5
Armenia			37		
Australia	58		63		5
Austria		63		53	–10
Azerbaijan			49		
Bangladesh			94	96	2
Belarus		47	31	21	–26
Belgium	62	58		60	–2
Bosnia and Herz.			52	72	20
Brazil		61	56		–5
Bulgaria		63	60		–3
Canada	63	62		63	0
Chile		55	57	47	–8
China		79	76	83	4
Colombia			49		
Croatia			22	56	34
Czech Republic		63	39	41	–22
Denmark	84	74		71	–13
Dominican Rep.			71		
Egypt				74	
El Salvador					
Estonia		59	49		–10
Finland		53	59	50	–3
France	58	54		54	–4
Georgia			47		
Germany (East)		74	51	67	–7
Germany (West)	60	52	39	51	–9
Great Britain	65	59		47	–18
Greece				36	
Hungary	78	53	36		–42
Iceland	64	53			–11
India		84	78	80	–4
Indonesia				87	
Iran				84	
Iraq					
Ireland	56	57			1
Israel					
Italy	80	66		61	–19
Japan	78	78	77	77	–1
Jordan				89	
Korea Republic	63	67	49	41	–22

	1981	1990	1995	2000	Change
Kyrgyzstan				55	
Latvia		58	25		–33
Lithuania		56	43	38	–18
Luxembourg				51	
Macedonia			64	69	5
Malta	93	92			–1
Mexico		30	47	49	19
Moldova			43	21	–22
Montenegro			49	42	–7
Morocco				82	
Netherlands	55	59		44	–11
New Zealand			64		
Nigeria		60	60	56	–4
Northern Ireland	69	72			3
Norway	80	75	70		–10
Pakistan				87	
Peru			46	54	8
Philippines			35	35	0
Poland		72	68		–4
Portugal		53			
Puerto Rico			75	81	6
Romania		63	67		4
Russian Fed.		52	35	32	–20
Saudi Arabia				57	
Serbia			54	58	4
Singapore				55	
Slovakia		46	29		–17
Slovenia		61	54		–7
South Africa			62	54	–8
Spain	56	62	68	57	1
Sweden	76	67	47		–29
Switzerland		78	59		–19
Taiwan			60		
Tanzania				90	
Turkey		74			
Uganda				66	
Ukraine			28	34	6
Uruguay			72		
USA	71	61	66	50	–21
Venezuela			72	56	–16
Vietnam				89	
Zimbabwe				83	

JUSTIFIABLE: CHEATING ON TAXES

(F116) *Please tell me for each of the following statements whether you think it can always be justified, never be justified, or something in between. Cheating on taxes if you have a chance*

Never justifiable (%)

	1981	1990	1995	2000	Change
Albania			44	58	14
Algeria				76	
Argentina	64	81	72	77	13
Armenia			41		
Australia	48		62		14
Austria		61		58	–3
Azerbaijan			48		
Bangladesh			96	98	2
Belarus		44	41	26	–18
Belgium	45	34		38	–7
Bosnia and Herz.			56	77	21
Brazil		61	47		–14
Bulgaria		57	65	67	10
Canada	67	59		67	0
Chile		76	64	70	–6
China		81	79	77	–4
Colombia			72		
Croatia			32	61	29
Czech Republic		69	41	59	–10
Denmark	68	57		66	–2
Dominican Rep.			70		
Egypt				80	
El Salvador			81		
Estonia		65	42	40	–25
Finland		40	55	53	13
France	49	46		48	–1
Georgia			53		
Germany (East)		67	54	59	–8
Germany (West)	52	40	40	57	5
Great Britain	57	54		56	–1
Greece				37	
Hungary		56	60	65	9
Iceland	56	56		58	2
India		82	77	80	–2
Indonesia				79	
Iran				89	
Iraq					
Ireland	45	49		58	13
Israel					
Italy	75	56		57	–18
Japan	82	82	81	84	2
Jordan				84	
Korea Republic	76	90	72	75	–1

	1981	1990	1995	2000	Change
Kyrgyzstan				58	
Latvia		64	31	60	–4
Lithuania		57	46	39	–18
Luxembourg				41	
Macedonia			61	68	7
Malta	84	84		80	–4
Mexico		37	51	69	32
Moldova			39	26	–13
Montenegro			48	46	–2
Morocco				96	
Netherlands	42	44		46	4
New Zealand			60		
Nigeria		63	68	58	–5
Northern Ireland	53	68		59	6
Norway	41	43	48		7
Pakistan				91	
Peru			63	64	1
Philippines			38	41	3
Poland		50	55	60	10
Portugal		40		55	15
Puerto Rico			74	78	4
Romania		68	64	57	–11
Russian Fed.		53	47	46	–7
Saudi Arabia					
Serbia			55	63	8
Singapore				67	
Slovakia		59	35	59	0
Slovenia		68	54	60	–8
South Africa		63	65	55	–8
Spain	50	58	70	57	7
Sweden	70	56	49	51	–19
Switzerland		64	54		–10
Taiwan			64		
Tanzania				85	
Turkey		90		92	2
Uganda				58	
Ukraine			41	41	0
Uruguay			80		
USA	67	68	74	62	–5
Venezuela			71	70	–1
Vietnam				88	
Zimbabwe				83	

JUSTIFIABLE: SOMEONE ACCEPTING A BRIBE

(F117) *Please tell me for each of the following statements whether you think it can always be justified, never be justified, or something in between. Someone accepting a bribe in the course of their duties*

Never justifiable (%)

	1981	1990	1995	2000	Change
Albania			46	53	7
Algeria				89	
Argentina	81	95	88	92	11
Armenia			63		
Australia	74		86		12
Austria		71		72	1
Azerbaijan			53		
Bangladesh			98	99	1
Belarus		72	67	39	−33
Belgium	62	60		68	6
Bosnia and Herz.			71	86	15
Brazil		87	46		−41
Bulgaria		80	67	78	−2
Canada	78	76		80	2
Chile		84	73	71	−13
China		86	90	83	−3
Colombia			81		
Croatia			60	79	19
Czech Republic		57	56	51	−6
Denmark	93	91		93	0
Dominican Rep.			76		
Egypt				94	
El Salvador			89		
Estonia		68	82	67	−1
Finland		74	83	80	6
France	58	63		67	9
Georgia			73		
Germany (East)		64	74	61	−3
Germany (West)	64	62	74	68	4
Great Britain	79	74		67	−12
Greece				64	
Hungary	72	64	34	53	−19
Iceland	85	84		87	2
India		85	79	85	0
Indonesia				82	
Iran				93	
Iraq				85	
Ireland	81	85		82	1
Israel				86	
Italy	69	76		79	10
Japan	69	70	76	83	14
Jordan				96	
Korea Republic	61	84	80	80	19

	1981	1990	1995	2000	Change
Kyrgyzstan				73	
Latvia		75	62	74	−1
Lithuania		59	69	67	8
Luxembourg				71	
Macedonia			82	87	5
Malta	98	96		94	−4
Mexico		52	57	73	21
Moldova			64	49	−15
Montenegro			78	84	6
Morocco				98	
Netherlands	66	67		73	7
New Zealand			82		
Nigeria		65	70	63	−2
Northern Ireland	90	85		78	−12
Norway	84	80	85		1
Pakistan				92	
Peru			75	73	−2
Philippines			35	40	5
Poland		80	85	77	−3
Portugal		73		74	1
Puerto Rico			88	90	2
Romania		67	73	80	13
Russian Fed.		85	81	70	−15
Saudi Arabia				77	
Serbia			83	86	3
Singapore				77	
Slovakia		53	46	39	−14
Slovenia		79	74	74	−5
South Africa		76	71	61	−15
Spain	77	80	83	72	−5
Sweden	74	74	69	68	−6
Switzerland		83	79		−4
Taiwan			75		
Tanzania				92	
Turkey		91		94	3
Uganda				73	
Ukraine			71	64	−7
Uruguay			91		
USA	80	80	89	80	0
Venezuela			67	75	8
Vietnam				94	
Zimbabwe				92	

Justifiable: Homosexuality

(F118) *Please tell me for each of the following statements whether you think it can always be justified, never be justified, or something in between. Homosexuality*

Never justifiable (%)

	1981	1990	1995	2000	Change
Albania			68	81	13
Algeria				93	
Argentina	68	60	32	40	–28
Armenia			71		
Australia	41		31		–10
Austria		48		26	–22
Azerbaijan			89		
Bangladesh				99	
Belarus		80	68	57	–23
Belgium	52	41		26	–26
Bosnia and Herz.			68	72	4
Brazil		70	56		–14
Bulgaria		80	51	60	–20
Canada	52	37		27	–25
Chile		77	44	37	–40
China		92	88	92	0
Colombia			61		
Croatia			40	70	30
Czech Republic		39	10	27	–12
Denmark	38	36		21	–17
Dominican Rep.			53		
Egypt				100	
El Salvador			81		
Estonia		76	66	57	–19
Finland		32	37	29	–3
France	52	39		23	–29
Georgia			82		
Germany (East)		46	27	22	–24
Germany (West)	45	33	15	18	–27
Great Britain	47	40	20	25	–22
Greece				24	
Hungary	87	73	46	88	1
Iceland	48	24		12	–36
India		93	77	71	–22
Indonesia				95	
Iran				94	
Iraq					
Ireland	61	51		37	–24
Israel				38	
Italy	66	46		30	–36
Japan	54	60	38	30	–24
Jordan				98	
Korea Republic	63	90	67	53	–10

	1981	1990	1995	2000	Change
Kyrgyzstan				81	
Latvia		82	55	77	–5
Lithuania		88	75	78	–10
Luxembourg				20	
Macedonia			81	76	–5
Malta		83		61	–22
Mexico		55	52	53	–2
Moldova			74	65	–9
Montenegro			68	86	18
Morocco					
Netherlands	25	13		7	–18
New Zealand			30		
Nigeria		72	79	78	6
Northern Ireland	66	65		42	–24
Norway	50	45	27		–23
Pakistan				96	
Peru			44	57	13
Philippines			29	29	0
Poland		78	60	60	–18
Portugal		65		43	–22
Puerto Rico			60	51	–9
Romania		86	67	80	–6
Russian Fed.		88	80	71	–17
Saudi Arabia				85	
Serbia			65	75	10
Singapore				55	
Slovakia		50	18	24	–26
Slovenia		60	50	42	–18
South Africa		73	61	48	–25
Spain	57	44	24	17	–40
Sweden	39	37	12	9	–30
Switzerland		40	17		–23
Taiwan			65		
Tanzania				94	
Turkey		84		85	1
Uganda				91	
Ukraine			71	71	0
Uruguay			46		
USA	66	54	45	32	–34
Venezuela			71	62	–9
Vietnam				82	
Zimbabwe				96	

Justifiable: Prostitution

(F119) *Please tell me for each of the following statements whether you think it can always be justified, never be justified, or something in between. Prostitution*

Never justifiable (%)

	1981	1990	1995	2000	Change
Albania			59	80	21
Algeria				93	
Argentina	67	73	43	51	–16
Armenia			65		
Australia	35		29		–6
Austria		45		36	–9
Azerbaijan			84		
Bangladesh				95	
Belarus		70	60	48	–22
Belgium	51	46			–5
Bosnia and Herz.			63	76	13
Brazil		74	68		–6
Bulgaria		70	61		–9
Canada	52	42		44	–8
Chile		77	51	48	–29
China		92	91	93	1
Colombia			64		
Croatia			37	82	45
Czech Republic		51	34	45	–6
Denmark	45	42			–3
Dominican Rep.			54		
Egypt				93	
El Salvador			85		
Estonia		61	54		–7
Finland		29	40	45	16
France	49	46			–3
Georgia			74		
Germany (East)		52	30	42	–10
Germany (West)	42	33	17	33	–9
Great Britain	50	42	20	42	–8
Greece				41	
Hungary	85	69	51		–34
Iceland	62	53		50	–12
India		83	74	74	–9
Indonesia				94	
Iran				95	
Iraq					
Ireland	70	61		58	–12
Israel				48	
Italy	71	59		57	–14
Japan	67	71	58	64	–3
Jordan				98	
Korea Republic	65	78	61	59	–6

	1981	1990	1995	2000	Change
Kyrgyzstan				74	
Latvia		64	45		–19
Lithuania		78	66	65	–13
Luxembourg				45	
Macedonia			76	81	5
Malta	95	94			–1
Mexico		48	53	61	13
Moldova			70	61	–9
Montenegro			61	80	19
Morocco					
Netherlands	30	20			–10
New Zealand			29		
Nigeria		66	75	77	11
Northern Ireland	77	65		69	–8
Norway	72	65	43		–29
Pakistan				96	
Peru			55	66	11
Philippines			44	43	–1
Poland		78	64		–14
Portugal		67			
Puerto Rico			71		
Romania		78	58	74	–4
Russian Fed.		77	69	61	–16
Saudi Arabia				87	
Serbia			64	76	12
Singapore				54	
Slovakia		57	34		–23
Slovenia		60	51	50	–10
South Africa		76	71	58	–18
Spain	59	50	29	30	–29
Sweden	54	65	31		–23
Switzerland		41	22		–19
Taiwan			66		
Tanzania				93	
Turkey		82			
Uganda				78	
Ukraine			66	67	1
Uruguay			44		
USA	65	60	57	47	–18
Venezuela			68	66	–2
Vietnam				92	
Zimbabwe				94	

Justifiable: Abortion

(F120) *Please tell me for each of the following statements whether you think it can always be justified, never be justified, or something in between. Abortion*

Never justifiable (%)

	1981	1990	1995	2000	Change
Albania			5	26	21
Algeria				79	
Argentina	48	45	46	66	18
Armenia			23		
Australia	29		24		–5
Austria		31		24	–7
Azerbaijan			30		
Bangladesh				90	
Belarus		25	19	18	–7
Belgium	37	22		30	–7
Bosnia and Herz.			26	35	9
Brazil		64	75		11
Bulgaria		25	22	20	–5
Canada	38	21		30	–8
Chile		75	69	67	–8
China		15	31	56	41
Colombia			74		
Croatia			21	44	23
Czech Republic		11	9	13	2
Denmark	23			13	–10
Dominican Rep.			59		
Egypt				56	
El Salvador			91		
Estonia		14	15	21	7
Finland		10	19	11	1
France	23	18		14	–9
Georgia			29		
Germany (East)		18	17	14	–4
Germany (West)	32	18	20	29	–3
Great Britain	32	19	15	26	–6
Greece				18	
Hungary	32	24	18	33	1
Iceland	23	11		12	–11
India		38	54	65	27
Indonesia				88	
Iran				77	
Iraq				77	
Ireland	79	52		52	–27
Israel				27	
Italy	33	24		32	–1
Japan	32	28	18	15	–17
Jordan				85	
Korea Republic	31	38	37	37	6

	1981	1990	1995	2000	Change
Kyrgyzstan				58	
Latvia		23	12	37	14
Lithuania		30	34	33	3
Luxembourg				18	
Macedonia			33	40	7
Malta	96	85		89	–7
Mexico		39	56	69	30
Moldova			36	42	6
Montenegro			26	32	6
Morocco				84	
Netherlands	32	14		15	–17
New Zealand			19		
Nigeria		52	70	74	22
Northern Ireland	43	40		46	3
Norway	19	14	15		–4
Pakistan				60	
Peru			64	74	10
Philippines			58	55	–3
Poland		44	43	44	0
Portugal		26		35	9
Puerto Rico			78	74	–4
Romania		23	27	40	17
Russian Fed.		19	18	17	–2
Saudi Arabia				62	
Serbia			17	21	4
Singapore				41	
Slovakia		20	24	25	5
Slovenia		14	25	19	5
South Africa		61	65	53	–8
Spain	51	30	33	28	–23
Sweden	16	13	5	5	–11
Switzerland		52	22		–30
Taiwan			46		
Tanzania				90	
Turkey		37		64	27
Uganda				76	
Ukraine			29	33	4
Uruguay			48		
USA	44	33	34	30	–14
Venezuela			69	71	2
Vietnam				61	
Zimbabwe				92	

Justifiable: Divorce

(F121) *Please tell me for each of the following statements whether you think it can always be justified, never be justified, or something in between. Divorce*

Never justifiable (%)

	1981	1990	1995	2000	Change
Albania			4	18	14
Algeria				26	
Argentina	30	24	17	25	–5
Armenia			18		
Australia	16		10		–6
Austria		16		11	–5
Azerbaijan			27		
Bangladesh			74	82	8
Belarus		20	14	9	–11
Belgium	29	17		13	–16
Bosnia and Herz.			13	15	2
Brazil		31	30		–1
Bulgaria		29	21	18	–11
Canada	19	14		11	–8
Chile		46	34	27	–19
China		15	14	57	42
Colombia			34		
Croatia			8	30	22
Czech Republic		10	4	7	–3
Denmark	12	13		7	–5
Dominican Rep.			27		
Egypt				16	
El Salvador			57		
Estonia		11	8	11	0
Finland		5	7	3	–2
France	15	11		7	–8
Georgia			21		
Germany (East)		12	11	10	–2
Germany (West)	15	8	7	14	–1
Great Britain	16	12	4	12	–4
Greece				7	
Hungary	20	23	9	24	4
Iceland	8	4		4	–4
India		51	47	51	0
Indonesia				54	
Iran				55	
Iraq				65	
Ireland	47	30		26	–21
Israel				12	
Italy	24	19		18	–6
Japan	22	17	9	6	–16
Jordan				42	
Korea Republic	33	38	27	21	–12
Kyrgyzstan				45	
Latvia		16	5	25	9
Lithuania		24	23	20	–4
Luxembourg				10	
Macedonia			33	36	3
Malta	82	73		59	–23
Mexico		26	37	40	14
Moldova			33	29	–4
Montenegro			12	9	–3
Morocco				43	
Netherlands	22	9		5	–17
New Zealand			6		
Nigeria		42	58	54	12
Northern Ireland	31	27		24	–7
Norway	16	14	6		–10
Pakistan				66	
Peru			29	42	13
Philippines			40	43	3
Poland		31	26	26	–5
Portugal		17		17	0
Puerto Rico			39	35	–4
Romania		23	23	33	10
Russian Fed.		16	13	11	–5
Saudi Arabia				27	
Serbia			11	13	2
Singapore				31	
Slovakia		15	9	14	–1
Slovenia		15	19	14	–1
South Africa		48	41	32	–16
Spain	29	20	16	12	–17
Sweden	10	7	2	2	–8
Switzerland		23	9		–14
Taiwan			33		
Tanzania				53	
Turkey		24		42	18
Uganda				62	
Ukraine			17	24	7
Uruguay			22		
USA	23	18	11	8	–15
Venezuela			36	30	–6
Vietnam				50	
Zimbabwe				74	

Justifiable: Euthanasia

(F122) *Please tell me for each of the following statements whether you think it can always be justified, never be justified, or something in between. Euthanasia (terminating the life of the incurably sick)*

Never justifiable (%)

	1981	1990	1995	2000	Change
Albania			46	47	1
Algeria				85	
Argentina	79	57	44	49	–30
Armenia			39		
Australia	23		15		–8
Austria		38		31	–7
Azerbaijan			47		
Bangladesh			92	97	5
Belarus		34	18	19	–15
Belgium	43	21		12	–31
Bosnia and Herz.			46	43	–3
Brazil		66	61		–5
Bulgaria		47	43	45	–2
Canada	35	23		20	–15
Chile		63	53	45	–18
China		15	21	53	38
Colombia			45		
Croatia			23	45	22
Czech Republic		34	13	18	–16
Denmark	20	21		12	–8
Dominican Rep.			53		
Egypt				78	
El Salvador			83		
Estonia		36	18	23	–13
Finland		12	16	18	6
France	28	22		12	–16
Georgia			57		
Germany (East)		37		29	–8
Germany (West)	30	30		28	–2
Great Britain	29	22		21	–8
Greece				30	
Hungary	65	39	14	44	–21
Iceland	31	20		18	–13
India		52	56	63	11
Indonesia				84	
Iran				76	
Iraq					
Ireland	70	56		49	–21
Israel					
Italy	58	44		40	–18
Japan	26	18	11	10	–16
Jordan				90	
Korea Republic	30		30	24	–6

	1981	1990	1995	2000	Change
Kyrgyzstan				55	
Latvia		41	13	30	–11
Lithuania		42	27	26	–16
Luxembourg				19	
Macedonia			62	56	–6
Malta	90	81		69	–21
Mexico		34	49	59	25
Moldova			58	50	–8
Montenegro			31	35	4
Morocco				93	
Netherlands	22	13		8	–14
New Zealand			12		
Nigeria		50	65	64	14
Northern Ireland	45	41		41	–4
Norway	55	30	18		–37
Pakistan				100	
Peru			49		
Philippines			51	50	–1
Poland		68	46	50	–18
Portugal		49		41	–8
Puerto Rico			65	69	4
Romania		49	44	56	7
Russian Fed.		49	30	23	–26
Saudi Arabia				80	
Serbia			28	35	7
Singapore				40	
Slovakia		42	21	25	–17
Slovenia		45	31	27	–18
South Africa		55	53	40	–15
Spain	54	38	29	23	–31
Sweden	29	19	6	10	–19
Switzerland		26	15		–11
Taiwan			27		
Tanzania				89	
Turkey		63		65	2
Uganda				83	
Ukraine			34	30	–4
Uruguay			40		
USA	45	32	29	24	–21
Venezuela			67	55	–12
Vietnam				51	
Zimbabwe				90	

Justifiable: Suicide

(F123) *Please tell me for each of the following statements whether you think it can always be justified, never be justified, or something in between. Suicide*

Never justifiable (%)

	1981	1990	1995	2000	Change
Albania			62	68	6
Algeria				94	
Argentina	81	82	70	78	–3
Armenia			60		
Australia	48		48		0
Austria		48		47	–1
Azerbaijan			73		
Bangladesh			98	99	1
Belarus		60	67	50	–10
Belgium	66	50		45	–21
Bosnia and Herz.			72	80	8
Brazil		89	87		–2
Bulgaria		66	68	71	5
Canada	66	52		52	–14
Chile		81	73	71	–10
China		54	52	83	29
Colombia			82		
Croatia			37	84	47
Czech Republic		49	25	48	–1
Denmark	55	56		51	–4
Dominican Rep.			76		
Egypt				95	
El Salvador			94		
Estonia		56	66	62	6
Finland		31	49	41	10
France	40	33		26	–14
Georgia			78		
Germany (East)		54	32	54	0
Germany (West)	50	41	25	54	4
Great Britain	51	39		39	–12
Greece				54	
Hungary	73	65	55	80	7
Iceland	58	57		63	5
India		81	70	72	–9
Indonesia				97	
Iran				95	
Iraq					
Ireland	76	63		69	–7
Israel					
Italy	77	69		62	–15
Japan	51	56	55	48	–3
Jordan				97	
Korea Republic	44	64	52	51	7
Kyrgyzstan				84	
Latvia		60	42	75	15
Lithuania		69	65	76	7
Luxembourg				38	
Macedonia			84	83	–1
Malta	97	92		93	–4
Mexico		48	74	82	34
Moldova			79	67	–12
Montenegro			47	53	6
Morocco				98	
Netherlands	49	32		28	–21
New Zealand			48		
Nigeria		73	79	76	3
Northern Ireland	69	58		68	–1
Norway	66	57	52		–14
Pakistan				97	
Peru			72	75	3
Philippines			61	57	–4
Poland		71	63	64	–7
Portugal		71		63	–8
Puerto Rico			87	90	3
Romania		76	75	87	11
Russian Fed.		66	68	67	1
Saudi Arabia				88	
Serbia			54	72	18
Singapore				69	
Slovakia		54	33	37	–17
Slovenia		55	47	47	–8
South Africa		74	71	65	–9
Spain	66	67	60	52	–14
Sweden	52	44	26	29	–23
Switzerland		54	38		–16
Taiwan			63		
Tanzania				96	
Turkey		80		90	10
Uganda				93	
Ukraine			69	73	4
Uruguay			71		
USA	73	61	61	57	–16
Venezuela			83	80	–3
Vietnam				85	
Zimbabwe				93	

JUSTIFIABLE: JOYRIDING

(F125) *Please tell me for each of the following statements whether you think it can always be justified, never be justified, or something in between. Joyriding*

Never justifiable (%)

	1981	1990	1995	2000	Change
Albania					
Algeria					
Argentina		94			
Armenia					
Australia					
Austria		93		92	–1
Azerbaijan					
Bangladesh					
Belarus				67	
Belgium	85	83		93	8
Bosnia and Herz.					
Brazil		90			
Bulgaria		85		90	5
Canada	89	82			–7
Chile		87			
China		85			
Colombia					
Croatia				91	
Czech Republic		68		67	–1
Denmark	97	96		96	–1
Dominican Rep.					
Egypt					
El Salvador					
Estonia		90		83	–7
Finland		78		82	4
France	82	83		86	4
Georgia					
Germany (East)		93		91	–2
Germany (West)	90	88		87	–3
Great Britain	92	89		89	–3
Greece				74	
Hungary		77		93	16
Iceland	76	72		75	–1
India		84			
Indonesia					
Iran					
Iraq					
Ireland	92	95		96	4
Israel					
Italy	86	82		80	–6
Japan		91			
Jordan					
Korea Republic		83			
Kyrgyzstan					
Latvia		91		92	1
Lithuania		93		93	0
Luxembourg				77	
Macedonia					
Malta	96	96		93	–3
Mexico		53			
Moldova					
Montenegro					
Morocco					
Netherlands	86	79		82	–4
New Zealand					
Nigeria		62			
Northern Ireland	97	98		93	–4
Norway	90	89			–1
Pakistan					
Peru					
Philippines					
Poland		89		91	2
Portugal		87		79	–8
Puerto Rico					
Romania		86		93	7
Russian Fed.		93		85	–8
Saudi Arabia					
Serbia					
Singapore					
Slovakia		60		42	–18
Slovenia		90		78	–12
South Africa					
Spain	75	80		71	–4
Sweden	89	97		87	–2
Switzerland		84			
Taiwan					
Tanzania					
Turkey				92	
Uganda					
Ukraine				82	
Uruguay					
USA	90	88			–2
Venezuela					
Vietnam					
Zimbabwe					

JUSTIFIABLE: TAKING SOFT DRUGS

(F126) *Please tell me for each of the following statements whether you think it can always be justified, never be justified, or something in between. Soft drugs*

Never justifiable (%)

	1981	1990	1995	2000	Change
Albania					
Algeria					
Argentina		95			
Armenia					
Australia					
Austria		85		75	–10
Azerbaijan					
Bangladesh					
Belarus				76	
Belgium	84	84		80	–4
Bosnia and Herz.					
Brazil		90			
Bulgaria		87		84	–3
Canada	63	64			1
Chile		90			
China		96			
Colombia					
Croatia				87	
Czech Republic		84		77	–7
Denmark	83	71		62	–21
Dominican Rep.					
Egypt					
El Salvador					
Estonia		87		81	–6
Finland		78		79	1
France	80	82		69	–11
Georgia					
Germany (East)		95		82	–13
Germany (West)	86	82		65	–21
Great Britain	80	76		52	–28
Greece				51	
Hungary		78		91	13
Iceland	79	80		72	–7
India		91			
Indonesia					
Iran					
Iraq					
Ireland	83	88		73	–10
Israel					
Italy	87	84		71	–16
Japan		91			
Jordan					
Korea Republic		93			

	1981	1990	1995	2000	Change
Kyrgyzstan					
Latvia		91		93	2
Lithuania		93		88	–5
Luxembourg				67	
Macedonia					
Malta	97	97		96	–1
Mexico		64			
Moldova					
Montenegro					
Morocco					
Netherlands	74	67		47	–27
New Zealand					
Nigeria		70			
Northern Ireland	92	91		69	–23
Norway	93	91			–2
Pakistan					
Peru					
Philippines					
Poland		90		84	–6
Portugal		81		70	–11
Puerto Rico					
Romania		91		95	4
Russian Fed.		93		88	–5
Saudi Arabia					
Serbia					
Singapore					
Slovakia		78		51	–27
Slovenia		87		68	–19
South Africa		78			
Spain	70	79		66	–4
Sweden	91	93		72	–19
Switzerland		77			
Taiwan					
Tanzania					
Turkey				93	
Uganda					
Ukraine				87	
Uruguay					
USA	71	74			3
Venezuela					
Vietnam					
Zimbabwe					

JUSTIFIABLE: LYING

(F127) *Please tell me for each of the following statements whether you think it can always be justified, never be justified, or something in between. Lying*

Never justifiable (%)

	1981	1990	1995	2000	Change
Albania					
Algeria					
Argentina		65			
Armenia					
Australia					
Austria		37		33	–4
Azerbaijan					
Bangladesh					
Belarus				20	
Belgium	39	29		31	–8
Bosnia and Herz.					
Brazil		59			
Bulgaria		70		80	10
Canada	52	45			–7
Chile		62			
China		32			
Colombia					
Croatia				56	
Czech Republic		36		34	–2
Denmark	67	58		61	–6
Dominican Rep.					
Egypt					
El Salvador					
Estonia		47		36	–11
Finland		31		40	9
France	41	33		34	–7
Georgia					
Germany (East)		36		34	–2
Germany (West)	34	24		29	–5
Great Britain	46	40		39	–7
Greece				33	
Hungary		37		48	11
Iceland	73	69		69	–4
India		57			
Indonesia					
Iran					
Iraq					
Ireland	53	52		55	2
Israel					
Italy	67	49		51	–16
Japan		54			
Jordan					
Korea Republic		69			
Kyrgyzstan					
Latvia		59		59	0
Lithuania		58		35	–23
Luxembourg				40	
Macedonia					
Malta	76	80		76	0
Mexico		29			
Moldova					
Montenegro					
Morocco					
Netherlands	32	25		27	–5
New Zealand					
Nigeria		41			
Northern Ireland	62	60		54	–8
Norway	63	56			–7
Pakistan					
Peru					
Philippines					
Poland		59		59	0
Portugal		37		56	19
Puerto Rico					
Romania		36		51	15
Russian Fed.		49		32	–17
Saudi Arabia					
Serbia					
Singapore					
Slovakia		37		31	–6
Slovenia		66		56	–10
South Africa		58			
Spain	39	45		41	2
Sweden	55	55		41	–14
Switzerland		50			
Taiwan					
Tanzania					
Turkey				84	
Uganda					
Ukraine				43	
Uruguay					
USA	53	55			2
Venezuela					
Vietnam					
Zimbabwe					

JUSTIFIABLE: ADULTERY

(F128) *Please tell me for each of the following statements whether you think it can always be justified, never be justified, or something in between. Adultery*

Never justifiable (%)

	1981	1990	1995	2000	Change
Albania					
Algeria					
Argentina		70			
Armenia					
Australia					
Austria		49		50	1
Azerbaijan					
Bangladesh					
Belarus				37	
Belgium	54	51		54	0
Bosnia and Herz.					
Brazil		63			
Bulgaria		46		40	–6
Canada	59	54			–5
Chile		60			
China		72			
Colombia					
Croatia				59	
Czech Republic		40		40	0
Denmark	66	66		67	1
Dominican Rep.					
Egypt					
El Salvador					
Estonia		29		35	6
Finland		41		53	12
France	27	34		37	10
Georgia					
Germany (East)		58		40	–18
Germany (West)	50	42		42	–8
Great Britain	55	52		55	0
Greece				43	
Hungary		58		66	8
Iceland	72	71		79	7
India		91			
Indonesia					
Iran					
Iraq					
Ireland	76	69		73	–3
Israel					
Italy	59	50		51	–8
Japan		46			
Jordan					
Korea Republic		71			

	1981	1990	1995	2000	Change
Kyrgyzstan					
Latvia		44		46	2
Lithuania		60		60	0
Luxembourg				56	
Macedonia					
Malta	96	95		94	–2
Mexico		39			
Moldova					
Montenegro					
Morocco					
Netherlands	53	47		49	–4
New Zealand					
Nigeria		54			
Northern Ireland	73	78		74	1
Norway	60	62			2
Pakistan					
Peru					
Philippines					
Poland		68		67	–1
Portugal		60		59	–1
Puerto Rico					
Romania		61		72	11
Russian Fed.		50		49	–1
Saudi Arabia					
Serbia					
Singapore					
Slovakia		45		36	–9
Slovenia		41		44	3
South Africa		68			
Spain	56	58		54	–2
Sweden	54	62		51	–3
Switzerland		54			
Taiwan					
Tanzania					
Turkey					
Uganda					
Ukraine				57	
Uruguay					
USA	65	70			5
Venezuela					
Vietnam					
Zimbabwe					

Justifiable: Throwing Away Litter

(F129) *Please tell me for each of the following statements whether you think it can always be justified, never be justified, or something in between. Throwing away litter*

Never justifiable (%)

	1981	1990	1995	2000	Change
Albania					
Algeria					
Argentina		85			
Armenia					
Australia					
Austria		66		57	–9
Azerbaijan					
Bangladesh					
Belarus				44	
Belgium		69		79	10
Bosnia and Herz.					
Brazil		85			
Bulgaria		77		76	–1
Canada		73			
Chile		81			
China		77			
Colombia					
Croatia				90	
Czech Republic		65		68	3
Denmark		79		80	1
Dominican Rep.					
Egypt					
El Salvador					
Estonia		76		62	–14
Finland		42		51	9
France		75		76	1
Georgia					
Germany (East)		65		70	5
Germany (West)		62		48	–14
Great Britain		63		49	–14
Greece				60	
Hungary		63		68	5
Iceland		66		63	–3
India		84			
Indonesia					
Iran					
Iraq					
Ireland		70		69	–1
Israel					
Italy		76		74	–2
Japan		71			
Jordan					
Korea Republic		87			

	1981	1990	1995	2000	Change
Kyrgyzstan					
Latvia		88		84	–4
Lithuania		69		63	–6
Luxembourg				71	
Macedonia					
Malta		96		95	–1
Mexico		54			
Moldova					
Montenegro					
Morocco					
Netherlands		65		66	1
New Zealand					
Nigeria		65			
Northern Ireland		61		53	–8
Norway		70			
Pakistan					
Peru					
Philippines					
Poland		86		69	–17
Portugal		73		68	–5
Puerto Rico					
Romania		84		86	2
Russian Fed.		69		75	6
Saudi Arabia					
Serbia					
Singapore					
Slovakia		50		39	–11
Slovenia		74		70	–4
South Africa					
Spain		75		65	–10
Sweden		51		44	–7
Switzerland					
Taiwan					
Tanzania					
Turkey				89	
Uganda					
Ukraine				66	
Uruguay					
USA		72			
Venezuela					
Vietnam					
Zimbabwe					

Justifiable: Driving Under Influence of Alcohol

(F130) *Please tell me for each of the following statements whether you think it can always be justified, never be justified, or something in between. Driving under influence of alcohol*

Never justifiable (%)

	1981	1990	1995	2000	Change
Albania					
Algeria					
Argentina		93			
Armenia					
Australia					
Austria		71		75	4
Azerbaijan					
Bangladesh					
Belarus				56	
Belgium		67		74	7
Bosnia and Herz.					
Brazil		90			
Bulgaria		85		81	–4
Canada		82			
Chile		87			
China		86			
Colombia					
Croatia				80	
Czech Republic		76		73	–3
Denmark		90		93	3
Dominican Rep.					
Egypt					
El Salvador					
Estonia		75		75	0
Finland		79		82	3
France		70		66	–4
Georgia					
Germany (East)		86		86	0
Germany (West)		64		77	13
Great Britain		86		81	–5
Greece				69	
Hungary		77		90	13
Iceland		80		78	–2
India		88			
Indonesia					
Iran					
Iraq					
Ireland		81		81	0
Israel					
Italy		85		81	–4
Japan		74			
Jordan					
Korea Republic		84			
Kyrgyzstan					
Latvia		75		79	4
Lithuania		73		76	3
Luxembourg				55	
Macedonia					
Malta		94		95	1
Mexico		56			
Moldova					
Montenegro					
Morocco					
Netherlands		79		75	–4
New Zealand					
Nigeria		73			
Northern Ireland		90		87	–3
Norway		88			
Pakistan					
Peru					
Philippines					
Poland		82		90	8
Portugal		76		69	–7
Puerto Rico					
Romania		83		87	4
Russian Fed.		83		77	–6
Saudi Arabia					
Serbia					
Singapore					
Slovakia		67		54	–13
Slovenia		71		67	–4
South Africa		80			
Spain		78		74	–4
Sweden		89		83	–6
Switzerland		73			
Taiwan					
Tanzania					
Turkey				93	
Uganda					
Ukraine				73	
Uruguay					
USA		82			
Venezuela					
Vietnam					
Zimbabwe					

JUSTIFIABLE: SEX UNDER LEGAL AGE OF CONSENT

(F135) *Please tell me for each of the following statements whether you think it can always be justified, never be justified, or something in between. Sex under legal age of consent*

Never justifiable (%)

	1981	1990	1995	2000	Change
Albania					
Algeria					
Argentina		70			
Armenia					
Australia					
Austria		69		64	–5
Azerbaijan					
Bangladesh					
Belarus				66	
Belgium	48	34			–14
Bosnia and Herz.					
Brazil		68			
Bulgaria		53			
Canada	59	50			–9
Chile		75			
China		75			
Colombia					
Croatia				73	
Czech Republic		75		78	3
Denmark	89	98			9
Dominican Rep.					
Egypt					
El Salvador					
Estonia					
Finland		36		43	7
France	36	36			0
Georgia					
Germany (East)		76		81	5
Germany (West)	56	52		54	–2
Great Britain	76	74		68	–8
Greece				20	
Hungary		78			
Iceland	47	39			–8
India		89			
Indonesia					
Iran					
Iraq					
Ireland	86	86		83	–3
Israel					
Italy	60	47			–13
Japan		54			
Jordan					
Korea Republic					
Kyrgyzstan					
Latvia					
Lithuania		71		72	1
Luxembourg				89	
Macedonia					
Malta	96	95			–1
Mexico		42			
Moldova					
Montenegro					
Morocco					
Netherlands	25	18			–7
New Zealand					
Nigeria		50			
Northern Ireland	86	88		78	–8
Norway	99	99			0
Pakistan					
Peru					
Philippines					
Poland		73			
Portugal		52			
Puerto Rico					
Romania		80			
Russian Fed.		63		53	–10
Saudi Arabia					
Serbia					
Singapore					
Slovakia		56			
Slovenia		27		22	–5
South Africa		68			
Spain	62	64			2
Sweden	96	98			2
Switzerland		60			
Taiwan					
Tanzania					
Turkey					
Uganda					
Ukraine				54	
Uruguay					
USA	65	65			0
Venezuela					
Vietnam					
Zimbabwe					

Justifiable: Political Assassinations

(F136) *Please tell me for each of the following statements whether you think it can always be justified, never be justified, or something in between. Political assassinations*

Never justifiable (%)

	1981	1990	1995	2000	Change
Albania					
Algeria					
Argentina		92			
Armenia					
Australia					
Austria		86		86	0
Azerbaijan					
Bangladesh					
Belarus				60	
Belgium	81	74			–7
Bosnia and Herz.					
Brazil		91			
Bulgaria		72			
Canada	79	72			–7
Chile		88			
China					
Colombia					
Croatia				81	
Czech Republic		79		82	3
Denmark	92	93			1
Dominican Rep.					
Egypt					
El Salvador					
Estonia		72			
Finland		57		81	24
France	75	69			–6
Georgia					
Germany (East)		90		85	–5
Germany (West)	86	79		85	–1
Great Britain	77	69		69	–8
Greece				64	
Hungary		76			
Iceland	91	88			–3
India		81			
Indonesia					
Iran					
Iraq					
Ireland	87	72			–15
Israel					
Italy	91	88			–3
Japan		73			
Jordan					
Korea Republic		71			
Kyrgyzstan					
Latvia		75			
Lithuania		80		88	8
Luxembourg				73	
Macedonia					
Malta	96	94			–2
Mexico		51			
Moldova					
Montenegro					
Morocco					
Netherlands	79	76			–3
New Zealand					
Nigeria		62			
Northern Ireland	94	78			–16
Norway	91	91			0
Pakistan					
Peru					
Philippines					
Poland		71			
Portugal		83			
Puerto Rico					
Romania		81			
Russian Fed.		77		78	1
Saudi Arabia					
Serbia					
Singapore					
Slovakia		71			
Slovenia		75			
South Africa		71			
Spain	82	82			0
Sweden	90	88			–2
Switzerland		82			
Taiwan					
Tanzania					
Turkey					
Uganda					
Ukraine				84	
Uruguay					
USA	81	71			–10
Venezuela					
Vietnam					
Zimbabwe					

JUSTIFIABLE: BUY STOLEN GOODS

(F139) *Please tell me for each of the following statements whether you think it can always be justified, never be justified, or something in between. But stolen goods*

Never justifiable (%)

	1981	1990	1995	2000	Change
Albania			46		
Algeria					
Argentina	75	90	81		6
Armenia			61		
Australia	71		77		6
Austria		84			
Azerbaijan			71		
Bangladesh			96		
Belarus		66	72		6
Belgium	74	68			–6
Bosnia and Herz.			70		
Brazil		85	87		2
Bulgaria		75	68		–7
Canada	75	73			–2
Chile		83	72		–11
China		72	78		6
Colombia			75		
Croatia			57		
Czech Republic		72	52		–20
Denmark	93	88			–5
Dominican Rep.			76		
Egypt					
El Salvador			87		
Estonia		77	82		5
Finland		70	73		3
France	67	64			–3
Georgia			61		
Germany (East)		86	73		–13
Germany (West)	79	69	59		–20
Great Britain	73	71			–2
Greece					
Hungary	87	71	65		–22
Iceland	82	82			0
India		83	77		–6
Indonesia					
Iran					
Iraq					
Ireland	81	80			–1
Israel					
Italy	82	74			–8
Japan	79	80	75		–4
Jordan					
Korea Republic	70	92	69		–1

	1981	1990	1995	2000	Change
Kyrgyzstan					
Latvia		74	58		–16
Lithuania		72	73		1
Luxembourg					
Macedonia			76		
Malta	94	91			–3
Mexico		47	59		12
Moldova			65		
Montenegro			69		
Morocco					
Netherlands	78	72			–6
New Zealand			79		
Nigeria		70	76		6
Northern Ireland	84	86			2
Norway	89	86	84		–5
Pakistan					
Peru			70		
Philippines			45		
Poland		85	80		–5
Portugal		72			
Puerto Rico			87		
Romania		77	71		–6
Russian Fed.		79	83		4
Saudi Arabia					
Serbia			73		
Singapore					
Slovakia		54	40		–14
Slovenia		84	71		–13
South Africa		64	70		6
Spain	63	74	79		16
Sweden	90	86	75		–15
Switzerland		86	79		–7
Taiwan			76		
Tanzania					
Turkey		87			
Uganda					
Ukraine			73		
Uruguay			82		
USA	77	77	82		5
Venezuela			78		
Vietnam					
Zimbabwe					

Geographical Belong First

(G001) *To which of these geographical groups would you say you belong first of all?*

Continent/The world (%)

	1981	1990	1995	2000	Change
Albania			2	2	0
Algeria				10	
Argentina	26	11	23	13	–13
Armenia			11		
Australia			11		
Austria		7		7	0
Azerbaijan			18		
Bangladesh			16	3	–13
Belarus		6	19	8	2
Belgium	9	18		17	8
Bosnia and Herz.			8	14	6
Brazil		22	29		7
Bulgaria		11	8	7	–4
Canada	33	13		16	–17
Chile		13	11	14	1
China		4	9	10	6
Colombia			14		
Croatia			5	10	5
Czech Republic		11	8	8	–3
Denmark	7	4		3	–4
Dominican Rep.			33		
Egypt				9	
El Salvador					
Estonia		5	19	5	0
Finland		14	12	8	–6
France	14	18		16	2
Georgia			13		
Germany (East)			7	3	–4
Germany (West)	13		15	6	–7
Great Britain	11	12		9	–2
Greece				16	
Hungary		9	10	6	–3
Iceland	3	5		5	2
India		9	0	5	–4
Indonesia				3	
Iran				7	
Iraq				6	
Ireland	5	5		3	–2
Israel					
Italy	20	20		13	–7
Japan	3	3	4	2	–1
Jordan				68	
Korea Republic	1		4	3	2

	1981	1990	1995	2000	Change
Kyrgyzstan				12	
Latvia		5	19	7	2
Lithuania		6	9	7	1
Luxembourg				21	
Macedonia			10	9	–1
Malta	7	4			–3
Mexico		18	20	19	1
Moldova			24	18	–6
Montenegro			11	4	–7
Morocco				9	
Netherlands	12	14		12	0
New Zealand			10		
Nigeria		20	12	11	–9
Northern Ireland	5	8		4	–1
Norway	3	4	6		3
Pakistan					
Peru			12	8	–4
Philippines			9	4	–5
Poland		6	9	3	–3
Portugal		14		6	–8
Puerto Rico			18	17	–1
Romania		5	6	5	0
Russian Fed.		33	16	16	–17
Saudi Arabia				14	
Serbia			8	11	3
Singapore					
Slovakia		8	7	9	1
Slovenia		4	6	6	2
South Africa		11	9	14	3
Spain	8	8	9	10	2
Sweden	3	6	7	9	6
Switzerland		12	23		11
Taiwan			15		
Tanzania				8	
Turkey		9	14	11	2
Uganda				19	
Ukraine			16	17	1
Uruguay			17		
USA	7	19	19	22	15
Venezuela			13	14	1
Vietnam				7	
Zimbabwe				10	

How proud of Nationality

(G006) *How proud are you to be (NATIONALITY)?*

Very proud (%)

	1981	1990	1995	2000	Change
Albania			57	73	16
Algeria				74	
Argentina	48	55	58	68	20
Armenia			44		
Australia	70		73		3
Austria		52		53	1
Azerbaijan			64		
Bangladesh			78	73	–5
Belarus		34	32	27	–7
Belgium	30	29		23	–7
Bosnia and Herz.			56	38	–18
Brazil		64	64		0
Bulgaria		39	51	34	–5
Canada	63	61		66	3
Chile		53	55	72	19
China		43	40	26	–17
Colombia			85		
Croatia			45	42	–3
Czech Republic		28	35	26	–2
Denmark	32	42		48	16
Dominican Rep.			76		
Egypt				82	
El Salvador			86		
Estonia		30	21	24	–6
Finland		38	48	56	18
France	35	35		40	5
Georgia			65		
Germany (East)		31	16	29	–2
Germany (West)	24	20	14	14	–10
Great Britain	57	54		50	–7
Greece				55	
Hungary	68	47	49	49	–19
Iceland	59	54		66	7
India		75	73	71	–4
Indonesia				48	
Iran				92	
Iraq				77	
Ireland	68	77		73	5
Israel				54	
Italy	42	41		39	–3
Japan	31	29	22	23	–8
Jordan				68	
Korea Republic	49	45		17	–32
Kyrgyzstan				43	
Latvia		49	22	40	–9
Lithuania		41	19	22	–19
Luxembourg				49	
Macedonia			69	61	–8
Malta	75	78		74	–1
Mexico		56	70	80	24
Moldova			36	23	–13
Montenegro			46	33	–13
Morocco				89	
Netherlands	21	23		20	–1
New Zealand			65		
Nigeria		68	63	72	4
Northern Ireland	50	54		28	–22
Norway	43	45	52		9
Pakistan			86	81	–5
Peru			80	77	–3
Philippines			74	87	13
Poland		67	70	72	5
Portugal		42		79	37
Puerto Rico			86	95	9
Romania		48	45	47	–1
Russian Fed.		26	30	31	5
Saudi Arabia				75	
Serbia			41	41	0
Singapore				44	
Slovakia		30	44	25	–5
Slovenia		59	61	56	–3
South Africa		64	83	75	11
Spain	52	46	65	53	1
Sweden	30	41	46	41	11
Switzerland		38	25		–13
Taiwan			15		
Tanzania				82	
Turkey		67	82	63	–4
Uganda				66	
Ukraine			25	24	–1
Uruguay			75		
USA	77	76	78	72	–5
Venezuela			94	92	–2
Vietnam				78	
Zimbabwe				78	

TECHNICAL NOTES

Questionnaire development

The Values Studies have been carried out in 1981–1984, 1989–1993, 1995–97 and 1999–2004. Each successive wave has covered a broader range of societies than the previous one, with the 1981 wave being carried out in 24 countries, the 1990 wave in 43 societies, the 1995 wave in 62 societies and the 2000 wave in 85 societies. Analysis of each successive wave has indicated that certain questions tapped theoretically interesting and substantively important concepts, while others were of little value. This led to the more useful items being replicated in future waves, while the less useful items were dropped, making room to add new items.

Suggestions were solicited from participants throughout the world, and expert groups developed the questionnaires used in the subsequent waves, giving particular attention to issues of comparability between and across countries, and allowing longitudinal analyses. An EVS methodology group also developed a methodological questionnaire to be completed by the principal investigators in each country, giving a detailed report on how fieldwork had been carried out in their country. These questionnaires can be found on the websites of both EVS (www.europeanvalues.nl) and WVS (www.worldvaluessurvey.org). We will not repeat all of these details here, but will simply give a general description of how the fieldwork was conducted.

In each wave, a final master questionnaire was prepared in English, and it was translated into the various national languages and, in many cases, the translated questionnaire was then independently translated back into English to check the accuracy of the translation. In most countries, the translated questionnaire was then pre-tested to help identify questions or concepts, for which the translation was problematic. In some cases, certain problematic questions were omitted from the national questionnaire. In many countries, country-specific questions were included; in two-thirds of the countries all core questions were asked and in almost all countries the order of the questions in the master questionnaire was followed. More details on questionnaire development and fieldwork is available from Halman (2001), and Inglehart, Basáñez, Díez-Medrano, Halman & Luijkx (2004).

Sampling procedures

In most countries, some form of stratified multistage random sampling was used to obtain representative national samples. In the first stages, a random selection of sampling points was made based on the given society's statistical regions, districts, census units, election sections, electoral registers, or voting stations, and central population registers. In most countries, the population size and/or degree of urbanization of these Primary Sampling Units was taken into account. In some countries, individuals were drawn directly from national registers. When no named individuals were drawn, various methods were used to select respondents, such as the Kish selection grid, the Troldhal and Carter-method, last or next birthday method, quota sampling on the basis of gender and age, and sometimes also on education or profession, and, in a few cases, random routes with age and gender quota. In most countries, substitution of respondents was allowed.

In all countries, samples were drawn from the entire population of 18 years and older. In most countries, no upper age limit was imposed. For a more detailed description of the sampling procedures, see the methodological questionnaires on the respective websites.

Fieldwork

Representative national samples of each country's public were interviewed using uniformly structured questionnaires. In most countries, the survey was carried out by professional survey organizations, using face-to-face interviews. In most countries, the sample was weighted to correct for deviations from national parameters. This weight factor was not constructed uniformly over countries. The following characteristics were used to construct the weighting factor in various countries: nationality, region, the urban/rural divide, town size, household size, sex, age, occupation, education, marital status, and economic activity.

Principal investigators

Survey organizations, fieldwork dates, sample sizes and the principal investigators for each wave and each country are shown below. If not otherwise noted, the investigator is affiliated with the institution that carried out the fieldwork.

1981–1984 wave

Argentina – Instituto Gallup de la Argentine; 1984. N = 1005. Principal investigator: Marita Carballo de Cilley, Gallup, Buenos Aires. The sample was limited to the urbanized central portion of the country, about 70% of the population.

Australia – The Roy Morgan Research Centre, Melbourne; 1983. N = 1228. Principal investigator: Greg Armstrong, University of Melbourne.

Belgium – Nationaal Instituut voor Dataverzameling/Dimarso; March to May, 1981. N = 1145. Principal investigator: Jan Kerkhofs, Catholic University Leuven. After selection of sampling areas, representative for all areas, people were selected at random from all inhabitants.

Canada – The Gallup Organization; 1982. N = 1254. Principal investigator: J.F. Kielty. After selection of sampling areas, representative for all areas, people were selected at random from all inhabitants.

Denmark – Observa, Instituttet for Erhvervsanalyser og Markedsforkning; March to May, 1981. N = 1182. Principal investigators: Nils Röhme and E. Petersen, Aarhus University. Simple random sampling. Random selection of sampling points was made, according to a geographical distribution, ensuring that all types of areas (rural, urban etc.) were represented according to their proportion in the population.

France – Faits et Opinion; March to May, 1981. N = 1200. Principal investigators:

Jean Stoezel and Helene Riffault, Paris. Quota sampling. stratification according to age, sex and/or occupation.

Germany-West – Institut für Demoskopie Allensbach; March to May, 1981. N = 1305. Principal investigators: Elisabeth Noelle-Neumann and Renate Köcher, Allensbach am Bodensee. Random selection of sampling points was made, according to a geographical distribution. Selection of individuals by quota sampling. Quotas set by age, sex and occupation on the basis of census data.

Great Britain – Social Surveys (Gallup Poll) Ltd; March to May, 1981. N = 1167. Principal investigator: Gordon Heald, Gallup, London. For the nationally representative sample of 1000, Gallup used a strictly random selection. The design was a two stage probability sample, with polling districts as the primary sampling units. The sample was stratified by region, and town size within region. The booster sample of 200 18–24 years olds was achieved by quota sampling, quotas set by sex and terminal education age. Sampling universe: Great Britain (England, Wales, Scotland).

Hungary – Hungarian Academy of Sciences; January to December, 1982. N = 1464. Principal investigators: Elemer Hankiss and Robert Mancin, Hungarian Academy of Sciences, Budapest.

Iceland – Hagvangur; 1984. N = 927. Principal investigator: Olafur Haraldsson, University of Iceland. After selection of the sampling areas, people were selected at random from all inhabitants.

Ireland – The Irish Marketing Surveys (Dublin); March to May, 1981. N = 1217.

Simple random sampling. Random selection of sampling points according to a geographical distribution, ensuring that all types of areas (rural, urban etc.) were represented according to their proportion in the population.

Italy – Doxa (Milan); March to May. N = 1348. Principal investigators: Claudio Calvaruso and Salvatore Abbruzzese, Trento University, Trento. A random selection of sampling points, according to a geographical distribution, ensuring that all types of areas (rural, urban etc.) were represented according to their proportion in the population. Then selection of individuals by quota sampling. Quotas set by age, sex and occupation on the basis of census data.

Japan – Yoka Kaihatsu Senta, Tokyo; March, 1981. N = 1204.

Korean Republic – Ewha University (Seoul); 1982. N= 970. Fieldwork was designed by faculty and interviewing was executed by students from Ewha University.

Malta – Data collection organisation: Gallup Malta Limited; Survey Period, November 1983 – February 1984. N = 467. Principal investigator: Gordon Heald, Gallup, London. Random sample from the adult population (over 18 years old) as published in the Electoral Register for the islands of Malta and Gonzo.

Netherlands – Nipo (Amsterdam); March to May, 1981. N = 1221. Principal Investigator: Ruud de Moor. A random selection of sampling points, according to a geographical distribution, ensuring that all types of areas (rural, urban etc.) were represented according to their proportion in the population. People were selected at random from all inhabitants.

Northern Ireland – Irish Marketing Surveys (Dublin); March to May, 1981. N = 312. Principal Investigator: Gordon Heald, Gallup, London. Random selection of sampling points, according to a geographical distribution, ensuring that all types of areas (rural, urban etc.) were represented according to their proportion in the population. People were selected at random from all inhabitants.

Norway – Central Bureau of Statistics; Survey period, November-December 1982. N = 1246. Principal investigator: Ola Listhaug, University of Trondheim. A random selection of sampling points, according to a geographical distribution, ensuring that all types of areas (rural, urban etc.) were represented according to their proportion in the population. People were selected at random from all inhabitants.

Spain – Data, S.A. Estudios de Mercado, opinion y sociologia aplicada; March to May, 1981. N = 2303. Principal investigator: Francisco Andrés Orizo, DATA SA. Use was made of quota sampling; quotas set by age, sex and occupation on the basis of census data. A random selection of sampling points was made, according to a geographical distribution, ensuring that all types of areas (rural, urban etc.) were represented according to their proportion in the population.

Sweden – Gallup Sweden / Sifo ab.; 1982. N = 954. Principal investigator: Karin Bush, SIFO, Stockholm. A random selection of sampling points was made, according to a geographical distribution, ensuring that all types of areas (rural, urban etc.) were represented according to their proportion in the population. People were selected at random from all inhabitants.

Usa – The Gallup Organization, Princeton, NJ; March 1 to 31, 1982. N = 2325. Principal investigators: Florence Rosenberg and Edward Sullivan, Center for Applied Research in the Apostolate (CARA), Washington. The sample was stratified by race, overrepresenting minority groups. The weight variable corrects for this.

1989–1993 WAVE

Argentina – Instituto Gallup Arentina (Buenos Aires); Februari 1 to April 1, 1991. N = 1002. Principal investigator: Marita Carballo de Cilley, Gallup, Buenos Aires. Sampling was limited to the urbanized central portion of the country, where about 70 per cent of the population is concentrated, and which also has above-average incomes. Within this region, 200 sampling points were selected, with approximately five individuals being interviewed in each sampling point through multi-stage probability sampling moving through zones, sections and dwellings to individuals.

Austria – Fessel - GfK Institut (Vienna); April 9 to June 1, 1990. N = 1460. Principal investigator: Paul M. Zulehner, Universität Wien. Random sampling was used.

Belarus – Institute of Sociology, Belarus Academy of Sciences (Minsk); October 1 to November 1, 1990. N = 1015. Principal investigator: Andrei Vardomatskii, and Hans-Dieter Klingemann, Wissenschaftszentrum, Berlin.

Belgium – Dimarso-Gallup; June 10 to 27, 1990. N = 2792. Principal investigators: Karel Dobbelaere and Jan Kerkhofs, Catholic University Leuven. Quota sampling by sex, age and occupation. Census data as a guide for the distribution for each group in the population.

Brazil – Instituto Gallup de Opiniao Publica (Sao Paolo); Oktober 1, 1991 to January 31, 1992. N = 1782. Principal investigator: Carlos Matheus.

Bulgaria – National Public Opinion Center, Sofia; August 1, 1990 to December 31, 1991. N = 1034. Principal investigators: Andrei Raychev, BBSS Gallup International, Sofia, and Kancho Stoichev, Index Group, Sofia.

Canada – Gallup Canada (Toronto); May 1 to June 30, 1990. N = 1730. Principal investigators: Neil Nevitte, University of Calgary, Canada, and Ronald Inglehart, Institute for Social Research, University of Michigan, USA. Random sample with three call backs.

Chile – Centro de Estudios de la Realidad Contemporánea (Santiago); May 1 to 31, 1990. N = 1500. Principal investigatosr: Carlos Huneeus and Marta Lagos, CERC, Academia de Humanismo Cristiano. The sample covers the central portion of the country, which contains 63% of the total population; the income level of this region is about 40% higher than the national average.

China – China Statistical Information & Consultancy Service Centre (Beijing); July 1 to December 31, 1990. N = 1000. Principal investigators: Jiang Xingrong, Xiang Zongde, and Ronald Inglehart, Institute for Social Research, University of Michigan, USA. The method used was stratified multiple-stage random sampling stratification by region and also by urban-rural criteria, sex, age, occupation and level of education. Each strata sampled by quota.

Czech Republic – Association for Independent Social Analysis (Prague); September 1 to 30, 1990. N = 924. Principal investigators: Vladimir Rak, Marek Boguszak, Ivan Gabal, and Hans-Dieter Klingemann, Wissenschaftszentrum Berlin. Sample stratified by sex, age, education, region and size of community, within 303 randomly selected sampling points.

Czech Republic – Czech Radio Research Unit, Faculty of Social Science, Department of Sociology and Social Policy, Institute for Social Analysis; August 26 to October 6, 1991. N = 2109. Principal investigator: Jan Rehak, Prague. Within the three basic strata the respondents were sampled with equal probability.

Denmark – The Danish National Institute of Social Research; April to May, 1990. N = 1030. Principal investigators: Peter Gundelach, University of Copenhagen, Ole Riis, Faculty of Religion University of Aarhus. A stratified random sample was conducted.

Estonia – Mass Communication Research and Information Center (Tallinn); June 1 to August 30, 1990. Principal investigators: Andrus Saar, Tallinn, and Hans-Dieter Klingemann, Wissenschaftszentrum, Berlin.

Finland – Suomen Gallup (Gallup Finland) Helsinki; April, 1990. N = 588. Principal investigators: Leila Lotti and Juhani Pehkonen, TNS Gallup Oy, Helsinki.

France – Faits et Opinion (Paris); June 25 to July 13, 1990. N = 1002. Principal investigator: Helene Riffault. Quota sampling by age, sex and occupation. Census data were used as a guide in distribution of each group in the population.

Germany East – Institut für Demoskopie (Allensbach); May 28 to June 16, 1990. N = 1336. Principal investigator: Renate Köcher, Institut für Demoskopie, Allensbach am Bodensee. Quota sampling by sex, age and occupation.

Germany West – Institut fur Demoskopie (Allensbach); April 23 to May 15, 1990. N = 2101. Principal investigator: Renate Köcher, Institut für Demoskopie, Allensbach am Bodensee. Quota sampling by sex, age and occupation, using census data as a guide to the distribution of each group in the population.

Great Britain – Social Surveys (Gallup poll) Ltd; June 1 to September 20, 1990. N = 1484. Principal investigators: Stephen Harding, ISR, London and Noel Timms, Leicester University, Leicester. Sample is randomly drawn from the Electoral Register for England and from the Electoral Register for Scotland and Wales.

Hungary – Gallup Hungary (Budapest); May and June, 1991. N = 999. Principal investigators: Robert Manchin and Elmer Hankiss, Hungarian Academy of Sciences, and Renate Köcher, Institut fur Demoskopie, Allensbach. Random sample.

Iceland – RI: University of Iceland, Social Science Research Institute; April, 1990. N = 702. Principal investigator: Fridrik Jonsson, University of Iceland, Social Science Research Institute, Reykjavik. Random sample.

India – Indian Institute of Public Opinion (New Delhi); July 1 to December 31, 1990. N = 1163. Principal investigators: Eric de Costa, V.P. Madhok, and Ronald Inglehart, Institute for Social Research, University of Michigan. The survey was stratified to cover 14 states representing different geographic and socioeconomic regions of the country. The interviews were stratified according to town size, allocating 90% of the interviews to be carried out with the literate part of the public. Within this segment, interviews were stratified according to education.

Ireland – Economic and Social Research Institute (Dublin) (ESRI); July 6 to October 26, 1990. N = 1000. Principal investigator: Chris Whelan. The used sample is random and based on the Register of Electors.

Italy – Centro internazionale di recerche sociali sulle aree montane (Trento); October 26 to November 26, 1990. N = 2018. Principal investigator: Renzo Gubert, University of Trento. Random sample based on the register of electors. Compared with the official statistics, the share of respondents with higher levels of education is disproportionately great in the study.

Japan – Nippon Research Center Ltd. [Gallup-Japan] (Tokio); September 10 to 28, 1990. N = 1011. Principal investigators: Kenji Iijima, Yuji Fukuda, and Seiko Yamazaki, Dentsu Institute for Human Studies, Tokyo. Stratified multi-stage random sampling. The country was stratified by both region and city size based on the 1985 Census data.

Korea Republic – Ewha University (Seoul); June 1 to July 31, 1990. N = 1251. Principal investigators: Soo Young Auh, and Sang-jin Han. Stratified multi-stage random sampling was used, with the samples being selected in two stages. First, a random selection of sampling locations was made ensuring that all types of location were represented in proportion to their population. Next, a random selection of individuals was drawn up.

Latvia – Public Opinion Research Group, Latvian Sociological Association (Riga); June 1 to August 30, 1990. N = 903. Principal investigators: Brigita Zepa, Baltic Institute of Social Sciences, Riga, and Hans-Dieter Klingemann, Berlin Science Center for Social Research.

Lithuania – Vilnius State University Sociological Laboratory; June 1 to August 30, 1990. N = 1000. Principal investigators: Rasa Alishauskiene, Vilnius, Lithuania, and Hans-Dieter Klingemann, Berlin Science Center for Social Research.

Malta – Gallup Malta Limited; 1991. N = 393. Principal investigators: Fr. Joe Inganuez and Richard Cachia-Caruana.

Mexico – Market and Opinion Research International [Mori de Mexico] (Mexico city); June-July 1990. N = 1531. Principal investigators: Miguel Basáñez, Instituto Tecnologico Autonomo de Mexico, and Ronald Inglehart, Institute for Social Research, University of Michigan. The sample was taken from a list of 73 cities with population larger than 50,000 and 42 cities were chosen. The total urban population is 72% and 28% rural, proportionately, surveyed.

Netherlands – Instituut voor Sociaal-Wetenschappelijk onderzoek (IVA) (Tilburg); June 1 to September 30 1990. N = 1017. Principal investigator: Loek Halman, WORC, Tilburg University. National representative multi-stage sampling of the Dutch population aged 18 and over.

Nigeria – Research and Marketing Services, Ltd [Gallup-Nigeria] (Lagos); May 1 to June 30, 1990. N = 1001. Principal investigator: Ronald Inglehart, Institute for Social Research, University of Michigan. The Nigerian sample was stratified with 90 per cent of the interviews being carried out with the urban and literate segments of the population. It was then stratified by age, sex and education, within 17 provinces representing the major ethnic groups in the country.

Northern Ireland – Economic and Social Research Institute (ESRI) (Dublin); July 1 to September 30, 1990. Principal investigators: Michael Fogarty, K. Kennedy, and Chris Whelan. The sample is random and based on the Register of Electors. Each element in the population has an equal probability of selection and the sample is therefore self-weighting.

Norway – Survey division of Norwegian Central Bureau of Statistics (Oslo); April to June, 1990. N = 1239. Principal investigator: Ola Listhaug, University of Trondheim. Random sample.

Poland – Osrodek Badania Opini Publicznej [Survey Unit of polish Radio-Television], University of Warsaw; November-December, 1989. N = 938. Principal investigator: Renata Siemienska, University of Warsaw, Warsaw, Institute of Sociology.

Poland (EVS) – Osrodek Badania Opinii Publicznej (survey unit of Polish Radio-Television); May-June, 1990. N = 1024. Principal investigator: Aleksandra Jasinska-Kania, University of Warsaw, Insitute of Sociology. Random sample.

Portugal – Euro Expansao S.A. Lisbon; May 11 to July 13, 1990. N = 1185. Principal investigators: Luis de França and Jorge Vala, Instituto de Cienciais Sociais, Avenida das Forcas Armadas - Edificio ISCTE. Use was made of quota sampling (with quota for sex, age and instruction grade, using census data as a guide to distribution of each group in the population).

Romania – Institute for Research on Quality of Life & Romanian Academy of Sciences (Bucharest); Spring, 1993. N = 1103. Principal investigator: Catalin Zamfir, Academia Romania. Pure quota sampling stratified by age, sex, occupation and size of the community within each of nine regions of the country.

Russian Federation – Institute for Social and Political Research, Soviet Academy of Science (Moscow); October 1990. N = 1961. Principal investigators: Vladimir Andreyenkov, Elena Bashkirova, ROMIR (Russian Public Opinion and Market Research).

Slovakia – Slovak Radio / Charles University, Faculty of Social Science, Department of Sociology and Social Policy / Institute for Social Analysis, Prague; August 26 to September 8, 1991. N = 1136. Principal investigator: Jan Rehak, Prague. First two regions were covered by interviewers network of the Czech Radio Research Unit and the latter by the fieldwork of Slovak Radio. Within the three basic strata the respondents were sampled with equal probability.

Slovenia – Center for Public Opinion and Mass Communication Research, University of Ljubljana; February, 1992. N = 1035. Principal investigator: Niko Tos. As sampling method was used a systematic multi-stage sampling of adults aged 18 to 70 years in the Central registry of citizens.

South Africa – Markinor (Johannesburg); October 1 to November 30, 1990. N = 2736. Principal investigator: Mari Harris. The universe and the sample size was 1236 whites throughout South Africa, urban and rural. 600 were blacks living in the PWV, Durban, Port Elizabeth East London and Cape Town, including squatters. 200 Coloureds, living in Cape Town and 200 Asians, living in Durban.

Spain – Análisis Sociológicos, Económicos y Políticos and Intercampo (Madrid); May 1 to 3, 1990. N = 1510. Principal investigator: Juan Diez-Nicolás.

Spain (EVS) – DATA SA; April 9 to May 14, 1990. N = 2637. Principal investigator: Javier Elzo, Universidad de Deusto, Bilbao, and Francisco Andés Orizo, Centro de Investigaciones Sociological, Madrid. Quota sampling by sex, occupation, age. Censuscdata as a guide distribution of groups in population.

Sweden – Svenska Institutet for Opinionsundersokingar (SIFO) (Gallup Sweden); April-May, 1990. N = 1047. Principal investigator: Thorleif Pettersson, Faculty of Theology Sociology of Religion, University of Uppsala. A stratified random sample was conducted.

Switzerland – Isopublic; November 1, 1988 to February 28, 1989. N = 1400. Principal investigators: Anna Melich, Dominique Dembinski-Goumard, Département de Science Politique, Université of Genève. The sample was representative of the Swiss population and comprised 1400 respondents of which 807 were German Swiss, 393 Romands and 200 Tessinois, ranging from 20 to 80 years old.

Turkey – Bogazici University, Department of Political Science and International Relations (Istanbul); November-December, 1990. N = 1030. Principal investigators: Ustun Erguder, Ersin Kalaycioglu, and Yilmaz Esmer. Stratified multi-stage random sampling.

Usa – The Gallup Organization (Princeton); May–June, 1990. N = 1839. Principal investigator: Ronald Inglehart, Dept. of Political Science, University of Michigan. A random sample was conducted. The sample was stratified by race, over-representing minority groups.

1995–1997 WAVE

Albania – Index Albania (Tirana); December 7 to 14, 1998. N = 999. Principal investigator: Hans-Dieter Klingemann, Berlin Science Center for Social Research. Stratified quota sampling of population aged 18 and over.

Argentina – Instituto Gallup de Argentina; August and September 1995. N = 1079. Principal investigator: Marita Carballo de Cilley, Buenos Aires. Random sample covering central region of Argentina, containing 70 percent of population.

Armenia – Sociological Research Center, Armenian Academy of Sciences (Yerevan). February, 1997. N = 2000. Principal investigators: Gevork Pogosian and Hans-Dieter Klingemann, Berlin Science Center for Social Research. Five-stage area probability sample.

Australia – Roy Morgan Research Center (Melbourne); Fall, 1995. N = 2048. Principal investigator: Alan Black, Edith Cowan University. Representative of total population aged 18 and over.

Azerbaijan – Ali Aliev, SIAR (Baku); February, 1997. N = 2002. Principal investigators: Ali Aliev and Hans-Dieter Klingemann, Berlin Science Center for Social Research. Five-stage area probability sample of total population aged 18 and over.

Bangladesh – Bangladesh Unnayan Parishad (BUP); August, 1996. N = 1525. Principal investigator: Q.K. Ahmad. A multistage random sampling procedure was used.

Belarus – Novak-Laboratory, Institute (Minsk); December 5 to 30, 1996. N = 2092. Principal investigators: Andrei P. Vardomatskii, and Hans-Dieter Klingemann, Berlin Science Center for Social Research. Five stage random sample of total population of Belarus aged 18 and over.

Bosnia and Herzegovina – Mareco Index Bosnia (MIB) (Sarajevo); February 14 to 21, 1998. N = 1200. Principal investigators: Hans-Dieter Klingemann, Berlin Science Center for Social Research, Andrei Raichev and Kancho Stoychev, Balkan British Social Surveys. Stratified random sample. Stratification criteria were region and type of residence (urban vs. rural).

Brazil – Instituto Gallup de Opiniao Publico (Sao Paolo); June, 1997. N = 1149. Principal investigator: Carlos Matheus. Representative sample of total adult population, aged 18 and over.

Bulgaria – Balkan British Social Survey [BBSS Gallup International] (Sofia); November 4 to 11, 1997. N = 1072. Principal investigator: Antony Todorov, Andrei Raychev, and Hans-Dieter Klingemann, Berlin Science Center for Social Research. A two-stage random sample was used.

Chile – Mori Chile; Spring, 1996. N = 1000. Principal investigator: Marta Lagos. Random sample of Central Chile, containing 68% of population.

China – Gallup-China (Beijing); Fall, 1995. N = 1500. Principal investigators: Michael Guo and Max Larsen. Random sample of Central China, containing 68% of population.

Colombia – Centro Nacional de Consultoria (Bogota); March to May, 1998. N = 6025. Principal investigators: Carlos Lemoine and John Sudarsky. Representative of total population aged 18 and over.

Croatia – Institute for the Culture of Democracy, Erasmus Guild (Zagreb); December 5 to 15, 1996. N = 1196. Principal investigator: Vesna Pusic. Stratified random sampling was used.

Czech Republic – Aisa (Prague); November 23 to December 15, 1998. N = 1147. Principal investigators: Hans-Dieter Klingemann, Berlin Science Center for Social Research, and Zdenka Mansfeldova, Academy of Sciences of the Czech Republic, Prague. Probability sampling combined with proportionate to size as a multistage cluster random sampling of cities and villages with less than 20,000 inhabitants.

Dominican Republic – Centro Poveda (Santo Domingo); April, 1996. N = 417. Principal Investigators: Josefina Zaiter, Marcos Villaman and Julio Valeiron. Four communities were chosen as representatives of the four main regions: Central South and Santo Domingo, Western South (Barahona), East (San Pedro de Macorís) and North or Cibao (Santiago). Individuals between the ages of 18 and 50 years old were selected.

El Salvador – Universidad Centroamericana José Simeón Cañas y FEPADE; September 1999. N = 1254. Representative of total adult population aged 18 and over.

Estonia – Center for Social Studies in Eastern Europe (Tallinn); October, 10 tot November 23, 1996. N = 1021. Principal investigators: Mikk Tittma, and Hans-Dieter Klingemann, Berlin Science Center for Social Research. One-stage random sample with random selection of the respondents from the National Population Register.

Finland – Suomen Gallup (Espoo); Spring, 1996. N = 987. Principal investigator: Juhani Pehkonen, Suomen Gallup, Espoo. Multistratified sampling. Individuals in households chosen with quotas.

Georgia – Georgian Institute of Public Opinion (Tblisi); December 16 to 29, 1996. N = 2008. Principal Investigators: Merab Pachulia, and Hans-Dieter Klingemann, Berlin Science Center for Social Research. Five-stage area probability sample of total non-institutionalized population of Georgia, 18 years and older, without citizens living in Abkhazia and Samachablo.

Germany (East) – Forsa – Gesellschaft für Sozialforschung und Statistische Analysen mbH Berlin/Dortmund; March, 28 to May 30, 1997. N = 1009. Principal investigator: Hans-Dieter Klingemann, Berlin Science Center for Social Research. Four-stage area probability sample of total non-institutionalized population of East-Germany, 18 years and older.

Germany (West) – Forsa – Gesellschaft für Sozialforschung und statistische Analysen mbH Berlin/Dortmund; March 27 to May 31, 1997. N = 1017. Principal investigator: Hans-Dieter Klingemann, Berlin Science Center for Social Research. Four-stage area probability sample of total non-institutionalized population of West-Germany, 18 years and older.

Great Britain – Mori (London); March, 1998. N = 1093. Principal investigator: Robert M. Worcester, MORI, London. Representative of total adult population of age 18 and over.

Hungary – Szonda-IPSOS Budapest; December 1998 to January 1999. N = 650. Principal investigator: Christian Haepfer. Sample of total non-institutionalized population of Hungary, 18 years and older.

India – Oases (New Delhi); 1995–1996. N = 2040. Principal investigators: Subhasah Misra, Anita Misra, and Ronald Inglehart, Institute for Social Research, University of Michigan.

Japan – Nippon Research Center (Tokyo); Fall, 1995. N = 1054. Principal investigators: Kenji Iijima, and Yuji Fukuda, Seiko Yamazaki, Dentsu Institute for Human Studies, Tokyo.

Korea Republic – Ewah Women's University and Seoul National University; 1996. N = 1249. Principal investigators: Soo Young Auh, Sang-jin Han.

Representative of the entire adult population, 20 years and older.

Latvia – Foundation for the Advancement of Sociological Studies (Latvia); October 25 to November 19, 1996. N = 1200. Principal investigators: Ilze Koroleva, and Hans-Dieter Klingemann, Berlin Science Center for Social Research. Five-stage area probability sample of total non-institutionalized population of Latvia (citizens and non-citizens), 18 to 85 years.

Lithuania – Baltic Surveys (Vilnius); May 23 to June 8, 1997. N = 1009. Principal investigator: Rasa Alishauskiene, and Hans-Dieter Klingemann, Berlin Science Center for Social Research. Five-stage area probability sample.

Macedonia – Ivan Hartjiisky Institute for Social Values and Structures (Sofia, Bulgaria), and British Macedonian Social Survey Ltd (BRIMA) (Skopje); February 2 to 9, 1998. N = 995. Principal investigators: Antony Todorov, and Andrei Raichev, Kancho Stoychev, Balkan British Social Surveys, and Hans-Dieter Klingemann, Berlin Science Center for Social Research. Respondents were selected by a stratified random sample. Stratification criteria were region and type of residence (urban vs. rural).

Mexico – Mori de Mexico and Reforma (Mexico city); September 20, 1995 to March 31, 1996. N = 2364. Principal investigators: Alejandro Moreno, Miguel Basáñez, Depto. Ciencia Politica, Instituto Tecnologico Autonomo de Mexico.

Moldova – Institute of Sociology, Moldovan Academy of Sciences (Chisinau); December 1 to 24, 1996. N = 984. Principal investigators: Ljubov Ishimova, and Hans-Dieter Klingemann, Berlin Science Center for Social Research. Two-stage random sample.

Montenegro – Institute of Social Science, University of Belgrade; October 1996. N = 240. Principal investigators: Vladimir Goati, Jovanka Maatic, Lilijana Bacevic, Dragomir Pantic, and Hans-Dieter Klingemann, Berlin Science Center for Social Research. Three stage area probability sample of total non-institutionalized population of Republic of Serbia and Republic of Montenegro, 18 years and older. Albanians from the Province of Kosovo boycotted the research.

New Zealand – The New Zealand Study of Values Trust in association with The School of Sociology and Women's Studies- Massey University; November, 24 to December 1, 1998. N = 1201. Principal investigator: Paul Perry (Massey University), Alan Webster. The sampling frame used was an electronic version of New Zealand electoral Roll. The defined age range was 18–90 years. A systematic sample of 225 was drawn from the Maori electorates.

Nigeria – Research and Marketing Services, Ltd. (Lagos); Fall, 1995. N = 1996. Principal investigator: Kareem Tejumola.

Norway – Norwegian Central Bureau of Statistics; Fall, 1996. N = 1127. Principal investigator: Ola Listhaug, University of Trondheim.

Pakistan – Department of Rural Sociology, University of Agriculture (Faisalabad); November, 1997. N = 733. Principal investigator: Farooq Tanwir. Random sample of the Province of Punjab, which contains 68% of Pakistan's population. The rural sample is half the size of the urban sample (the weight variable corrects the urban/rural balance).

Peru – Apoyo, Opinión y Mercado, S.A. Gerente; May 10 to 13, 1996. N = 1211. Principal investigators: Alfredo Torres, and Catalina Romero, Instituto Bartolome de las Casas, Lima. The sampling method was stratified by town districts within urban scope. Within each town, sampling was polytopic, with computer selected squares and systematic selection of housings within each square. The selection of the respondent was made using non probabilistic sex and age quotas.

Philippines – Social Weather Stations (Quezon City); March 01 to April 30, 1996. N = 1200. Principal investigators: Mahar Mangahas and Linda Guerrero.

Poland – Centrum Badania Opinii Spolecznej (CBOS) (Warsaw); October 25, 1997 to March 03, 1998. N = 1153. Principal investigator: Renata Siemienska, University of Warsaw, Warsaw. Stratified random sample of total non-institutionalized population of Poland, 18 years and older. Stratification was done by a combination of twelve macro-regions and three groups of cities of different size.

Puerto Rico – College of Social Science, University of Puerto Rico (Rio Piedras); September 15 to October 31, 1995. N = 1164. Principal investigator: Angel Rivera-Ortiz. Multi-stage structured random sample, representative of total population aged 18 and over.

Romania – CSOP Ltd Market, Media and Opinion Research (Bucharest); June 8 to 22, 1998. N =

1239. Principal investigators: Russell J. Dalton, School of Social Sciences, University of California, USA, and Andrei Raichev, Kancho Stoychev, Balkan British Social Surveys, Sofia, Bulgaria. Respondents were selected by a stratified random sample. Stratification criteria were region and type of residence (urban vs. rural).

Russian Federation – Russian Public Opinion and Market Research [Romir] (Moscow); November 17, 1995 to January 25, 1996. N = 2040. Principal investigators: Elena Bashkirova, and Hans-Dieter Klingemann, Berlin Science Center for Social Research. Five-stage area probability sample of total non-institutionalized population of the Russian Federation, 18 years and older, without citizens living in the Far North and in inaccessible regions of Siberia.

Serbia – Institute of Social Science, University of Belgrade; October 1996. N = 1280. Principal investigators: Vladimir Goati, Jovanka Maatic, Lilijana Bacevic, Dragomir Pantic, and Hans-Dieter Klingemann, Berlin Science Center for Social Research. Total non-institutionalized population of Republic of Serbia and Republic of Montenegro, 18 years and older (Albanians from the Province of Kosovo boycotted the research). Three stage area probability sample.

Slovakia – Aisa (Prague); November 23 to December 15, 1998. N = 1095. Principal investigator: Zdenka Mansfeldova, Institute of Sociology, Czech Academy of Sciences, Prague, and Hans-Dieter Klingemann, Berlin Science Center for Social Research. Probability sampling.

Slovenia – Survey Research Center, University of Ljubljana; September 1 to November 30, 1995. N = 1007. Principal investigator: Niko Tos. Three-stage probability sample. The sample was split-half by a random procedure. One half of the interviews were used for the study under consideration.

South Africa – Markinor (Stellenbosch); Spring, 1996. N = 2935. Principal investigators: Mari Harris, and Johann Mouton, Centre for Interdisciplinary Studies, University of Stellenbosch, and Anneke Greyling, Centre for International and Comparative Politics, Department of Political Science, University of Stellenbosch, and Robert B. Mattes, Public Information Centre, Institute for Democracy in South Africa.

Spain – Análisis Sociológicos, Económicos y Políticos and Intercampo (Madrid); October 2 to 8, 1995. N = 1211. Principal investigators: Juan Diez-Nicolás, ASEP, and Juan Diez-Medrano, ASEP, and Jose Ramon Torregrosa-Peris, Facultad de CC. Politicas y Sociologia, Universidad Complutense de Madrid, Campus de Somosaguas. Stratified polytopic sampling, built from 1986 census data. Proportional distribution of the sample was done by Autonomous Communities and town size.

Sweden – Temo (Solna); 1996. N = 1009. Principal investigators: Prof Thorleif Pettersson, Faculty of Theology, Uppsala University, and Bi Puranen, Institute for Future Studies, Stockholm.

Switzerland – Geselleschaft für Socialforschung; Fall, 1996. N = 1212. Principal investigators: Simon Hug and Pascal Sciarini, University of Geneva.

Taiwan – Survey Research Center, Academia Sinica (Taipei); Summer, 1994 and Summer 1995. N = 1452. Principal investigators: Hei-yuan Chiu, Jin-yun Liu, Ronald Inglehart, Institute for Social Research, University of Michigan, and Pi-chao Chen, Taipei.

Turkey – Survey Research Center, Bogazici University (Istanbul); December 1, 1996 to January 31, 1997. N = 1907. Principal investigator: Yilmaz Esmer. Random sample of Turkey except for South-Eastern (predominantly Kurdish) region.

Ukraine – Social Monitoring Center, National Institute for Strategic Studies (Kiev); September 12 to October 1, 1996. N = 2811. Principal investigators: Olga Balakireva, and Hans-Dieter Klingemann, Berlin Science Center for Social Research. Probability sampling. Two-stage random sample.

Uruguay – Equipos Consultores Associados (Montevideo). October, 1996. N = 1000. Principal investigators: Cesar Aguiar, Jose Arocena, Augustin Canzani, Rafael Mendizabal. Representative of people of 18 years and more, residing in Montevideo and nine more towns. Selection of respondents using random tri-stage sampling. First stage selection of census regions. Second stage, selection of housings. Third stage selection of persons.

USA – The Gallup Organization (Princeton); Fall, 1995. N = 1542. Principal investigators: Alec Gallup, Max Larsen, and Ronald Inglehart, Institute for Social Research, University of Michigan.

Venezuela – Doxa (Caracas); March 01 to April 30, 1996. N = 1200. Principal investigators: Gustavo Mendez, Friedrich Welsch, and Jose Molina, Zulia University, Idf. Urano.

1999–2004 WAVE

Albania – Index Albania; February 17 to March 5, 2002. N = 1000. Principal investigator: Kosta Barjaba. A nationally representative multistage random probability sample of the population aged 18 and over.

Algeria – University of Algiers; March 1 to May 31, 2002. N = 1282. Principal investigators: Abdallah Bedaida, Mark Tessler. Respondents were selected by quota in each district based on sex and age.

Argentina – Instituto Gallup de Argentina; January 22 to February 9, 1999. N = 1280. Principal investigator: Marita Carballo, Buenos Aires. A nationally representative sample of the population aged 18 and over. The sample was stratified according to two criteria, using multistage random selection of the sampling units.

Austria – Fessel-GfK Austria; August-October 1999. N = 1522. Principal investigator: Paul M. Zulehner, Universität Wien, Vienna. A multi-staged, stratified sample method was used with clustered addresses. The target person within the household was selected using the Kish method.

Bangladesh – Bangladesh Unnayan Parishad; August 20 to September 15, 2002. N = 1499. Principal investigators: Q. K. Ahmad and Nilufar Banu. Population 18 years old and over, representative of Bangladesh. Stratified random sampling.

Belarus – The Centre of Political and Sociological Researches of Belarus State University; March-April 2000. N = 1000. Principal investigators: David Rotman and Larissa Titarenko, Belarus State University, Minsk. Stratified sampling was used.

Belgium – Nationaal Instituut voor Dataverzameling/Dimarso; March-June 1999. N = 1912. Principal investigators: Karel Dobbelaere and Jaak Billiet, Catholic University Leuven, and Bernadette Bawin, Université de Liège. A two-stage sampling procedure was used. The primary units were districts, the secondary units were addresses.

Bosnia-Hercegovina – Mareco Index Bosnia; December 3 to 10, 2001. N = 1200. Principal investigator: Hans-Dieter Klingemann. The survey interviewed in 16 cantons/regions, ensuring the required ethnic and demographic structure of the sample.

Bulgaria – Institute of Sociology at the Bulgarian Academy of Sciences; June-July 1999. N = 1000. Principal investigators: Georgy Fotev and Mario Marinov, Bulgarian Academy of Sciences, Sofia. Two-stage cluster sampling was used. In first stage random selection was made with probability proportional to size of 1000 statistical regions. Then a street (block of flats) was selected and from a definite number of addresses one respondent of 18 years or older has been selected.

Canada – Dept. of Political Science, University of Toronto; August 3 to September 24, 2000. N = 1931. Principal investigator: Neil Nevitte, University of Toronto. National probability sample of Canadians aged 18 and over.

Chile – Latinobarómetro / MORI Chile; November 9 to 19, 2000. N = 1791. Principal investigator: Marta Lagos. Modified probabilistic sample, random in the first and second stage, by age and sex quota on the last stage.

China – Research Center for Contemporary China, Peking University; March 18 to June 25, 2001. N = 1000. Principal investigator: Shen Mingming. Population 18 years old and over, representative of China.

Croatia – Market Research Agency "Target"; March–April 1999. N = 1003. Principal investigator: Josip Baloban, Universitatis Zagrabiensies, Zagreb. Use was made of two-stage probability sampling. In second stage, respondents aged 18 years or older were selected randomly within the household (using the Throdal and Carter method - balancing gender and age) from a list of addresses in each location.

Czech Republic – SC&C Ltd., Statistical Computations and Computing; March-May 1999. N = 1908. Principal investigator: Ladislav Rabušic, Masaryk University, Brno. Use was made of a three-stage sampling method within 29 strata. The stages were 1) Census Units; 2) households and 3) person. Population between 18 and 75.

Denmark – SFI, the Danish national institute of social research; April-November 1999. N = 1023. Principal investigator: Peter Gundelach, University of Copenhagen, Copenhagen. The sampling procedure was based on simple extraction.

Egypt – Emac Research and Training Center in collaboration with Women's College, Ain Shams University; July 1, 2000 to January 1, 2001. N = 3000. Principal investigators: Abdel-Hamid Abdel-Latif, Mansoor Moaddel. A random sample of households in each PSU's was first selected. Eligible individuals who were 16 years old and over with certain educational level were then selected.

Estonia – Saar Poll, Ltd.; October 1999. N = 1005. Principal investigator: Andrus Saar, Saar Poll, Tallinn. A staged sample method was used. In the third stage, the respondent was selected using the principle of "youngest man'. If no man in the house, then 'youngest woman'.

Finland – Suomen Gallup Oy; September-October 2000. N = 1038. Principal investigator: Juhani Pehkonen, Suomen Gallup Oy, Helsinki. A multi-stage sample was used excluding Åland (Ahvenanmaa) covering all administrative districts in Finland. There were quota controls for age and sex.

France – Research International; March-April 1999. N = 1615. Principal investigator: Jean-François Tchernia, Tchernia Etudes Conseil, Paris. Sample has been drawn by the method of quota sampling after stratification according to region and size of town.

Germany – Infass (Bonn); October-December 1999. N = 2036. Principal investigator: Wolfgang Jagodzinski, Universität zu Köln, Cologne.

Great Britain – Quality Fieldwork & Research Services; October-November 1999. N = 1000. Principal investigator: Helmut Anheier, London School of Economics and Political Science, London. Cluster sampling, sex quota.

Greece – Department of Psychology, School of Philosophy, the University of Athens; March-June 1999. N = 1142. Principal investigators: James Georgas, Kostas Mylonas and Aikaterini Gari, the University of Athens, Athens.

Hungary – Szonda-Ipsos Média-, Vélemény- és Piaclutató Intézet (Budapest); November-December 1999. N = 1000. Principal investigator: Miklós Tomka, Hungarian Religious Research Centre, Budapest. Two-staged sample method using Kish-grid method.

Iceland – The Institute of Social Research at the University of Iceland; June-December 1999. N = 968. Principal investigators: Fridrik H. Jonsson and Stefan Olafsson, University of Iceland, Reykjavik. Random sample from the National Register, population aged 18 and over.

India – Political Science Faculty, Bangalore University; August 20 to October 15, 2001. N = 2002. Principal investigators: Sandeep Shastri, Pradeep Chibber. National representative sample of Indians aged 18 and over.

Indonesia – Institute of Quranic Studies; March 1 to September 30, 2001. N = 1004. Principal investigator: Nadra Muhamad Hosen. Stratified sample.

Iran – Institute of Social Research and Studies, University of Teheran; January 1 to February 28, 2000. N = 2532. Principal investigators: Taghi Azadarmaki, Mansoor Moaddel. Representative sample of population aged 18 and over.

Iraq – The nation Wide Poll M-27; November 16 to December 16, 2004. N=2325. Multi-stage probability-based sampling of population aged 18 and over.

Ireland – The Survey Unit, The Economic and Social Research Unit (Dublin); October 1999 to February 2000. N = 1012. Principal investigators: Tony Fahey, ESRI, Dublin, Bernadette C. Hayes, the Queen's University, Belfast, and Richard Sinnott, Trinity College, Dublin. A two-stage probability clustered sample of population aged 18 and over.

Israel – B.I. Cohen Institute for Public Opinion Research; September 1 to November 1, 2001. N = 1199. Principal investigator: Noah Lewin-Epstein. Population 18 years old and over, representative of Israel. Multistage sampling using Kish-grid method.

Italy – Centro Ricerche Sociali di Moncomo G. e C. SaS (Milan); March-May 1999. N = 2000. Principal investigator: Renzo Gubert, University of Trento, Trento. Stratified multistage sampling.

Japan – Nippon Research Center; July 11 to 26, 2000. N = 1362. Principal investigators: Seiko Yamazaki and Toru Takahashi. Population 17 years old and over, representative of Japan. Stratified multistage sampling.

Jordan – Center for Strategic Studies, University of Jordan; September 15 to 21, 2001. N = 1223. Principal investigator: Fares al-Braizat, Mustafa Harmaneh. National representative multistage sampling of population 18 years old and over.

Korea Republic – Dpt. of Political Science and Diplomacy, Ewha Women's University; November 10 to 21, 2001. N = 1200. Principal investigator: Soo Young Auh. Population 20 years old and over, representative of the Republic of Korea. Selection of 120 clusters with a sample of 10 chosen from the household of each of the selected clusters.

Kyrgyzstan - East-West Center for Research, American University; June 15 to September 10, 2003. N = 1043. Principal investigator: Temirlan Moldogaziev. Five–stage probability sampling of total population of the Kyrgyz Republic, 18 years and older.

Latvia – Latvia Social Research Centre; March 1999. N = 1013. Principal investigator: Brigita Zepa, Baltic Institute of Social Sciences, Riga. A three-stage sampling method was used, respondents were selected using the principle of "youngest man'. If no man in the house, then 'youngest woman'.

Lithuania – Baltic Surveys Ltd.; November-December 1999. N = 1018. Principal investigators: Stanislovas Juknevicius, Lithuanian Institute of Culture and Arts, and Rasa Alishauskiene, Institute for Social Research, Vilnius. Multistage sampling using Kish-grid method for male and female sub-samples separately.

Luxembourg – Ilres Market Research; July-October 1999. N = 1211. Principal investigators : Pol Estgen and Michel Legrand, SeSoPi Centre Intercommunautaire a.s.b.l., Luxembourg. Quota controls for age, sex, profession and nationality, communities used as stratification factors.

Macedonia – Brima Skopje; November 28 to December 2, 2001. N = 1055. Principal investigator: Hans-Dieter Klingemann. A nationally representative multistage random probability sample of the population aged 18 and over.

Malta – Misco International; March-May 1999. N = 1002. Principal investigator: Anthony M. Abela, University of Malta. A random selection from a file containing all registered voters of the Maltese islands (18 years and over).

Mexico – Instituto Tecnológico Autónomo de México; January 28 to February 7, 2000. N = 1535. Principal investigator: Alejandro Moreno. Multi-stage sampling procedure. Population between 18 and 94 years of age.

Moldova – Institute of Sociology, Moldovan Academy of Sciences (Chisinau). N = 1008. Principal investigators: Ljubov Ishimova, Hans-Dieter Klingemann.

Montenegro – Institute of Social Sciences, Belgrade; November 1 to 17, 2001. N = 1060. Principal investigators: Dragomir Pantic, Hans-Dieter Klingemann, Ronald Inglehart. Three-stage stratified probability sample, 18 years old and over.

Morocco 1 – Serec, Bureau d'études; August 2 to 28, 2001. N = 1247. Principal investigator: Juan Diez-Nicolas (ASEP, Spain). The sampling method is based on sex, age, education level, socio-economic and professional level and place of residence.

Morocco 2 – Serec, Bureau d'études; February 8 to March 7, 2002. N = 1013. Principal investigator: Mansoor Moaddel. The sampling method is based on sex, age, education level, socio-economic and professional level and place of residence.

Netherlands – Survey data (Tilburg); March-August 1999. N = 1003. Principal investigator: Loek Halman, Tilburg University, Tilburg. National representative multi-stage sampling of Dutch population aged 18 and over.

Nigeria – Research and Marketing Services; October 13 to November 22, 2000. N = 2022. Principal investigators: Bukola Bandele, Kareem Tejumola. Population 18 years old and over, representative of Nigeria. Multi-stage sampling method was observed until the final respondent selection. The final respondent was selected by quota by age and sex in all locations

Northern Ireland – Research and Evaluation Services (Belfast); July-November 1999. N = 1000. Principal investigators: Bernadette C. Hayes, the Queen's University, Belfast, Tony Fahey, ESRI, Dublin, and Richard Sinnott, Trinity College, Dublin. Two-stage probability based sample utilising probability proportionate to size (PPS) was used.

Pakistan – Faculty of Agricultural, Economics and Rural Sociology, University of Agriculture; August 15, 2001 to February 28, 2002. N = 2000. Principal investigator: Farooq Tanwir. Combination of purposive, random and quota sampling.

Peru – Instituto Bartolomé de las Casas / Datum International; July 19 to 25, 2001. N = 1501. Principal investigator: Catalina Romero. Combination of random and probability sampling method. Kish method used to select final respondent.

Philippines – Philippine Social Science Center; July 9 to September 27, 2001. N = 1200. Principal investigators: Linda Luz Guerrero, Felipe Miranda. Voting age adults (18 years old and over), representative of Philippines. Multistage probability sampling was used in the selection of sample spots.

Poland – CBOS-Public Opinion Research Centre; February-March 1999. N = 1095. Principal investigators: Aleksandra Jasinska-Kania, Mira Marody and Joanna Konieczna, University of Warsaw, Warsaw. Three-stage random sampling.

Portugal – Euroteste-Marketing E Opinião; October-December 1999. N = 1000. Principal investigators : Jorge Vala, Alice Ramos and Manuel Villaverde Cabral, Instituto de Cienciais Sociais, Lisbon. There was stratification by region and habitat and the sample was defined in order to be proportional to the population.

Puerto Rico – Dept. of Political Science, University of Puerto Rico; April 15 to May 15, 2001. N =

720. Principal investigators: Jorge Benítez-Nazario, Ángel Rivera-Ortiz. National population representative of Puerto Rico, without age cut-offs. Structured random sample.

Romania – The Research Institute for the Quality of Life; July 1999. N = 1146. Principal investigators: Malina Voicu, Cătălin Zamfir and Lucien Pop, Romanian Academy, Bucharest. Combination of stratified and random sampling of population aged 18 and over.

Russian Federation – Romir (Moscow); April-June 1999. N = 2500. Principal investigator: Elena Bashkirova, Bashkirova & Partners, Moscow. Stratified multistage sampling.

Saudi Arabia – Pan Arab Research Center; April 20 to May 10, 2003. N = 1502. Principal investigator: Abdullah A. Al-Otaiby, Umm al Qura University, Makkah. Sampling by clusters.

Serbia – Institute of Social Sciences, Belgrade; October 29 to November 8, 2001. N = 1200. Principal investigators: Dragomir Pantic, Hans-Dieter Klingemann, and Ronald Inglehart. Three-stage stratified probability sample, 18 years old and over.

Singapore – Faculty of Arts and Social Sciences, National University of Singapore with the assistance of Joshua Research Consultants; March 14 to August 7, 2002. N = 1512. Principal investigator: Tan Ern Ser. Stratified, random sample of Singapore citizens.

Slovakia – Agentúra MVK (Bratislava); June-July 1999. N = 1331. Principal investigator: Zuzana Kusá, Slovak Academy of Sciences, Bratislava. Two-stage random sampling, quota controls for gender and age.

Slovenia – Public Opinion and Mass Communications Research Center, Faculty of Social Sciences, University of Ljubljana; October 1999. N = 1006. Principal investigators: Niko Tos and Brina Malnar, University of Ljubljana, Ljubljana. Systematic multi-stage sample with random start of adults aged 18 years or older living at non-institutional address in Slovenia.

South Africa – Markinor (Stellenbosch); March 1 to May 22, 2001. N = 3000. Principal investigators: Mari Harris, Hennie Kotzé, University of Stellenbosch,. National representative sample of South Africa's population aged 16 and over. Random sample according to a selection grid used by Markinor.

Spain (WVS) – Análisis Sociológicos, Económicos y Políticos, S.A. (ASEP); November 6 to 13, 2000. N = 1209. Principal investigators: Juan Díez-Nicolás, Jose R. Torregrosa, Juan Diez-Medrano. National representative multistage random sample of the Spanish population aged 18 and over. Kish-grid method used.

Spain (EVS) – Data SA (Madrid); March-April 1999. N = 1200. Principal investigators: Javier Elzo, Universidad de Deusto, Bilbao, and Francisco Andrés Orizo, DATA, Madrid. Multi-stage, random (semi-probabilistic) sampling procedure, stratified by means of conglomerates.

Sweden – ARS Research AB, Stockholm; November 15, 1999 to February 13, 2000. N = 1015. Principal investigators: Bi Puranen, Theseus Institute, Sophia Antipolis (France) and Thorleif Pettersson, Uppsala University. A two-stage representative sample of Swedish population aged 18–75 years old.

Tanzania – University of Dar-es-Salaam, Tanzania; May 30 to November 6, 2001. N = 1171. Principal investigator: G. K. Munishi. Multistage representative sample of Tanzania's population aged 18 and over.

Turkey (WVS) – Bogazici University (Istanbul) and Birim Arastirma; December 2000 to January 2001. N = 3401. Principal investigator: Yilmaz Esmer. Multistage representative sample of Turkey's population aged 18 and over.

Turkey (EVS) – Bogazici University (Istanbul) and Birim Arastirma; September-October 2001. N = 1206. Principal investigator: Yilmaz Esmer, Multistage representative sample of Turkey's population aged 18 and over. In the last stage, quota-sampling was used.

Uganda – Markinor (Stellenbosch, South Africa); March 3 to 18, 2001. N = 1002. Principal investigator: Mari Harris (Stellenbosch). National representative sample of Uganda's population aged 18 and over. Random sample according to a selection grid used by Markinor.

Ukraine – Social Monitoring Centre (NGO) and Ukrainian Institute for Social Research; December 1999. N = 1195. Principal investigator: Olga N. Balakireva, Ukrainian Institute for Social Research, Kiev. 100 voting stations were selected randomly (random figure method) from the national list of the voting stations. In the second stage, 20 named individuals have been selected by systematic selection.

USA – Institute for Social Research, University of Michigan; first phase: November 19 to December 23, 1999; second phase: August 4 to September 25, 2000. N = 1200. Principal investigators:

Virginia Hodgkinson, Ronald Inglehart and Miguel Basáñez. A nationally representative multistage random probability sample of the population aged 18 and over.

Venezuela – Red Interuniversitaria de Cultura Política, Universidad del Zulia; November 30 to December 20, 2000. N = 1200. Principal investigator: Jose Molina. Random sample stratified by States and Municipalities within locations of 5000 inhabitants and over.

Vietnam – Institute of Human Studies; August 28 to September 30, 2001. N = 995. Principal investigators: Pham Minh Hac, Pham Thanh Nghi, Russell Dalton and Nhu-Ngoc Ong. Multistage probability sample.

Zimbabwe – Markinor (Stellenbosch, South Africa); February 2 to March 28, 2001. N = 1002. Principal investigator: Mari Harris (Stellenbosch). National representative sample of Zimbabwe's population aged 18 and over. Random sample according to the traditional Kish-grid method.

Creating the integrated dataset

After the fieldwork, data cleaning was carried out by the principal investigators. Further cleaning for the European surveys was performed at Tilburg University and the Zentralarchiv in Cologne and by JD Systems in Madrid, for the other countries.

To combine the various datasets from all waves into one integrated dataset, a master codebook was created, based on the national data sets, the national questionnaires, and the master questionnaire. First, merged data files were created for each wave. For the European datasets, this was done by Tilburg University in collaboration with the Zentralarchiv in Cologne. In September 2003, Zentralarchiv released the European Values Study 1999/2000 wave (see Luijkx, Brislinger & Zenk-Moeltgen 2003). Since 2007, the three waves of the European Values Study including full documentation are available for free online analysis and data download via the ZACAT platform (http://www.gesis.org/Datenservice/zacat.htm).

The other surveys were merged by JD Systems in Madrid. Then, all European and non-European surveys were combined into one integrated dataset containing all values surveys from 1981 to 2004. This data set, fully documented, can be downloaded from the websites of EVS, WVS and ASEP/JDS (http://www.jdsurvey.net/bdasepjds/PrinHome.jsp); online analysis is available as well.

References

Halman, Loek 2001. *The European Values Study: A Third Wave. Source book of the 1999/2000 European Values Study Surveys.* Tilburg: EVS/WORC, Tilburg University.

Inglehart, Ronald, Miguel Basáñez, Jaime Díez-Medrano, Loek Halman & Ruud Luijkx (eds.) 2005. *Human Values and Beliefs: A Cross-Cultural Sourcebook based on the 1999–2001 Values Surveys.* Mexico City: Siglo XXI.

Luijkx, Ruud, Evelyn Brislinger & Wolfgang Zenk-Moeltgen 2003. European Values Study 1999/2000 – A Third Wave: Data, Documentation and Databases on CD-ROM. *ZA-Information* 52:171–183.

ABOUT THE AUTHORS

Miguel Basáñez, Ph.D. (1990), London School of Economics, is president of Global Quality Research Corp, an international survey research firm based in Princeton, NJ, USA. He helped found the Latin-Barometer (1995) and the Asia-Barometer (2004) and is member of the World Values Survey's Steering Committee. His research deals with changing belief systems and their impact on social and political change.

Jaime Díez Medrano, Eng. (1987), Universidad Politécnica de Madrid is the president of JD Systems, director of the ASEP/JDS Archive and responsible of the World Values Survey data cleaning since 2000. He participated in the construction of the WVS1995 and WVS2000 official files and the construction of the four wave EVS/WVS aggregate. He is expert in data dissemination.

Loek Halman, Ph.D. (1991), Tilburg University is Associate Professor of Sociology at the Department of Social Cultural Sciences at the Faculty of Social and Behavioral Sciences at Tilburg University. He is general secretary to the European Values Study Foundation and Program Director of the European Values Study. His research deals with issues of modernization, individualization, and secularization of (Western) societies, attitudes and values.

Ronald Inglehart, Ph.D. (1967), University of Chicago is professor of political science and program director at the Institute for Social Research at the University of Michigan. He helped found the Euro-Barometer surveys and directs the World Values Survey. His research deals with changing belief systems and their impact on social and political change.

Ruud Luijkx, Ph.D. (1994) Tilburg University, is Lecturer of Sociology at Tilburg University, the Netherlands, and data manager for the European Values Study. He has published on inter- and intragenerational social mobility, social inequality and stratification, the dynamics of value change and on categorical data analysis.

Alejandro Moreno, Ph.D. (1997), University of Michigan, Ann Arbor, is professor of political science at the Instituto Tecnologico Autonomo de Mexico (ITAM), and head of the department of surveys at newspaper Reforma, both in Mexico City. His main publications and current research deal with public opinion, voting behavior, and political values in Mexico and other new democracies.